D1121317

Sowing the American Dream

SOWING
the AMERICAN
DREAM

*How Consumer Culture
Took Root in the
Rural Midwest*

David Blanke

Ohio University Press

ATHENS

Ohio University Press, Athens, Ohio 45701
© 2000 by David Blanke
Printed in the United States of America
All rights reserved

09 08 07 06 05 04 03 02 01 00   5 4 3 2 1

Library of Congress Cataloging-in-Publication Data

Blanke, David, 1961–
    Sowing the American dream: how consumer culture took root in the
rural midwest / David Blanke.
        p. cm.
    Includes bibliographical references and index.
    ISBN 0-8214-1347-3 — ISBN 0-8214-1348-1 (pbk.)
    1. Consumption (Economics)—Middle West—History. 2. Consumer behavior—
Middle West—History. I. Title.

HC107.A14 B553 2000
306.3'0977—dc21   00-040672

CONTENTS

TABLES

PREFACE AND ACKNOWLEDGMENTS

My reliance upon the work of other scholars is developed more fully in the book's endnotes. Still, some terms and expressions used throughout *Sowing the American Dream* require more explicit remarks. For example, when discussing the "rural consumer ethos" or "agrarian mentality" associated with consumption, I am assuming first that such a distinction can be made between farmers and other Americans. While less formal than a stated ideology or political platform, the essence of this ethos runs parallel to the notions of producerism that were so deeply ingrained in midcentury thought. The many paradoxes and inconsistencies in the expression of this agrarian ideology seem to constitute an entire branch of rural studies. But from Richard Hofstadter's well-known attack of farm anxieties to Lawrence Goodwyn's advocacy of a regional movement culture, it is clear that an intangible harmony exists for many who experience similar economic and social conditions. Such was the case for Midwestern farmers. As examined in the first three chapters of this book, the rural consumer ethos that developed was a reflection of these shared experiences with settlement, commercial farming, and the established distribution network.[1]

Institutional history can also be problematic. The separation between an institution's organizational goals and those of its members or clients is never absolute. The history of the Grange, Montgomery Ward, and Sears, Roebuck is no different. In chapters 4, 6, and 7, institutions loom large in the narrative. I endeavor to make clear when and how the formal structure differed from the goals of the individual. In additional, institutional rhetoric often went far beyond the real and intended activities of rank-and-file members. Generally, however, these institutions are useful for developing the relative importance that participants placed on their communal versus individual goals.[2]

When discussing "rural" Midwesterners, it will soon become clear that I am referring more specifically to farmers who were involved in commercial agriculture. While they comprised an overwhelming majority of most Midwestern counties (the opposite of today's rural regions), planters were not the only ones living in the countryside. Laborers, tenants, and nonpersisting subsistence farmers clearly had differing goals and ambitions. Small-town inhabitants faced a different set of challenges than their farming cousins. As a result, their consumer experiences were based on a values that often conflicted with commercial farmers. These tensions are examined more fully in chapters 1 and 5.[3]

The term *modern consumer culture* denotes more than the physical requirements of mass-produced consumer goods, a mature distribution network, and the use of sophisticated advertising techniques. Modernity suggests something qualitatively different. As Jackson Lears, Roland Marchand, and William Leach have demonstrated, modern consumption also entails a visceral and very personal relationship between the purchaser and the goods. This relationship can be influenced and manipulated, but certainly the goods stand for something more than simply their utilitarian characteristics. Modern consumer culture is explored throughout the text and is at the heart of chapter 7.

Finally, the adjective *Midwest* generally refers to the states of the Old Northwest—Ohio, Indiana, Michigan, Illinois, and Wisconsin—originally chartered by the Ordinance of 1787. I have added Iowa to my use of the term because the Hawkeye State shared almost every key characteristic, such as population demographics, topography, soil fertility, market access, the role of central cities and river towns, and access to the marketplace via the transportation network, with its Eastern neighbors. Ohio and Michigan are largely excluded from this analysis not because they failed to share in the region's qualities but in order to maintain a more organized narrative from early settlement through to the formation of state and local organizations. Relying on states as key units of reference supports the historic perception of place used by most antebellum Americans, an abstraction that only gains strength during the Civil War. The analysis treats a wide range of local communities as representative of the Midwest in an effort to discover an aggregate voice. Hopefully the sum of these narratives is greater than what is lost in local, state, or regional distinctiveness.[4]

Yet political and geophysical boundaries do little to capture the emotions that the region aroused in many throughout the era. Hamlin Garland, the nineteenth-century writer on Midwestern life, came closest to grasping the sense of change and modernization, of what he would no doubt term progress, in referring to this same territory as the "Middle Border." Garland later confessed a near-sensual pleasure in breaking the

Iowa prairie sod; "There was something epic, something large-gestured and splendid" in how the "thick ribbon of jet-black sod rose upon the share and rolled away from the mold-board's glistening curve." While Garland admitted sadness in the destruction of "all the swarming lives which had been native here for untold centuries," the joyous themes of individual potential and fulfillment, liberation, action, and economic opportunity course through his autobiography.[5] For many European-stock Americans, these feelings left an indelible impression, both for good and ill, on the psyches of those who established their commercial farms in the Midwest. Still, it was the development of commercial farming that united the Midwest. Garland's emotional reminiscences of the land's "virginity" do little to temper his criticism of the social costs that were later exacted by the regional Jezebel known as the market.[6]

A large volume of substantial and influential scholarship has been done to provide a more concrete basis for defining the Midwest. William Cronon, Allan Bogue, Andrew R. L. Cayton and Peter S. Onuf, and John Mack Faragher represent a rich, and at times provocative, historiography of the region.[7] If there is an overarching thesis to be taken from this mature body of work, it is that the burgeoning market forces of the nineteenth century significantly altered the rural society and culture that settlers brought with them to the region. It is also well accepted now that the Midwest's strong commercial character was in no way the result of a grand or unified policy. As Hal Barron noted for the rural North, regional development is "a story of change and continuity, and of accommodation and resistance, which took place under conditions that were not always chosen or anticipated." Still, as this study tightens its focus on commercial farmers and then again on those who were active consumers, "pecuniary benefits" were far and away the leading motivational force behind their collective behavior.[8]

I wish to thank Loyola University Chicago, the Arthur J. Schmidt Dissertation Fellowship, and the American Heritage Center for providing funds that were instrumental to the completion of my research. In addition, the following institutions and their staffs proved indispensable: the American Heritage Center, Laramie, Wyoming; Briar Cliff College, Sioux City, Iowa; the Chicago Historical Society; the Chicago Public Library; the Crerar Library at the University of Chicago; the Illinois State Historical Library; the University of Illinois Library, Champaign-Urbana; the Illinois Regional Archives at Northern Illinois University and Northeastern

Illinois University; the Indianapolis Historical Society; the Indiana State Library; the State Historical Society of Iowa, Iowa City; the interlibrary loan staff at Loyola University Chicago; the National Archives and Records Administration, Chicago Branch; the Newberry Library; and the State Historical Society of Wisconsin.

I am deeply appreciative to the Department of History at Loyola University Chicago. In particular, Timothy J. Gilfoyle has been both supportive and demanding since I first took up the topic of rural consumerism in one of his seminars. I am forever indebted to his willingness to polish my writing skills, ability to spot the logical inconsistencies within my arguments, and advice to constantly seek new ways in which to practice these skills. I am appreciative of his friendship. Susan E. Hirsch demonstrated to me the potential of quantitative research for consumer studies. Her critical review of my methodology and the relevance of my findings opened up a variety of potential sources that otherwise could not have been used for a study of consumer culture. Harold Platt, as my adviser, provided indispensable criticism of the many drafts of this work, at the same time keeping me focused on the "bigger picture." Even while separated by the Atlantic Ocean, I benefitted greatly by his enthusiasm, keen sense of region and place, and pointing out of numerous "opportunities" for me to rethink my conclusions. His friendship, advice, and optimism kept me focused on the project when the distractions were the greatest. In spite of such capable assistance, any errors or omissions that remain are my responsibility alone.

Ted Karamanski and Lew Erenberg provided critical advice at early stages of the research that helped me to justify and clarify the questions that I was asking. For Ted, an additional thanks for welcoming me into his office in 1990 when all I brought with me was a dream. From beginning to end, their comments and friendship sustained me throughout graduate school, the origins of this book, and my development as a historian. My only restitution to them is that I promise to work as hard with my students as they did with me.

As the research, public presentations, and writing of this study progressed, valuable comments and critiques were provided by Hal Barron, Bob Blahut, Linda Borish, Greg DeBenedicitis, Jim Farrell, Phil Hey, John Hoffman, Steven James Keillor, Gordon W. Kirk Jr., Mark A. Mastromarino, Harriet Moster, the dissertation and rural-history seminar groups sponsored by the Newberry Library (in particular the written comments of Robin Bachin and John Wills), Steven Reschly, Richard

Schneirov, Susan Schroeder, and several anonymous readers who made many helpful recommendations. Additional thanks go to Denise Burhoop, Paul Ives, Dawn Luensmann, Molly Moberg, and Mark Martin, students in my rural history seminar for their thoughts and suggestions. David Sanders at Ohio University Press merits high praise for making the process of editing and revising a creative, rather than limiting, experience.

I would also like to give special thanks to my parents, Paul and Gloria Blanke, sister, Barbara Blanke, and Bob, Joanne, John, and Mariann Moster for their support over the years. To Alex and Benjin, thank you for teaching me to work productively so that we had time for each other. The joy you afforded me may not be apparent within the text, but I assure you that it sustained me throughout the entire project. My greatest debt is to my wife, Janet. Her love, hard work, and determination kept me in touch with our own "roots."

Sowing the American Dream

Introduction

The Problem Itself

The farmer is endeavoring to solve the problem of a livelihood by a formula more complicated than the problem itself. To get his shoestrings he speculates in herds of cattle. With consummate skill he has set his trap with a hair spring to catch comfort and independence, and then, as he turned away, got his own leg into it. This is the reason he is poor; and for a similar reason we are all poor in respect to a thousand savage comforts, though surrounded by luxuries.
—Henry David Thoreau, Walden (1854)

For Thoreau, "the problem itself" was obvious. Rural America, and by extension the rest of the nation, had made a deal with the devil. Rather than trust themselves to grow their food, fabricate their clothes, maintain their homes, and find spiritual and moral sustenance in their self-sufficiency, planters aspired to a "livelihood" that promised tangible proof, in the form of wealth, that supposedly exemplified these transcendent strengths. The profession, also known as commercial farming, required ceaseless speculation about an uncertain future, intense and often illogical specialization, competition with one's neighbors, and dependency on a host of insatiable suppliers, most of whom knew that the farmer was incapable of stocking even his own "shoestrings."[1]

To Thoreau, the willful entry of rural America into the cash-market economy was akin to renouncing a birthright of virtue and enlightenment. The famed essayist's greatest concern, however, was the permanent loss of the United States' independence from the forces of capitalism. The agrarian ideal was not a simple abstraction to his generation. Obliged to reconcile natural rights with slavery, Western imperialism, and a growing industrial proletariat, Thoreau and others looked to the countryside as a refuge for simpler, more equitable answers to modernization. The "Puritan-republican" values espoused by Thoreau sought individual redemption through group harmony. Commercialization, therefore, not only threw

Americans out of paradise but threatened to destroy the only means of restoring grace.[2]

Before the end of the century, writers such as Hamlin Garland openly questioned this consummate faith in the countryside. In *A Son of the Middle Border*, his autobiography on rural Midwestern life from 1864 to 1893, Garland cautioned "those who think of the farm as a sweetly ideal place" might find time to consider the "disturbing" reality of child labor, family disintegration, misogyny, and rampant materialism. To Garland, neither farm living nor the pastoral "beauty of nature" had any positive effect on the moral fiber of the nation. Commercial farming had already installed a cultural thralldom to the marketplace; attempts to build rural solidarity or strengthen communal expression, such as the Patrons of Husbandry, in which his father actively participated, were pointless, he felt, because of the grinding realities of farmers' chosen "livelihood." As Garland somewhat caustically noted, "There [is] no escape even on a modern 'model farm' from the odor of the barn." Garland found his personal salvation in the busy streets of Boston and devoted much of his life's work to debunking the rural mythology.[3]

Thoreau and Garland grappled with some of the most vexing questions facing rural Americans in the nineteenth century. Central to their analysis was an understanding of how farmers maintained a sense of community while meeting the challenges of market capitalism. To Thoreau, the conservation of precapitalist social values was paramount. To Garland, farmers instead ought to concentrate on progressive reforms of their provincial culture. To both, the consumption of goods was a pivotal factor in the ultimate success or failure of their quest. Consumerism, whether expressed only as a simple desire for "shoestrings" or through the creation of a complex and "modern 'model farm,'" provided a clear gauge that measured the countryside's connection to the marketplace.

The link between consumption, community, and traditional republican values in the United States is well established. Republicanism formed the backbone of America's civic religion by cherishing incorruptible simplicity, equality of opportunity, economic independence, commonweal, and citizenship. To early critics, such as Thoreau and most notably Thomas Jefferson, consumerism destroyed community through rampant individualism, created economic dependencies through rising consumer debt, and fostered large and threatening corporate bureaucracies. Later reviewers, such as Thorstein Veblen, claimed that the black art of modern advertising was manipulating the isolated purchasers. Moreover, Veblen's influential 1899 work *The Theory of the Leisure Class* highlighted the extremely unproductive nature of "conspicuous consumption" (Veblen's phrase) as practiced by families of more than moderate means. Sheltered by their considerable assets, these individuals were blind to the larger needs of the community, he claimed. Their fashionable purchases drained capital away from the mass production of goods desired by the vast majority of Americans, thereby increasing unit costs and stultifying the economy. To Veblen, this prodigal behavior squandered a rare evolutionary opportunity for the capitalist order to progress. He held out little hope that the organic nature of U.S. society or a harmony of economic interests might correct these disruptive practices.[4]

Yet many people in the United States did not see materialism as a threat to republican values. Consumption, properly harnessed, could be a powerful and useful tool in supporting communal goals. In his novels *Looking Backward: 2000–1887* (published in 1888) and *Equality* (1897), Edward Bellamy predicted that the United States would realize economic justice and true republican virtue. The author's socialist vision, termed "Nationalism," was expressed most directly in his predictions regarding future consumer practices. In Bellamy's twenty-first century, all interest in fashion and elitist luxuries were excised from material goods. For example, women were freed from the gendered clothing, jewelry, and cosmetics that constituted their earlier cultural prisons. Further, retail outlets for the general consumer consisted of "public stores" that offered a wide variety of low-cost and guaranteed goods. As with gendered products, these changes liberated patrons from their dependency upon the modern distribution network. To Bellamy, consumption aided Americans in their attempt to regain self-control and resulted in a population that again cherished simplicity and utility. Significantly, in his sequel, *Equality,* Bellamy recognized that the changes to industrial capitalism and individual materialism could not transpire without a revolution. Incited by farmers who rejected the high-priced technology needed for their craft, Bellamy saw the agrarian unrest of 1873 as the "beginning of the final or revolutionary period of the pseudo-American Republic which resulted in the establishment of the present system."[5]

These impressions were supported by the active consumption practiced by the nation's farmers, particularly those of the Midwest. As a young man working for the trade journal *Agricultural Advertising*, the writer Sherwood Anderson suggested in 1902 that many contemporary retail suppliers overlooked the consumer élan of their neighbor farmers.

Anderson noted that only recently had "big, general advertisers" become aware that rural journals were "tucked up close to the hardest reading, best living class of people in the World, the American farmer." Driving home the point in later contributions to the journal, Anderson asked, "Don't you remember how your old daddy used to settle himself down before the fire . . . and spend long hours pouring over the advertising columns of the farm papers?"[6]

Oddly, given the concern over rural consumption at the turn of the century, little attention is evident in the modern historiography. The contemporary study of materialism in the United States developed rapidly once David Potter, Marshall McLuhan, John Kenneth Galbraith, Daniel Boorstin, and several others reanimated the debate in the 1950s. Intent on finding a unified "national character" within the postwar opulence, many of these early studies impatiently surveyed the austere countryside before turning their full attention to the cities. By and large, more recent studies have continued this trend while splitting the analysis of material abundance into three broad patterns. The first seeks to explain, much as Thoreau, the ideology and normative values associated with growing consumption. Jackson Lears, Roland Marchand, James D. Norris, and, most recently, Pamela Walker Laird look to unbundle these mores from the complexities of modern advertising. William Leach, Leigh Eric Schmidt, and Lendol Calder have studied department stores, holidays, and consumer credit, respectively, in a similar fashion. As a category, these works tend to revise or refute Warren Susman's claim that modern consumer culture replaced the Puritan-republican values of the nineteenth century for ones that supported industrial capitalism and justified the pursuit of personal gratification. But they also support the contention that individualism alone, not collective action, is the primary measurement of a modern consumer ethos.[7]

A second general pattern is evident today in the examination of the infrastructure that brought about mass marketing. An offshoot of the research by Samuel P. Hays, Robert Wiebe, Alfred Chandler Jr., and Carl Degler, these works explore the organizational changes to business practices and manufacturing processes that set the parameters for modern consumer culture. David Hounshell, Olivier Zunz, and Timothy Spears, for example, explore the fundamental transformations that manufacturing, corporate management, and distribution underwent in the late nineteenth century. This approach concedes that the suppliers of the retail economy controlled, as much as was possible, the pace and direction of change. In short, the maturing distribution network of the Gilded Age reached out and transformed the local customer into the national consumer. This method, potentially more deterministic—and certainly so, if misappropriated—contends that modern consumerism requires an infrastructure that largely was not in place in the United States until the close of the nineteenth century.[8]

Finally, some current studies look to local communities in an effort to register the actual consumption practices of the typical modern shopper. From Roy Rosensweig to more recent works by Lizabeth Cohen, Andrew Heinze, and Dana Frank, these sophisticated and detailed works have done much to substantiate the claim that consumerism significantly altered American society. By giving voice to the individual consumer, this breed of analysis has increased our awareness of the profound choices open to many urban shoppers. Driven by recent changes in the history of organized labor and urban ethnicity, most of these works are concerned with how class affects an individual's status as consumer. Still, each work shows how the determined efforts by a motivated population to direct the nature of consumerism was possible by the twentieth century.[9] Taken together, these three strands confirm that modern consumer culture was growing in importance from 1865 to 1930. Augmented by stable business platforms, armed with a motivated sales force, made accessible through rail, credit, and mail links, and backed by enticing advertisements, this new fashion of cultural expression made profound and rapid changes to the accepted social practices and beliefs systems of many Americans.

Yet what of rural America and the fears expressed by Thoreau and Garland? As noted, political and economic historians before 1970 generally ignored rural consumers and instead focused on a seemingly straightforward progression from frontier settlement to commercial stability in the countryside. Quick to identify benefits and barriers—posed by industrialization, the transportation and financial revolutions of the midcentury, urbanization, and the expanding global demand for U.S. food products—most inquiries sought only to find out who won and lost in the high-stakes contest over commercialization. While few early rural historians even stopped to consider the social costs associated with consumption, their work was neither insignificant nor in vain. Based on a mountain of early research, contemporary historians like David B. Danbom can now readily conclude that nineteenth-century U.S. farmers "might choose to be in the market a lot or a little, but they could not choose to be out of it completely."[10]

The market assumptions underlying these initial works came under intense criticism by "New Rural Historians" who rejected the conclusion that all rural Americans had an instinctive desire to participate in capitalism. By focusing on the smaller, interpersonal changes to rural society, recent historians have revitalized the questions and warnings first posed by Thoreau, Garland, and a multitude of others. They assume nothing was determined and ask whether and how the various communal and domestic links of transplants, persisters, and transients affected and addressed the growing materialism of farm individuals and families. The new paradigm interjects complexity and contingency on material and political change. Again, Danbom speaks for a large sentiment of contemporary scholars when he observes that "Agriculture, rural culture and society, and agrarian politics are so intertwined . . . that separation of them is misleading and excessively artificial."[11]

It is here, I believe, that agrarian consumerism emerges as a significant and largely undervalued component to both rural history and materialism in the United States. Only relatively recently have historians even addressed the changing purchasing patterns of rural consumers. In particular, William Cronon and Hal Barron have both helped to reestablish the central role that nineteenth-century farmers had in the formation of modern U.S. society and culture. In the process, both rely on extensive treatments of rural consumerism to support their theses. In *Nature's Metropolis* (1991), Cronon establishes a clear connection between the structural changes described above and buyers in the rural hinterland. Yet as the market economy took hold, most farmers lost their ability to identify the source of their economic ills. In Cronon's words, the market "concealed the very linkages it was creating . . . making it harder and harder to keep track of the true costs and consequences of any particular product." Cronon's depiction of Midwestern planters buying pancake mix (consisting largely of wheat grown in their own fields) from Chicago mail-order firms suggests that rural consumers were poorly prepared to come to terms with the forces of modern consumption. By contrast, Barron does show, in *Mixed Harvest* (1997), that farmers possessed a unique understanding of these changes but that their localism and small-businessman perspective prevented most from articulating, much less enacting, any viable organized response. In both texts, rural consumption is finally posited not as a deterministic backlash to urban change, but rather an integral part of this transformation.[12]

The central thesis of this book builds upon and revises this historiography by arguing that Midwestern farmers, between 1820 and 1900, consciously took advantage of the evolving modern consumer culture in order to better compete in the marketplace. At the same time, they protected what they believed to be vital notions of community. This population of commercial planters did not assume that they needed to discard communal ideals for the sake of individual gain, nor that market participation undermined rural solidarity. Rather, farmers' responses as consumers to the challenges of modernization were rooted in their traditional, vocational activities—behaviors shared by most of their rural contemporaries. In this way their collective consumer ethos was actually sharpened by modernization. As farming was transformed by the spread of railroads, urban centralization, currency retraction, middlemen, rising debt, modern advertising, and new technologies, so too did rural consumer strategies evolve and refine. As a result, Midwesterners expressed one of the earliest and most forceful modern consumer sensibilities of any population in the United States. Farmers not only intended to survive these changes, but thrive by them. They believed that collective consumer reform provided both the best method by which to succeed within the new economic order and, more importantly, the means to control and direct change to their own advantage. This doctrine was much more than an odd assemblage of shopworn credos and slogans; rather, it was a unique and highly modern ideological construct. Finally, *Sowing the American Dream* contends that rural Americans developed bold and active institutional strategies to bring about the required adjustments to the nation's consumer economy. While these organizations ultimately proved incapable of maintaining the delicate mix between communal and individual values, their failures were due more to operational and systemic errors, or timely adaptations by the private sector, than to a rejection of modern consumer culture by Midwestern farmers. In this way, rural consumerism directly molded America's early consumer economy in profound and long-lasting ways.

The consumer practices of Midwestern farmers are important for a number of other reasons. Most notably, the population under discussion was large and commercially active. By 1870, the four states most closely examined in this study—Illinois, Iowa, Indiana, and Wisconsin—encompassed more than five million rural citizens. This subset of men and women represented almost a greater number of like-minded planters from neighboring states and territories. In the same enumeration, Illinois alone claimed more than two hundred thousand farms, valued at $750 million (not including livestock), that produced 30 million bushels of wheat, 130 million bushels of corn, and 43 million bushels of oats. The leading farm institution for the region and era, the National Grange of the Patrons of Husbandry, claimed more than 858,000 dues-paying members, with savings from their collective consumer practices estimated in the tens of millions of dollars per year. Midwestern commercial farmers were neither a marginal group nor without economic means. Their collective consumer vision represented a powerful voice of dissent over the emerging purchasing practices in this country.[13]

In addition to the size of the population, its economic bearing was overwhelmingly capitalist. While families migrated west for a variety of reasons, following the Civil War few Midwesterners practiced subsistence agriculture. Even before this time, as Andrew R. L. Cayton and Peter S. Onuf recently noted, "The idea that [regional] settlers were ever fully self-sufficient is now generally discredited." By the 1850s, most planters were thoroughly aware that distant market conditions, the cost of money, productivity enhancements, and the extended distribution network were key components of their bottom line. Barron, Winifred Barr Rothenberg, and Christopher Clark, for example, show how many eastern farm communities were split earlier by the lure of market participation.[14]

By and large, those who remained to farm the Midwest had few of these divisive doubts about participation. Most had to pony-up more than a thousand dollars, usually by means of credit, even to begin working their stake in the Old Northwest. These were not protocapitalists or reactionaries hoping to arrest the cash economy, but rather knowledgeable planters searching for competitive strategies to provide themselves with the greatest degree of control over their lives. Their awareness ensured neither consensus nor success. Opinions varied as to how little or how much market participation was desirable. Many dissenters moved on. The history of the region's consumer campaigns is generally one of frustration and ultimately defeat. Yet the contest between commercial farmers and the market was played out using rules with which all were familiar. While they may not have been capable of sustaining their own local consumer outlets or urban supply houses, Midwestern farmers generally understood the financial reasons for such an effort. Their singular status as experienced capitalists supports the notion that their purchasing strategies were also novel.

It is important to note that while this large regional population did advance an extraordinary and well-founded consumer strategy, this study is not concerned with establishing Midwestern farmers as "the first" modern consumers. Too many other populations, such as those described by Clark, Rothenberg, T. H. Breen, and Carole Shammus, predate these activities to justify such a claim. But ultimately, any discussion of "firsts" are academic and largely pointless exercises. To avoid simply becoming parlor trivia, any assertion of originality should touch on the deeper themes developed within the historical scholarship. For example, the study of modern consumer culture is dominated by an analysis of mass-produced merchandise, mature distribution and sales networks, and sophisticated advertising techniques. On the other hand, the history of rural America has focused on the many ways in which the farm society struck a balance between communal and individual goals. I believe that the consumer practices of Midwestern farmers links these seemingly separate commentaries and offer ways in which to expand the debate beyond traditional "firsts" to more substantial questions rooted in the broader historiography.[15] For example, this examination suggests that the rural unrest of the 1860s and 1870s has been inordinately overlooked by recent scholars. If, as many contend, the "democratic promise" and movement culture of the Farmers Alliance was a direct challenge to the economic hegemony of large, urban capitalists, then their actions were pre-dated by nearly a full generation in the rural Midwest. While often slighted for its clumsy organizational skills, confused political directions, and screwy Masonic secrecy, the Midwestern Grange articulated a tenable and modern consumer policy that was in direct conflict with the established providers of retail wares. It is reasonable, and not trivial, to note that this large, regional community, organized through an extensive, national institution, came to terms with the forces of modern consumerism as early as 1868, much sooner than either urban shoppers or Alliance members.[16]

Finally, the study of rural consumerism in the Midwest returns to the troublesome themes introduced by Thoreau and Garland. In many ways, the relationship between the market, the countryside, and the commercial farmer has remained "the problem itself." Both writers saw rural America in terms of its potential rather than its reality, a problem that exists to this day. For Thoreau, the countryside was a place where the innocent yeoman accidentally "got his own leg" caught in the trap of materialism. Unwary of either the perils of capitalism or the Arcadian benefits of the countryside, the unfortunate bumpkins became the very agent of their own, and the nation's, enslavement. Yet this common misinterpretation fails to account for the day-to-day individual choices made by a host of husband-men and women who actively sought out and participated in the market-place. To Garland, by contrast, rural America retained no uplifting communal spirit to succor its citizens. As a result, individual farmers found comfort only in the base calculations of yields, prices, and labor, transportation, and storage costs. Regardless of his heritage, Garland's commercial farmer was incapable of connecting to social realities that were not first identified on a balance sheet. Garland ignored the strong sense of place and community that persisting farmers felt toward the land and each other. Both writers were guilty of a common mistake in consid-ering rural America. They looked to the countryside as a means to deci-phering America's future, a place to house the nation's potential, promise, and hope. In reality, rural America was a place rich in meaning for those who lived there.

Similar problems exist in our contemporary appreciation for rural America. Popular culture, in the form of books, television documentaries, and movies, tends to view the countryside as a testing ground for Amer-ica's commitment to a set of core values: independence, simplicity, democracy. In reality, life on the farm is as complex and paradoxical as any other place on the globe. While born and raised in the city, I have had nu-merous experiences with rural Americans and life in the country. As a young man I worked for more than three years as a groom for horses at a racetrack outside of Cincinnati. There I got more than an olfactory sense of the work patterns, commercial values, and unyielding responsibilities that came with the care of livestock. Not surprisingly, my co-workers, mostly from the city's collar of rural counties, expressed a strong sense of fellowship to everyone from what they called the back side; they showed little toleration for those unwilling to commit themselves fully to the par-ticular kind of hard work that was needed for success. If a task took many hours to accomplish, then so be it: we did not "punch the clock." We dif-fered from others certainly not because of some innate wisdom imparted by animal husbandry but, more probably, because we shared many occu-pational duties, goals, and values that are absent from more traditional commercial occupations.

While an undergraduate, I studied veterinary science and spent an-other three years following large-animal vets around central Kentucky. I recall numerous examples of exacting commercial farmers, willing to quibble over pocket change, demanding expensive and "illogical" medical treatment for their aging horses or inefficient dairy cows. While the reasons for their decisions were no doubt complex, many admitted that the afflicted animal represented something more to them than simply a broken cog in the agricultural factory. My college roommate hailed from a nearby family farm that grew tobacco on nearly two hundred acres. He and his relatives graciously allowed me access to their farm, their work, and their lives. While typical in almost every way to those whom I knew from Chicago or Cincinnati, his family, too, saw their work in both individual and regional terms. Rural communalism was and is distinctly a part of the country life, work patterns, and family history. It may be impermanent, contradictory, and, at times, self-delusional, but it exists.

Finally, my current home in northwestern Iowa is a region where agriculture, farm living, and the economic challenges of commercial planting are manifested daily. Here, county and state fairs are not places merely for city slickers to wallow in homespun nostalgia but energetic arenas for future farmers and cattlemen publicly to gauge their mettle and learn from each other. While attending the 1999 Woodbury County Fair, I was struck by how many of the characteristics displayed by nineteenth-century expositions still hold true and resonate within the rural community. This is not to suggest that rural America today is living in the past, but rather that past agrarian communities should be granted their own "present" that is free and clear of idyllic yeoman farmers.[17]

1 Buying the Farm

*The Midwest, Midwestern Farmers,
and the Origins of a Regional
Consumer Heritage, 1825–1860*

When William Clark first established his farm near Bloomington, Illinois, in March 1831, he owned an ox, a young heifer, and an iron hoe. Forty years later, Clark's prosperous son recalled that in the earliest days his family subsisted on a mere five acres of improved land that rarely produced a surplus harvest. He and his kin were compelled to travel "as much as 4 days to find where [we] could get corn to make bread," and what little maize they did work from the soil was coarsely ground at home. William Clark's neighbor Rachel Durbin similarly struggled to support her relations. In addition to the daily demand to "get up a meal out of almost nothing," Durbin searched "creek bottoms [to] gather nettles . . . after they had rotted through the winter, [took] them home, [broke] them the same as flax, [to] spin and weave and make clothes for her children."[1]

These dramatic episodes are important not only as demonstrations of the personal tenacity of Midwestern settlers but especially because of what these farmers soon accomplished. Within a few short months, Clark used the currency earned from his first cash crop—twelve bushels of corn—to purchase a modern rifle lock. Later, following more substantial yields, he invested in a team of oxen with which he could bring more of his land into cultivation. Durbin harvested sumac leaves for tanning and wild hops to sell to various Springfield merchants. Clark wrote that "a man in these times with a woman who possessed anything like the saving qualities [Durbin] did would not nor could not fail to get rich." Iowa settler Sarah Brewer mirrored Durbin's efforts in 1848 when she harvested wild roots and plants such as bitteroot and indigo and sold them in Des Moines and Dubuque. The money she earned from locating, "digging, drying, and selling" the produce was converted first into "a set of delftware dishes—twenty-four each of cups, saucers and plates" and later a large stove. Collectively, these efforts illustrate the central tasks of commercial farming in the Middle West: to correctly identify the marketplace, to use the land as productively as possible, and constantly to improve one's access to the market's benefits.[2]

The aggressive economic footing of the Midwestern farmer has rarely been disputed. In many ways, Carl Köhler, a German immigrant to the region, approached the heart of the matter when he surmised that "when doing business" his new neighbors had "no conscience at all, and follow implicitly the advice an Old Yankee once gave his son: 'Boy, make money; if you can, make it honestly—but make money!'" The region is frequently pictured by its frank materialism. In some accounts, the Midwest is even defined as being the "most American" of regions because of its affinity for market capitalism. Clearly, such a portrayal does little to explain *how* regional farmers became such ardent businessmen.[3]

Consumerism and market participation were not predetermined qualities of the region or of the rural inhabitants. The choices made by Clark, Durbin, and Brewer were not cold calculations based on the logic of an advancing marketplace but decisions deeply influenced by the particular challenges they faced in the Middle West. Regional folkways, immigration and ethnic legacies, governmental policies, and the very nature of prairie farming all acted as shunts and dams in the flow of the region's development. Moreover, sources simply do not exist to measure accurately the frustrations, hopes, and gratification that these consumers faced when considering material goods. We can only speculate on the feelings of the homesteader who, as was the case with one Iowa woman, painstakingly saved enough money to purchase a modern stove only to find that the device was primarily used as a place for her children to play. In addition, the inexact yet powerful values of agrarianism—such as economic independence, simplicity of life, and republican virtue—colored farmers' perceptions and recollections of rural society. One man from Henry County, Illinois, fondly remembered, under the title "Old Timer," his frontier community as a pristine oasis, unblemished by the evils of mass consumption. According to his account, the first settlers had "no amusements" to corrupt them—no "brass bands," no "theatrical troupes or concert company," not even a "daily paper." Ethnicity in the form of distinct material goods was not expressed, neither by "Germans, nor French, nor English, nor Irish," and "no Jews and no Negroes" were present to undermine their consensus. This chaste, yeoman community, according to the pioneer, never witnessed "a law suit between neighbors, never an accusation of crime, and never a family scandal. The community was an example of men living virtuously without government. Everybody did as he pleased, and no man trespassed on the rights of another, either in respect to person or property."[4]

With such an inflexible adherence to the "agrarian ideal," the thought of combining rural republicanism with consumerism seems almost ridiculous. Yet the two concepts are not mutually exclusive. The lives of nineteenth-century Midwesterners rarely posed such contradictory choices. Time and again, scholars have demonstrated the subtle balance between market participation and communal autonomy. Moreover, the ideological construct of producerism frequently crossed back and forth between the poles of community and marketplace. Dating back to (at least) the Jacksonian era, the producer ethos championed social harmony and communal order over capitalist individualism. Crushed by the depression of 1837, producerism was revived and modified during the 1850s under the new Republican Party. This second iteration was different from the first in that leaders expressed an opinion that property owners and labor might peaceably coexist within a capitalist frame. Through the GOP, producers found a home in market capitalism. In short, the accumulation of wealth by rural Midwesterners was neither the direct indication of moral decay nor a prophecy of the United States' capitalist future.[5]

More importantly the region was, in the words of Andrew R. L. Cayton and Peter S. Onuf, undeniably "a veritable bastion of liberal capitalism" by the middle of the nineteenth century. The potential for profits from the countryside were almost limitless. Even a brief list of regional capitalists—Cyrus McCormick, James J. Hill, Phillip Armour, and Richard Warren Sears—indicates the lush market opportunities afforded to those who met the needs of commercial farmers. Nor was prosperity only for the very rich. From 1840 to the end of the century, the Old Northwest boasted the highest annual rate of per capita economic growth (1.61 percent) of any region in the United States. Early market conditions were robust and generally egalitarian in distributing wealth. In Appanoose County, Iowa, initial settlers recalled how "homes, provisions, cattle, and swine were to be bought from the pioneer farmers; breaking-plows, clothing, and other articles from the dealers; lumber from the nearest saw-mills, and all paid for in hard cash. . . . It was the hey-day of the financial millennium." Although the Midwest may not have been created as a capitalist utopia, it quickly convinced many that it might become one.[6]

Yet, there were few early indications that the antebellum Midwest was any better suited than other regions of the country to advance a new, broadly conceived, consumer ethos.[7] In reality, most contemporaries assumed that settlers forfeited all claims to a modern society when they took a stake in Midwestern agriculture. As the *New England Farmer* assured its readers, "no man in his right sense would think of going west and taking up government land at $1.25 per acre. The chances are, as a general thing, that he will die before he gets anything like his good New England civilization." Most early manufacturers, peddlers, advertisers, and lenders shared in these apprehensions over the mud, shaky currency, high concentrations of Native Americans, and mysterious characters that were found in both fact and fiction. Their hesitancy and anxiety had profound effects for the economy and consumer practices of the region. If necessity promotes invention, then the absence of consumer alternatives for farmers loomed large in the formation of a unique purchasing strategy.[8]

One reason that the Middle West eventually did develop into such an economic dynamo was the intense concentration of new settlers who migrated to the region after the close of the War of 1812. With the fear of British-sponsored Indian uprisings temporarily assuaged, Easterners looked to the comparatively well-known territory of the Northwest for safe occupation. With the completion of the Erie Canal in 1825, the expansion of the National Road, and the continued improvement of harbors, rivers, and smaller canals, the bottlenecks to the human passage gradually cleared. As a result, between the second decade of the nineteenth century and the start of the Civil War, more than three million people resettled in the Old Northwest.[9]

The colonization of the region by native-born Americans took place during two distinct periods. The first occurred roughly from 1825 to 1838; the second began in the mid 1840s and lasted until the 1857 depression. The physical and temporal differences between settlement in Ohio, Indiana, and Michigan and those in Illinois, Iowa, and Wisconsin provide numerous exceptions to any gross generalizations about periodization. Still, the migration patterns and customs identified by historians such as John Mack Farragher, Jon Gjerde, and Kathleen Neils Conzen do suggest some broad similarities between both eras that contributed greatly to the formation of a distinctive Midwestern culture.[10]

The first phase of Midwestern settlement was girded by the completion of the Erie Canal and the Panic of 1837, when most state-financed internal improvement projects halted. The period saw the most dramatic population increase directly attributable to migration (rather than a natural increase). Although the migrant population consisted of both Yankees and Southerners, Midwest culture in these early years reflected much more of the latter. Borrowing their ballot qualifications from Kentucky, voting primarily for Democratic candidates, using Cincinnati as a regional trade center and New Orleans for access to world markets, the early Midwest plainly displayed its Southern sympathies. Preferring to raise livestock, particularly hogs that could care for themselves for most of the year, settlers from the South tended to allow the marketplace much less control over their farming decisions than will be seen in later generations.[11]

The second wave of settlement was precipitated by a variety of factors. The Michigan Copper Rush and the California Gold Rush, the Illinois-Michigan Canal, the effects of "Slave Politics" and the accelerated promotion of Western settlement by Northeasterners, the opening of the British grain market, and increased immigration into the United States—all these were instrumental in revitalizing the parade of pilgrims.[12] Unlike the earlier movement, which concluded only a few short years before the second commenced, this phase of Midwestern settlement was dominated by Northern migrants. Chain migrations, which targeted and drew family members to the West, were much more active in places like New York, Connecticut, and Vermont than in the South. The use of family credit and the limits to new farming opportunities in New England probably made the decision to move more compelling to Yankees. Susan Short May, who settled in Kendall County, Illinois, from New York, was typical of other Northern transplants when she remarked that her "residence was probably decided by the circumstance that a number of New York city people . . . had preceded" her.[13]

One particularly meaningful consequence was the rise in regional prejudice shown against the earlier arrivals. For example, May believed that Southern-born pioneers were "generally a poor set of farmers. . . . Many of them raise large crops and leave them to spoil in the fields." Another, a native of Plymouth County, Massachusetts, recalled how her Southern neighbors in Hillsboro, Illinois, lived well off the abundance of the land but showed no interest in improving their farms. Content with mere subsistence, she feared that "by another winter [they] should be able to sit by the fire most of the time. . . . Such was the standard of at least nine-tenths of the inhabitants that were our neighbors." References to slovenly, lazy, and generally dull-witted neighbors were common in the private letters and diaries of the recently transplanted Northeasterners.[14]

Regional tensions were also sparked by more personal considerations. For example, the Hillsboro farmwoman mentioned above took exception when her Southern-born neighbors referred to her miserly portions of food as "Yankee pies" or laughed at her dialect. Another woman confided to her mother the shock she felt when she learned that her neighbors made no observation of Thanksgiving. Only after "a family from good New England" arrived did she organize a party; only the New Englanders attended. Alvan Stone, another Massachusetts migrant, went so far as to suggest that because much of the southern Midwest was "peopled chiefly with emigrants from Virginia, Kentucky, and Tennessee," the "state of morals [was] generally very low" if compared with areas where Northeasterners were becoming dominant. Regional chauvinism was not universal, however. One Illinois settler attested that "upon going to [our] new home west of Galesburg, [we found ourselves] in the midst of Tennessee and Kentucky people—the most hospitable set of folks of the earth—and with the kindest hearts." Still, settlers were keenly aware of the origins of their neighbors and often were quick to apply stereotypes. The sectional tensions that arose in the 1850s only exacerbated this trend.[15]

Regional prejudice takes on greater significance when considering the two separate phases of Midwestern settlement. As the Yankee population grew in relative size, the biases took on normative and didactic roles. Cautionary tales about the improvident first wave served to reinforce the growing logic of capital investments and scientific farming in the postwar Midwest. For example, at the close of the first agricultural fair of Buchanan County, Iowa, held 21 October 1858, speakers reported that the earliest settlements were now "worn out by age and debility." Unlike their Southern predecessors, who seemed comfortable in just living off the land, the more recent arrivals came west "certainly, not to repeat the old system of decay that is urging the soil of the east into sterility, but to grow luxuriant crops and yet retain the pristine vigor of the fields by nourishing them with proper ailment." The carefree harvest of nature's abundance would be replaced by "farming [that] must be done on more wise and scientific principles. Scientific . . . is becoming deservedly popular in agriculture." The agricultural press, rural organizations like the farmers' clubs, state agricultural societies, and the Patrons of Husbandry, and even the Republican Party returned again and again to the symbol of the Southern wastrel, first established during the initial settlement of the region, in promoting their respective institutional goals immediately following the Civil War.[16]

While not concentrated enough to be termed a third wave, the constant flow of regional migrants westward within the Middle West merits at least tidal status. More than a quarter of a million people passed through and then moved out of the region by 1860, many to what they saw as greater opportunity in the Great Plains and Far West. By 1860, Ohio and Indiana were net exporters of people, with Illinois to follow by the next enumeration. Based on the census data, this itinerant population had some discernable characteristics. Few owned land: most were either squatters, tenants, or renters. On average, they were older than the persisting population. According to their self-declared occupational status, few saw themselves as farmers, choosing instead to turn toward other vocations that might bring them greater returns. Although it is hard, if not impossible, to draw any definite conclusions based on such sketchy data, one study reported that these "migrants seemed to be acutely aware of economic opportunities and strove to maximize their economic advantage." In short, it would be wrong to conclude that most of these travelers moved on because they rejected the strong market forces that developed in the Midwest.[17]

Decidedly, the single most important legacy of initial settlement was the local cooperation that it engendered. Writing about the Midwest, historian William N. Parker concluded: "Of all the puzzles in the frontier character, the paradox of individualistic neighborliness is the most striking and potentially pregnant with promise of strength for the industrial culture to come."[18] The ambiguous relationship between the community, their collective actions, and classic economic individualism remains at the heart of one of the most contentious issues surrounding our understanding of the region. In reality, the uneven market penetration in the Midwest from 1820 to 1860 makes a clear and distinct separation of cooperation and individualism nearly impossible at the regional level. While many came to the Midwest specifically to compete as commercial farmers, certainly others did not. Communal cooperation, therefore, often served both purposes, depending on locality, ethnicity, and personal preference. In one area, barn raisings, tool sharing, and labor trading might represent efforts to avoid the pressures of the marketplace, while in other locales these activities might serve simply as stopgap, emergency measures taken so that one might better compete in the coming years. What seems clear is that, as the Midwest developed, many local community associations became much more concerned with material objectives. As Hamlin Garland noted after moving to Iowa in February 1869: "We held no more quilting bees or barn-raisings. Women visited less that in Wisconsin. The work on the new farms was never ending, and all teams were in constant use during the week days. The young people got together on one excuse or another, but their elders met only at public meetings." Although it would not be true to think that Garland's account means that all Midwesterners abandoned all connections with their pre-market past, increasingly these elders met to discuss what they grew and how best to sell it in the modern marketplace.[19]

Ethnicity adds a further levels of complexity and ambiguity to Midwestern communalism. Foreign immigrants, after 1820, made up a sizable percentage of the white settlement in the region. Although fewer than 100,000 foreign-born pioneers had arrived by 1820, the Old Northwest saw a doubling of its immigrant population by 1840, and it doubled again by 1850 and yet again by 1860. By the time of Fort Sumter, the Midwest claimed more that 1.2 million souls born beyond the U.S. border. Collected chiefly from the German Empire, the British Isles, and Scandinavia, immigrants were drawn to the Middle West for a multitude of reasons. Although access to land was obviously a prerequisite, the simple promise of republican government, while often overshadowed, lured many, and the regular inducements emanating from the United States suggests that economic opportunity also ranked high in immigrants' decisions. Letters from family and friends added authenticity to the more official appeals being circulated by shipping firms, local boosters, and later the railroads and the Republican Party.[20]

The distinctive by-product of foreign migration to the Midwest was subtle but, in places, significant. Immigrants to the Midwest did not markedly differ in their demographic makeup from most other regions of the country; the "chain migration" experience was not all that atypical from that in the Southwest, on the border with Mexico, or the industrial Northeast. While the percentage of foreign-born citizens was high in the Midwest, hovering at around one-fifth of most states, it was not significantly greater than any other region in the United States and even lagged slightly behind that of the Pacific Coast. Once established, regional immigrants were more likely than the native-born to remain in one location. But this may be more of a statement concerning their American neighbors, who were well accustomed to moving within the United States, than any particular characteristic that immigrants brought to the Midwest.[21]

Rather, it was in the formation of what Jon Gjerde recently titled the "minds of the West" that immigrants most deeply affected the territory. Gjerde's analysis of the Upper Midwest builds on a wealth of previous work (notable contributions have come from Kathleen Neils Conzen, Robert C. Ostergren, and Walter D. Kamphoefner) that shows that immigrants to the Midwest rarely assimilated into the established culture. Instead, most of them transplanted and adapted their familiar culture to fit the new circumstances as best as possible. Gjerde's research supports the conclusion that, in the Midwest, ethnic communal integrity was strong and often acted as a bulwark against ideas perceived to be too individualistic or materialistic—clearly relevant to modern consumerism.

Still, it is difficult to find a striking divergence between immigrants and native-born rural people in their consumer habits. Undoubtedly, ethnicity affected how one lived in the antebellum West. From weighty decisions such as religious practices or crop selection to the more commonplace ones such as dress or diet, the customs that immigrants maintained did determine how they viewed and interacted with the growing marketplace. Yet very often it appeared that the distinctions between Yankee and Southerner, owner and tenant, or farmer and rancher were more substantial than those between native-born and foreign-born.[22] Moreover, the volatile national politics of the era seemingly aided many native-born Midwesterners in their acceptance of immigrants as full-fledged citizens. While the Know-Nothings flourished briefly as a frenzied response to the sudden rise of immigration in the 1850s, the equally strong rebuttal by Free Labor advocates and the demonstration that Roman Catholics could live as both citizens and communicants generally compensated for the bigotry.[23]

When taken together, regional migration patterns, communal cooperation, and ethnicity provide important clues about the establishment of a Midwestern consumer character. First, the size and scope of the human traffic within the region was unprecedented to that point in U.S. history. As a result, by the start of the Civil War many parts of the Midwest remained "a region of strangers." These strangers relied, of course, on their personal histories and experiences but also availed themselves of the fluid social conditions in the West to forge new institutions and relationships based on their recent and shared heritage. The rapid growth also accelerated the pace of change in Western society, its political culture, transportation needs, and market opportunities. But with so many new migrants, each cherishing their own dreams for the future, the social institutions of the region remained muddled. While their aspirations may or may not have included market participation, they certainly could not have predicted the intense competition from so many others willing to brave the challenges of resettlement.

Secondly, migration was directly supported by a variety of governmental and semipublic institutions intended to spur the economic growth of the West. From the building of the Erie Canal to federal land policies such as the Preemption Act of 1841 and the Homestead Act, settlers came to see governmental and other collective actions as fiscally beneficial and protective instruments. Richard Vetter and Lowell Gallaway noted about Midwestern migrants that they "appeared much more sensitive to economic opportunities, in particular to per capita income differentials, in making their location decisions than persons from any other region." Given the many uncertainties of prairie living, these monetary considerations remained as important indicators of a person's desire to come to or remain in the region. In spite of a strong Jacksonian-Democratic tradition, the Midwest was a region generally comfortable with an active state role in the regulation of the marketplace.[24]

Finally, the manner in which people borrowed to purchase land, moved to gain wealth or access to markets, and used the political process to fund internal improvements strongly suggests that Midwesterners had little if any long-term interest in creating self-sufficient, island communities set off from the marketplace. In many respects, newer settlers were even more interested in maintaining contact with the world around them, if only to stay in touch with relations left behind. Given the constant replenishment of new homesteaders, the drive to remain in contact with more developed regions was reinforced with each new arrival. Much like Robinson Crusoe, relocated Midwesterners did not look to create new institutions from scratch but rather worked to fashion together facsimiles of those that they remembered from their experiences in Europe or in the Eastern states. Failure to meet these expectations was no doubt deflating, but setbacks and consumer frustration also drove many to search for new ways in which to improve on, and profit by, existing access to remote goods.[25]

The market orientation of Midwesterners soon established itself as a distinguishing feature of the region's culture. Since the publication of E. P. Thompson's *The Making of the English Working Class*, an abundance of scholarship has added to the depth of our understanding of the "subsistence verses commercial farming" debate. The importance of Jeffersonian idealism concerning U.S. agriculture and society only adds intensity to this debate.[26] The crux of the problem is whether and how farmers chose to participate in economic activities that ceded control and undermined the moral authority of traditional social structures, such as the extended family and immediate community, in return for cash and individual freedom.[27]

What seems clear from local studies of frontier settlements is that few pioneers traveled west in order to immerse themselves in market economics. A desire to conserve tradition played as important a role in why people relocated westward as the desire to make money. Yet while these early squatters may have shown no preference for modern capitalism, the rapid spread of highly-capitalized agronomy thrust Midwesterners, willingly or not, to the fore of commercial farming. Allan Kulikoff's study *The Agrarian Origins of American Capitalism* represents a wide body of research that suggests that those who strenuously rejected market participation soon left the Midwest for regions that were, at least for a time, beyond the reach of capitalists.[28] The transformation to market-oriented farming did not transpire quickly, nor was it the result of a single, conscious decision.[29] Yet, as noted above, most Midwesterners were fully committed to commercial agriculture by the start of the Civil War and seemed willing to bear the burdens of dramatic social change in order to do so. The subsistence-versus-market debate rings somewhat hollow by 1860, as few Midwesterners had real options. While the economic prerogatives lasted later in Wisconsin and Iowa than in the more settled eastern and southern regions, there, too, farmers were soon forced to play the only economic game in town. As a result, the regional consumer culture was particularly well honed for the fundamental changes to America's industrial output in the years following the Civil War.

Subsistence farming, or the practice of economic self-sufficiency known as safety-first farming, was a prerequisite for early settlement. Accounts by and about early settlers reflect the need to grow or hunt most of their own food, make their own clothes, build and repair their own tools and shelter, and basically to trade what was a growing risk—participation in the Eastern marketplace—for the self-esteem that came with material independence. Yet as is clear in the accounts of Rachel Durbin and William Clark, while subsistence was an early reality in the Midwest, market participation was also an acceptable ambition. As Cayton and Onuf succinctly note: "The idea that settlers were ever fully self-sufficient is now generally discredited." Even such seemingly premarket characteristics as barter, shared labor, and the borrowing and use of a neighbor's oxen and horses were carefully chronicled by most diarists. These debts needed to be accurately repaid, not simply wrapped within a moral economy of communal obligation. Frequently, the meager cash earned from surplus grain and the natural bounty of the environment was used to improve the farm and, hence, to increase the settler's reliance on the marketplace rather than insulate the homestead from the outside world.[30]

Overshadowing these admittedly speculative factors was the capital-intensive nature of Midwestern farming. While some assistance could be expected from family members in the East, the typical homesteader in the Midwest expected to spend at least $1,200 in start-up costs for a farm of average 40-acre size. This price included land, housing, fencing, livestock, and domestic and field machines, plus the teams of horses or oxen needed to drive them. Larger homesteads of 80 and 160 acres required greater outlays of cash—approximately $2,000 and $3,000, respectively. Capital goods, including domestic articles, often accounted for nearly one-quarter of these totals. This kind of money, one historian surmised, was "more than was possessed by a good percentage of the population, and, although time could be substituted for some of this capital, the poorest households could still not enter Midwestern farming as farm operators." While the earliest years in breaking Midwestern land may sometimes appear to be isolated from the marketplace, it is highly unlikely that those with the wherewithal to spend or borrow these sums were interested in keeping their investment from bearing dividends.[31]

High start-up costs lent Midwesterners an ancillary benefit: a heightened knowledge of the emerging financial systems. Farmers forced to borrow money to buy land or machinery soon found it in their interest to be businesslike with creditors, merchants, dealers, and the government. Frontier merchants were forced to deal with payments in kind, but farmers soon came to appreciate the financial rewards that came with cash payments—rewards that took the form of discounts and avoidance of loans. Eastern capitalists increasingly pumped venture capital into the

Western economy, making the transition to a cash economy easier. As a result, the Midwest's agricultural surplus ballooned. From a mere 23.4 tons of annual agricultural export via the Erie Canal in 1835, by 1849 this amount had grown to 377.7 tons, or 72.3 percent of total exports shipped via the great waterway. The money invested in the prairie often took the form of first, second, and third mortgages, deferred payment for manufactured items, and investment capital for Western brokers. As Allan Bogue wrote: "From the late 1850s onward, more and more eastern businessmen, professional folk, and prosperous farmers came to cherish the Midwestern farm mortgage as an investment. For some the mortgage business was a natural outgrowth of western land speculation or investment in tax titles." Farmers became active borrowers, often holding up to five separate lines of credit on their property. Bogue held that the "suggestion that the very act of mortgaging was an indication of agricultural distress is, of course, quite erroneous." These extensive financial links provided Midwestern farmers both a logic and a financial incentive to develop new consumer strategies to tap into the existing marketplace, rather than try to invent their own institutions from scratch.[32]

Much as immigration complicates an understanding of the region's settlement patterns, so too does tenancy affect an appreciation of farmers' market orientation in the antebellum era. While the forms and afflictions of tenancy varied, on average it tended to increase the pace of market participation in the Midwest. Tenant farming generally fell into three broad categories: sodbusters, who improved land for resale before they moved on to other short-term opportunities; young families starting out, who often rented land from parents or other close relations as an interim strategy toward ownership; and a true rural working class. The latter—who were not, strictly speaking, tenant farmers—owned nothing except their labor and they tended to work for the largest "factory farms." Tenancy did not automatically mean poverty or an avoidance of the market, which, given such disparity, is little wonder. Wealth among tenants varied greatly, but no more so than among owners. The economic equity of Midwestern planters makes distinctions based on proprietorship difficult to gauge. Many of the most mobile tenants were those most willing to experiment with market economics. Only on the largest plantations was tenancy practiced in ways that related to the more familiar concept seen in the Reconstructed South or the Great Plains. Examples of two such spreads were in Champaign County, Illinois: the 70,000-acre farm of Michael Sullivant (of which a mere 23,400 acres were improved) and the 27,000-acre estate of magnate John T. Alexander that contemporaries remarked "might almost be called a principality." Tenants, while frequently more mobile that their landowning neighbors, were equally if not more enmeshed in the economy of the region and its emerging consumer culture.[33]

Regardless of land-ownership patterns, all farmers had to market something in order simply to remain on the land, let alone to become active consumers. The two most reliable cash crops in the Midwest were wheat and corn. Wheat was the easiest crop to get into the ground and to ship to market, but it suffered due to critical labor shortages at various stages in its production. Missing a harvest by a matter of days could result in the grain going to seed or its destruction due to foul weather. Corn yields were higher than wheat, but the product's bulk made it more expensive to market in distant cities and also required additional labor to harvest. As a result, many corn producers chose to sell their produce locally to livestock owners. The leading stock investments were swine, dairy cattle, and, for the more fiscally daring, beef cattle fed with planted pasture (grazing lots) or stored corn and silage (feed lots). Smaller markets existed for a variety of other products, led by oats, barley, flax, potatoes, rye, poultry, sheep, and wool. Most farmers grew and raised some mixture of these products. The Midwest was a patchwork of regional crops, herds, and various feeding and production methods.

Probably the best indication of vitality in a capitalist market is the dedication displayed by individual producers to maintain high levels of productivity. For example, while early Midwesterners were no doubt concerned about yields, breeding, and market prices during the settlement cycle, few invested their time and money on improving production. By contrast, in the period between 1850 and 1880, commercial farmers mechanized and investigated their craft with an intensity almost unrivaled by any other field or epoch in American history. Mechanization took the region by storm, and little in their recent past prepared Midwesterners for ways in which to deal with such change. This extraordinary transformation lent momentum to the search for still more means of increasing productivity.[34]

A brief account of the practices used will serve. The initial job of any prairie farmer was to break the sod. This living crust of the earth was the accumulated and interlocked roots of plants that had lived largely untouched for centuries. The turf was so tough that one Iowa settler joked that "a yoke of oxen could have been hitched to an end of a prairie-sod turned by plow, and a strip twenty rods long [about 110 yards] snaked from the field without breaking it in two."[35] Between 1830 and 1860, a series of innovative plows were developed, most notably by John Deere and William Oliver, that used a polished or "chilled" iron blade to cut the earth and to prevent the moist and matted prairie sod from clogging the apparatus. A skilled team of men and animals using this plow could break land at the rate of about 1.5 to 3.0 acres per day.[36]

Once the prairie was scarred and the farmer was convinced that the wound would not heal (that is to say, that the turf would not need to be broken again), the field was sown with seeds. For wheat and other small cereals, this was accomplished by broadcasting the grains and then, twice, either hand harrowing or using a horse-drawn drag to cover the furrows to protect the seeds from the colossal flocks of birds (particularly pigeons) that once existed on the prairie. Corn kernels, which were dropped by hand into the furrows, required greater precision in planting but were more reliable in their germination than the smaller, and more easily exposed, grains. During the 1850s, both planting styles were mechanized, allowing for one man and a team to plant nearly ten acres per day.[37]

Harvesting is probably the greatest and most obvious example of the benefits of mechanization. Before the 1830s, the only reliable method of harvesting was, for corn, to use the simple sickle, and, for wheat, the scythe, which often added a cradle to catch the cut stalks and had a slightly less bulky blade. Performance for a trained reaper ranged from about .5 of an acre to 2 acres per day, depending on the technology employed. Remarkably, some New England farmers warned against using the more modern, cradle scythe as late as 1837. But following the demonstration of Cyrus McCormick's mechanical reaper in 1831, and the patenting of Obed Hussey's competing design two years later, the mechanized harvester was seen to have truly arrived. With a performance of about 12 to 15 acres per day, mechanical reapers made it possible for farmers to gather produce from larger fields in a timely and economical manner, something that had limited commercial wheat production until then. In the final stages of grain production, the smaller grains such as wheat and oats needed to be threshed from their stalks. Originally performed manually, using flails or tethered animals, by the 1840s grain separators and fanning mills (to detach and blow away the chaff) completed the job of extracting a nutritious and marketable product from the prairie soil with half the effort. Corn was manually husked and then cribbed or left on the stalk to dry until spring. Because much of the labor and time-sensitive work had been accomplished by this time, mechanized threshing was the slowest technology to be fully implemented in the Midwest.[38]

Unlike other "revolutions," the agricultural revolution that ensued from mechanization truly affected all levels of rural Midwestern society. At its most basic, the change dramatically increased the productivity of the husbandman. As Allan Bogue marveled, by 1860 "the man who could sickle less than an acre of grain a day could cradle at least two; place him on the seat of a Virginia [McCormick] reaper, and he could cut ten to fifteen acres per day." Thomas Isern estimates that more than eight hundred thousand mechanical reapers were in operation west of the Appalachian Mountains by 1860. One firm, the Marsh Harvester, reported sales of more than one thousand machines per year in Illinois alone.[39] Estimates for improved productivity range from 25 to 35 percent for the average agricultural worker from 1800 to 1850. Between 1840 and 1900, work hours expended per hundred bushels of wheat fell from 233 to 108; for corn, they fell from 276 to 135. What made technology truly revolutionary, however, was how it multiplied change across so many other facets of life. Not only did production yields skyrocket in the Midwest, but farmers also found increased free time for other pursuits (which often included seeking knowledge of more productive methods of work). Immense amounts of hardware were ordered, most of which was purchased on credit; railroad construction was financially justified by Eastern manufacturers and capitalists; U.S. foreign policy began its slow change away from isolationism to the capture of distant food markets; and a small army of territorial agents were dispatched by manufacturers to comb the countryside in an effort to drum up additional business.[40]

Radical changes to the farm industry brought with it fundamental shifts within rural society at large. For example, while farm women rarely worked in the fields or outside of the home, and therefore did not benefit from the productivity enhancements that came from agricultural mechanization, they were integrally involved in the ultimate success of the farm venture. The growth of the family's awareness and appreciation of the market (discussed more fully in chapter 2) was of pivotal importance in providing women a greater voice in the fiscal management of the farm. The mechanized farmer also often cashed in his productivity gains on the cultivation of more land, rather than less work for mother. As Garland noted, reflecting the bitterness he felt toward his mother's hard life, while their new yields "were enormous and prices were good . . . [and] a constantly improving collection of farm machinery lightened the burdens of the husbandman, the drudgery of the house-wife's dish-washing and cooking did not correspondingly lessen."[41]

Mechanization also changed other traditional communal practices of the Midwest. Local boys continued to be the primary source of seasonal labor, but it was less likely that neighboring farmers had either the time or the need to assist each other during plowing or harvesting times. Although it is clear to anyone who spends time reading the various diaries, ledgers, and account books of rural Midwesterners that visiting patterns, contact with neighbors and relations, and participation through church remained relatively high, increasingly the shared public time of the community was dedicated to commercial interests. In short, localities were less likely to be linked by citizens' desires to conserve customs of the past than they were in a growing desire to adjust to, and often embrace, the future.

The source of this shift can be seen in the rapid rise in productivity and resulting fluctuation in prices. Particularly in the years before, during, and immediately after the Civil War, a period when most Midwestern planters had completed the first stages of mechanization, demand for wheat and corn shifted so radically that many farmers looked to formal organizations to try to gauge future market conditions. In addition, the new machines brought with them greater financial obligations and the need for new technical knowledge that was quite unforeseen by the pioneer generation. The formation of agricultural societies and farmers' clubs became the leading form of local association during these years.

Finally, the profound changes brought about by mechanization no doubt created or added to a heightened sense of anxiety. With the increased immigration to the region, a rapid transformation in the nature of work, a vast expansion of market economics, and massive shifts in production and prices, it would be remarkable if Midwestern farmers did not feel a little ill at ease. For example, in 1856 Francis Morse, a shoemaker of meager but stable means in Southbridge, Massachusetts, emigrated to Genoa Bluffs, Iowa, at the recommendation and financial assistance of his brother. According to family correspondence, Francis and his wife Sarah found many greater causes for concern in the West than they had experienced through his low-paying profession back East. As their fretting and homesickness grew, Sarah wrote increasingly despondent letters "back home." After six months, she complained that though "I try hard to drive the bad feelings off they will come on sometimes, & were it not that I hope it will be better for Francis on some accounts bye & bye I could wish I had never seen Iowa." The couple could not benefit by a moral economy of informal cooperation because they had "scarcely any society here [and] have not got acquainted with any of the neighbors yet." One month later, Sarah confessed that she tried "not to think of the luxuries I am deprived of any more than I can help," while Francis concluded, "In regard to living here I would say I did not come out here expecting to get rich so that I am not at all disappointed in that respect. I came here hoping that we might get a place that we could call home and if we are favored I think we shall succeed though we may get in debt some." Francis and Sarah Morse abandoned the uncertainties of the West and returned to Southbridge. Once there, while their prospects for wealth undoubtedly did not improve, they most certainly benefitted by the ease and comfort that family, friends, and predictability provided.[42]

Although the worst misappropriations of Richard Hofstadter's thesis concerning the "status anxiety" of American farmers have been corrected (as well as his errors in regard to Populism), it is hard to dismiss the regular, regional eruptions of nativist and reactionary movements such as the Know-Nothings or leaders such as Ignatius Donnelly as simple aberrations. Here again an appreciation for the growing influence of modern consumerism is instructive. Midwestern farmers knew how the market economy and distribution networks operated. They not only wanted to participate as capitalists but needed to take part at the fore of a movement that relied on modern and expensive technologies, complex credit and marketing networks, and protected worldwide markets. They were well aware that changes external to their local environment were occurring— that others, mostly monied interests in the East, controlled these vital aspects of their industry. In short, they knew that as individual entrepreneurs they were vulnerable to those with greater influence. Certainly such a population would be anxious about their status in society. While no doubt there were reactionaries, demagogues, and crackpots touting their own agendas, by and large the anxieties unleashed in the Midwest were those generated by fears that someone, somewhere, was profiting from the farmers' growing monetary dependency.

Midwesterners developed a variety of consumer strategies that either minimized their vulnerability or augmented their advantages. Their actions were based on the regional experiences of settlement, market conditions, and farming that constituted an internal, coordinated, and logical response to modernization. For example, agricultural presses developed locally to spread reliable technical and marketing information. Mirroring the early efforts of Edmund Ruffin, who circulated the *Farmer's Register* to Southern planters, and Northeastern presses such as the *Country Gentleman*, *Moore's Rural New Yorker*, and the *American Agriculturalist*, Midwestern farmers subscribed to the *Prairie Farmer*, the *Wisconsin Farmer*, the *Western Rural*, and the *Iowa Homestead* in large numbers after 1850. By the dawn of the Civil War, the nation claimed nearly sixty thriving journals that touched approximately 350,000 readers. On average, one in ten of all U.S. farmers were subscribers, with the proportion probably being significantly higher for those who were actively involved in commercial farming.[43] In addition, rural capitalists not only sponsored agricultural societies and their ancillary fairs, land-grant colleges, and political organizations, they acquired new relationships with manufacturers' territorial agents—all as reformative responses to the "financial millennium" that had descended upon them. When the Patrons of Husbandry exploded onto the scene in the late 1860s, Midwesterners benefitted greatly from the extensive heritage of rural associations initially founded to aid farmers with modernization. In short, these actions suggest that while Midwestern farmers were anxious about change, they energetically responded to the challenge in ways that reflected an internal logic. Their consumer patterns were only the most forceful evidence of this trend.

All told, by 1860, the Midwest proved to be a region that was uniquely receptive to changes in the consumer marketplace. In settlement, economic outlook, formation, operation, and communal disposition, commercial farmers gave voice to a rough consensus concerning the means, quality, and purpose of modernization. This does not mean, of course, that communities within the region did not promote competing economic or social values. Rather, the dominant consumer ethos that developed in the Midwest was elastic enough to encompass many parochial variations, while firm enough so that formal institutions could effectively marshal the ideals into a powerful movement culture. An analysis of the shared, everyday experiences that supported this ethos is vital in demonstrating the potential for an organized response by Midwestern consumers.

2

Breaking the Prairie and Taming the Market

The Formation of a Consumer Ethos in the Rural Midwest

The experience of mail-ordering, or sending away for goods, whether via U.S. mail or other shipper, using an 800 number from a catalog or through Internet shopping, is familiar to most Americans today. The pleasures of selecting goods, securing shipment, and anticipating a package's arrival can appear to be near-magical, and that they are relished is evident from the billions of dollars in annual sales tallied by mail-order providers.[1] Yet long-range shopping is far from being a new phenomenon. Rural Midwesterners have been availing themselves of "sending away" since the arrival of modern mail-order catalogs in the late nineteenth century, and accounts of the hopes and frustrations of rural catalog customers are legion. Obligatory references are made in most historical surveys of the period.

But although the process is well known, it will be useful here to consider the experiences of three antebellum Midwestern women: Mary Bradford, Susan Short May, and Jane Morse. The goods they requested were typical for the region and era. Bradford selected "an abundant stock of household articles," blankets, and clothing that remained "precious heirlooms" and family keepsakes for generations—a sentimental description that suggests the magic sometimes endures. May's description of her requirements was more detailed, although most of the goods were commonplace: "rice, tea, coffee, flour, salted meats, and loafed sugar, which

meant great cones of hard sugar, weighing many pounds, all kinds of gar-
den seeds, apple seeds and locust seeds." She also told of a request for
"furniture, a three-ply ingrain carpet, a high post bedstead of some dark
wood, parlor chairs of curled maple, and a very large mahogany bureau
with brass handles, a looking glass in a gilt frame with acorn pendants
across the top, and another mirror in mahogany frame." May concluded
her list with "Dutch ovens, copper tea kettles, cranes, andirons, and other
appliances for cooking in a primitive way." The third woman, Morse, related an experience common to all three, and no doubt many others: she
repeatedly "went to the depot" only to be frustrated by the fact that her
"goods have not come yet. . . . I hope my things will come soon for I shall
need my tools."[2]

I relate these stories because Bradford, May, and Morse were not
members of well-settled commercial farm families but pioneers, coloniz-
ing the Wisconsin frontier and the Illinois and Iowa prairies, respectively,
in the 1850s and 1860s. They were not buying these goods: they and
their neighbors were requesting the merchandise from their relations in
the East, playfully termed "plunder," not buying the goods from a retail
outlet. In all other ways, however, the experience of "sending away" was
analogous to that described above. Clearly, even early settlers to the region brought with them a keen sense of what goods were available, how
to gain access to them, and the costs associated with such a transaction.

Although these narratives do not demonstrate market participation,
nor any desire to participate, they do suggest a unique perspective that
Midwesterners accumulated on the unfolding consumer economy. As
farm mechanization proceeded, as the transportation infrastructure expanded, and as manufacturers and suppliers increasingly reached for farmers' pocketbooks, consumers who did participate developed a broader
appreciation for their place within this new marketplace. Correspondence
between early Midwesterner settlers and their Eastern kin teems with references to the type of goods available, their comparative prices, and relative
ease of access via the market. By 1860, one popular publisher remarked
that "the intelligent western people . . . , having done with speculations
and pioneer life, are prepared to devote themselves to the interests of their
farms and homes." This uneasy transition from frontier survival to industrialized commercial agriculture greatly influenced the consumer behavior
of rural Midwesterners.[3]

Critical considerations emerge, therefore, about the effect of commercial agriculture upon the developing rural consumer ethos. For
example, did Midwestern farmers publicly debate the logic of acquisition

in light of their unique market position? If they did, what ideological constructs did they use? How was this regional philosophy expressed? and were distinctions made between capital goods, such as machinery (both field and domestic), and noncapital consumer goods? How did the commencement of the Civil War influence the perceptions and economic reality of those who survived? How did economic and monetary changes after the war influence rural consumers in the Midwest?

We can be thankful that ideology and generalizations about the character of Midwestern consumerism are not necessary to demonstrate this process: the evidence is extensive that farmers were exposed to a host of new experiences that fundamentally changed their behavior and attitudes as consumers. For example, an open and conscious appraisal of husbandry, known as scientific farming, attended the explosive growth in commercial agriculture. Scientific farming was actively debated in almost every rural publication, and, invariably, consumer choice was a central consideration in how rural people were to modernize. Farmers' clubs and agricultural societies, sympathetic to "book farming," mushroomed throughout the Midwest, giving power to these new and pragmatic spending policies. The clubs sponsored fairs and other public displays that further liberated the discourse surrounding consumption and commercial farming. Of course, the centrality of the Civil War lent profound passions to these deliberations. We also get brief glimpses of people who were less than enthusiastic about the material changes to their lives. For example, the expanding commercial role of rural women and the faint voices of farmers who feared rising debt give us a sense of the growing complexity that surrounded the illusion of dependable progress on the Middle Border.

The term that commercial farmers used to describe their pursuit of economic efficiency was *scientific farming*. The central mission of this modernizing doctrine was to circulate practical information and to engender a shared logic for industrialized farmers to use by which they might better understand, discuss, and take advantage of the rapid changes taking place on their land. One contemporary wrote that the "improvement of agriculture need[ed] the aid of the wider range of knowledge which the advancements of the age have placed within its reach. But the farm has neither the text books, apparatus nor teachers necessary to impart it."[4] Scientific farming appealed to those who sought the "knowledge"; it castigated those who did not as backward, wasteful, and negligent. Information concerning soil conditions and conservation, better care and breeding of livestock and plants, crop rotation, and mechanization was distributed. Motivating those who sought these educational opportunities was a desire to compete better in the increasingly complex and competitive economy. Scientific farming, therefore, touched on all aspects of commercial agriculture, especially consumption.

In concept, scientific farming—derisively termed *book farming*—had genuine problems. For one thing, it could hardly claim to be a new doctrine. Many of the editorials pertaining to progressive farming only reiterated themes and practices first discussed by Eastern, and even European, planters. Moreover, the state of agricultural science was crude, leading Allan Bogue to conclude that "the advice of the editor sometimes was only an illustration of the blind leading the blind." A further problem was that the sharp criticism leveled by reformers against "dirt farmers," many of whom participated in the earlier and primarily Southern migration, carried with it clear class and regional biases: it excluded many marginal operators. Exhorting Iowa farmers to employ "more wise and scientific principles," C. A. L. Roszell closed the 1858 Buchanan County agricultural fair with the reprimand not to "stoop to farming" as had earlier settlers. Subtly contrasting scientific farmers with the presumed loafers who preceded them, Roszell concluded that progressive planning would "elevate [farming], with yourselves, to a plane of commanding dignity, by combining intellectual capacity with physical energy."[5] The *Prairie Farmer*, too, cautioned reluctant farmers to be aware that a new breed of husbandman had arrived—one who "by a judicious system of management, produces better crops, grows better stock, and consequently makes more money." The editorial concluded that if farmers chose to remain in a "quiet 'unconsciousness,'" willing merely to "plod on in the footsteps of [their] father[s]," they would be summarily dispossessed by the rational hand of market capitalism.[6]

Yet another consideration was the long period of time between specific improvements and finite measurements of success. For example, in the 1840s, the Osage Orange hedge plant became a reasonable, "scientific" alternative to expensive wood fencing. Many traveling salesmen, and more than a few grifters, took to selling the plant cuttings wholesale. The hedge became wildly popular, especially with the Illinois-Central Railroad. One "Model Farm" was celebrated at the Iowa State Fair for "quite a quantity of young Osage Orange hedge in a thrifty condition." After several years, however, the honeymoon was over. The plant required too much pruning, too much water, and tended to exhaust the soil more than forty feet from the fence line. Moreover, its lower branches were thin and allowed industrious pigs and cattle easily to find their way through the hedgerow and onto a neighbor's fields. By 1857, one Illinois farmer came to the conclusion that "the Osage Orange will answer for a hedge so long as you have a good rail fence on one side and a board fence on the other." By 1881, more than thirty years after the introduction of the progressive hedges, the import was being described as a "nuisance" by most Mid-westerners.[7]

Still, in the Midwest, scientific farming was most appealing when it demonstrated an optimism that was in rhythm with the growing expectations of material benefits that were to accrue from commercial farming. Prospective innovators were to be rewarded if they delivered the most cost efficient and desirable commodities to trading areas where demand for goods was greatest. In short, their challenge was not in breaking the sod, but rather in braving financial competition as no previous generation of husbandmen. While whistling past the graveyard, advocates of scientific farming used the speculative terminology and comparative descriptions of the marketplace to highlight the benefits of modernization and to popularize their doctrine. The *Prairie Farmer* insisted that "the spirit of competition must be aroused" among enterprising farmers. Scientific farming "must be talked of, agitated."[8] Some "efficient mode of instruction" was needed that would "concentrate, increase and diffuse this knowledge . . . and ultimately make itself felt upon every farm and through every industrial pursuit."[9]

The widespread dissemination of scientific farming among commercial farmers created and reinforced a set of strong normative boundaries. Success was the measure of a good citizen, and success was defined as applying farming techniques that were new and productive. Expanding acreage and yields contrasted sharply with the old ways, which valued stasis and independence. Criticism of these powerful assumptions was largely muted. In most instances, those most easily identified as being "backward" were poorer farmers or tenants who generally moved out of the region within a few years. These social constraints became particularly evident when scientific farming was brought before the public.

Agricultural journals were the first vehicles to carry this philosophy to Midwestern farmers. As with scientific farming, trade journals made their first appearance in the East and migrated westward with the settlers. Yet by 1860, Midwestern journals were reaching a far higher percentage of commercial farmers than those in any other region.[10] Historians have long paid close attention to these popular new publications. For the most part, they found that editors were chiefly propagandists for their readers' economic causes and proponents of modern farming techniques. While some editors and publishers professed disgust for "book farming," their columns were generally filled with practical advice on how to keep farm ledgers, conserve soil, use fertilizer, and the like. Much more than other rural institutions, the journals frequently advocated political solutions; for example, stricter fencing laws, a national system of internal improvements, and mandatory primary education.[11]

The *Iowa Homestead*, a bellwether regional publication, provides a useful example of the origins and evolution of a typical rural press. Started by Mark Miller in Milwaukee in 1849, the journal was first published as the *Wisconsin Farmer*. Under this title it dealt almost entirely with Eastern methods of farm improvements and scientific farming such as crop rotation and fertilization, presented as means by which to reanimate deteriorating soil. When Miller moved to Dubuque in 1856, he was one of thousands flocking to the state. Between 1850 and 1860, Iowa's population exploded from a relatively modest 200,000 to nearly 675,000. Appealing to these new farmers, who hailed mostly from Ohio, Indiana, Pennsylvania, and New York, Miller changed the title of his weekly to the *Northwestern Farmer and Horticultural Journal*. He expanded its coverage to include a wider variety of Midwestern concerns: the care and marketing of fruit trees; regional commodity prices; editorials on the effect of national politics on the Midwest. Echoing the traumas of the market crash in 1857, the press temporarily scaled back its boosterism and concerned itself with more pedestrian chores and even dabbled in fiction. But with the return of boom years and the inevitable bust after the close of the Civil War, the journal took on added zeal in its promotion of organized improvements and demands for more active and democratic controls over farmers' economic destiny. When William Duane Wilson purchased the sheet in 1869, he fully committed the renamed *Iowa Homestead* to the Patrons of Husbandry and associated political activity.[12]

The bindings of farm journals and account books were often covered with pasted-on pages taken from journals. The pages presented articles of particular interest to a progressive farmer. Illinois planter Asa Abbot's diary was typical when, between 1849 and 1850, he collected information on topics ranging from "Ashes for Peach Trees" and "The Culture of the Pea" to "Improvements in Farm Implements: The Plow, the Thrasher, The Horse Rake" and more straightforward pieces culled from the *Albany Cultivator*. Abbot attached the following quote to his diary—words that could have served as a mantra for his commercial efforts: "Let every farmer who has a son to educate believe and remember that science lays the foundation of every thing valuable in agriculture."[13]

Unfortunately for the rural community, the frenzied promotion of scientific farming by the farm press did not always profit its readers. The combination of persuasive advice, misleading advertising, and rising competitive pressures convinced many credulous farmers to gamble their homesteads on untried technology and spurious quick fixes. One historian noted that unprincipled salesmen used the journals readily to "fleece unsuspecting farmers." Often, charlatans would sell a "non-existent journal to the public, or, after one or two issues, escape with the subscription money." Periodicals were also guilty of political demagoguery that undercut their nonpartisan, practical recommendations. However, despite these and other pitfalls, agricultural journals made practical knowledge readily available to commercial farmers and provided substantiality to the philosophy of scientific farming.[14]

By 1850, the merger of scientific farming with the agricultural press created a powerful scripture for the evolving Midwestern economy. When taken in conjunction with the arrival of hundreds of thousands of new migrants and the firm establishment of mechanized farming, the era took on the feel of a movement. The backbone of the crusade was the judicious evaluation, purchase, and use of modern agricultural machinery. The emergence of a staple-crop agriculture led to a standardization of the technology with which to process the crops, cook the food, and market the surplus. Propelled by the growing demand for wheat, corn, and hay, farmers turned to machinery that predictably and steadily increased yields. Commercial farmers were not, however, encouraged by the market to innovate with untried equipment: those who attempted to change technologies gambled with their very livelihood in the event of failure. Farmers sought information in periodicals to temper this risk.[15]

The use of agricultural machinery was the most visible evidence that farmers conformed to the principle of market efficiency. The largest farms, such as Michael Sullivant's 70,000-acre estate, teemed with mechanical apparatus. In 1866 one reporter wrote that most of Sullivant's work "is done by machinery. He drives his posts by horse power, cultivates his corn by machinery, ditches, sows and plants by machinery, so that all his laborers can ride and perform their duties." Sullivant boasted that he employed two hundred farm hands, two hundred horses, "and a large number of children" to run his operation. Farms of moderate size were proportionately mechanized. Even the smallest holdings, from forty to eighty acres, believed that they benefitted by investing in capital improvements. One farmer in Christian County, Illinois, opined that "prairie breaking is something of a job and requires a good steel plow." While the farmer believed that, before 1857, it was not possible to do the job alone, "it has been since found that 12-inch plows of peculiar construction, and two or three good horses can do the same work as a 24-inch plow and five yoke of oxen." Territorial agents such as J. M. Wilcox noted that the introduction of machinery such as the Marsh harvester created "considerable interest" throughout the Illinois farm community and that selling was simplified because "all [farmers] seem to like the principle of the machine." The desire to use the latest agricultural technology permeated the entire range of commercial farms.[16]

The tales about purchase and evaluation of threshers, seed drills, and reapers are important, but it should not be forgotten that capital investments were not limited to machines used in the fields. Scientific farming was holistic: economic efficiencies in the domestic sphere had to equal those of the pasture. Probably the best example of the symmetry between field and farmhouse was when the crops were harvested. One typical Illinois farm, occupied by Myron and Jane Farnham Boughton in late 1850, consisted of 60 acres of wheat, 80 acres of oats, 120 acres of corn, and 200 acres of "tame hay." Boughton required up to eleven men to bind and shock the wheat, thresh the oats, and harvest and store the corn and hay.[17] The arrival in the fall of these skilled teams comforted farmers knowing that their crops would soon be secured, but they also created intense disruption for the family, and particularly for the matron of the house. Boughton recalled how, "one night about 10 o'clock, without warning, the thresher came. There were four men to be fed and lodged and four spans of horses to be stabled and cared for. To carry out the work properly we required a gang of thirty men or more." Most of Boughton's helpers were day workers from the village, but they, too, had to be fed. They were given three meals at the farm. Hamlin Garland remembered that "the gathering of the threshing crew was a most dramatic event to my mother." Teams often spent two to three weeks on each farm. Domestic chores, such as preparing and cooking meals and cleaning for so large an army of hands, often necessitated "extra helpers for the work of the house."[18]

Come fall, accounts by farm women who had to accommodate the crews dominate their diaries and letters. Lydia Moxley, for example, who toiled with her husband raising wheat, oats, corn, and hogs on a farm in Grinnel, Iowa, saw her seasonal duties for 1877 begin on Monday, 13 August. She "did up work and Kate W. came over to help me cook for threshers." The following day, what reads like a seemingly endless litany began: Tuesday, "I did up work. . . . We had 5 hands to supper. Made cake, pies, etc."; Wednesday, "did up work . . . made 6 pies and 4 loaves of bread, cooked beans, beef, etc. Kate Walker was here. We had 7 to supper. Mrs. Rowe called. I baked all the things myself." By the end of the month her entries simply read: "Worked hard all day." Lydia's last reference to the harvesters and threshers for the year was not until 5 September; she simply concluded, "Had 9 men here to dinner & 5 to supper. Baked 5 pies and 2 rice puddings." An Illinois farm woman, Catherine Durin, who self-consciously wrote with "sutch a poor pen," was shocked to learn how, in California, when "Men folkes ar . . . thrashing their barley they donte halve many men hardley [and] they halve onley twentey two for dinner . . . this is rather difrent from our thrashing."[19]

The sudden saturation by large numbers of laborers pressured women to keep the farm running at peak efficiency. A Chicago publication, the *Chase Western Rural Handbook,* noted that "before the introduction of agricultural machinery, farming operations were conducted upon a limited scale. . . . But now, how changed!" With the arrival of the reaping and threshing teams needed to collect the larger yields, "the western farmer's home is often converted into an Irishman's boarding-house, and the kitchen, contracted [in space] and illy furnished, becomes a sort of dutiful penitentiary." The same article asked readers if their farm kitchens were "the latest and best, and equipped with a troupe of new-fangled contrivances for doing the baking, broiling, roasting, steaming and boiling? What special facilities do you [have] for washing, drying and ironing the clothes . . . ?" Although farm work had been revolutionized by new inventions, "farmers' kitchens seem to have withstood the insinuations of genius, and derided all attempts at material improvement." Household work was included in the scope of scientific farming— indeed, was seen by this Chicago publication as presenting "the most pressing demands of a farm establishment" because it directly affected the commercial farm's bottom line. Publications pressed farmers to conform to the rigors of commercial agriculture by modernizing the domestic workplace.[20]

The contribution of women to the financial success of family farms was fundamental. In addition to feeding and clothing the family, women were responsible for growing, harvesting, and preserving most of the fruits and vegetables, manufacturing medicines, soap, and candles, and maintaining important social connections to the community. Garland recalled that his mother never enjoyed "a full day of leisure, with scarcely an hour of escape from the tugging hands of children, and need of mending and washing of clothes." He recalled her passing "from the churn to the stove, from the stove to the bedchamber, and from the bedchamber back to the kitchen, day after day, year after year, rising at daylight or before, and going to her bed only after the evening dishes were washed and the stockings and clothing mended for the night."[21]

By embracing the economic importance of these household duties, scientific farming reconstructed the functional role of women in the farm family: the woman was now a competent consumer. In Rochelle, Illinois, a female settler remembered, somewhat romantically, "farming was being done on new and different lines. Improved farming machinery was invented and bought. . . . The spirit of improvement and progression was abroad in the land. Homes were made more comfortable, and women found relief from much drudgery by the use of the many household helps." Unlike long-term improvements in the field, productivity gains through the use of stoves or sewing machines were more easily noticed and appreciated. They directly affected the family's basic needs. Above, we took time to study a detailed description of farm tasks in order to fully appreciate the potential for mechanization; here, a survey of women's "duties" will be instructive in appreciating the connection between the farmhouse and consumption.[22]

Yet in reviewing women's work on the farm, it is important to keep in mind that, as researchers like Ruth Swartz Cohen have demonstrated, while women were as susceptible as men to the lure of scientific and progressive improvements, many of them were still concerned with preserving family autonomy and a sense of place for themselves and their relations. Consumption often served several tasks. Sharp distinctions did not exist between the farm wife's household chores, her duties involved in raising a family, participation in the community, and fulfilling individual hopes.[23] One Iowa woman listed her duties as a "regular routine of water carrying, cooking, churning, sausage making, berry picking, vegetable drying, sugar and soap boiling, hominy hulling, medicine brewing, washing, nursing, weaving, sewing straw platting, wool picking, spinning, quilting, knitting, gardening and various other tasks"; but notwithstanding the apparent even tenor of this woman's comprehensive "routine," in other accounts some activities stand out because of their ubiquity and reported monotony and drudgery (not to mention their especial relevance, for this study, to consumption). Sewing and the care of clothing was a daily routine. Emblematic was Matilda Paul, who moved to Wisconsin in 1854 and then Iowa seven years later. She recalled the stitching she did just to make herself "ready for housekeeping. I made enough quilts, sheets, and pillow cases for two beds"; this, in addition to hemming and adorning her clothes, kept her "quite busy sewing." Sarah Ann Davidson lamented in a letter from Carthage, Illinois, to her sister that she could not keep up with the continual mending. Davidson's recourse—in order that that her "own sewing would be so caught up with"—was paying for "the assistance of a 'girl' [then] I could get along nicely." Although Davidson had "an entire infants wardrobe to make up" while her son "Willie [wore] out nearly everything he had," financial considerations prevented her from hiring a seamstress. Christina Ann Rook summed up her day's work of preparing to make a rug with the terse recollection that "I have been cutting rags all day. My arms aches a good deal tonight."[24]

The introduction of the sewing machine by Isaac Singer in 1851 (an invention that was to be endlessly improved, patented, and manufactured from then on) revolutionized the nature of home clothing production. It cut the time spent handsewing by nearly 90 percent. Records left by many farm women indicate that they welcomed the autonomy associated with the automation of their drudgery. An Indiana farm woman, Ellen White, in a series of letters between her and her mother Sarah Tyner, discussed the rationale for her desire to purchase a sewing machine. The traditional practice of hand sewing had mangled her fingers and wracked her body with pain; she wrote that, as a result, "my side is so bad [that] I do all my sewing at the neighbors." The neighbor owned a machine, but this proved to be only a temporary solution: Ellen admitted that she was too "ashamed to go anymore," and her thoughts turned to owning a machine of her own. She wanted "to have a little something to be *independent*." After she finally refused to sew at all, the family bought her a seventy-dollar Singer, and with it, in one season, she completed "five full suits of little clothes."[25]

Another task involving extensive labor that women believed should be scientifically improved was the treatment of animal fats to produce soap and candles. In the old process, women first manufactured lye by leaching, in boiling water, wood ash that had been conscientiously collected over a period of months. Once the caustic chemical was clarified, they boiled it up with animal fats and entrails to produce soap. If soap making was a chore; candle making was nearly intolerable. In addition to the subtle chemical engineering required to fashion a tallow that was neither too soft in warm weather nor too brittle in cold, wives and daughters spent countless hours holding racks of wicks at arm's length, executing a repeated dipping process. Pioneer Christiana Tillson estimated that rural women averaged making four hundred candles each per year. She recalled: "Were I to attempt to tell you the process, or the labor bestowed on these 'nocturnal luminaires,' you would not comprehend it." Tillson and her contemporaries must have greatly welcomed the distribution to local stores of mass-produced candles and soap flakes.[26]

Food preparation was, of course, a constant task for most women. Just accumulating the raw materials for cooking must have seemed to be almost a full-time job. This involved growing vegetables and herbs in the truck patch, churning butter, grinding corn, collecting eggs, and even "search[ing] the fields and woods for herbs, roots and fruits." Once the ingredients were assembled, cooking itself was an assembly-line-like process that was undertaken two to three times per week. Some baked or cooked foods were stored in as cool a place as possible in sealed containers. Most freshly made entrees, such as pork and "corn doggers" or johnny-cakes, were fried in grease just before the family sat down to eat. Sarah Brewer-Bonebright of Newcastle, Iowa, recalled how "Mush and milk, or fried mush," rounded out many meals; she called them "staples which recurred almost with diurnal persistence." Frequently, large kettles were kept filled with stews or "coffee" (often, but not always, made with real coffee beans). The kettle "bubbled all day long on its nest of coals for the benefit of tired or belated hunters." Women's culinary knowledge was drawn upon not only to meet nutritional needs but also to fashion home remedies such as "bitters," using barks and natural herbs: water pepper, pennyroyal, and velvet dock concoctions all were liberally diluted with corn whiskey. Probably many knew their limitations as pharmacists because, as Brewer-Bonebright confessed, they increasingly purchased "home-remedy preparations, as soon as they could be procured from the apothecary shop."[27]

It is thus not difficult to see why farm women were strongly attracted to the progressive principles of scientific farming. Francis Gaston wrote to the *Prairie Farmer* that in a typical day, when many rural women rarely had time even for trips "in and out" to the bathroom, they demonstrated "the patience and skill necessary for a general." She lamented that "In this age of inventions, nothing seems to meet the demands necessitated by a

large family, living too far from town." Yet women were increasingly turning to solutions offered by the marketplace to ease their burdens.
Whether they bought patent medicines at the local store or a stove or
sewing machine from a traveling agent, farm women, through their purchases, became knowledgeable about the consumer marketplace and were
quick to use their social connections to compare prices, quality, and conditions of sale. When Anna R. Morrison, the wife of a well-to-do New Orleans merchant settled in Jacksonville, Illinois, in 1840, she was stunned
to meet women who were like "living table[s] of prices current"; they
could often "talk nothing else" than the costs for consumer goods. Morrison marveled that when she sat with prairie women in the parlor, she
was less likely to be asked about "some philosophic or scientific idea" than
be queried: "What does butter sell for in the city?" Of one woman in particular, Morrison remarked: "If I were an editor, I should consider her a
valuable wife; for she is perfectly competent to give a daily table of prices.
. . . She is to me truly formidable." Women soon discovered that as well as
being able to purchase goods, they had marketable skills. Younger farm
women worked outside the home to earn a little extra money. In a few instances, they pooled their resources and opened shops in town as
"milliners, dressmakers, seamstresses, and fancy goods merchants." As
Lucy Eldersveld Murphy recently concluded, Midwestern businesswomen
of the era "capitalized on activities that were extensions of their duties as
mothers and homemakers."[28]

Many farm men were not comfortable with these activities, believing
that "one employment after another is taken out of the hands of women
folk by the innovations of machinery and associated labor." Nostalgic for
the days when their grandmothers spun and wove (and, although this was
probably less well remembered, in Rachel Durbin's case collected nettles
from creek bottoms), they groused that now "our wives barely recollect
homespun; [and while] they *can* make up their own garments . . . little is
left for our daughters to do but wear them out."[29] Not surprisingly, the
contributions of women frequently went unobserved. Lydia Moxley—the
woman cited above for her contribution to feeding and caring for harvesting teams—is a case in point. Less than a month after she finished her
cooking, cleaning, and mending, "3 men came with a sewing machine. I
got dinner for them and they went off [with her husband] to hunt prairie
chickens." While the men prowled, Lydia no doubt experimented with
the gadget; the men had "left their sewing machine here" for her to ex-
amine. The price asked was thirty dollars. Lydia recorded soberly that

"Anson would not buy it." Interestingly, only days later, farmer Moxley sold three hogs—fattened by the plants so economically harvested by his well-fed workers—for $27.50.[30]

The dual role of maintaining both home and community probably aided in women's growing participation as modern consumers. Mary Neth, Steven Hahn, and Jane Marie Pederson have shown how the visiting patterns and social skills of rural women were key in maintaining local links between families. No doubt this community socializing did much to convince men to support women's desire to automate their chores. Christiana Tillson humorously records how her "first few months' housekeeping was made uncomfortable by the Sunday visiting."

> By the time our breakfast was over and our morning work disposed of there would be a tremendous knocking at the door, accompanied by sonorous demands of "who keeps the house?" Sometimes with the knocking would come, "housekeepers within?" sometimes nothing but a loud, drawling, "h-o-u-s-e-k-e-e-p-e-r-s!" and when the door was opened a backwoodsman would walk in with a big baby on his arm, followed by the wife with the youngest in both her arms, would introduce his lady, and let us know they had come for a day's visit. . . . [Often they] would go about the house taking up things and ask, "whart's this 'ere fixin?"

By combining their requests for store-bought, labor-saving improvements (sewing machines, stoves, and so forth) with the needs of the family, many rural women were able to serve both objectives.[31]

Public and press were mute about these unintended social consequences, but editorials nearly crackled with progressive advice about the vital monetary skills that were required for market participation. The cost of acquiring capital goods was not insignificant, accounting for nearly one-quarter of the start-up costs for a typical Midwestern farm (see chapter 1). Entrepreneurs turned to the logic of scientific farming to find ways in which they could best evaluate and acquire essential gear.[32] Insolvency was rarely a problem for owners of commercial farms in the antebellum Midwest—a point important to note in this study of rural consumerism. Further, researchers have found that wealth distribution among all regional farmers, both tenant and proprietor alike, was much more egalitarian than at any other time in the nation's history.[33] Farmers temporarily strapped for cash could often find some method by which to obtain goods. As discussed in chapter 3, local and regional agents extended liberal credit terms to farmers in their efforts to secure sales. Another source of financing is revealed in an 1858 article titled "The Cost of Operating an Illinois Farm." The author observed that it was "customary for a number of farmers to join together in purchasing . . . expensive implements, and to work them in common." Still, there was plenty of motivation for planters to seek ways to buy outright: the specter of foreclosure on an article as integral as a reaper or the frustration of being last in line to use a group-owned wheat thresher was tantamount to a loss of economic control.[34]

Purchasing strategies, like the devices they were designed to purchase, were an integral part of the educational doctrines of scientific farming. The two topics went together, and the sites of this fusion were the agricultural societies and farmers' clubs. These rural associations, first seen in New England during the 1840s and 1850s, began in most Midwestern states as informal bodies comprised of regional farmers who met to discuss current agricultural practices, coordinate political and economic activities, and, most importantly, to organize local and county fairs.[35] Members believed that these democratic organizations "raised the standard of farming . . . and expanded, and liberalized, and in every way improved the minds of farmers." As Allan Bogue noted, "the most significant aspect of membership may well have been the discussions that took place." At their monthly meetings, experienced farmers tutored their neighbors on the utilitarian aspects of irrigation, fertilizers, and plant husbandry.[36]

Although clubs circulated general agricultural information, their main focus quickly turned to the mechanical arts. In the 1856 edition of *Transactions of the Illinois State Agricultural Society,* a state body that coordinated the actions of local farmers' clubs, the society's correspondence secretary, John A. Kennicott, held that clubs could "hardly be called 'educational institutions,' though [a] great number of ignorant farmers and mechanics receive [their] first lessons in progressive agriculture and art through their agency." Kennicott wrote that the clubs' "true mission" was to "draw public attention to great improvements in the arts of production." His view was endorsed by the *Prairie Farmer.* In forming a club, said the journal, "the most effectual method of getting up an interest among farmers" was by holding county and town fairs to display new machinery.[37]

The staging of local fairs was the single most important contribution made by farmers' clubs to Midwestern consumer culture and the spirit of scientific farming. Agricultural fairs were the most likely places where the average commercial farmer would be enlightened on the purchase and availability of modern machinery. These expositions were the most widely publicized and attended events in the farm community from 1850 until 1870, a period once termed the Golden Age of agricultural fairs. At first, organizers were glad simply to see that their efforts were met with local participation. Herbert Blakely, secretary of the Ridott Agricultural Society, in Illinois, claimed to have organized the first local fair in 1857. It was "numerously attended . . . everyone was astonished that [the] town alone could produce such an exhibition." Midwestern states soon became the most active in organizing and attending fairs. Not even the Civil War interrupted the pattern of annual fairs in many locations. By 1867, the region was home to more than half of the 1,032 national agricultural societies hosting a fair.[38]

An important element of these galas, not to be lost in a discussion of rural consumerism, was the ensuing social benefit. Mary Lane, attending her first agricultural fair in 1868, wrote: "All the country lasses are arrayed in their best, to figure at the most important yearly event in their lives." Fairs made rural Americans feel good about themselves and their neighbors. Farmers came to view the goods on display as a visible validation of their economic status when compared with the larger U.S. population. One editorial noted that the fair was "an occasion when the farmer's worth to the community is best appreciated; at fair time, if at no other, the farmer can regard himself as the equal of other men." Other narratives echoed these sentiments, stating that fairs "contribute[d] to social feelings and good neighborhood" and broke down class lines between owners and laborers. Willis Boughton recalled buying "a season family ticket" to the state fair that admitted "a Democrat wagon load, including our hired men" as well as his family. He noted that "on the promise to attend the Fair our hired men were given a holiday."[39]

Fairs also lent communities a spirit of carnival. Schools often proclaimed Friday or even the entire Fair Week to be a holiday so that teachers as well as pupils had "no excuse for not attending." Garland wrote that "the crowds were the most absorbing show of all. We met our chums and their sisters with a curious sense of strangeness, of discovery." Like someone visiting a crowded city for the first time, Garland found that "our playmates seemed alien somehow—especially the girls in their best dresses walking about two and two, impersonal and haughty of glance."

One farmer noted in his diary his dutiful attendance at the implement expositions and cattle judging, then went on to record that he spent much of his remaining time engrossed in the "very fast trotting" horses being raced at the event. Garland echoed the farmer's sense of priorities, recalling that his "interest in the races was especially keen, for one of the citizens of our town owned a fine trotting horse called 'Huckleberry'"; whereas his "survey of fat sheep, broad-backed bulls and shining coats was a duty," Garland's desire to "to cheer Huckleberry at the home stretch was a privilege." At the 1869 Buchanan County Fair, the first day was initially deemed "not in all respects the success of former years" until more than nineteen hundred tickets were hawked for the next afternoon to patrons unwilling to miss a day at the races. At an 1868 fair located outside Davenport, Iowa, one female visitor recalled that "excitement during [the races] was tremendous, everyone rose to their feet, men shouted, women screamed, one lady near the spot where [one horse] jumped the fence, fainted dead away." Fortunately for the afflicted woman, she "was worked by application of water and a little whiskey" and was soon back to the show. While some attendees were comfortable with these pursuits, including those who spent the time playing baseball, picnicking, or simply drinking, there were calls for restrictions to be placed on such unrefined pursuits and for the removal of "vagabond showmen who infest [our] fairs." The recorded clashes of views confirm that fairs were serious public forums for expression and debate among the farm community.[40]

Pageantry and pastime aside, the expositions generally concentrated on the display of agricultural machinery. Editors at the *Prairie Farmer* observed that "no part of an exhibition is more thoroughly studied by those who visit it, than the machinery for the farm." Visitors marveled that "Art seems to have brought machinery for cultivation to perfection." At a fair in Springfield County, Illinois, an observer noted the "various novel agricultural implements exhibited in the show yard," including plows, "seed-planters of ingenious construction," and "little hand machines for washing clothes upon, which are said to economize labour 100 per cent." Devices drew praise if they were "simple, cheap, and efficient." Sewing machines and other household appliances exhibited at the 1868 Illinois State Fair were intended to lead to "a greater willingness to adopt for the wife every machine which can lighten the burden of household toil." It was the exception, not the rule, for the display of implements not to be "abundant."[41]

Manufacturers helped the farmers' clubs by making their wares easily available for public trial. Ostensibly, suppliers provided their goods in order to compete for the cash premiums, or prizes, awarded for the best device in a particular category: reaper, thresher, and so forth. True to the "scientific" mien, machines were publicly analyzed for their relative strengths by manufacturer's agents and then evaluated by an independent panel of farmers. Often the testing could be quite extensive. The Indiana State Board of Agriculture, for example, which regulated more than sixty-seven county and district fairs, ruled that only during the trials could plows "be held by the competitors, or persons appointed by the Committee"; there was to be no practice time before the fair. Each plow was to "open and plow four rounds" and "the following points will be considered . . . gross draught, weight of plows, loss of power in overcoming friction, net power required to cut and turn furrow slice, width of furrow slice, depth, simplicity of structure, materials, workmanship, durability and price." Similar restrictions, tests, and evaluations were enumerated for corn plows, shovel plows, wheat drills, harrows, and mowers. There were specialty tests for devices of "general purposes," for those to be used on "alluvial or muck soil," and those for exceptional conditions such as on hillsides. Other trials tested machines that were manned by a gang or by single operator.[42]

Backers of the fairs professed that the premiums alone were effective in drawing a wide range of competitors, but manufacturers such as plowwright William B. Young put a higher value on the opportunity to best his rivals openly. In a circular entitled "The Farmer's Friend" issued well after the conclusion of the 1865 Illinois State Fair, Young complained that "no field trials of Plows were held" and that the prize for "Best Plow for general use . . . was awarded *without trial*, to Deere & Co." Using italic type to emphasize his message, Young told the Illinois planters that "*the same identical plows* were taken to the Iowa State Fair, the following week, where a field trial was held"; in open competition, he reported, the superiority of his plows was "exhibited and tested." Needless to say, Young's circular was not an effort to obtain the trifling premium but to inform Illinois farmers that his plow had routed Deere's.[43]

Often, mere visibility of their goods at the fairs was sufficient reason for suppliers to participate. Once given access, manufacturers such as grain-drill maker D. E. McSherry, of Dayton, Ohio, staffed their exhibits with territorial agents who could extol the virtues of their product to passers-by. McSherry told an associate that he "hope[d] to find a good fair at Quincy [Illinois] and trust[ed] to find there *our* crowd in full force, and to get from them all the assistance & *pressure* needed" for sales. John Deere & Co. took more than sixty plows to a single fair, both right-handed and left-handed models, including all of the "implement[s] for every variety of work for which the plow is adapted." Not all of these displayed goods were entered into performance tests. These manufacturers clearly were not motivated by the relatively small premiums being offered but by the revenues to be extracted from the farmers' strongboxes.[44]

Manufacturers went to great lengths to publicize their participation at the county and state fairs. As early as 1853, secretary Kennicott informed local farmers' clubs that suppliers were pressing him for dates and locations of upcoming festivals. Many firms helped to underwrite the fairs by advertising in the fair guides and premium lists. By so doing, merchants presented their goods with the institutional blessing of the popular farmers' clubs. One officer of the Illinois State Agricultural Society wrote that "the very act of advertising shows a liberality of spirit at variance with all penuriousness, and a confidence in the intrinsic value of his goods and articles to which he had invited public investigation." By placing "their names before the world," according to the official, participants "will rarely attempt to deceive [the people]; for they know that one single act of dishonor, with their names so prominently displayed before the public, will blast them forever." Through the fairs, manufacturers staged demonstrations of their wares that won for their products the prestige of scientific farming. Their efforts were seen not as opportunistic huckstering but as a further contribution to the functional education of consuming farmers.[45]

Not only farm machinery was touted. The tremendous success of the fairs, both social as well as financial, coupled with the assertive participation of manufacturers, blurred the distinction between consumption as practiced by "scientific farmers" and the pursuit of less-essential goods. Merchandise such as stylish boots and shoes, cloth, clothing, millinery goods, books, and an assortment of other products that did not qualify as capital investments were displayed adjacent to the sanctioned reapers, sewing machines, and stoves. Advertisers of the 1861 Illinois State Fair included outfitters of "fine watches," furs, musical instruments, sporting goods, wigs, and perfumes. The Chicago Mercantile Bakery cloaked its loaves in efficiency and modernity by advertising its bread as a product of a "monster labor saving machine." Remarkably, the image transference was a two-way street: luxury household objects could be used as a way of conferring distinction on farm machinery—a telling comment on the emerging consumer perceptions of farmers. For example, a report on the display offered by John Deere, cited above, noted that "embraced in [their] display were two extra finished plows for exhibition, that far surpassed anything ever yet brought out at a fair in this country for elegance of workmanship and finish. . . . Farmers remark[ed] that they were fine enough for parlor ornaments."[46] The association of capital and noncapital goods lent farmers an expansive understanding of scientific farming. Not only were goods justified for their utility in maximizing profits on the farm but also for their aesthetic appeal. One McCormick agent wrote in 1868: "Say what you will in favor of plain machines for work, in nine cases out of ten if you find a piano in a farmer's house and a silver-plated carriage in his barn, just so often does a farmer buy a mower because it is polished, burnished and painted fancifully."[47]

Progressive, normative values were reinforced during these galas— but not without challenge and even some conflict. Evidence of this can be found in reports quoted below (the first, about a "Model Farm," further demonstrates the clear link between scientific farming, the clubs, and the fair). At the 1853 County Fair in Jefferson County, Iowa, the eighty-acre homestead of John Andrews won first prize for the "good rail fence" and the judicious division of his farm into lots "so situated that stock can be readily watered." His crops gave "evidence of superior cultivation; his buildings [were] conveniently arranged, and consist[ed] of a neat and commodious dwelling, a large and spacious barn, milk-house, smoke-house, hen-house, piggery, and carriage-house, workshop and shed for utensils, of which there was a large quantity in thorough repair, and well housed when not in use." Finally, Andrews was praised for fertilizing his land, using vegetable and fruit varieties "adapted to this country," and, as a forerunner of the suburban fantasy to come, for a "front yard well laid down in grass, and interspersed with shrubs and flowers, fine shade trees around the house, all in a clean and thriving condition." One year later, a second Jefferson County husbandman earned the top award for the "most numerous collection of agricultural implements."[48]

Model farmers, in addition to being recognized with premium awards for their produce, were also applauded less formally. For example, at the second Iowa State Fair, held in October 1855, a "superb silver-mounted plow" was at first received with muffled laughter from some who held the device to be an example of "injudicious ornamentation." In response, one marshal was quick to ask if those who giggled were not more than likely to be those idlers who "leave their plows in the fence corner until the spring plowing reminded them of the old rusty occupant . . . devoid of paint and all overgrown with weeds? If so, [then] they should have been laughed at, not the plow." The device was sold, and to a farmer who, according to the sponsors, "has a farm of which one might be proud, for the farmer who buys such articles generally expects to take care of them, and he who takes care of his plows, . . . keeping them safely housed from the effects of the weather, is, almost invariably, the possessor of a nice clean, tidy farm, on which grain grows ranker than weeds, and where the fence corners are as clean as the meadows." Given these bene- fits of modern management, the marshal suggested, "a silver-mounted plow is not so far out of the way after all." While these normative values were subtle, they also were powerful. Consumption, the fairs preached, was that best way for commercial farmers to attain prosperity, respect, and pride.[49]

Women's participation at the fairs—limited though it was—was packed with meaning for rural consumerism. As we have seen, women's work on the farm was extensive and their connection to scientific farming close; their representation at these expositions, however, was for the most part trifling. Early categories offered premiums for the best twenty-five yards of carpeting, bed quilts, loaf of bread, "best specimen of cooking," fancy push pins, embroidered collars, and silk embroidery. Little had to do with the scientific management of the hearth. Most of the prizes ranged in value from fifty cents to ten dollars, or about one-third of men's awards. A Dixon, Illinois, visitor whose neighbor had worked three days on a single handkerchief commented in 1858: "The premiums offered are not at all suitable for the article for which they are intended." Yet women usually attended the fairs in droves: their attendance was critical to the success of most early fairs. As paying participants and attendees, women were the best represented segment of the farm community. One periodi- cal noted of a sparsely visited fair that "had the community in general manifested the same zeal as the ladies in particular, the fair would have been all that could be desired." Women proved more than willing to par- ticipate when, as rarely happened, a contest was offered that actually matched their skills against others for efficiency and cost effectiveness. In a particularly compelling example, fourteen-year-old Hattie Winslow won an eight-dollar premium for the woman who could "cook a meal in the shortest time." While the money no doubt justified Hattie's efforts, her salary for the forty-eight minutes it took to prepare the warm biscuits, fried chicken, tomatoes, potatoes, cabbage, tea and coffee (all "heartily enjoyed by the committee") in no way prepared her for the contemptible "wages" she would earn as a farm wife. The contest is painfully patronizing from our current perspective, but the young lady no doubt entered the competition of her own free will.[50]

Women often bridled at such limited opportunity, especially in view of their prominent role in attending and promoting the fairs and their commitment to progressive farming. A measure of this was shown in one especially rowdy competition in "female horsemanship [*sic*]." The problem began with the omission of a woman's equestrian category by the organizers of Iowa's first state fair in 1854. When informed of the growing public indignation by many young women—who ingeniously used the agricultural journals to publicize and defend their objections—the fair president, Thomas W. Clagett, magnanimously offered his own gold watch as the premium for "the boldest and most graceful female equestrian." The ten women who competed, ranging in age from early teens to late twenties (three of them being married) took Clagett's offer in ways that he may not have intended. Wearing colored ribbons on their caps and saddles to avoid using names that might provide regional information to the notoriously biased crowds, the women quickly revealed what they thought of the omission of their sex from the virile pursuit of "horsemanship." Ordered by the committee to parade into the ring quietly and individually, perform four riding styles of their choice, and then demurely depart, the women chose instead to assemble themselves into a posse, gallop in formation into the arena, wheel, and halt in unison before the stunned judges and frenzied audience. Clagett rose from the stands to chide the women for their recklessness and suggested that the best riding characteristics for women were "coolness, self possession, gracefulness and posture," not an emulation of ol' "Rough and Ready" Zachary Taylor. After Miss Belle Turner, of Lee County, had been named winner (the runners-up received gold rings as consolation prizes) the crowd selected their own champion, fourteen-year-old Eliza Jane Hodges, based on her youth, daring in the ring, and ability to control the animal beneath her. Topping the used gold watch, the assembly gathered up a collection of $165 and promises for free enrollment at the Female Seminary of Fairfield for three terms and the Female Seminary of Mount Pleasant for one term. The next year, a "Female Equestrian" event was formally added to the state fair, but "Breakneck or otherwise daring riding" was officially barred under penalty of expulsion. Miss Hodges defended her informal title against sixteen others, but she won neither the judges' nor the crowd's approval.[51]

These anecdotes and reports from the regional fairs illustrate the ongoing maturation of the region. Unlike the rather cloistered early settlers, second-generation Midwesterners were increasingly confident of their place in the world and their ability to master the market on terms that had meaning to them. As consumers, rural Midwesterners developed a unique ethos that was based on the shared experience of commercial farming. The idea of scientific farming, which aimed for efficient, market-oriented homesteads, focused on the modernizing function of domestic and field machinery. Farmers' clubs sponsored agricultural fairs largely to evaluate and purchase these goods. Farmers prospered in relation to the demands of the national economy, yet clearly the strong normative values of the market doctrine did not go unchallenged. The outbreak of civil war, however, greatly transformed these traditional perceptions and experiences.

The tragic effects of the war—the anguish over the thousands killed and wounded, the physical destruction, and the missed opportunities of Reconstruction for millions of African-Americans—drive home the pain of the period to even the most callous observer. Contemporaries such as Henry Adams noted the severe psychological confusion suffered by his generation. "Society," Adams wrote, "from top to bottom, broke down." By comparison with the backdrop of this solemn tableau, the economic dislocation of the war and the resulting unintended consequences for rural consumers seem inconsequential. Still, these changes were as real and long-lasting as the more painful ordeals of war.[52]

The economic influence of national (i.e., federal) policies on the Midwest can appear at first glance to be deterministic. For example, the Union Pacific Railroad Act, the Morrill Land Grant College Act, the Homestead Act, and the formation of the Department of Agriculture all displayed a new utilitarian leaning by Washington with regard to the West. Many of these actions, while aiding in the war effort, were aimed at placating an increasingly vocal body of Western representatives in the Union Congress. Although the direct beneficiaries of much of this legislation lived in the Great Plains and the Far West, Midwesterners also profited from the economic subsidization that federal laws provided.[53]

But for many, the fiscal repercussions of the war were more subtle and personal, bluntly challenging many traditional rural perspectives on consumption. Attitudes were most directly affected by the visible increase in the sheer volume of goods made available to prosecute the war. Economic shifts, most notably the inflation of currency, were more silent harbingers of changing purchasing patterns. Together, even for those not yet converted to scientific farming, these forces magnified the general tendencies of Midwesterners to act as modern consumers. They sought a greater access to, knowledge of, and desire for a wider range of manufactured goods. Just as the isolated farmer, upon enlistment, was first exposed to the viruses that caused measles and chicken pox, so too was this a "contact period" for millions of rural Americans with the powerful force of mass consumption.

The primary stimulus that transformed consumer opinion was the immediate need for vast amounts of manufactured goods in order to furnish the Union army. Records from Midwestern quartermasters, attempting to provide for the rapid surge in enlistments at the outset of the conflict, suggest that even experienced merchants had no preparation for such an undertaking. Indianapolis hardware merchant and manufacturer J. H. Vajen, named state quartermaster general, was nearly overwhelmed by the need for everything from tents, haversacks, canteens, and infantry equipment to clothing, food, and animal fodder.[54] Massive orders were the norm. On 24 May 1861, Major Jefferson Davis, an Indiana quartermaster and namesake of the man who that same year became president of the Confederacy, procured from the Bowen Stewart Company 270 boxes of paper, 3,000 envelopes, 99 dozen steel pens, and enough sealing wax and ink to stock them. In addition, that same month he was responsible for the purchase and distribution of 24,803 pounds of fresh beef, 29,241 pounds of bacon, 17,383 pounds of ham, 60,000 pounds of flour, 5,291 pounds of rice, 7,661 pounds of coffee, 11,400 pounds of sugar, 754 gallons of vinegar, and 3,344 pounds of soap. While orders such as these may have been placed by a handful of antebellum urban wholesalers, nothing before had reached this level for breadth and duration of procurement.[55]

The vast scale of the conflict made the army's previous experience in the Mexican War inconsequential. General Vajen confided to his superiors that "it was impossible to do business strictly according to the 'army Regulations' [for to] have been any more stringent with our officers and troops would have retarded volunteering." In order to move a single regiment through the city and onto Camp Morton, Vajen and Davis were required to negotiate and coordinate the efforts of scores of local merchants, various railroads, and numerous wholesalers.[56]

Such a vast quantity of goods created new perceptions about the range of possibilities for the average consumer. At one time, farmers were forced to choose from a limited stock of goods at the local depot. Now, as enlisted men, they saw mountains of goods passing them in freight cars and commissary wagons. Most noticeable to many of these men was the relative stylishness of their various state and regimental uniforms. In light of the severity of the war to come, the early disputes over swank uniforms took on a darkly comical air. One Indiana private wrote to his mother that "we have had a big battle at last, not with the Rebels but with our Colonel about our uniforms. We have got them at last, [and they] are the very best kind." Illinois servicemen, too, were concerned about the fashion of vestments on parade. Private Andrew Bush, writing to his sister, noted that "it looks nice when we go on battalion drill. Everyone has to have his best clothes on and his shoes blacked."[57]

Wartime machismo may explain the interest in smart battle fatigues, but other goods, too, were commented on by Union soldiers. Unremarkable items such as food and undergarments became talking points when made so readily available. One soldier wrote to his family that he and his five brothers were "getting quite fat" on the liberal army provisions. Enlisting at a lanky 148 pounds, the private gleefully observed that he had since gained thirty pounds "and I think if I stay my three years out I will weigh eight hundred pounds if nothing happens . . . don't fret about me or [my] brothers, for we will live well." Clothing was seen as cheap and bounteous. Unlike earlier wars, infantrymen rarely requested garments from home for they could get them more easily and cheaper in the service than their relatives could get them at home. One infantryman noted: "Uncle Sam will sell us good boots . . . socks . . . flannel drawers . . . and everything else in proportion [to the low costs for other consumer goods]." The war forced these men to view in a new light not only fancy uniforms, but also common items such as food and clothing. What were once merely basic items were transformed into objects of consumer desire.[58]

A similar change occurred regarding less-essential consumer goods, and these, too, were described in servicemen's letters home. Whether it was the cookware of the camp, the personal utensils used by the men, or the actual implements of warfare, Midwestern soldiers relayed to their kin the measureless volume of unusual merchandise. After listing an inventory of his gear in a letter, Private James Vanderbilt related this wartime consumer knowledge to his previous experience as a mechanized prairie farmer: "We have got all our riggings . . . and I never was harnessed before I got them on but I was surely harnessed then." Just as Vanderbilt once trained his teams at home to utilize a new agricultural machine, so too was he being conditioned by the army to this material abundance.[59]

Rural consumers were undoubtedly tethered to their goods in other new and potentially revolutionary ways. Patrons tried to square wartime abundance with their unique antebellum consumer experiences: scientific farming, agricultural clubs, and fairs. This new knowledge, provided through their ordeals in the war, merely expanded the potential for acquisition of more goods by using these established antebellum patterns. Just as farmers had once worked to evaluate and purchase farm implements, so too, rural veterans determined, would they acquire their goods in a progressive and modern fashion. William Pankhurst, the commissary sergeant for the Seventy-fifth Illinois Volunteer Regiment, will serve as an example of this trend. He wrote from Whiteside, Tennessee, to a hometown retailer to procure penknives that he could sell to his compatriots. He asked his supplier to "sell them as low as you can as I want to sell them again and do not want to run the risk for nothing." As a result of such opportunism, the army required servicemen to vouch to their quartermaster that commissary stores were bought solely for personal use. Such a sweeping proclamation hints that this new activity among federal troops was widespread.[60]

Noncombatants were not sheltered from these changing perceptions: the federal cornucopia instructed many in the modern ways of mass consumption. At the most basic level, advertisers used the war as a device in advertising their products. Pitches like the Cornell Sewing Machine Company's in the premium list of the 1861 Illinois State Agricultural Society were common. The company avowed to readers that "the soldier is speedily uniformed" through the use of their machine. Other examples abound.[61]

The war also forced many people to participate in a much larger world than had previously existed for them. As one Illinois women recalled, they "worked day and night, busily filling boxes and barrels with comforts for [the soldier]. Wives and children with strong faith that they would be cared for at home took up their part of the burden."[62] A good example of this broad trend is Louisa Jane Phifer. From October 1864 until September 1865, while her husband was away with the Thirty-second Illinois Volunteer Infantry, Phifer not only managed her seven young children but also every operation of the family farm near Vandalia, Illinois. In letters to her husband George she relates how she was able to get the corn harvested, fields fertilized, accounts settled, and a sheep stable constructed. While the letter is loving and concerned in tone, Louisa demonstrated a growing awareness of her own ability to make decisions independent of her husband. Whereas earlier letters sniffle, "Now if we have done any thing that you do not like I want you to forgive me for We intend to take as good care of the things as is possible till you get back," later in the year she demonstrates a clearer willingness to exercise independent thought and action. Commenting on horse riding, Phifer protested: "Now George you wrote for me to get a side saddle. I would not ride one if I had one. . . . We will keep the Old Mare well till you get back and then I want you to get you a saddle. And then I want to learn to ride behind you." Phifer later made decisions about when to sell the produce, when to slaughter the pigs, and how to pay for and reconstruct the family's well.[63]

An economic reality also stemmed from the war that was meaningful to rural consumers. Augmenting the effects from urbanization and the recent opening of foreign markets, the Civil War further boosted the demand for all forms of agricultural surplus. Commercial farmers, among many others, found that war brought with it economic prosperity. At the ninth annual exhibition of the Illinois State Agricultural Society, regional farmers were asked to plant "every productive acre of your soil. Let no excitement, no interest in the stirring events of the day interrupt your operations of the farm. . . . Your market is certain, and all History is a lie if it shall not be remunerating. We urge you, then, to strain every nerve; your interest financially cannot fail to be promoted by it"—a prediction that was aided by an unexpected boost from the federal government.[64]

In an effort to pay for the provisions and wages needed to prosecute the war, the government turned to printing legal tender. Historians have noted the immense expansion of "greenbacks" in the wartime economy. The speed with which money was suddenly brought into circulation was in some cases startling. In one month, the governor of Indiana, O. P. Morton, made $500,000 in federal notes available for use by his quartermaster general, Vajen. The result, of course, was inflation. Letters from servicemen attest to the rising costs for many goods later in the war. Indiana volunteer Cyrus Jackson McCole, writing to his sister from the battlefield of Murfreesboro (1862), reported that a "five cent loaf of bread at [home] is worth twenty cents here." McCole dourly added that most provisions that were available were of poor quality (butter "so strong that it can hold itself out at arms length") or scrawny in size (pies "about as thick as a very thin knife").[65]

Farmers, as debtors, were able to utilize this inflated currency. Flush with cash, farmers liquidated debts incurred by their pursuit of scientific farming. Benjamin Gates, of the Thirty-third Illinois Volunteer Regiment, was typical when he sent much of his pay home to square debts incurred for machinery and goods. Further, as the *Prairie Farmer* noted four years after the war's end, using these opportunities "to obtain the ready cash, farmers were not only able to wipe out the old scores set against their names, but to pay the money for everything they bought. And so it came round that the war that found so many farmers in debt left them with no store accounts to settle and with money in banks or in their pockets."[66] The cash books of rural merchants substantiate these claims. The records of retailers J. B. Jolly & Lewis Mayo, of Mount Erie, Illinois, suggest a pattern of purchases inflated due to easy availability of federal notes. At the start of the war, Jolly & Mayo had average weekly cash sales of approximately $40 per week. By 1865 this average had skyrocketed to more than $200 a week, and in one transaction alone a patron paid $2,000 in cash. The cycle of purchases appears to have been sustained, with pauses in early spring of both years, despite inflation.[67]

Much as today, inflation pressured consumers to spend their money or see it devalued over time. The *Prairie Farmer* reported that farmers supported a new and "expensive habit of living" during the war. Rural patrons dressed in "imported clothes. . . . They set a better table and rode in finer carriages than they were wont; while pianos and melodeons found their way into thousands of farmers' houses than had ever heard other music than simple songs and hymns." Clearly, the rush of currency had a profound effect on the economics of consumption.[68]

For the perceptions and economics of rural consumers, the Civil War was certainly an important and rousing event. It generated and sustained a high level of demand for both consumer goods and the agricultural produce that would eventually pay for them. The war effort provided a rationale for consumption and the experience of a wide range of consumer options. The application of federal notes to pay for the conflict fueled rural consumer demand while it liquidated much of the debt incurred from the practice of commercial agriculture. But the merger of wartime consumer experiences with the "logic" of scientific farming led farmers to expect these patterns to continue. Farmers hoped that the public evaluation of goods, their liberal access, and low costs might endure into the postwar era.

Unfortunately for these aspirations, the Civil War bequeathed a profoundly different legacy. The focus of federal legislators turned away from the West and toward Reconstruction in the South. Further, the artificial demand generated by the war effort ceased, and with it went the need for huge amounts of farm yields to maintain the army. Servicemen returned to their farm livelihoods only to see the fruits of their labor add to a glutted agricultural market. Many young, single men chose to set out for opportunities in the Far West. This caused a depletion of the hired labor force and increased harvesting expenses for many commercial farmers. One correspondent stationed in Champaign County, Illinois, noted that the "demand for labor and farm hands is at the present time as strong as it has ever been known to be. Were our small grain harvest as large as it has previously been here it would be impossible to secure it in a satisfactory way."[69]

The introduction of federal notes had elevated the rural economy; now their withdrawal from circulation resulted in a host of negative consequences for regional farmers. Led by President Johnson's secretary of the treasury, Hugh McCulloch, the department quickly retired greenbacks in favor of coins and bullion notes. While Congress lackadaisically resisted full retraction, the deed was a fait accompli by 1869 with the passage of the Public Credit Act, which redeemed federal notes and war bonds with specie. As one economic historian noted, currency reform in Washington was the single most important source of "external disturbance" to the nation's economy from 1865 to 1873.[70]

The years subsequent to the war inaugurated a thirty-year period of intense rural unrest. The debate over the causes of this strife is wide-ranging and far from settled. Most historians agree that economic motives—extending from high interest rates and low commodity prices to increased tenancy and overspecialization—predominated. The Midwest led in the political struggle from the outset. The region was prominent for its many farmers' clubs and, later, the granges, which pressed for reforms to ease the economic burdens as they were perceived by farmers.[71] Yet, oddly, the immediate postwar years, from 1865 to 1873, were ones of relative prosperity. Why then did Midwesterners feel that they had to turn to such associations in order to express their discontent? The affiliation between independent farmers' clubs and the established rural consumer patterns holds the answer to this question. Through their progressive purchasing practices, ensconced for decades in the doctrine of scientific farming, agronomists first expressed their discontent not as producers but as consumers. As the *Chicago Tribune* wrote in 1873, "if [a farmer] cannot sell dear, he can certainly, when he wills to do it, buy cheap. Herein lies the whole kernel of that nut." Farmers understood the changes in the nation's economy, and their relative status in that continuum, through the teachings of their unique consumer ideology.[72]

From 1865 to 1873, Midwesterners clearly recognized that the leading source of their fiscal troubles was currency retraction. Wartime prices endured while the government failed to keep its hand to the pump that primed this fledgling consumer economy. Regional newspapers such as the *Oshkosh City Times* ran articles that foreshadowed the fertile use of the currency issue in future political campaigns. More importantly, rural consumers saw that the scarcity of money made consumption of all goods more difficult.[73] A farmer in White Hall, Illinois, Henry A. Griswold, left telling evidence of this rural perceptivity. Griswold began farming and raising hogs in 1850. As a conscientious businessman, he kept records of his yearly savings and annual currency deposits, and luckily the records from 1869 to 1877 survive. Clearly, Griswold experienced a steady decline in his ability to obtain cash to deposit in his local bank. Most notably, his annual savings fell in harmony with this shortage of cash. By January 1872, Griswold had barely enough reserves to pay for the capital expenses of his farm. Between January 1869 and January 1873, his currency deposits fell from $1,025 to $136.11 and his year-end balance crashed from $436.50 to $15.19. In 1874 there was a slight easing of his fiscal constraint, but Griswold's records through 1877 indicate that his finances never rebounded to the robust levels of 1869. He did have speculative landholdings in Nebraska, but there is no indication from the records that these investments, or any other on the farm, were the cause of his near insolvency. Griswold's record keeping, a trait espoused by many agricultural periodicals and ingenuously practiced by most commercial farmers, could not have failed to inform him that his operation was imperiled by the restriction of currency.[74]

Farmers were not the only witnesses to the profound effects on consumerism from the withdrawal of greenbacks: manufacturers' agents also suffered from the want for cash. These middlemen, unlike the jobbers discussed in chapter 3, were often assigned specific territories and sold specialty goods. Hardware drummer John Kirk complained that "I have scarcely ever in the eight years that I have sojourned in this New York Jr. City [i.e., Chicago] had so universal a complaint of . . . [a] scarcity of money." Further, Kirk noted that merchants were in dire need for cash, more so than "since before the war. All complain of scarcity of money & poor collections from the country. . . . I think my trip this far has been one of the most unsuccessful I have ever made." As a result, he predicted that "there seemed to be very little demand for goods of any description" until the issue was resolved.[75]

Rural merchants were hit with concerns about both supply and demand as a result of the national policy. On the one hand, they found it difficult to maintain their cash payments to territorial agents, such as Kirk, and manufacturers. Numerous examples attest to the fact that "country merchants" were falling behind in paying their bills following the war. The ledger of one general store, headed by William Schneider and George Naas, in Saint Wendel, Indiana, gives an example of the rapidly shifting cash flows between 1864 and 1866. In 1864, the firm transacted more than $4,000 in sales. The following year, this figure ballooned to $9,185. Yet in 1866, the firm's posting returned to $4,191 in annual receipts, and only $119 in profits. Unquestionably, such enormous fluctuations made paying suppliers in a timely fashion extremely difficult.[76]

Merchants of course also suffered because of the want of cash among their customers. As one farm woman wrote, "the merchants are receiving their fall goods but I do not think there can be any great demand for large stocks of goods unless money was more plenty." Even the best customers experienced strained relations with their suppliers. One such patron, the Peru House, a hotel in Miami County, Indiana, regularly transacted large-volume purchases with mill owner and general store operator Charles Stowman. Throughout the war, Stowman allowed the Peru House to rack up huge debits for the use of his milling services and for various sundries. At its peak in August 1864, the hotel owed Stowman $7,749, which less a credit of $2,062 amounted to a real debt of more than $5,600. This deficit was not considered a loan in Stowman's ledgers: throughout the war, no interest was charged to the Peru House account.[77] Beginning in 1865, however, Stowman's permissiveness changed markedly. That December, Stowman began demanding payments from the Peru House managers for each individual purchase. Their deficit remained around $4,700 until late in 1867. At this point the retailer began charging 7 percent interest on the balance of the account. By 1869, the last entry in Stowman's log, the account was down to around $1,200. There is no indication that the Peru House had suffered a severe economic setback that might have frightened Stowman into demanding payment. The most likely conclusion is that the postwar retraction of currency forced the retailer to restrict purchases that were not secured by cash or guaranteed loans.[78]

The direct effect of currency restrictions was a change in the purchasing patterns by rural consumers. Where once farmers were free to indulge themselves in more luxurious goods, they now were increasingly restricted in their purchases. For example, by 1867 rural resident Adeline Clark spent as much as $400 for "incidental" wares such as gloves, hats, stereoscopes, and perfume, including a "Chicago spree" that netted nearly $200 in goods. But by 1871, these nonessential expenses were roughly halved. Significantly, by 1878 her spending had surpassed her earlier levels, suggesting that the 1871 experience was caused by a sharp recession in family expenses, which she, in turn, responded to. Others took to creative financing and short-term loans in order to afford the goods that once came so easily. Illinois farmer Thomas Richardson, in Macoupin County, asked his McCormick supplier for a new machine "without paying nothing down until the 1st of October. I will give you good security, but money I have not got."[79]

With such a pervasive lack of capital, rural consumers began fearing that consumption might lead to ruinous debt. Further, in the days before Keynsian economics the specter of consumer debt was not seen as an investment in manufacturing jobs and future growth but rather as a loss of economic stability. One newspaper described a typical farmer's reaction to inflation and currency constriction: "If I have to pay these prices, where am I to get my balance to meet other expenses? Where does the money go to, and why the necessity for these prices?" Farm families took pride in their avoidance of these expenses. Ellen White wrote to her mother: "I cannot boast of broad acres and money but can boast of a good name, credit, and many friends." Editors of the *Prairie Farmer* echoed the lofty place that avoidance of debt had in the farm community, writing that it was better to "live poorly, to dress plainer, better in short to deny one's self most the luxuries and pleasures of life, than to get in debt, live in debt, and die in debt."[80]

Farmers such as Henry Griswold were left with few alternatives, however, if they were to maintain the productivity required by commercial agriculture. As noted earlier, the intensive use of capital goods ranging from reapers to sewing machines had become a necessity to farmers' economic viability. Examples abound of men such as Bartholomew Applegate, of Johnson County, Indiana, who, despite operating profitably for years, suddenly found themselves facing high deficits simply by meeting the basic requirements of their trade. In one year, Applegate incurred nearly $2,000 in loans in order to get his crops and pigs to market. They were sold for only slightly more than $900. When fashioning a simple balance sheet of assets and debits, Applegate found that his net worth was less than $60. In an era of commercial farming and inadequate currency circulation, the average farmer simply could not avoid debt.[81]

The retailing firm of Schneider and Naas provides convincing case evidence that rural Americans took on consumer debt at an astounding rate (see table 2.1). Steadily, from 1867 to 1872, the firm extended credit to an ever-widening pool of consumers. By 1872, the merchants had transacted nearly $5,000 in business for both basic and luxury goods, but more than one-third of this was sold on advance. In their most active lending period, between 1870 and 1872, the average advance amount nearly doubled each year. The relatively high standard deviation in 1872 indicates that the loan amount ranged considerably, from a low of $8 to a high of $338. This suggests that the need for assistance was widespread among the assortment of husbandmen. Trends at other retail establishments support these findings.[82]

For a variety of reasons, rural patrons directed their anguish over this trend not at the merchants themselves but at the territorial agents of major firms who supplied the retailers. Most tellingly, the roving peddlers were suddenly more noticeable, pressing farmers into decisions made by farmers for products ranging from agricultural machinery to the most basic personal goods—although not all accounts describe their role as entirely unsatisfactory. Olivier Zunz noted that many "enduring contacts" were established between the agents of the McCormick Reaper Company and Midwestern wheat growers; and agent F. G. Welch, who represented the Champion "Self-Raker" and reaper, was praised for hosting an extravagant party for his clients in July 1868. Welch's fete was applauded by the *Prairie Farmer:* "Farmers need more such opportunities for cultivating the social graces and enlarging the circle of their acquaintances." Others praised the role of agents in bringing goods to the region in a timely manner.[83] However, when farmers were forced into debt in order to acquire the suppliers' wares, familiarity bred contempt. Beginning in 1865 and

Table 2.1
Retailer Schneider & Naas, Loans Extended, 1866–1872

Year	# of Loans	Sum of All Notes	Avg. per Note	Median	Std. Dev.
1867	1	$44.39	$44.39	$44.39	$0.00
1868	5	$290.30	$58.06	$70.90	$33.71
1869	9	$852.70	$94.74	$29.70	$163.03
1870	14	$538.83	$38.49	$40.95	$16.04
1871	19	$1,102.93	$58.05	$40.00	$49.53
1872	28	$1,900.91	$67.89	$46.18	$71.16

increasingly thereafter, periodicals related negative experiences with rural agents. Newspapers such as the *Oshkosh City Times* warned farmers by citing examples of jobbers' chicanery. Their news report, said the paper, was only the half of it—only "one of the many plans pursued" by corrupt agents whereby "many thousands of dollars have been taken from farmers." Other publications suggested that the drummers were taking unethical profits from their advantageous place in the distribution network. The *Chicago Tribune* wrote: "Nothing [the farmer] needs escapes [agents'] greedy claws, whether quinine for a sick wife or child, or iron and steel and lumber and paint for a wagon or plow." In the face of such attacks, the image of the traveling salesman began to tarnish in the eyes of many farmers.[84]

There were other kinds of criticism, too—adding to the reasons for farmers' distrust. As early as July 1862, the *American Agriculturalist* had warned that a Midwestern farmer's consumer needs "var[ied only] with the size of the family . . . and their propensity to gratify pride—an expensive article in a new country." Following the war, many critics objected that agents used "smooth-tongued" sales pitches to get farmers to overconsume. The persuasive jobbers were seen as a direct challenge to a farmers' autonomy, thwarting the central tenet of scientific farming: control over purchasing decisions. James Creighton, of Wayne, Illinois, held that the agents' "fancy rig and handsome salary are rung from our hard earnings. The manufacturer does not pay a cent of this expense." An observant farmer who made a survey of properties only "a short day's drive" from his Illinois homestead, said he tallied more than 168 agricultural implements left unused in the fields. One woman contributed a poem to the *Prairie Farmer*—an ode to the commercial traveler. Her account reveals the underlying concern of many consumers: that they would be overrun by salesmen and rack up ruinous debt if they surrendered to the agents' appeals. She concluded:

> *So if we sometimes turn away*
> *Abruptly, Sirs, you must remember,*
> *That we have heard your tale each day*
> *From Early Spring to late December.*
> *Why! If we listen to you at all,*
> *And give you the required attention,*
> *I think 'ere long each one would call*
> *The "country house" the best invention.*

The agents' place in the distribution network made them the flashpoint for conflict.[85]

In many ways, this rancor was simply the accumulation of frustrations that farmers had incurred since the close of the war. The withdrawal of greenbacks undercut what was a prosperous period for many farmers. Commercial farmers were well aware of this capital retraction and attempted to change their purchasing patterns accordingly; unfortunately, they found it impossible to avoid debt when practicing market-oriented agriculture. These developments generated obvious frustrations and farmers vented their feelings on the conspicuous territorial agent.

In sum, we can see that from 1840 to 1873, rural Americans expressed and codified a set of consumer patterns that were based on substantive experiences. Hoping to expand as capitalists, farmers developed a doctrine of scientific farming that was expressed in agricultural periodicals and discussed in farmers' clubs. These clubs fostered fairs that featured the required capital goods along with less-essential consumer wares—acquisition of which was aided by the advantageous market conditions afforded by the war effort. The collapse of this support in 1865 led to an awareness of the limits farmers faced in achieving their consumer goals.

When the mature farm communities of the Midwest began to assess what lay at the root of their problems, they did so with a clear sense of what goods they wanted, the manner in which they were prepared to acquire them, and the prices they were willing to pay. Based on these perspectives, they targeted the existing distribution system, comprised primarily of local stores and agents. Yet farmers failed to comprehend the risks and responsibilities that stores and agents had assumed over the preceding decades. These duties, essential in maintaining a responsive consumer marketplace, had evolved and expanded with commercial farming. Regional middlemen were the first to respond to the demands of farmers. They also were the first to be targeted for reform as rural Midwesterners sought greater access to consumer goals.

3 The Men in the Middle

Agents and the Development of a Demand-Driven Consumer Economy, 1840–1861

Brothers Charles and Isaac Harmon were risk takers. Leaving the relative comforts of New Hampshire in the early 1830s for the fur-trading post that would soon be the town of Chicago, the Harmons dived into nearly all of the political and economic opportunities that the village had to offer. Undeterred by failed land speculations, frustrated bids for alderman, and, as Whigs, largely shut out of local politics by William Ogden's Jacksonian Democratic machine, the Harmons found their niche as regional wholesalers and retailers. In partnership with Horatio Loomis, Isaac operated a dry-goods store at the southwest corner of South Water and Clark Streets; he ran another in a nearby settlement founded by Joseph Naper. Charles controlled a large agency in close cooperation with the two stores, offering a wide variety of basic goods, commercial scales, stoves, and pane glass for distribution throughout the Midwest. Another brother, J. D. Harmon, the youngest of the three, joined his siblings in the early 1840s and acted as their traveling representative, making purchases and securing loans in the East and closing deals and collecting bills in the West. Within fifteen years, the Harmons' business connections stretched from Saint Louis to northern Wisconsin and from central Iowa to New York City.[1]

The brothers lived in a community that prized wealth accumulation over all else. The town in which they lived and planned was the creation of canal builders, land speculators, army engineers, fur traders, and other entrepreneurs. If a Chicago "moral economy" existed at this stage (Ogden wanted to create a cultured and respectable settlement), it was not what attracted the Harmons.[2] In a telling and unusually reflective exchange between Charles and J. D., the elder Harmon confessed that he was in the process of underbidding a rival Saint Louis agent for the business of a sugar refinery. Charles wrote that despite the fact that the competitor "& myself are on *first* rate terms, love each other like h_ll; nevertheless, feeling the most benevolent sentiments toward him; I would like to make [the] $1,000 com[mission] . . . even if he was minus the am[oun]t. . . . You will understand that this is in the way of trade, and without the slightest disposition to do a dishonorable act to produce as desirable a result." Charles's seemingly cold rationality extended to family relations as well. He rarely supported, and repeatedly expressed frustration with, his father's business ventures in New Hampshire. In October 1848, the Harmon sire requested several hundred dollars to fund a carpetbagging expedition to Texas following the conclusion of the war. Listing his current debts, including the many loans extended to potential Midwestern clients, Charles surmised to his brother: "Under these circumstances I do not feel warranted in furnishing him with funds which I feel certain will not be repaid. You know his incompetence in the management of business, and to my mind it seems folly to entrust funds to his control with any expectations of a favorable result." To his father's request that the male children attend him to Texas, Charles curtly responded: "It is entirely out of the question. Every day involves me in some new transaction which requires my presence here." Later, Charles parted with seventy-five dollars in cash toward the Texas affair, but it was never again mentioned in the surviving records. Nor was Harmon Senior.[3]

That middlemen were preoccupied with the bottom line is not, in itself, remarkable. What makes these men and others like them unique was the transformative effect their actions had on the consumer marketplace of the rural Midwest. Between 1840 and 1861, while many second-wave commercial farmers were just beginning to pawn their "scientifically" managed crops, middleman in the form of urban wholesalers, jobbers, traveling salesmen, and store proprietors were creating the physical, managerial, informational, and credit links required to supply them. In many ways, middlemen like Charles and Isaac Harmon acted as midwives, delivering the market economy that the rural population had produced. The desire, capability, and natural resources were present in abundance. What was needed were ways in which to make more viable the connection between Eastern suppliers of manufactured goods and Western consumers.[4]

Middlemen accomplished several tasks that were critical in changing the Midwestern consumer economy. Agents liquidated the raw materials sent to them by local developers, such as lumber, grain, or livestock, and saw to it that consumer goods were shipped back to the rural frontier. At both ends, buying and selling, brokers assumed the largest share of the financial risk, thereby insulating both the prairie farmer and the capitalist from the vagaries and pressures of market economics. Remarketeers also took an active role in providing credit for the purchase and sale of goods. Additionally, in order to keep sources of capital open, middlemen were information brokers: they provided useful information about the availability of goods to the rural providers and about the state of local credit to backers in the East. Their further accomplishment was that they nurtured and grew the latent consumer demand that was at the core of commercial, progressive farming in the rural Midwest. Jobbers pressured local retailers to make consumption easier, with more choices and more reliable merchandise for their clients. As Tim Spears notes in his well-researched account of traveling salesmen, these agents were the "aggressive, logical consequence of the expanding national market system."[5]

It is important to keep in mind the contingent role that rural consumers played in the middleman's early success. Farmers seeking their economic destiny came face-to-face with the agent's desire to profit by rural consumption. Conflict was inevitable and misunderstandings were common as the two groups vied for control over the access to goods. At the same time that agents sought more stable business relations with local providers, farmers worked to expand their options as progressive patrons. Still, the means employed by both groups often worked toward the same ends. The ways that farmers expressed themselves as consumers were closely linked to the changing role of middlemen in the expanding economy. Moreover, while the shared and internally sustained logic of rural consumption pushed many farmers into more modern economic relations, agents did much to pull their rural cousins along. To understand how these two groups indirectly cooperated in challenging the rural marketplace, we need a better picture of how the pioneer store failed to provide the services required by scientific farmers. These deficiencies, as expressed by husbandmen and -women, provided opportunities for enterprising middlemen. The agents looked to profit by meeting the suppressed demand.

Through it all, the risky yet powerful market forces that attracted both commercial farmers and middlemen generated a multitude of unexpected adversities. By identifying what farmers did and did not see of the evolving consumer network, we can better understand what they wanted to change after the war.

It is interesting to speculate on how the Midwestern consumer economy might have developed had middlemen not played such an active role. Without middlemen to assume the risk of reaching isolated communities, the cost of accessing the hinterland would undoubtedly have remained high for manufacturers. Higher marketing costs would have resulted in higher prices, and fewer new and innovative goods would have been adopted within the region. At a minimum, the rate of innovation would surely have been slowed.

Commercial agriculture was founded on the rapid spread of productive machinery; hence, without middlemen, fewer farm surpluses would have been marketed in regional towns such as Saint Louis, Cincinnati, and Chicago. Eastern manufacturers would have been less likely to gamble in this slower-paced, more speculative economy. Faced with rare and expensive merchandise, rural consumers would have been less likely to participate in the market, possibly opting instead for homemade wares. As a result, merchants who did supply "scientific" goods would have found near-monopoly conditions in many locales. As credit was extended to patrons when the inevitable years of poor harvest came around, it is conceivable that a debt-peonage system similar to that of the postbellum South would have appeared. An example from Sheffield, Illinois, demonstrates the ease with which a retailer might accomplish just such a scenario. The Corner Store was the creation of Albert Boyton, who owned and operated the Sheffield Coal Company. Boyton required that his miners be paid through the store, and most of them soon "carried accounts." One farmer recollected that "although Sheffield could boast of no bank, Albert Boyton did a business that eventually developed into a local bank." In addition to the miners, "the trainmen had their pay accounts settled there," and even farmers quickly realized that "it would be wise to keep in touch with the group that daily gathered around this store, for the builders of the town were also there." Thankfully for the residents of this town, Boyton was unable, or unwilling, to maintain a coercive grip over the retail and financial markets of Sheffield.[6]

The predominant reason that this scenario did not commonly develop was because of the active and astute consumption practiced by rural Midwesterners. Letters and diaries of the earliest settlers to the region testify to the fact that they knew they were limited in their purchasing decisions. As discussed earlier, in letters to family in the East, Midwesterners regularly discussed the availability of goods, the prices they paid relative to those in Eastern markets, and their trips to town for necessary purchases. The feeling behind these remarks was overwhelmingly one of frustration with the obvious limits of Western consumerism: Midwesterners wanted more.

The spread of ideas promoting progress and scientific farming gave strong support to rural Midwesterners who saw consumption not as a threat to their republican virtue but as a liberation from dependency. Thurston Chase, author of a series of Western handbooks, rhetorically asked rural consumers: "Surely your own family ought to be dearest to you, and worthy of the best the house affords." Even many who might traditionally be seen as ascetics, such as clerics or members of strict denominations, found ways to use the market to their advantage. Samuel D. Guengerich, a Mennonite homesteader, made no less than thirteen trips to Iowa City in his first ten months of settlement in Kalona, Iowa. On every trip he stocked up on basic supplies, and he often bought other items, too. His accounting for 25 January 1866 is typical: "Bought a cooking stove $33.00. Stove pipe and tin wear $11.50. Plates, cups and saucers $4.00. Dry goods $5.00. Hardware $3.00. Drugs, oil varnish paints $1.80. Paid for dinner." His orders often exceeded $100, much of which he offset by selling his labor and some produce; he also dipped into the savings from his previous farm.[7] Such active consumption suggests that farmers were quite comfortable within the expanding consumer economy. Luxury items and one-of-a-kind purchases were demanded by farm patrons. One historian noted that researchers "cannot turn many pages in a merchant's day book without realizing that such goods were in steady demand." By 1859, a Canadian traveler noticed that there "seems to be a market for everything in the West, the spirit of 'trading' is so thoroughly ingrained in the people." Midwesterners clearly had an early itch for the "goods life."[8]

Then, as today, consumption was linked with the deep emotions of gratification and pride. Shopping liberated these feelings in ways few other experiences could. Hamlin Garland recalled, when he overheard his father planning the family's first trip to town to buy school supplies, that the "words so calmly uttered filled our minds with visions of new boots, new caps and new books, and though we went obediently to bed we hardly slept, so excited were we, and at breakfast the next morning not one of us could think of food. All our desires converged upon the wondrous expedition." Residents of many rural villages had similarly excited recollections of new consumer goods. By 1860, the topic of consumption was well and truly in the air: agricultural newspapers, journals, books, and speakers were praising the "progressive farmer" for his parlor filled with "appropriate" goods such as "minerals, and other curiosities . . . a variety of useful and entertaining books, drawings, engravings, paintings and the like." One contributor to the *Prairie Farmer* concluded that such goods were "an important agent in the education of life; it will make a great difference to the children who grow up in it, and to all whose experience is associated with it." Early shopping was less a form of entertainment and more like an actualization, fulfilling personal potential that was temporarily held back by the austere conditions of the West.[9]

The arrival of a teamster in town or village was an event loaded with meaning as well as the latest urban wares. One such driver, Bill "Blossom" Stanley, traversed the 120 miles separating his home in Pendleton, Indiana, from Cincinnati, his primary destination, using teams of four to six horses. Leaving Pendleton, the wagons carried a variety of agricultural articles for the Cincinnati market: grains, beeswax, ginseng, dried fruit, feathers, and "many other products of the country." Pendleton merchants used the empty wagons returning from this seasonal pilgrimage for the drayage of their consumer stocks. Residents recalled how draftsmen often "secured a row of bells . . . over the shoulders of their horses, and as they moved, these bells kept up a continued jingle which could be heard for quite a distance." On one memorable occasion, Pendleton consumers waited several weeks for "Blossom's" chimes to toll the scheduled approach of their consumer wares: while in Cincinnati, Stanley had found other profitable work that delayed his commission. A resident noted that "days passed but still no tidings. Stores ran out of tea, coffee, sugar and other necessities but still no tidings. It became a town trouble with nearly all on short rations or foreign goods." When Blossom did return, it was reason for the locals to celebrate: his caravan "was greeted by almost the whole population of Pendleton. The crowd, to expedite the unloading, all helped and the load was soon in the stores to be distributed." Teamsters usually timed their arrivals to coincide with the seasonal harvests of their neighboring farms. Prospective patrons often "rush[ed the wagons] to see the quantity of new goods." These biannual odysseys confirmed the consumer dependence that all antebellum rural residents had toward the distribution network.[10]

As this story indicates, the problems of the early rural consumer marketplace were due not to a lack of knowledge or desire on the part of farm patrons but rather to the fact that most local stores and the distribution network that supplied them were too limited to meet these needs. Teamster Blossom's delay was exasperating. People, regardless of their faith, grew tired of repeated, time-consuming trips to central cities. And while the itinerant peddlers offered some solace, bringing basic goods for barter and trade, they hardly represented progressive commerce. Sarah Brewer-Bonebright noted that when peddlers first arrived in her town, their backpacks "bulg[ed] with the small and more valuable articles . . . everything from jew's-harps to andirons." But such trade was not the full line of goods or services required by rural consumers. It was not until the arrival of a formal "more pretentious peddler's wagon," driven by Cy Smith, that Brewer-Bonebright saw the potential for a local store that offered real consumer choices. She seemed both pleased and proud that Smith selected her town to found a permanent store, and that his eventual success as a "prosperous merchant-banker" reflected well on the fortitude of regional consumers.[11]

Consequently, early settlers to the Midwestern countryside faced a particularly vexing problem in regard to local suppliers. For their commercial farming efforts to thrive, farmers needed merchants to provide access to a variety of staple goods not produced on their homesteads. "Good" farmers also sought technical improvements, from plows to candles, that would make the ventures more productive and, hence, more profitable. Equally important, farmers required the assistance of merchants in order to market surplus agriculture; they were subject to the success of these local depots in ways that limited their ability to demand change. This led to the insulation of local merchants from the traditional market pressures of supply and demand. Retailers did not have to respond to consumer needs for specific goods because they had often captured this clientele through their other services. As a result, most country stores were slow to develop business practices that supported the growing consumer consciousness of their patrons.[12]

Complicating this picture was a three-tiered distribution network for consumer goods. In the center were "middlemen," contractors who assumed the risk and evaluated the opportunities for profit via consumption. Representing a second node were speculators and developmental financiers. Often based in the East, these men funded Midwestern development in an effort to improve the value of their landholdings, or to more profitably control and harvest the natural resources of the West. This group often wholesaled bulk-processed and manufactured goods that were then shipped to the interior. These basic goods, such as packed pork, ready-made clothing, and light hardware, were in constant demand. The only market pressures facing these speculators, therefore, were those expressed within the Eastern markets as wholesalers battled for control of the various sources for goods. As a result, operators at this level of the distribution system were generally free from the economic pressures stemming from local consumer demand. At the local level, stores and other direct retailers provided access, information, and usually short-term credit by which Midwesterners might acquire merchandise.

The term *store* is so familiar to us today that the basics of how a store operates seem not to require explanation. Yet central to our understanding of a retailer is the belief that consumer demands drive the proprietor's business decisions: in this relationship, the supply of goods in relation to customer wants creates a reliable pattern that vendors can then use to establish profitable inventory controls. (The contemporary comedian Paula Poundstone often implores her audience to leave her performance, walk to a local convenience store en masse, and for each person to purchase one of the same item [a Slim-Jim]. Her punchline rests on the next night, when the expectant vendors will surely be surrounded by crateful of the overstocked item, waiting for the hordes of customers due "any minute now.") The modern assumption is that, ultimately, the consumer propels the decision of what a store carries, and when it will carry it; that is, not the other way around—with stores forcing customers to accept the goods presented to them at the time most advantageous to the retailer. But, essentially, it was the second scenario that was the norm for most early stores in the Midwest.

During the formative years of the region, between 1840 and 1860, most local storekeepers were affiliated with economic mainstays such as the grist or lumber mill—operations that generally were not dependent on customer satisfaction. If the store failed, owners fell back on their primary venture, and consumers awaited another speculator to assume the mantle of "town merchant." The earliest retailers habitually provided only the most basic provisions in return for bulked agricultural surplus. Such a "store" had little intention, and even less ability, to respond to individual consumer demand. One typical establishment, set up in an Illinois farming town in 1836, was housed in a simple log cabin. According to an early settler, it opened exclusively "for the sale of liquor, [yet] in those days [was] called a grocery." A second local vendor marginally expanded his stock of goods to include a small inventory of "general merchandise." In one Iowa village, the contents of the general store were regularly used as collateral for bets on the numerous horse races and shooting matches that attracted men to town. Such owners were often required to post bonds in which they promised to "keep an orderly house, and . . . not permit any unlawful gaming or riotous conduct."[13]

As evident from the company store in Sheffield, the reasons proprietors opened their stores varied according to temperament. Most common were family operations that imported "such goods as the natives were needing and [took] in exchange butter, honey, beeswax, maple sugar, and such things as they could raise . . . [as] a convenience and benefit to the neighborhood." While more benevolent than company stores, these backroom operations were no more beneficial to the long-term consumer goals of the region. Many operators neither enjoyed working for the "suckers," as one operator referred to her patrons, nor were good businesspeople. Their inexperience placed unmanageable financial burdens on both the store and its clients. Elizabeth Fancher related her experience with her brother-in-law, Joseph Fancher, who in 1854 ran their Waterloo, Iowa, family store into bankruptcy. Joseph found it easiest to move the merchandise by extending loans to anyone who would ask. As Elizabeth and her husband soon discovered, "few of those credit debts were ever paid." That was not all. "If a customer came for a dollar's worth of sugar and Joe was busy he would say: 'There's the barrel and there's the scales. Help yourself.'" The patron often figured: "Well I'll take a few pounds extra for waiting on myself and just charge it." When the Fancher store closed, local farmers went more than a year without one. Lacking any clear motivation to respond to consumer demand and practicing poor management, early stores showed no ability to advance even the most basic consumer services to Midwestern farmers.[14]

By contrast, the middleman Isaac Harmon ran a well-managed store in rural Illinois. Located in Naperville, which today is an affluent suburb of Chicago only twenty miles southwest of the Loop, in 1836 Harmon's store was certainly rural: the crossroad settlement was a full day-and-a-half's journey from the sodden streets of Chicago. Certainly, in developing a more responsive retail establishment Harmon benefitted by his relative proximity to Lake Michigan transports and his close association with his brother's business. But he also practiced a number of management techniques that indicated his willingness to meet the burgeoning rural consumer demand. The Harmon store stocked a wide variety of goods. The sale of alcohol nearly monopolized his early invoices and ledger books, but a range of more luxurious items were also sold. Typical were orders from the farmer Silas Lyman, who between April and October 1838 purchased goods worth more than $34.00 ("paid in full using note") such as plates, a tea set, sugar bowl, creamer, "Jamaica rum," and specialty items such as a "Britannia" pot and "Thunder Mug."[15]

Harmon's store was capable of surviving the financial fluctuations that existed in the protomarket conditions of early settlement. Isaac proved willing to barter for goods when necessary, a custom that was common to country stores, but he was strict in demanding a full accounting and enforcement of his loans to ensure that the store remained solvent. Accordingly, when an L. M. Clayes used a note to pay for his $54.11 invoice, brother J. D. Harmon quickly appended to the ledger a note that the borrower "lives at Mount Hally [and] was introduced by Norman Hawley who is considered accountable for the goods to be paid in 4 weeks, J. D. H." Moreover, the Harmons proved all too willing to use the power of the law to enforce collection. B. R. Begun was "sued & in judgement" in July 1839 for a delinquency of $29.00. Augustine Porter followed Begun to the dock days later for an overdue balance of $12.31.[16]

The Harmons were able to manage the intense speculative costs associated with supplying their rural depot. Running a store that was responsive to consumer demand proved expensive. Characteristic was an entry in Harmon's records for 17 January 1838, when $1,211.99 was spent to provide the store with "locks, screw drivers, cork screws, bolts, hammers, gun wormers, razors, candles, nails, horse brushes, fish hooks, 6 styles of tea and table spoons, coffee mills, percussion caps, knives, cow bells, pans, waffle iron, cloth, buttons, thread, shot, batting, sugar, apples, cologne, ink wells, brandy, [and] hats." Account books record that the brothers expended $25,669.01 between 1836 and 1838 to fill the shelves of the Naperville establishment, owed $16,129.57 to the canal commissioners to ship their merchandise, and managed $12,215.84 in bills payable, or credit vouchers extended to their customers. The latter two figures no doubt include portions of Charles Harmon's agency business, but still the financial acumen and wherewithal needed to remain solvent, much less profitable, was considerable. Periodic references to the Naperville store in their sales books indicate that a large quantity of cash also flowed into Harmon's accounts. These funds needed to be accurately managed, quickly reinvested, and used to liquidate debt to avoid bankruptcy.[17]

Isaac Harmon's long-term success as a retailer no doubt was aided by a number of factors. The financial and business connections established through his brothers were critical to replenishing his stock and securing his large orders on credit. In a letter from Illinois agent Peter Wheelock to the Fairbanks Scale Company, located in Johnsbury, Vermont, the middleman assured the supplier that while he was sick and unable to attend to sales in Naperville, he had "left the business there with Mr. Isaac L. Harmon, a brother of C. L. Harmon of Chicago. He is a regular safe business man." Within six years, the Harmons had supplanted Wheelock's agency and were conducting more than $7,000 in business per month with Fairbanks, most of which was on credit and some of which was sold through their Naperville store.[18] In addition, access to Chicago's growing port and canal facilities and fading concerns about local transportation soon made the Naperville experience unique. As a result, the region's wealth was more fungible and Harmon's sales garnered him cash and reliable credit rather than "butter and eggs." Harmon's proximity to the growing city also resulted in a more diverse client base that made his business less susceptible to the sudden pitches of the rural economy: his account books read as a who's who of early Chicago, including men such as Gurdon S. Hubbard, Jean Baptiste Beaubien, and Joseph Naper (women rarely attended his stores, and when they did and made purchases, they were noted). Still, Harmon's long-term success rested largely upon the fact that he was able to meet the consumer demand of the rural marketplace.[19]

The career of Isaac Greene, another Midwestern middleman, demonstrated the economic perils of brokerage. This case illustrates how prudent risk assessment was absolutely critical to running a profitable store. Greene's initial prosperity and eventual bankruptcy were closely linked to the risk he assumed in moving his retail operations deep into the Midwestern hinterland. His experiences indicate two other things: that agents profited by their astute management of rural consumer demand; and that many within the distribution network were insulated from financial disaster as a result of the middleman's speculation.

Greene's focus centered on the milling town of Saint Croix, in northwestern Wisconsin, a region rich in natural resources—white pine forests, fertile farm land, copper ore. The site was attractive primarily due to its physical location. There, the Saint Croix River dropped more than fifty-five feet in elevation in less than six miles, making "the Falls" an excellent location for mill works. Following a surveying expedition in 1832 led by Henry Schoolcraft, in 1837, a lumber company was formed. Construction began on a mill the next year.[20] Investors in Saint Croix saw the potential for easy profits. Ownership of the mill repeatedly changed hands between speculators. One historian of the region noted that by 1846 "who was actually in possession of title to the land was a question which kept Wisconsin law courts busy with suits and countersuits for many years to come." By 1849, William S. Hungerford and Hamlet H. Perkins owned and operated the Saint Croix timber mill and its associated store. In Boston, Robert Rantoul Jr., Benjamin H. Cheever, and the notable Caleb Cushing claimed joint title to the mill and to some nearby copper lodes. Both groups indicated that they intended to utilize the Falls as an investment that could be easily liquidated.[21]

Yet, as with other regional improvements, excellent opportunities did not always translate into quick profits. Local developers failed to reckon with the river's strength. As a result, from 1838 to 1842 little finished lumber was sent downstream except for what the river tore from the foundations of local construction. Further, legal battles between Boston-based businessmen and those in Wisconsin slowed efforts to rebuild the mill. By June 1849, only half of the constructed housing was occupied; other, nonresidential, structures moldered for want of use. The boomtown's Grand Hotel, lacking human guests, housed cattle in its unfinished basement.[22]

Isaac Greene, meanwhile, actively involved himself in developing the rural hinterland. He established a reliable system by which Perkins was supplied with consumer goods and the Eastern investors were funded from the sale of whatever finished lumber was delivered. Greene's efforts were representative of the activities of agents: he provided Perkins with the necessary credit to transact business, sought to improve the transportation of goods (both up to the logging town as well as downriver delivery of their surplus), and pressed provincials to practice prudent business practices when selling manufactured goods to local loggers.

Yet even such a description of Greene's activity covers only half of the significance that agents had in the developing economy: it fails to explore adequately the relationship between consumer demand and the agents' role in assuming the risk of meeting those needs.[23] Greene and Perkins did not suffer from a lack of local consumer desire for manufactured goods. Materially, rural patrons demanded a variety of wares from their suppliers. Surviving invoices and account books record the predominance of orders for staple goods such as sugar, rice, and salt. But surprisingly, at least in regard to the images of a desolate and debilitating existence on the frontier, luxury goods were ordered equally as often, if in smaller quantities. As early as 1847, with fewer than four hundred settlers and itinerant loggers for patrons, Perkins repeatedly placed orders for satin clothing, silk handkerchiefs, and "fine linen." By the fall of 1847, such luxury merchandise filled more than sixteen trunk loads over and above the regular demand for goods. Only eight months later, Perkins hastily ordered more such items, noting to his Saint Louis supplier that the goods were "absolutely necessary as soon as they can be sent to keep our business alive."[24]

But market facilitation of this kind, while potentially profitable, was extremely risky. The supply of raw goods was unpredictable and Eastern money markets highly volatile. Middlemen stood to suffer if either end of this distribution network failed. Eventually, Isaac Greene was stung by these economic perils. He found himself indebted to Eastern manufacturers while his unconsigned merchandise upriver went unsold. When his supplier of timber met with an unforeseen delay, Greene's ability to cover these credit gaps stretched beyond his limit. Writing to his Wisconsin associate on 28 May 1849, Greene was candid: "I wish you would write me on receipt of this letter how soon you can pay me the amount of your note, for I am suffering for the want of money. I have not got a dollar in the world to buy any lumber with. . . . I wish in this you would be positive and explicit, for I have no business now, and must get to doing something immediately." Unlike Harmon, Greene saw little use in legal action, possibly a reflection of the distances involved between his Eastern associate in Boston, his home in Saint Louis, and Perkins in Saint Croix. Greene reasoned: "It is evident that both parties here and there at St. Croix should be paid, and it belongs to the same parties to pay them, and hence it is all nonsense to go to quarreling among one or the other in regard to it." Greene's efforts came to naught: he was forced to declare himself bankrupt and close his business. Adding to his disappointment, the insolvency came at the same time as the Saint Louis fire, when the city's demand for lumber and the services of general middlemen was the greatest. Greene no longer had a business with which to profit by these opportunities.[25]

If the consumer market was expanding in the Midwest, why did

Greene fail? The answer highlights the pivotal nature of middlemen in the expression of rural consumer behavior. The economic engine that brought about these changes was the assumption of business risk by the multitude of independent agents. As demonstrated in Saint Croix and Naperville, agents staked their money, in the form of orders placed to Eastern wholesalers, against the promise of a marketable agricultural surplus from the hinterland. Obviously, they gambled not for hidden altruistic reasons but in the hopes of earning profits. Still, the antebellum agent can appear today more honest and courageous than the "heroes" promoted during that period, from Davy Crockett to the odd assortment of Indian-fighters, gunslingers, and filibusters that haunt U.S. folklore. Harmon's ability to manage and Greene's failure to plan for the risk that felled him spell the difference between success and failure. With an optimistic belief in the pledges of their countrymen to deliver the goods, and in expectation of a fair return for their efforts, agents shouldered huge personal liabilities. Their efforts sometimes led to great wealth, but usually agents either only got by or failed outright. Isaac Greene noted that the psychological stress associated with these risks was "enough to move the equilibrium of any one." One woman, writing to her agent brother, "fear[ed] so much care & anxiety as you must have in purchasing goods and getting started in trade will be too much for you. . . . I was glad to hear you were so well pleased with your purchases in NY."[26]

Recent scholarship provides a more detailed account of how this risk was managed. Jeffrey Adler relates that in antebellum Saint Louis, many Yankee traders maintained their economic viability by relying heavily on their family ties to Eastern markets and credit. Another study, Timothy Mahoney's skillful account of regional development, explains two other important examples of risk management by local dealers: the transportation factor, and credit. These, Mahoney concludes, deeply affected the direction of regional growth.[27] Jobbers and other urban suppliers practiced risk assessment most directly by predicting the costs and hazards of transportation. Mahoney demonstrates that these providers gained some stability through the use of short-haul transports, generally within a couple of hundred miles of their point of origin. These smaller journeys were less likely to run the risk of stranding shipments due to bad weather or low water. In a very real sense, this problem directly affected Isaac Greene, whose business relied on an extremely long trade route between Saint Louis and Saint Croix: more than five hundred miles. His miscalculation resulted in the failure of his business.[28]

In a second example, Mahoney shows how agents established predictable timetables during which they might transact their regional business. Timing of shipments, in conjunction with the length of the haul, were pivotal in netting profits. Managing receipts through intricate timing schedules was one way to mitigate the unpredictability of the Midwestern marketplace. The Dubuque *Herald Express* wrote that "it required a merchant of more than ordinary firmness and judgement to buy and sell goods on the western market. Unfortunately, we have, especially in smaller towns, a class of merchants utterly inexperienced in business who are led into serious errors in buying and selling, and on selling on letters [with] insufficient security." Agents exploited this business opportunity by assuming this risk for profit. By doing so, they insulated many town merchants from this same danger.[29]

As a result, regional agents were deeply concerned with changing the traditional, limited role of a store into a more responsive vehicle for rural consumers. Given their unique position and vulnerability to the financial loss, agents such as Greene demanded that their merchants "look very closely into affairs at [the] store, t'is *very important* that it should be clearly looked after, pardon our anxiety on this head."[30]

Middlemen, exerting a subtle leverage over the flow of goods into a region, induced local merchants to change their marketing styles in several ways. First, agents pressed retailers to cultivate local methods of inventory control. Briefly, this business method was important as a means to spur sales of goods by making them easily available to consumers at the desired time. Turnover of goods was essential for the profitability of each node of the distribution network: store, middleman, manufacturer. If merchandise was desired but unavailable, then manufacturers would lose sales. On the other hand, if goods were stocked months in advance of being needed (for example, if winter boots were kept on the shelves in July) retailers would have unprofitably tied up both money and precious storage and display space.[31] Because few Midwestern retailers could afford such a luxury, they often erred on the side of caution and stocked only the most basic goods.

Charles Harmon described to his brother how a balanced inventory was achieved. The drummer provided an understanding of "the nature of business operations here, character of stock wanted, & time of sale" without "wast[ing] many words." First, Chicago agents needed to be wary of carrying off-season stock without the prospect of quick sales. Harmon noted that, "on the contrary I think it best to order as the articles are wanted." The best time to order "for the fall trade" was "about the 1st of Sept[ember] and calculate to dispose of a very large proportion of the stock by the first of Dec[ember] in fact to nearly close it up." Notably, the timing coincided almost exactly with the harvest, transport, and sale of the region's agricultural surplus. Despite more vigorous sales than in the preceding year, Harmon urged caution not to overstock. The products that he saw as the most profitable—in his letters he referred to them as "trimmings"—reveal that agents responded to consumer demands not met by the providers of staple goods. Harmon concluded that "it is an object, for profits, to have as complete a stock of 'trimmings' and to sell as large a proportion of that class of articles as possible. I have therefore added to the list sent several articles not usually kept by the trade in NY."[32] Inventory management was central to the profitability of agents and one of the leading tenets directly supporting consumer demand. Agents worked hard to compel retailers to use this method of merchandising control.

The role of agents in bringing about this change is seen in the correspondence between dealers and rural retailers during this era. For example, Isaac Greene wrote to Perkins, in Saint Croix, urging him to anticipate his customers' demands for sugar, molasses, tobacco, tea, and sundry other goods. More important than simple reminders to resupply his stock, Greene actively encouraged Perkins to carry a wider variety of goods to create and meet potential demand. In addition to an order for basic commodities, Greene noticed that he "had no order from [Perkins] for Beans, but we know that are wanted for the woods, and have no knowledge of any being purchased for you, so we took the liberty to send them." Two weeks later, Greene sent an additional two dozen axes "in case you are short, new article, said to be superior, cost high, try them and see how they go." An associate of Greene's more forcibly stated the agent's indispensable role in balancing inventory and consumer demand along the distribution network. The middleman lamented that their "eastern friends have not had much experience in purchasing evidently, or they would have anticipated our want and provided for them with greater punctuality." G. S. Howell, a Dixon, Illinois, agent wrote to his brother that "the time will come when we will not have to go east" for the goods required by Midwestern consumers, because the agents were "coming thicker & faster."[33]

The increased and diversified inventory of goods provided to retailers by regional agents was closely allied to the burgeoning consumer preference for specialty goods. As was the case with Harmon's "trimmings," luxury items were increasingly required to fill out a firm's inventory.[34] Again, agents both instigated and then responded to this need by supplying retailers with fashionable goods. The label "Eastern-bought" became a mark of a product's desirability. Illinois retailer John Bennett, in a letter to his father about a missed meeting, explained that he had had to leave for New York to fill his orders before others beat him to it: "It would not sound well in the peoples ears for all the rest of the merchants to be getting their goods from the east and for us to buy exclusively in St. Louis. As all you have to do with some is to say that your goods were bought in the east."[35]

A second important capacity of agents was that they helped stabilize and balance the prices for locally available goods. Fair pricing was advised by agents to keep customers happy while providing just compensation for everyone along the distribution network. The records indicate that agents generally discouraged price gouging (that is, obtaining the highest price the market would bear) in favor of increasing the volume of sales. Again, the relationship between Greene and Perkins demonstrates this attempt. Greene repeatedly chided and corrected storekeeper Perkins on the pricing structure of his inventory. He was painfully aware that his "freight bills . . . [were] $5,800! besides insurance" and therefore "we must, *we ought* not let an article go out of the store [for] less than 50 pr ct sum from invoices, and much should bring 75 pr ct." Greene wrote that the fashionable, Eastern-manufactured, ready-made clothing procured "mostly for cash and at extremely low prices . . . will bring 60 to 70 per cent profit, I think we can easily get 100." Yet for caps and hats, much more common stock, Greene later suggested that "we think about 50 or 75 per, not too much profit on this bill, especially the caps." Greene's position in Saint Louis gave him additional data, enabling him to add the cost of transportation and the element of risk into the pricing of goods. He thus could figure a fair market value.[36]

It is important to note that most agents did not recklessly pursue greater sales volumes at the expense of business stability. Agents were intent on securing profitable turnover of stocked goods but not at the expense of extending too much credit, or of extending credit to those incapable of repayment. This was logical. Agents were demonstrably the most vulnerable to fiscal collapse when the network experienced a local failure of payments. This was especially evident after agents had shipped large consignments to store operators and merchants were most likely to be rushed to sell their new wares. Greene boldly stated that "we must caution you strictly in regard to the county you are in, not to credit one dollar unless you have property to move [i.e., logs for export] . . . put in your possession." Two weeks later, following another large consignment, the agent reiterated: "Be very careful and not let [the shipment] get scattered without first having the pay for them, you are in a county noted for grabbing." With some sarcasm, Greene advised Perkins to just "give the goods away," rather than to sell them on shaky credit.[37]

Agents were key in the formation of the true retail stores that replaced the more authoritarian or foolhardy frontier outlets. By demanding that rural retailers provide greater inventory control, more reasonable pricing, and safer credit practices, agents hoped to secure a sheltered environment in which they could expect a reasonable profit. Although in no way were these efforts intended to be for the direct benefit of the rural consumer (for example, Greene instructed Perkins to extend no credit "unless it is to loggers [who will need the mill] and then so bound that you control their logs above the mill"),[38] inevitably they improved the economic position of the customers. Their actions allowed for the more direct expression of real consumer desires. By unleashing the governing forces of supply and demand into the relationship between retailers and rural consumers, agents unwittingly gave patrons a new and important economic role that had been absent in earlier country "stores." Still, the full effect of these changes in the market position of consumers required further reform of the entire distribution network.

Manufacturers and suppliers of finished goods also needed to recognize and respond to the consumer demand of the hinterland. Many manufacturers during this period were willing to reap only the easiest sales from nearby urban and local markets, ignoring the more distant rural consumer. To some extent, this advantage was the key difference between the retail experiences of Isaac Harmon and Isaac Greene. Agents helped to turn manufacturers' attention toward this new and potent opportunity. They did so not by merely filling orders and dispensing products but, hoping to increase the profits of all involved, by actively pressing manufacturers to change their business practices. As one old hand put it: "These Chicago Jobbers are just as cunning as an old Red Fox, and whenever they find any manufacturers, whether east or west, hard up for 'material aids' . . . they always stand ready to lend them a helping hand, in a

friendly & business way." Two attempts by Charles Harmon, one a failure
and the other a success, illustrate how agents hoped to transform their
suppliers.[39]

Harmon was an early advocate of extending business to the remote
countryside. His sizable correspondence with the glass manufacturing
firm of Smith & Wilkins, of Southport, Wisconsin, makes this clear. In a
letter dated 8 September 1846, Harmon wrote: "I have no doubt that
your glass can be introduced in this market to almost the entire exclusion
of other kinds, at an advance on the price that you name." Further, Harmon promised firm orders from rural towns along the most accessible
trade routes. Hoping to entice the skeptical producer with a vast new hinterland market, Harmon told him: "I shall be able to send your glass
through all the country between here and within 100 miles of St.
Louis."[40] Despite Harmon's pleas, the Wisconsin firm failed to act. The
agent's frustration was evident: he expostulated at the firm's inability to
"keep a full supply of glass here, and the more because I think you misap-
prehend the importance of the Market."[41] Harmon concluded his correspondence with complaints about lost sales and in one of his last letters he
chided his erstwhile partners for not allowing him to meet promises he
had made regarding deliveries to the interior, for "it is extremely unpleasant to endure the importunities I am subjected to" because of the glass
maker's delays. Given the daily risks assumed by most middlemen, it
would be hard to imagine a more disconcerting scenario than Harmon's
futile attempts to convince this supplier to vend a sure-fire product to
such willing consumers.[42]

Harmon had more luck elsewhere. A. J. Dunham & Company, makers of parlor stoves, were more receptive to Harmon's suggestions regarding the Midwestern marketplace. Correspondence between the two
reveals that Harmon directed the manufacturer in response to specific
consumer demands. For example, he suggested that the firm concentrate
their production on the "copper & tin trimmings & stove pipes" rather
than the stove itself, which were "sold in this market at very low rates, indeed without profit, and whatever is made in the trade is on the trimmings."[43] In an effort to further the sale of these stoves, Harmon pressed
the supplier to provide credit and terms available to other agents in markets "wholly given them" (i.e., where they had a territorial monopoly).
Again, Harmon's first concern was with the potential profits to be earned
through the venture, but in the process, he aided rural access to a wider
variety of goods, and on good terms. At an early time in the economic de-

velopment of the Midwest, by pressing manufacturers to contend in more wide-ranging markets for consumer dollars, agents reduced the stifling effects of local manufacturing monopolies.[44]

By thus pressing manufacturers to expand their services and reach into the countryside, agents helped amplify the receptiveness of the distribution network toward rural consumer standards. As the easily accessible local markets were glutted, manufacturers, agents, and suppliers all faced stiffer competition in the more distant, yet profitable, lands. Those who met the challenge by expanding and competing were more likely to survive than those who ignored the needs of the rural consumer. Again it was a matter of reducing the insulation factor: as in their dealings with local merchants, agents put the manufacturers more in touch with the demands of the farm community—the consumers themselves.

A third, and relatively minor, role played by agents in the transformation of the rural consumer landscape was their impact on transportation facilities. Throughout the antebellum era, poor roads, rail, and water transport were the peril of business operations in the Midwest.[45] Still, agents negotiated the intricacies of rural shipment while earning a profit. In one letter to his brother, Chicago agent Edson Keith reported in December 1855 how he traveled throughout Wisconsin in order to make sales of his millinery goods, using almost every Midwestern means of locomotion: lumber wagon, carriage, rail, horseback. He related how once, "going up a steep hill," his traveling partners were "sitting in the back of the wagon leaning against the tail board . . . [when] out bursts the board & down those fellows went heals over head. It bruised them up some . . . we had a capital laugh and went on." Keith had had a relatively safe position in the fore of the wagon, but he too had been shaken "to a pomace and I was never so lame in my life."[46]

Given their experiences, agents were in a good position to identify and cite the business costs associated with poor transportation facilities. Their advice might decide for or against the development of a trading connection. For example, representatives for the Fairbanks Scales Company awaited the coming of rail transportation before moving their venture deeper into the rural marketplace outside of Chicago. The agent of Dixon, Illinois, merchant P. M. Alexander kept Alexander informed with updates on the rates and insurance figures for seasonal travel on Lake Michigan. Merchant Milo Custer, in McLean County, Illinois, received similar information regarding the prospects for commerce via the Illinois-Michigan Canal from agent John Mayers. Charles Harmon, among many others, regularly lamented the seasonal rains that made "the roads . . . nearly impassable, and consequently, trade . . . very dull & collections nothing."[47] Agents were keenly aware that when adequate transportation facilities existed, trade did a booming business and their urban businesses prospered.[48]

Agents could also provide insightful market intelligence, pointing directly to the advantages of surmounting a particular difficulty. Harmon reported to one of his suppliers, the New York wholesaler Wood & Sheldon, that because the "Illinois river is very low, and has been for two months past . . . the Interior dealers have been unable to procure supplies of any kind from St. Louis, and further, the price of Sugar and Molasses is very high in the market. These causes will compel the traders from a larger territory to come here for such articles, who usually go the other way." Harmon frequently sent in such reports. Six months after the Illinois River report, he related that while roads to the interior were almost impassible "and business has entirely ceased," as soon as they cleared "I think I shall be able to make rapid sales of the consigned goods."[49]

Undoubtedly, the transportation network in the Midwest would have developed without the pressures from the jobbers. Still, their voice was added at an early date and reached the ear of Eastern investors, who may not have noticed the immediate business consequences had improvements been only the pet project of Western politicians. When aggressive agents overcame the obstacles of poor transportation facilities and turned a profit on their sales to the interior, they offered compelling evidence to others of the latent consumer demand. This, no doubt, emboldened others to press for improvements to infrastructure and fueled the grassroots drive for economical, physically easier access to these markets.

But the single most important contribution made by agents to the antebellum business condition was their ability to gather and disseminate credit and market information efficiently. Typical was an account mailed by agent Charles R. Blake to his Springfield, Illinois, hardware supplier on 6 December 1868. In a single letter he informed his associates about four bad accounts. Of one store operator, he wrote: "I am sorry to say, [he was] a dead duck and I doubt very much if he ever squares up with us"; another's "note [was] probably a dead loss"; a third was "doing nothing and is very poor"; and finally, another regional agency had "got up entirely and turned their shop over to Crain & Mauson. Nearly all their notes and [accounts] have been gobbled up by a Springfield house. The best I could do was to take their note at six months." Letters such as these were common. They functioned as the mortar that held together the different branches of the distribution network. Midwestern agents bridged the gap between local merchants and Eastern wholesalers. They also demonstrated to both the means by which profitable businesses must proceed under such conditions. These efforts resulted in an accumulation of credit and market experience that was unique in the West. By disseminating this information, agents stabilized the region's distribution ties and paved the way for consumers to take advantage of the tremendous future growth in manufacturing output and rail delivery following the Civil War.[50]

Saint Croix provides a further example of this essential role linking the day-to-day needs of everyone along the distribution line. Isaac Greene supplied local retailers with personnel, cash, and goods. In one instance, in a single letter to Perkins, Greene provided $9,000 in credit by which the Boston wholesalers continued to outfit the mill town, forwarded $2,000 and "a lot of goods" to Perkins at Saint Croix, discussed the need for more lumber to be sent downstream, and even produced a source of labor ("some carpenters & Dutchmen") to meet the construction needs of local boosters. In other letters, Greene supplied additional laborers as well as skilled river pilots in order to bring lumber to market.[51] Greene's position in Saint Louis gave him a complete view of the network and allowed him to anticipate the needs of both local merchants and remote suppliers. Agents dealt with complex issues: a typical transaction by an agent balanced a variety of credits, debits, interest, and consumer demands. In a letter to Messrs. Wood & Sheldon, Charles Harmon granted the firm credit for fifty bags of coffee, advanced two checks for cash totaling more than $1,800, and distributed the appropriate interest and profits to the various parties involved. Through the independent action of a host of agents, the staggering complexity of the pioneer market slowly became predictable.[52]

The region's fickle money supply played havoc with the network. In the Midwest, a throng of small banks printed bills backed by little more than speculative fervor and unimproved land, a risky and volatile asset at best. Illinois alone had dozens of these small operators circulating notes. More secure Eastern institutions made safer money available for the larger wholesalers. Yet even these bills were heavily discounted when transacted for goods or specie.[53] The inevitable failure by many of the Western outfits struck at the heart of the utility of these early greenbacks. The trust invested by the bearer (in this case the merchant), that he or she would be repaid for accepting this consumer convenience, vanished.

Careless or uninformed agents who accepted the sundry currencies were often left with worthless guarantees. The normally cautious Harmon was left holding forty-five dollars in notes, a relatively small sum in comparison with other failures, from a bank in Sandusky, Ohio. In a letter to an associate, Harmon bemoaned the fact that he was "unable to use any of it. Please advise me by return mail, what disposition you want made of it. The reputation of the bank is growing worse every day in this place." William Blair, a Chicago agent for hardware supplies, wryly noted that as experience with risky funds spread, "Merchants generally have a good deal more confidence in *nails* than in Illinois Bank Notes."[54] These merchants came to rely more on the use of gold or notes from the more reputable, Eastern firms for their large business transactions. Edson Keith, speaking of retailers, nicely summed up the feeling that sales should be restricted when he advocated: "Stick to the cash system principally on Customers you don't know perfectly about the liabilities & assets & honesty." Illinois retailer Junior Ellis sounded a common warning to patrons when he circulated a notice that, due to "the unsettled state of currency, on and after this date, I will receive no money for any Goods, or Accounts due me, except such as will buy NEW YORK EXCHANGE OR GOLD." This ordinary practice led to a downward spiral in the value of local notes and the increased scarcity of specie. The inescapable outcome was to make purchases by rural consumers more expensive and more difficult.[55]

Keith's foray into rural Illinois, Missouri, Iowa, and Wisconsin in the summer of 1856 showed the stultifying effects that poor currency had on the consumer economy. Here Keith found that most merchants refused to pay for his wares using gold or sound Eastern currency. Keith recognized that without a change in local conditions, he did not "think [he would] sell many more goods to the newest part of the wooden country as it [was] more than it [was] worth to collect it, unless they [were] uncommonly obliging men." Frustration over lost sales and delinquent accounts receivable was galling to a veteran like Keith. After being repeatedly refused sales by formerly good customers, he confessed in a letter to his brother that "collections are mighty hard. I feel almost discouraged in trying, [soon] they will think the Border Ruffians are after them if they don't pay for I am getting desperate."[56]

Such conditions were more or less pervasive throughout the heartland and agents were obliged to find ways to respond to the difficulty in order to spur sales and take care of their own survival. Faced with customers "troubled with the shorts worse than a man would be with the 7 year itch," agencies extended credit to merchants who they deemed most trustworthy. The cautionary tone in many letters of the era suggests the alarm that gripped most agents as they were forced to assume an even greater financial liability to support the distribution of goods. Keith reminded his brother: "I should not want you to rely upon [my efforts alone] to give credit, for you ought to ascertain from every customer their real responsibility." Agents usually based their evaluations on a merchant's ability to sell the products that were suggested by the jobber.[57] The means employed to balance the agents' personal accounts and provide this fiscal bridge to local merchants were often as trying as the physical access to the consumer markets. In order to keep on top of the state of their customers' credit, agents had to make long trips into the hinterland. Keith believed that no "man ever worked, coaxed, pled & took old Job as a pattern [as much as] I did" when he hit the trail in 1856. Agencies were forced to rely on—in the words of one agent—"some pretty sharp work financing" the various shortfalls, credits, risks, and benefits associated with providing goods to the rural marketplace.[58]

Nevertheless, by extending currency information into the Midwest, agents were helping to stabilize rates enough for businessmen and speculators to feel comfortable in investing in the West. The risk that was involved would not, by itself, have prevented Easterners from seeking profits in the prairie. But a total lack of information would scare all but the most foolhardy gamblers. Letters collected for the Illinois hardware dealer Alexander, Howell & Company span more than two decades from 1854 to 1876 and show how the risk associated with trade in the Midwest gradually diminished. Throughout their correspondence with both local retailers and Eastern partners, the firm kept everyone informed of the relative values of currency and gold in the various regional markets. They suggest the cumulative effects that more logical market conditions had on the final price for many goods. For example, their Boston suppliers wrote in 1855 that the going rate for Western loans was 3 percent above that available on the Atlantic seaboard, a premium that the Midwestern firm dutifully passed on to the stores. Five years later, a firm from Troy, New York, lowered the transaction costs to less than 1 percent. By 1871, Alexander, Howell & Company were procuring most of their goods through Chicago suppliers, who often, as was the case with one firm, actually *discounted* their sales to the interior. As the Chicago firm wrote: "We do not offer the 1% as a cash discount because we don't want the money—and would rather you would take an equivalent in time, but we know you don't want the time any more than we do the money therefore you will only consider it as a concession in price." Certainly the combined effects of hundreds of agencies processing thousands of letters had assuaged much of the fears of transacting business.[59]

The consequences of these efforts were profound for the rural consumer, and the region proved to be one of the most important in the consumption of capital and consumer goods throughout the rest of the nineteenth century. To reiterate what was noted earlier—for this point cannot be overstated—agents played an important role in spurring national sales through their efforts at extending credit. But more directly, the selective use of credit by agents shifted the relative economic importance away from the supplier in favor of the consumer. Agents extended credit primarily to merchants who responded to the loans with increased sales. In this way, the distribution network was further transformed from one on a supply-driven footing to one driven by demand.[60]

A second and associated benefit to consumers was the agent's ability to distribute accurate information about current and future market conditions. As evidenced above, the general correspondence between agents, merchants, and suppliers often gave vital information about each firm's honesty, creditworthiness, and volume of business transacted. But the letters also indicate that agents were atypical in their active pursuit of market stability through more accurate sales projecting and marketing techniques.[61]

Forecasting the current and future sales volumes for a region was, in large measure, the economic niche that the middlemen exploited for their profits. The greatest share of the correspondence preserved in agents' letter books reflected their need to inform local merchants and distant suppliers of new business opportunities. Harmon's firm was characteristic. Numerous examples survive of dispatches sent across the region calling attention to sales opportunities and possible liabilities. In one instance, the firm warned that some goods, such as sugar and molasses, were "entirely inadequate." They also listed other goods that could be expected to generate "considerable sales . . . not entirely depend[ing] on their scarcity." The timing of shipments was often the critical factor in gaining a profitable market advantage. In 1846, the clothing markets proved to be "overstocked at present, although there maybe a demand before winter sets in." One item that happened to be ordered without this rule in mind—black cashmere sweaters—resulted in paltry sales because the "low prices of woolen goods in NY induced large purchases for this market & it is overtaken with every description of woolens." In another letter, Harmon contemplated the bare essence of this vital exchange of information: "Would you inform me what it can be sold for, speedily, in your market[?] The charges and expenses of selling, and if you are doing a commission business. If not, please name a House to whom it would be advisable to consign."[62]

Successful agents were ones who accurately aligned the distribution network to the needs and desires of consumer demand. Rarely were goods ordered or even accepted on consignment that did not meet the consumer's needs for quality or price. Further, agents' intimate contact with Western economic conditions added veracity to their judgments regarding consumer tastes. In many instances, agents wrote to their suppliers along the following lines: "Dealers have too many old goods left from last fall and people I think will not feel able to indulge very extensively in anything that is not positively needed. I am afraid from accounts from the country that the wheat crop will be quite poor and the farmers will have to rely upon corn for their exports." In this instance, the delay in the farm cash cycle postponed consumer demand. The agent prevented merchants from assuming the economic hardship of owning excess inventory during such a momentarily dull season. Instead, the agent promised little "risk however in buying a fair fall stock as I have no doubt we shall be able to sell a larger extent of the trade [at that time] than we did last spring."[63]

It bears repeating that, in supplying this critical market information, agents were acting to further their own economic interests. Harmon himself used his knowledge of the local Chicago markets to profit by two speculative ventures as a retailer of oysters and tallow candles.[64] Yet, as with their use of credit, the combined action of these entrepreneurs led to profound changes in the timing of the development of the Midwestern consumer economy. Credit-rating services and market analyses were eventually to become institutionalized into business ventures of their own. Tappan & Douglass and R. G. Dun were only two firms that provided such services for Western merchants in the late antebellum era. Equally, regional newspapers such as the *Chicago Tribune* and independent wire services provided comprehensive market data.[65] Undoubtedly, these aids were used by some retailers in the rural Midwest to further their ability to react to the changing market conditions. Yet it is probable that these formal institutions were more useful to national suppliers and speculators than to the final consumer.

The effect of these labors for rural patrons was both important and often overlooked in the rush to place the middlemen's actions in a national context. Agents kept suppliers free from the stagnating effects of a glutted consumer market. As with the case of the New York woolens, Harmon warned one Gotham wholesaler that there were "several articles in the stock sent me [by them] on which a profit cannot be realized in the market over the invoice cost. To wit currants, peanuts, bitters, blanking [blanket material?], twine, & caps. Most of these articles are sold as low here as they are billed." In anticipation of their response, Harmon offered "a list of a few articles which will be wanted by the time they can be got here."[66] By creating a responsive network to supply consumer goods, agents freed rural customers to express their demands on a more pliable marketplace. Middlemen provided credit to local merchants who responded to their customers' wishes. Finally, agents also provided wholesalers with information on how well their products were being accepted in the rural marketplace, and where they might more profitably sell their merchandise.

Agents such as Harmon, Greene, and Keith were no more determined to expand consumer involvement in the acquisition of goods than any other economic participant of the era. Still, as a class of businessmen, successful agents employed precise and sometimes rigid business practices to meet their needs. They pressed merchants to adopt a new conception of their stores. Agents increased the involvement by manufacturers in the wider distribution of their goods. They communicated to others along the distribution network what were the transportation limitations of the region. Finally, as a group, they circulated news of credit and market conditions. All of these were attempts to lower the risk that they assumed in order to get goods into the hands of rural consumers.

Agents largely succeeded in their task because they were able to change the behavior of those on the margins of the network. Supported by the agents' use of credit, merchants ordered a wider variety of goods, practiced inventory control, and sold their merchandise at fair market values. Many manufacturers expanded their commercial reach into the hinterland—resulting in greater competitive forces. Agents demonstrated to Eastern speculators the profits to be found in the West, in spite of its transportation woes. Finally, the distribution network itself became self-correcting. Through the advice of agents, markets were less likely to be glutted or empty of specific consumer goods. Equally, credit information stabilized the chain's economic solvency, as fewer firms were likely to be caught unaware by questionable rural merchants.

Combined, these changes cultivated the prominence of consumer demand in the region's economy. By 1861, escalating competitive pressures and the increased availability and awareness of goods ended the opportunity for rural merchants to maintain local monopolies. Supply gave way to demand as the governing force in the consumer economy. This was accomplished by agents who spread the risk of doing business to others along the supply line. Merchants, wholesalers, and manufacturers assumed this risk by becoming beholden to rural consumer preferences. The success of agents in extending the consumer market into the hinterland, in fact, gave real economic power to rural Americans. By diluting and decentralizing the distribution network, agents democratized the control over mass consumption.[67]

Ironically, the systematization of consumer demand made agents appear to be less important to the maintenance of this relationship. Rural consumers failed to comprehend much of the risk assumed and care taken by agents to open the countryside to consumer options. When economic conditions worsened after the war, and especially after 1873, farmers focused their ire on the concept of the middleman without fully understanding these costs. In large part because of the overall success that agents had in changing the retail market in the Midwest, shopping excursions to Chicago or Saint Louis became the paradigm of rural consumption. With the integration of urban suppliers, the individual consumer, local retailers, and the developing transportation network, the role of the middleman became problematic. Firms such as those run by Charles Harmon and Edson Keith either transformed themselves into wholesalers of specific goods or, as with Greene and many others, faded from view—or at least from the historian's view.[68] With their passing, the source of change in consumer practices shifted from antebellum agents to the newly empowered rural patron.

4 An All-Consuming Vision

The Expression of Rural Consumer Ideology, 1865–1875

Braving the harsh Wisconsin winter, Grange organizers from Oshkosh traveled to neighboring Ripon to promote their new agrarian fraternity in February 1873. Their hosts met the delegation at the train depot "with a capacious sleigh, in which all were soon snugly packed; and dashing off at a lively rate" soon reached the meeting place some four miles south of the terminal. A local reporter for the *Oshkosh City Times* noted that the session was attended by more than three hundred men, women, and children. Graciously offering their guests "first chances" at a meal, the throng then ate their dinners in shifts "as only about thirty could be seated at once . . . so great the jam indeed that it was after midnight before the last served could obtain a mouthful." Addresses from the visiting Oshkosh "Patrons" enlivened the feast and were met with "unbounded applause." First, J. W. Sanders spoke of the "monopoly of implement makers" and agents who were "sapping the lifeblood of the agriculturalists." Joseph Osborn followed with an oration on the methods of ensuring profitable cooperation based on the shared needs of regional farmers. The assembly disbanded shortly after three o'clock in the morning with "many pleasant interchanges of social feeling . . . all heartily entertained, and enthusiastic over the prospect and advantages" of the new Ripon chapter.[1]

In Green County, Illinois, a less festive but equally constructive convention was held. Local farmer and diarist Henry Griswold wrote in his distinctively terse style: "March 4, 1874: Clear hauled some hay and straw out, went to the church to organize a Grange." Griswold remained busy in the resulting chapter, the White Hall Social Grange No. 1308, as a founder and officer of their purchasing cooperative until 1887. The "Social Grange" endured as one of Green County's most vital social and economic associations for the next forty years.[2] The actions of Griswold and his Wisconsin affiliates reveal the clarity with which grassroots rural institutions reflected the life experiences of most Midwestern farmers. Like many of his neighbors, Griswold spent his day pursuing the independent, market-based agriculture that secured his family an income. He and his brethren chose to gather, however, not at a convenient work site, or at an influential farmer's residence, but at a community church. Here they set about forming one of the most dynamic institutions for consumer activism, a Grange purchasing agency.

Purchasing cooperatives operated through the Patrons of Husbandry offered the clearest example of the dramatic synthesis that took place between rural Midwesterners' consumer behavior, economic outlook, and communal fidelity. Based on their shared experiences with scientific farming and the customary need by commercial planters to purchase a wide variety of goods, Patrons constructed a simple yet insightful agrarian philosophy that attempted to balance collective and private needs. The fabric of this rural consumer ethos was woven with the threads of four sentiments: to instill a greater deference in suppliers and manufacturers for consumer demand, to justify individual consumption by the benefits it provided the broader rural community, to reform the existing distribution system with an eye toward eliminating unfair pricing and other market inefficiencies, and to shore up rural America's public virtue and republican heritage through open and democratic consumer institutions. While Grange organizers had to contend with existing and often apathetic farmers' clubs, the merger of this modern consumer doctrine with the order's unique purchasing practices propelled their "agrarian union" to the pinnacle of national rural organizations by 1875.[3]

Separating the many causes, influences, hopes, and misconceptions that led to this groundswell of organized activity drives the analysis of rural consumption toward some tangled, if familiar, questions about the Midwest. For example, what led a region largely dominated by independent commercial farmers to adopt a communal cooperative strategy to deal with the problems of materialism? Were rural Americans aware of a new "consumer ethos" and did their actions change as a result of this knowledge, or is this simply an artificial and ahistorical arrangement of unconnected behaviors? Who participated in the movement and were they representative of the region? How did the rise of institutional powers affect consumer behavior and, connected to this, can the rhetoric and bombast of these organizational leaders be separated from "real" sentiment? Finally, how to explain the relationship between communal harmony and individual economic prosperity that was at the core of the Midwestern Grange movement?

The dynamic growth of formal rural associations in the Midwest was due primarily to the profound economic downturn and political changes of the immediate postwar years. The recession produced a lasting deflation of commodity prices for commercial suppliers. In Iowa, prices for a bushel of corn fell from $0.70 in 1864 to $0.24 in 1872. Returns for live hogs and wheat suffered as well, falling from $7.75 per animal and $1.57 per bushel in the late 1860s to $3.44 and $0.77, respectively, by the mid 1870s. The Panic of 1873, brought on by blundering speculation in railroads and real estate, was largely to blame and heralded a new age in rural unrest. Farmers came to be considered "chronic revolutionaries." Coinciding with the retraction of federal greenbacks, depression and deflation threatened commercial farmers with unmanageable debt. The economic anxiety generated by the crisis aroused resentment between farmers, rail transporters, financiers, and territorial agents that lasted for generations. Exaggerated tales of a complex international conspiracy, known later as the "Crime of '73," were widespread in the region, and this, plus political corruption, added to the distrust that attends systemic economic downturns.[4]

These cyclical economic shifts led to fears of increased dependency that further compounded the recession and amplified the sense of crisis. Commercialization and the centrality of cash transactions for transportation, consumer goods, farm equipment, and, more importantly, for the compensation that their produce brought in the futures market accelerated during the decade before the Civil War. The indispensable role that these components played in commercial farming compelled even the most isolated planters to participate in the market at some level. Moreover, as William Cronon notes, the new and expanding distribution web "concealed the very linkages it was creating," making it even more difficult for farmers to recognize and adapt to the transformation. Concerted action, it was hoped, might thwart these potentially sinister forces and regain a sense of economic agency for the embattled farm population.[5]

The underlying political instability in the Midwest and the nation also contributed to farmers' growing desire to seek greater representation and influence (and sometimes refuge) in formal organizations. For the Democratic Party, the dishonor of the "rebellion" loomed like an albatross and damned its members to permanent minority status in the Midwest. John Kirk, a territorial agent based in Chicago in 1868, reflected a popular sentiment when he longed for "the Devil Democratic Party & Slavery and Traitors and Rebels all [to] go to hell together." The Democrats were never fully eclipsed. They retained significant political strength in many local jurisdictions, but they suffered at the state and national level from the winner-take-all polling system that was distinctive of American politics. While the Republicans gloried in the Union's victory on the battlefield, they, too, suffered, enduring divisions and in-fighting as the party sought to balance Reconstruction with that era's own return to normalcy. As a result, enterprising politicians brandished new and provocative issues such as currency, transportation, and banking reform, which often bred fusion movements between the dejected Democrats, frustrated Republicans, and other temporarily nonaligned factions. In one noteworthy example, Illinois's John McAuley Palmer represented, either as a candidate or elected official, no fewer than five separate and distinct political parties between 1854 to 1900. Agricultural journals and daily newspapers exacerbated these trends by increasingly presenting politics as sporting contests that only propagated controversy, and hence the sales of their publications. All told, the era was blighted with overambitious promoters and provocateurs who offered apprehensive Midwesterners a full range of panaceas guaranteed to cure their economic ills.[6]

Supporting these materialistic and political changes were subtle shifts, or more precisely a settling in the rural community. Hal Baron and John Mack Faragher show that "those who stayed behind" often constructed strong communal links between families and other regional farmers based on values that honored continuity, stability, and conservation. A representative sample of charter members in the Delaware County (Indiana) Grange discussed below shows that by 1873 the average span of residency was more than twenty years. As Jane Pederson showed, such continuity led many rural Americans to seek ways to control their changing society rather than try to stop or prevent change.[7]

Few, if any, regions within the Midwest even remained open to farming that was not in some way a precursor to staple-crop agriculture. This uniformity of economic outlook was supported by, and in turn upheld the moral economy of, persistent families. In a very real sense, the visible divisions between the two useful historical concepts of market and moral economy broke down. Their economic relations were conducted in cash, and because of the widespread knowledge gained through scientific farming, many were more confident of their ability to succeed. The discourse within most Midwestern farm communities changed from answering how to prevent or limit the market's influence to asking how farmers might overlay their mores onto capitalism. Sally McMurry, in *Transforming Rural Life*, details a similar phenomenon in the cheese-making communities of Wisconsin between 1820 and 1885. There it was often the families most committed to community and local solidarity that succeeded at dairying; indeed, it was the chief source of their success.[8] Accordingly, farmers looked to new institutions to check rising material threats by using their strengthened sense of community as an asset. In short, they sought to guarantee the benefits of market participation for the individual farm family while at the same time staying true to the ethos of community, equality, and collectivity.

Collective consumer behavior through formal institutions was only one component of this modern philosophy. Cooperative selling, formal education for farm children, a continued dispersal of progressive farming techniques, and expanded social opportunities were equally important. But unlike these other pursuits, consumer cooperation showed the greatest potential in restoring many of the social controls that had worn away under the torrent of modern market forces. Purchasing cooperatives were not intended to swim against the historical currents that led farmers to promote agricultural fairs and to marvel at Model Farms, that led agents to risk their money in the pursuit of Midwestern purchases, and that enfeebled the two-party political system. Rather, rural consumers wanted to benefit by their unique experiences.

The National Grange of the Patrons of Husbandry was the most committed disciple to this exacting vision. Its rise from obscurity to the most dominant rural organization of the era (detailed below) remains an impressive feature of the order. When founded in 1868, the Grange consisted of merely 2 small, indifferent, and withering assemblies. By January 1873, the national institution claimed 1,362 subordinate chapters concentrated in Illinois, Indiana, Wisconsin, Iowa, and Minnesota. Twelve months later, subordinates numbered more than 10,000. Iowa alone, the state with the largest following at the peak of the movement, claimed a mere 40 affiliates in 1871 but 1,823 by 1873. From 1874 until 1875, the Grange was at its peak in membership and influence with more than 858,000 members belonging to more than 21,000 regional chapters.[9]

Due in large part to the complex causes of their overnight success, as well as their sudden collapse, many contemporaries of the Patrons of Husbandry had a hard time categorizing just what was happening in the countryside. Significantly, many writers used the motif of a prairie fire to explain the order to a curious audience. The image is a powerful one and suggests a natural force that was uncontrolled, irrational, destructive, and possibly vindictive. After the fire was put out, the analysis shifted to identifying those who participated. A typical rendition, written in 1878 while potentially many embers still drifted in the air, believed that the Grange was made up of three types of principle miscreant. The first were failed commercial farmers, losers who "hailed the Grange movement as a means for bolstering their credit through fraternal feelings, and look forward to the day when their brethren would sign their notes simply because they were members of the same Order." A second group was dismissed as "suppressed candidates in the political parties with which they had acted, and believed they could lead the guileless farmer whithersoever they would chose." Finally, there were the simple fools, "whose ideas were numerous enough, but lacking in practicability, yet really well-intentioned at heart, recognized the educational feature of the grange as a means for ventilating their crude and visionary schemes, and thereby, in their own opinion, setting the world to revolving according to a better system."[10]

Many historical interpretations of the Grange and its purchasing activities did little better in their analyses. Early historians of the movement held that the purchasing agency was an irrational attempt to bridge the emotional gap between an idyllic, preindustrial past and a utopian, democratically controlled future. Even contemporary scholars, and certainly most textbooks, tend to view the Grange as little more than a "hopeful monster." The term, coined by the twentieth-century German geneticist Richard Goldschmidt, describes a hypothetical organism that actively attempts to evolve by traversing the genetic span from one species to the next (hence, hopeful). Goldschmidt reasoned that only one in a million of these mutations (monstrous, to its peers) might actually lead to a new breed. This unusual term, discredited as a scientific concept, describes the common interpretation of the Grange's role in agrarian unrest: a hopeful but ungainly creation that failed to acquire the stature of the later Populists. But such an explanation does a disservice to the thousands of Grangers who indeed held and expressed a unique and insurgent economic doctrine.[11]

While indeed hopeful, the structure of the purchasing cooperative was neither radical nor without precedent in the buying practices of Midwestern farmers. In its most simple form, a rural purchasing agency banded consumers together in order to create a more cost-efficient link between manufacturers and the patrons of their goods or services. The agency obtained discounted prices for its efforts in collecting orders and distributing shipments. Manufacturers benefitted through large orders and by the reduction in commissions paid to their sales force. Some providers also slashed prices if the agency paid with cash, thereby avoiding the liability and expense associated with extending credit. Significantly, any profits accrued by the agency were dispensed to the consumer in the form of savings at the time of the transaction. Rarely were profits funneled back into the agency system.

This loose structure, hardly unique to the Midwestern farm community, allowed early members to interpret the role of the agency in their own fashion. Those who hoped to "eliminate the middleman" or nurture an "agrarian union" were able to use the purchasing agency equally with those who merely wanted to improve their personal bottom line through discounted purchases. Cooperative stores were often little more than locations for farmers to order and pick up their goods, or to purchase supplies that had been bulked by special request, free from the glare of the local merchant. The term *cooperation* was frequently given to these nebulous associations by rural consumers in the middle of the nineteenth century.

Nor was the generic concept of communal consumption a new one. Entire antebellum populations—Hopedale and Brook Farm in Massachusetts, or New Harmony in Indiana—were based on communitarian principles popularized by Robert Owen and Charles Fourier. Similarly, independent "Union Stores" were stationed even in the most remote districts of the rural Midwest. However, these stores and communes differed from Grange purchasing agencies in that they centered more on neighborhood solidarity and less on cost savings for their economic viability. Cooperation was based on like-mindedness, not on the desire for economic efficiency. Cooperatives of this kind hinged on three aspects of community fellowship: religion, ethnicity, and the desire to form a perfected society—none of which took into consideration the market forces that were swirling around them.[12] Agencies based on these shared social creeds were rarely flexible enough to withstand the changing economic conditions of the region. Studies have suggested that ideological cooperatives thrived only when populations remained static and market pressures were minimal. The fact that many of these groups channeled the profits back into the organization further destabilized their efforts and doomed most of these more ideological cooperatives in the Midwest.[13]

At the other extreme, farmers' clubs erred on the side of materialism. Independent farmers' clubs, the earliest agrarian leagues built at the grass-roots level, heartily supported the concept of scientific farming. Often forming around conventional community functions, such as fairs or for the organization of Independence Day celebrations, the clubs grew to be a formidable force by 1860. On the eve of the Civil War, Illinois alone claimed more than seventy-five clubs totaling more than two thousand members; bordering states showed similar numbers. Officials at the Illinois State Agricultural Society opined in 1862 that local "Farmers' Clubs are to county, state and national agricultural associations what families are to the more extended social organizations: the church, the state and the nation."[14]

These early associations and purchasing agencies provided rural Midwesterners the context through which they might express a shared consumer goal. Commercial farmers had traditionally relied on local clubs, and then granges, to bargain collectively with agents. First practiced at the county fair, planters hoped to convert their greatest assets as consumers—the common need for standard goods that allowed salesmen to bulk their orders—into greater control over the access to those goods. In short, scientific farmers believed that they knew what they wanted; it was simply for the middleman to supply them with a timely and efficient gateway. In an effort to instill a greater deference in suppliers and manufacturers to individual consumer choice, farmers looked to the purchasing cooperatives to tighten their control over the acquisition of merchandise. The desire was strengthened through monetary and price deflation and the growing awareness by rural Midwesterners that they shared many consumer experiences. One farmer wrote that the "fact that [we] should have a say in the matter, or have any rights that manufacturers were bound to respect, [was] entirely ignored" in the postwar years.[15]

A more determined course was taken by the purchasing agencies to respond to these perceived offenses. Postwar agencies collected orders and payments and then arranged for the transport of all manner of goods. They boycotted disagreeable firms and formed their own depots in order to recapture their lost consumer prerogatives. One activist humorously noted that "it was tauntingly said [that farmers] raised too much produce and so reduced the price. Now, suppose we turn in and use the old corn planters for a few years, won't there be a surplus of corn planters?" Personal consumption was seen as an answer to achieving greater market controls. One farmer wrote that "there can be no doubt of the disposition of the farmers to go without new machinery to a great extent unless the manufacturers will . . . deal with them on the same terms as they now do with their regular agents."[16]

Seeing a lucrative opportunity, and greatly aided by the region's mature rail network, many suppliers reacted favorably to these efforts. Potential increased sales led manufacturers to consider listening to consumer representatives rather than the middlemen. Moreover, agents were increasingly being publicly criticized by farmers and suppliers alike for the dampening effect that their overhead had on the consumer economy. The same individuals who first made manufacturers sensitive to rural consumer demand were now castigated for evaluating market opportunities based solely on their ability to profit by the commission of goods. The bond between manufacturers and agents was relatively weak, except in a few notable cases such as the McCormick Reaper Company. Grange purchasing agent G. L. Waterman, of the Highland Grange, in Seneca, Illinois, saw that farmers "certainly have more right to say who shall be their agents than anybody else. And manufacturers who will not deal with such agents, but insist on sticking an agent of their own between themselves and the farmer, let them wear out their own tools." Rather than buck the trend, Waterman believed, suppliers would gladly cede control over the access to goods to the farm representative as it "would insure a better article for farmers and better profits to the manufacturers."[17]

Some nonaffiliated general contractors were also responsive to the call by farmers. Firms such as the Chicago-based Z. M. Hall & Company took up the opportunity presented by the purchasing agencies to offer price lists for nearly every conceivable consumer good. As early as March 1873, Hall was viewed by the *Prairie Farmer* and many local organizations as "a reliable wholesale house . . . who will sell to Farmers' Clubs and Granges . . . [through a] reliable purchasing agency perfectly familiar with all the different lines of trade." In almost every town, regardless of the size of its retail hinterland, commission houses contacted granges and clubs with letters of introduction, circulars, and free samples. The *Prairie Farmer* warily noted that "scarcely a day has passed that this office is not the recipient of requests for a list of the Granges and Clubs." These list seekers, said the paper, were agents who wanted to contact the cooperatives on how they "may save money, or make money, without limit" on a variety of new products. Thereafter, the paper routinely provided information, often based on mere hearsay, about firms reported to have contacted farmers, including such potentially fly-by-night operators as "The Union Furnishing Company, Geo. B. Hodge & Co., proprietors, and the firm of Montgomery, Ward & Co." Clearly, the times suggested that farmers were capable of changing their relationship to the distribution network, and that many suppliers were willing to assist them in this reform.[18]

A second notable feature of the developing consumer ethos emanated from the savings associated with collective buying. The money conserved by organized rural shoppers was considerable. Discounts ranging from 30 to 50 percent on domestic and farm implements or household supplies were not unusual. One leader of the Illinois State Farmers Association (ISFA), a body formed in 1872 to represent the state's most active clubs, claimed that individual members over the years had each economized "over $2,000 by buying directly from the manufacturers . . . about $10 on ploughs, $30 on reapers, $13 on corn-planters, $20 on sowing machines," and so on. The Iowa State Grange concluded that by the end of 1873, in their state alone, farm operators saved an average of 27 percent, or $60,750, on purchases of $225,000 in farm implements, and that families saved an additional 18 percent, or $80,210, on purchases of $445,612. The *Prairie Farmer* cited these price reductions as the driving force behind the strength of the more materialistic ISFA. The slogan of the institution spoke to this single-minded economic purpose: "We mean business."[19]

Yet individual profits were only part of the formula that made rural consumerism so appealing. Farmers found that buying and saving by means of bulk orders promoted not only personal prosperity but also communal solidarity. According to Major H. P. Burroughs, a prominent member of the Elk Prairie Farmers' Club in Illinois, planters "resolved to combine and cooperate not for the purpose, as it claimed by some, to infringe upon the rights of others, but to protect themselves and their own rights." Similarly, at the first state meeting of the ISFA, club members noted how they were favorable to the growth of purchasing agencies "to effect for our class what organization has done for others." As another noted, demand-based consumer tactics practiced in the countryside "lessened the cost of living" to farmers "and to some extent [everyone] in the county."[20]

The common, everyday experiences of rural Midwestern consumers acted as a bridge by which these associations linked the fiscal benefits of cooperation to the citizenry. The collective nature of their cultivating, the stability of the families that remained in the region, and the closeness of the community, as seen through the important visiting patterns of rural women, all contributed to the feelings of fellowship. As a result, consumer activism was driven not by the various rural organizations themselves but rather by the shared and "deep-felt feeling[s] that the times demand a change." Farmers came to agree that "this change must be brought about by concerted action." Iowa State Grange Master A. B. Smedley suggested to the order that when commercial farmers first moved to Iowa, "strangers to each other, urged on by the absolute necessity of making from the soil, homes and a standing in the community, we put all of our lives into the material work before us, forgetting that any life purely material in its character must be practically a failure."[21]

Unlike most clubs, and certainly the ISFA, the national, state, and local granges placed a strong emphasis on combining pecuniary benefits with social ones. As a result, for many the grange provided a communal context that justified or absolved their individual, material pursuits. Evidence of their broad appeal often marched right past them. In Eldora, Iowa, "not less than five thousand people" turned out to parade in a Grange-sponsored picnic in June 1873. The Fourth of July procession by neighboring Henry County Grangers that same year measured five miles long. The slight but noticeable differences between the ISFA slogan and these more local affiliations draws out these subtle connections between social and economic prosperity: "By industry we live, by honesty we thrive"; "Farmers glory in their occupation";"Equal and exact justice to all men, special privileges to none"; "The farmer pays for all." While Grangers, too, "meant business," their economic efforts were projected more to the rural community than directly upon individual operators.[22]

Determining which factor, solidarity or individual gain, dominated the equation that made the Grange purchasing efforts a success is pointless. Both considerations were vital and each supported the other. Yet it is ironic how their efforts to gain collective consumer control relied so heavily on the individual's affirmation of classical, free-market economics.

Midwestern communal consumer strategies required individuals to make the fiscal compromises necessary successfully to manipulate the supply and demand curve to their common advantage. One rural contributor to the *Western Farmer* noted that there was "no good reason why the simple fact that a farmer belongs to any organization, agricultural, political or religious, should secure him anything at a less price than that for which any one else can obtain the same article." The contributor concluded that if "reduced prices be secured it must be . . . because something is given in return." What was very often "given" was a greater reliance upon one's neighbor. An editor at the *Prairie Farmer* echoed this sentiment when he wrote that through collective action individual "farmers and manufacturers will be brought directly together and occupy that relation that they should, a relation that would insure a better article for farmers and better profits to the manufacturers." Rural solidarity could not mask the fact that the farmer's role as capitalist was at the core of his purchasing strategies, nor could these entrepreneurs succeed without the aid of the community at large.[23]

As a result, despite the obvious success by the various clubs in fostering a demand-based consumer market and addressing notions of class solidarity, farmers began to abandon them in favor of the Patrons of Husbandry, slowly up until 1873 but with increasing speed thereafter. The reasons why one movement grew at the expense of the other cuts to the heart of the blossoming consumer ethos in the region. While the implacable drive for greater individual market advantages was a reflection of farmers' commitment to scientific farming, it represented only one portion of the influences that precipitated their consumer anxieties. Accordingly, independent clubs proved unable to move beyond local concerns and address, for example, the need for progressive reforms to the larger distribution network. Coordinated action through the national grange promised farmers a more comprehensive consumer strategy that blended with traditional republican principles. These final two planks of agrarian consumerism anchored the Grange-sponsored purchasing cooperative and were integral to the order's success in the Midwest.

A progressive reform of the distribution network was a third longstanding ambition of the extended farm population. Unlike their efforts at making suppliers responsive to local consumer demand, which often required the circumvention of territorial agents, farmers also focused on rehabilitating the improprieties contained within the entire distribution network. Midwestern husbandmen argued that by either removing or modernizing the most offensive and immoral characteristics of trade, "legitimate" consumers, manufacturers, and distributors would reap even greater profits. Through consumer cooperation, they hoped to exert intense pressure on suppliers that were once "far beyond [the farmers'] reach."[24]

The practice by wholesalers and manufacturers' agents of restricting the general availability of goods was of particular concern. For example, sales of specific capital goods—harvesters, reapers, sewing machines— were usually restricted to specific territorial agents. Farmers regularly lamented that the extension of these privileged, private networks was underwritten by the exorbitant prices paid by rural consumers. In the words of one husbandman, "the worst thing that has come of the [exclusive territorial] system is that many manufacturers depend upon their 'oily' agent to sell their goods instead of the goods selling themselves." Listing layer after layer of needless middlemen, all of whom assessed a 5 to 10 percent surcharge for their efforts, the farmer concluded that the huge markups were used only "to pay a host of useless and expensive servants, whom men of any other calling would have had the economy and good sense to have discharged long ago." As one Illinois activist noted, by 1874 farmers were tired of incurring "the expenses both ways." A more centralized, and therefore more powerful, rural purchasing method was the only sure way that progressive reforms could be established.[25]

Middlemen and agents fiercely defended their traditional rural sales territories. Those allied with specific manufacturers often blacklisted farmers who placed orders through rural organizations. In addition, as the Iowa State Grange purchasing agent, J. D. Whitman, noticed, many recalcitrant manufacturers "put their agents under bonds to sell no implements outside of the limited territory given them, the violation of which involved a penalty of $25 on each machine thus sold." The result of these artificial limits on supply and demand—for example, a farmer had no recourse if the territorial agent for his area was unfit or unwilling to fill orders—was that "no competition could arise" and the farmer soon found himself back in the days of the frontier store.[26]

Some industrial producers looked more favorably on the idea of cutting out the middleman's profits. Whitman reported in 1873 that "most manufacturers, and particularly those of Illinois, from whence we had drawn most of our implements for years, were in sympathy with the movement." One year later, Whitman boasted prematurely that the "practical result" of these modernizing reforms was "secured"; no further difficulty "need be anticipated from manufacturer's rings, or middle men's interdictions or intermeddlings. . . . I have yet to receive the 'cold shoulder' from any manufacturer."[27]

Although Whitman may not have received the cold shoulder, these efforts had not fundamentally restructured the distribution network. Many of the initial savings earned by farmers on their bulked purchases came as the result of expediency. For example, while committed Grangers served faithfully as purchasing agents, often at high personal expense and risk, they were prohibited from profiting by the efficiencies that they delivered to the country. When the Iowa Grange executive committee recommended, in 1874, to bar Grange agents from any financial rewards beyond their meager stipends, it concluded that "to pay agents commissions tends to destroy the confidence so essential to our success and prosperity." That same year, agent Whitman foreshadowed some of the problems in store for the reforms when he bragged: "The very idea of establishing a State Business Agency, and attempting to direct the great bulk of purchases of one hundred thousand Patrons through a given channel, without one dollar of actual cash capital, appears to men of business, to say the least, preposterous." State granges were attempting to provide reform on the cheap. The long-term expense to institutional stability would soon become evident.[28]

Finally, the farmers' commitment to republicanism permeated their consumer vision as well. Combining the three previous components of agrarian consumerism, this ethic sought an underlying fairness and honesty, a concept fresh in the minds of post–Civil War Americans recently challenged to provide their nation with a "new birth of freedom." In addition, as Paul Johnson demonstrated for Rochester, New York, religious virtue can be utilized by a relatively homogeneous society in an effort to stave off rapid social and economic change. Here, the Grange excelled at providing an intricate mixture of virtue and monetary value, community and individual improvement. Notions of honor, character, and moral decency were integral to the Grange purchasing cooperative.[29]

Isaac Beeson, a charter member of the Nettle Creek Grange of Dalton, Indiana, insisted that traditional consumer cooperation outside of the order, such as those practiced by the clubs, resulted in economic advantages to some but unjustly harmed others. In a speech, he argued that only if all of Dalton township traded at one store regulated by local farmers, would business be fairer and "goods afforded at a lower percent than under the present system." In a penetrating analysis, Beeson reflected his maturity as a rural consumer when he saw that "merchants as a class do not make too much for the amount of work that they do, the number who become rich & remain through life are very few, their trade is all uncertainty—rich today and poor tomorrow." The caprices of the profession were "evidence that their profits are not honestly earned. But simply a game of fleece & get fleeced. The goods are marked high & the price at which a sale is made depends altogether on the shrewdness & brass of the purchaser." By contrast, Beeson believed that at a Grange-sponsored cooperative store it was "evident that the same goods can be sold to one person just as cheap as another, and no cheaper. . . . [The Grange believes in] stores where we all are interested in its success . . . [as opposed to] a store run on the usual plan [where] everyone's interest is against the interest of the store." Such an analysis succinctly illustrates the combination of virtue and commerce embraced by Midwesterner farmers.[30]

The moral decay associated with market abuse also supported rural consumer protection. In a second speech, Beeson added that "the old system of competition or everybody skin everybody else" should be ameliorated by Grange purchasing practices. The wasteful practice by suppliers who "regard[ed] *any profit* they can obtain as legitimate" was found to be "too expensive for [farmers] to have to foot the bill." The republican virtue of this practice, bypassed by the clubs, was heralded by many as the central justification for the pursuit of individual savings via the Grange purchasing agency. A contributor to the *Prairie Farmer* reckoned that "the feeling 'How can I help my neighbor?' predominates as a necessary result. The wants of a neighbor are known, and a brotherly or sisterly pride taken in satisfying that want. Everyone is willing to do his or her part, and a little more if necessary, [so that] many dollars are saved in ways too numerous to mention."[31]

Farmers and farm journals, like other advocates, soon multiplied the moral benefits of cooperative consumption well beyond any demonstrable effect. James Creighton of the ISFA rhapsodized that "cooperation in buying" could save "hundreds of thousands, if not millions, of dollars . . . to the farmers of Illinois in a single year." These reserves could "enable many a poor man to lift the mortgage from his farm, and save a home for his little ones. By it, many a father will be enabled to send his bright-eyed son or daughter to the college or academy, and the neat new cottage will take the place of the cabin or hovel." According to Iowa state master Smedley, college-bound Patrons would not need to study law since cooperation would nearly eliminate personal lawsuits. Smedley said that because of "the good coming to us in this connection," it was estimated that "among members of the order in our state, nine out of every ten cases of [legal] dispute, which, under the old system, would be litigated in the courts, are settled in subordinate Grange by friendly and fraternal arbitration."[32]

Even if their predictions were correct, the dominant role of consumption in these associations was problematic. As the differing elements of rural consumerism attest, the balance between communal and individual benefits was often paradoxical and full of tension. For example, fair and equitable treatment does not follow from the determined efforts to remain within the boundaries of industrial capitalism. In addition, demand-based controls and democratic reforms often run counter to established communal norms. As such, the preeminent position of consumerism in rural ideology led to a tremendously fluid interpretation by the many members of these farm organizations. Every purchase entailed a constant reevaluation, whether consciously or not, of the individual and communal sacrifices demanded of participants. Institutional control was even more difficult since leaders were forced to support the parochial foundations of their organization while farmers evaluated these goals upon a changing set of social and economic criteria. Nevertheless, although these tensions would, in the end, make it impossible to maintain an institutional control over consumption, the period from 1865 to 1875 witnessed a tremendous growth in institutional purchasing activities and the parallel spread of the rural consumer ethos.[33]

The growth of the Grange offers some of the strongest evidence that Midwestern farmers were drawn to this communitarian vision of consumption. Although the expansion of the order—like a "prairie fire"—is often related, the numbers bear repeating. A newborn institution in 1868, the Patrons claimed allegiance from more than 21,000 local associations by 1875. In the Midwest this growth was even more pronounced and, a fact often overlooked, was accomplished in the presence of an existing and thriving rural institution in the form of the farmers' clubs. As noted above, the clubs were closely aligned with many of the most important elements of commercial farming: regular meetings to discuss scientific farming; sponsorship of the local fairs; purchasing cooperatives. If there was a central characteristic to describe their efforts, it would surely be that of materialism. Their concern for the provable, the reformable, and the profitable overshadowed all others. Why and how, then, did the Grange supplant the clubs as the chosen institution to promote the rural consumer vision?

As the Patrons of Husbandry spread and became better known as a preferable alternative to clubs, the criticism leveled against the older institution became more pointed. Most often mentioned was the fact that the autonomous clubs found it difficult to conceive and coordinate an effective regional purchasing strategy. Acting independently, each club negotiated discounts based only on the aggregation of a small number of orders. Exasperated manufacturers were inundated by a chaotic hodgepodge of requests, each demanding recognition based on rural solidarity. One Midwestern businessman, generally sympathetic to the farmers' efforts, wrote that he was "flooded with letters, [but] have got no business from them. They don't amount to anything. We make machines to sell. We have had too much of their correspondence. They can't do anything in this way of writing for machinery. They must have a system of doing business, and then we will trade with them when we know who we are dealing with." The Grange promised organizational representation for "a people," or at least a vocation, rather than the seemingly petty interests of the few adjoining townships that generally made up a club.[34]

A second significant and identified problem of the clubs was their crass partisanship. Initially, between 1850 and 1870, many members found that the political fusion between clubs and organized parties was a constructive activity. Club promoters held that the "farm problem" could be solved by removing offending legislators who "clos[ed] our ports to commerce, [and gave] to manufacturers and speculators the control of the markets." Political mobilization would remove "Radicals" bent on "support[ing] monopolies and a horde of speculators and operators, who live upon the industry of the country." Illinois club leaders, probably the best organized of the Midwest, challenged farmers to "put your votes where they will do the most good."[35] As a result, Midwestern planters formed the backbone of many third-party movements and often held the balance between the traditional coalitions in local and state elections. In Illinois, this led to the selection of Judge David Davis as a compromise candidate for the U.S. Senate. In Wisconsin, reform candidate William R. Taylor—relying on clubs, the Milwaukee business community, and an inept campaign by the competition—won the race for governor.[36]

Yet even with the formation of the nationally active Anti-Monopoly Party in 1873 and the Greenback Party in 1874, farmers rarely found that high-profile political contests resulted in any significant relief. Railroad and granary-rate regulation in the Midwest (which later would be seen as the lone substantive legacy of the Grange) bred much controversy but did little to ease the real source of unrest: falling commodity prices. These campaigns often sacrificed the authentic rural agenda in order to broaden their urban and national appeal. S. M. Smith, the firebrand secretary of the ISFA, talked repeatedly of "blood and anarchy," naming it as the ultimate goal of farm mobilization. Mass meetings staged by such leaders rarely addressed the communal needs of most farmers; when they did, it would be through only perfunctory comments. One convention commissioned by Smith and J. A. Noonan, the editor of the *Industrial Age*, broke down into a Hamiltonian nightmare of mob ascendancy over the democratic process. A witness of the melee, William Orlidge, writing to the state purchasing agent of Wisconsin, drolly noted that the troublemakers Smith and Noonan "must have had a nice time" since attendees "took possession of the chair by force, lifting [one speaker] out bodily"; the door keeper "was taken up bodily and put down quietly in one corner of the room and told to stay there." Such displays, where "the most kindly expressions . . . used by each to the other [were] Damn Sirs, Infernal Thieves, and Sons of Bitches," may have redounded to the basic character of nineteenth-century popular politics but not the socioeconomic requirements of most Midwestern farmers. Orlidge concluded: "I should think that any man possessing only common decency must have felt disgusted with the whole thing."[37]

The year that proved decisive in regional farmers, breaking with the clubs in favor of the order was 1873. Planters openly chastised clubs. One spoke of "danger [caused by their] diversion from the true objects of the organization. If allowed to do so, politicians will rend [farm cooperation] to fragments before next fall's election." Later in the year, the *Chicago Evening Journal* reported that the "majority of our farmers are displeased with the sell-out Democratic resolution adopted at the [ISFA] convention of Farmers at Decatur last week, and openly declare that if the clubs are to be used solely for the purpose of helping broken-down demagogues into office, they will have nothing more to do with them." Others saw the clubs as anachronisms, leading a "forced existence" and dependent upon "being resurrected once a fortnight" by political opportunists.[38]

A conspicuous problem of the clubs, identified by many converts to the order, was that political storms flared, unintendedly, from their partisanship. Demagogues like the ISFA's S. M. Smith were widely condemned for all rural efforts at reform, including the clubs' relatively impartial purchasing agency. In Iowa, when upstarts rejected the established, and incumbent, political parties to form the rival Anti-Monopoly Party in 1873, they summarily named the state Grange master, Dudley

Adams, as their leading candidate. A stunned Adams immediately rejected the offer, but not before local incumbents and office seekers alike singled out the commercial farmer as a potential political foe. A grand master of the national grange, D. Wyatt Aiken, recollected that clubs in the Old Northwest at this time were "composed of men who could not or would not join the Grange, whose province seemed to be to wage war against transportation companies." Aiken regretted that "anathemas thick and heavy were hurled upon the Grange for making this attack, whereas every Patron of Husbandry knew that the Grange, as such, was not a participant in the fight from beginning to end."[39]

While many farmers were bothered that the clubs further politicized the agricultural press, an institution that was hardly free of bias, planters would not tolerate the rising partisanship at the sacrosanct agricultural fair. Farmers opined in their local papers that "these political blood-suckers are not satisfied with running all the caucuses [and] conventions . . . but now propose to take possession of the agricultural societies. Let the honest farmer step to the front and head off these greedy candidates for political preferment." Such overt partisanship led many farmers to question the very essence of these independent associations. As one planter grumbled, in the clubs "there are no bonds of union except that of buying cheap." Clearly, for this man and many others, by 1873, rural allegiances were to be broader than just to their pocketbooks.[40]

It was at the height of these tensions between the clubs and the granges that the rhetorical flourishes of many leaders seemed to be the most strident. If we read too much into the charges and countercharges leveled in the press, we run the risk of overlooking the more level-headed and evenhanded rural population. When the *Prairie Farmer* piously reassured the nation that the Midwestern "Farmer [was] not a Communist," one can almost see the slow shake of the head and a quick roll of the eyes by the average commercial planter. Skepticism regarding the pretentiousness of these and other pronouncements surely sapped the zeal of many Midwesterners. While Red-baiting was a new and serious problem in the United States, particularly following the Paris Commune, it is doubtful that such posturing did much to forward the debate over the economic plight of regional producers. Part of the appeal of the Grange to many was their exclusion of partisanship from within the gates of the order.[41]

In contrast to the clubs, then, the Patrons of Husbandry was able to more faithfully and coolly represent the full range of the farmers' consumer experiences and the philosophy that they generated than the existing associations. The convictions of control, community, reform, and virtue united the farm community's concern over economic, political, and social unrest. Rather than being bifurcated into elements of moral or market economics, agronomists experienced both: the individual market-based practices of consumption and the communal hopes and fears that their unique need for purchased goods would overrun their traditional social customs. Relying on shared experiences and expectations, Midwesterners implemented this new ethos through the order's purchasing agency and placed consumerism at the center of their thoughts and actions. Still, it is critically important to note that the Patrons' approach to consumption was learned in the Midwest and not an organic goal of its national founders. The order appended the regional purchasing cooperative to its movement as a means of gaining the support of Midwestern farmers, a fact that would prove critical to the national association's long-range commitment to rural consumption.

Attesting to the contingency of this shift, it can be claimed that the initial success of the National Grange of the Patrons of Husbandry rested on the purchase of a lone Minnesota jackass. Grange founder Oliver Kelley's plan for a national, fraternal organization dedicated to the "knights of the plow" had its roots in his experiences as a frontier farmer and Washington bureaucrat. Born in Boston, Kelley migrated west to Itasca, Minnesota, in 1849. There, as farmer, speculator, and newspaper editor, Kelley experienced first hand the vicissitudes of commercial agriculture. He demonstrated his original beliefs in fraternalism and commercial farming by founding a local chapter of the Freemasons, as well as a farmers' club. In 1864, discouraged by his lack of prosperity at home, Kelley accepted an appointment to Washington as a clerk in the new Agricultural Department. Two years later, after touring the war-ravaged South to collect economic data for Andrew Johnson's administration, upon his return to the nation's capital Kelley formed the Patrons of Husbandry.[42]

Oddly, rather than tap into the frustrations that had built up over two generations of commercial farming in the Midwest, Kelley's new institution was based on more esoteric and privileged Masonic principles. As a result, the Grange was slow to catch on with many whose primary interest was in economic protection. If the clubs erred by being overly materialistic, then the early Grange was too fraternal. Kelley wanted to maintain strict secrecy in the order, with highly ritualized and formal meetings. Members could attain to seven Grange degrees at three hierarchical nodes in the organization: the subordinate (the first through fourth degrees), the state (the fifth and sixth), and the national (the seventh). In spite of his roots, Kelley seemed to be genuinely shocked at the "pecuniary" interests of Midwestern farmers. The only real deference to established rural institutions of the day was the creation of a position of lecturer, an official who was responsible for passing along information on agricultural improvements. Local chapters were strongly regulated by the rules of the central leadership, but in another respect the order was relatively liberal-minded for its day: subordinates could be chartered through the participation of nine men and four women. This fifteen-person membership was, however, a required minimum, and state granges were to be formed only after the successful establishment of fifteen subordinates. The states were to be tightly controlled by the national grange, which instituted protocols, prioritized agendas, and collected and distributed money. Many farmers were hesitant to pay dues to both club and grange, and existing clubs were not allowed simply to claim grange status: they had to charter, apply, and pay dues like all other new granges. Exceptions or allowances for existing institutions were rarely granted.

The high hopes of Kelley and his colleagues notwithstanding, the institution was not heard as a clarion call by the farm community until it joined with the rural consumer ethos. "Paper" granges, formed in the cities of Washington and Chicago, lacked connection to rural America and simply were not sustainable. As the *Chicago Tribune* later wrote, the local chapter, housed in the offices of the *Prairie Farmer,* "was puny from the first, and city air and habits soon stifled it to death." Not until summer 1868, after Kelley had resigned from his federal position and returned to Minnesota, were the national Grange principles aligned to meet the needs of regional farmers.[43]

Kelley was met in Minnesota by farmers' clubs determined to pursue their provincial agenda. In a letter to his Washington associates, Kelley noted that farmers asked "what pecuniary benefit are we to gain by supporting the organization?" While "protection" and "pecuniary benefits" soon became watchwords for the order, Grange organizers were hesitant to append this strict materialism to their pure social union. Still, farmers were intent on establishing a centralized purchasing agency with or without Grange leadership. Kelley directed the Minnesota leaders on 10 March 1869 that "it will be premature to make any appointments for Minnesota until you are further advised [by the national grange]. It is looked upon as a movement of vital interest to the Order, and involves its success or ruin; hence we must be cautious." As soon as the local farmers learned that the national grange had tabled the plan, they moved to form an independent state agency.[44]

The correspondence between Kelley and F. M. McDowell, a national grange officer, indicates that local members clearly articulated their demand for a purchasing agency. Kelley wrote that the farmers believed that the "State Grange has a right to appoint such an agent, and the National has no right to interfere." More importantly, Minnesotans claimed that "if they can't do as they please . . . they will withdraw from the organization in a body, and run it on their own hook." With mutiny looming, which would undoubtedly have dealt a deathblow to his last-ditch efforts, Kelley supported the purchasing-agency concept within the order. On 2 April 1868, the Grange's first state purchasing agent was appointed and immediately commissioned to "go down on Robert Street and purchase a jackass." The state grange secretary, William Paist, playfully observed that the "purchasing business commenced with buying jackasses; the prospects are that many will be sold."[45] As Kelley then noted, the effort was wholly local and could therefore be disowned by the national body if it failed. At the same time, he reasoned that it would generate enormous free publicity. Kelley wrote that "If it proves a good thing, then, (if we like) we can pass some law hitching the system on the [national] Order." With their fraternity firmly yoked to the purchasing-agency system, coupled with aggressive recruiting campaigns at the local level, Grange activity exploded across the Midwest.[46]

The rapid development of the purchasing agency at the state level led to heightened expressions of rural consumerism and an oftentimes giddy focus on reform. Following the dramatic defection of club members to the Grange in 1873, state purchasing agents reported a boom in business volume. It made sense that it was the state granges, not the national body, that first unlocked the regional consumer potential. The Indiana State Executive Committee, the ranking assembly within the Grange, provided its state agent, Alpheus Tyner, with instructions to begin to coordinate all local purchasing efforts immediately. County agents were requested to combine and forward their orders to the state agent "promptly on the first of each month." Responding in kind, the state agent furnished "printed price lists to the county agents who are requested to place one copy . . . on file in each Subordinate Grange . . . so that orders can be filled up from them." Payments for goods were to accompany the invoice in cash or post office order. The state agency was pledged "not to give any special preference to any particular manufactured article." A Chicago daily reported that all Grangers would "hereafter make their purchases . . . through an agent selected by the Grange."[47]

The day-to-day operations of the regional state agents were relatively uniform. Paid either by salary or by a small commission on sales, the agents were required to be bonded (up to $25,000 in the case of Tyner) to establish a centralized depot accessible to both mail and rail traffic and to hire clerks to process the orders. The agents readied informal agreements with manufacturers. They focused on agricultural implements, but also arranged for the purchase of dry goods and other foodstuffs. Bulk supplies such as soil conditioners (e.g., "agricultural plaster" and peat), binder twine, and even coal were often acquired through the state agency. The agent was also required to travel throughout the state, chartering "Grange stores" and helping to ensure their early success.[48]

The cooperative stores established by these agents were highly representative of their patrons' wishes. Although some farmers questioned the ordering of anything other than capital goods, the stores provided a wide selection of merchandise, from basic wares to luxury goods. In one instance, Grange sales of musical instruments were "so great . . . that many machines [organs], not patronized by the order, [were] run out of the rural markets. Members indicated that they intended to use providers who responded to demand-based consumer needs. *The Patron's Hand-Book* said that in many cases "it is the practice of [granges], where they can effect it, to make contracts with the other merchants, to supply their members with goods for cash, and return to the co-operative society a percentage (usually ranging from 7½ to 15 per cent.) of what they receive from these society purchasers." One outside observer, writing from New York to Joseph Osborn, the Wisconsin state purchasing agent, questioned whether "doing away with the merchants as a class" was a good idea. After examining Osborn's system, the New Yorker observed that many other articles obtained through existing suppliers "at your own village . . . may be on the whole as cheap as to get in large quantities and divide up as freight, labor of handling, waste, have to be borne unavoidably by the consumers."[49]

But the Grange commitment to republicanism, a vital characteristic of agrarian consumerism, ensured that members would retain control of their operation and not allow traditional market forces to dominate their activities. "County Councils"—first formed in Wisconsin and then propagated regionally—conveyed local desires up through the agency's management. The *Prairie Farmer* noted that this neighborhood emphasis was the basis for a "strong and efficient system." Officials of the national order could only sit by and watch as local groups, "so much in earnest in this matter of cooperative stores," inaugurated their own agencies through the county council format "without waiting for the [national] plan to be completed."[50]

The combination of market and moral economies, of individual savings and communal ethics—in short, the fusion and expression of Midwestern farmers' distinctive construct of consumerism—made the Grange a success. An Indiana farmer, who refreshingly likened the movement to a "tidal wave," saw local chapters "springing up with great enthusiasm." The *Prairie Farmer* commenced a new column, "The Business Feature of It," that reported local consequences of the movement. Although the series was later discontinued, the editors proclaimed that "we have before us more than one hundred reports from Granges and clubs in response to our call, which form conclusive proof of the general interest that exists throughout the country in the business success of organized effort." For good reasons, then, Midwestern Grangers were optimistic about their purchasing program. Leaders deduced that every one of the more than seven hundred thousand families in the order, "allowing $1,000 worth of necessary articles for home consumption for each family," would net "a saving of $175 to each . . . or a total of $122,500,000!" Taking a deep breath, the authors dutifully reported that "owing to imperfect organization, this estimate is excessive; but that an annual saving of $25,000,000 cannot be considered a high estimate."[51]

The impassioned rhetoric of Grange organizers insinuates that average farmers, farm families, and rural communities were fundamental to the spread of these new purchasing activities. Modern scholarship has so far little to show about the relative economic rank and basic social characteristics of early Midwestern members. Steven Hahn shows that, in the South, affluent landowners "played the major role" in Grange affairs. An analysis of charter members who joined during the earliest growth phase from one Indiana county indicates that this was not the case for the Midwest: "ordinary farmers" comprised the bulk of Grange membership. This supplies tangible support for a claim that the order's egalitarian rhetoric had some basis in fact.[52]

In Indiana, the pattern of early Grange participation took on a geographic predictability. Growth in 1873 was most apparent along two broad corridors. The first stretched between the cities of Chicago and

Indianapolis (continuing across state lines into north-central Illinois and southern Wisconsin) and was greatly influenced by the transportation links between these urban markets. The eight Indiana counties within the belt contained 141 of the 344 local chapters formed from January to August of that pivotal year. The second convergence was in east-central Indiana and surrounded the emerging town of Muncie. Encompassing Grant, Madison, Blackford, Delaware, Henry, and Randolph Counties, the region was home to 99 branches, or 29 percent of the state total.

Delaware County, in the heart of this second grouping, was representative of the early settlement patterns established in the Midwest. Pioneers arriving from the East were isolated from each other for much of the 1810s and 1820s. Settlers recalled how, in Hamilton Township, "each family [considered themselves] . . . the sole tenants of the woods; for in very few cases did [their] lands . . . adjoin those of their neighbors." Determined simply to survive the frontier conditions, few farmers progressed past subsistence cultivation and therefore required few manufactured goods or processed foods. Correlated to this behavior, few merchants or jobbers braved the wilderness to provide for their limited needs. Common were tales of early stores such as that run by John Mitchell: his establishment was patronized mostly by "the lovers of strong drink."[53]

As the decades past, homesteaders in Delaware County, as elsewhere, began to see the fruits of their labor. A cash economy replaced bartered trade as the primary means of economic exchange and more than a few Hoosiers were able to amass substantial wealth. Railroad and canal networks were the principal cause of this transformation. One early settler of Washington Township noted that after the local canal was completed in 1840, "farmers began hauling their grain to . . . market, receiving cash payment for it." The development of urban trading zones such as Fort Wayne, Muncie, and Indianapolis also spurred the use of currency. Farmers observed that "money began to circulate and to be exchanged for merchandise, and the homespun and farm produce became possessed of a cash value, and no longer stood in lieu of currency."[54]

Local planters, by the 1850s, enthusiastically supported farmers' clubs and other rural associations. The Agricultural Society for Delaware County, organized in March 1852, included most of the "leading farmers" of the district. True to form, these prominent men focused their energies on promoting regional fairs, studying modern agronomy, and slandering the early settlers. The society's secretary, John C. Helms, wrote that "more attention was being bestowed on the manner of farming" by club members so "that our former loose, slovenly, and careless habits were being reformed, giving place to systemic and scientific farming." Suffering many of the same tribulations as the ISFA, by 1873 most Indiana clubs had unwillingly ceded their influence and authority to the Patrons of Husbandry.[55]

Based on data tallied by the Indiana State Grange and the federal census of 1870 (see appendix 1), an analysis of the Delaware County Grange members provides strong support to substantiate the order's claims that the new association better represented the totality of the farm community. First, and most obviously, the Delaware granges were much more representative of rural women than their club rivals. While the Agricultural Society for Delaware County claimed no female members, as was the case for most if not all of the Midwestern clubs of the era, nearly one-third of the 859 charter members of the Grange were female. While the vast majority of these women joined with either their husbands or fathers, a good number—such as Ellen Stifler and Catherine Jones, of Liberty Township, and Elvina McCormick and Elizabeth Watson of Washington Township— paid dues and joined on their own. Of the sixteen charter members to form Mount Pleasant Grange No. 265, five were married women who joined the order independently, not paired with their husbands.

The general characteristics of the membership also suggests certain tendencies for those who associated with the Grange. Of the 257 Patrons tracked through the 1870 census, 72 percent enlisted with at least one other family member. By and large, these were husbands and wives, but in some instances adult brothers and sisters worked together to help found a subordinate chapter. Full families—such as William and Elizabeth Nottingham, who signed up with the Mount Olive Grange accompanied by their son George, aged sixteen, and daughter Katie, aged thirteen—were rare as charter members. Possibly the depth of community interest in the early days of the Grange provided communities a glut of willing notaries. With so many eager to form granges, perhaps some places did not need to enlist children to meet the basic criteria. Still, children were certainly a key component of the subordinate chapters. Nearly two-thirds of charter members, or 169 of the total, were recorded as having at least one child. William and Harriet Ribble, of Smithfield Grange No. 174, had the most children—nine; the overwhelming majority had three, or fewer. These numbers suggest that the Grange used the rural family to strengthen its advantage, rather than challenge this traditional institution. Single people and people without children did participate, but by and large those with strong domestic obligations were first in line to establish these farm cooperatives.

An analysis of members' ages also attests to the chapter's social stability. The census indicates that by 1873 the typical age of participants was a well-seasoned forty-one. The youngest charter member, Charles Thorne, was a native Hoosier who had seen fifteen years; the oldest, Phillip Woodring, was born in Maryland in 1802. Moreover, these farmers had resided in Indiana (although possibly not in their current location) for an average of 20.1 years. This number places their arrival in the midst of the second great wave of regional migrants, a group seen to be highly attentive to commercial agriculture. Grange founders in Indiana were steeped in the very economic and social debates that led to organized resistance following the 1873 depression.

A further set of data from the Indiana State Grange deals with the activity of its subordinate chapters based on quarterly dues payments. Regular and consistent payment of dues indicated a willingness and ability of the chapter to continue to abide by the standard authority of the state and national granges. The Delaware County granges remained active, on average, for more than three years. This figure is above average for the state and may reflect the fact that Delaware County was in the heart of an active Grange corridor. At any rate, these institutions were formed neither capriciously nor were they quickly abandoned. Delaware County charter members seemed determined to form and operate their chapters conscientiously and for the long term. Married, with children, residing two decades in the state, and relatively advanced in age, the Indiana Patron represented a mature and balanced Midwestern society.

Granger wealth, in the form of personal property and real estate values, was also recorded in the 1870 census.[56] Table 4.1 gives the total and average for estimated (self-declared) real estate (improved and nonimproved land) and personal property values for 162 charter members reported as heads of household. The average of $5,265 in real estate holdings and $1,306 of personal property owned by Grange members represented significant personal assets. Nearly all of the members surveyed reported at least some net worth in one of the two categories. For comparative purposes, a random sample of wealth for 110 male, non-Grange, heads of household from four Delaware townships who declared themselves to be farmers is included in table 4.1. In only two instances, the average real estate value for Union Township and the average personal property for Center Township, did the average wealth of the Patrons exceed those of their nonmember neighbors. While the differences were usually minimal, this certainly supports the conclusion that, in the Middle West, the Patrons of Husbandry was not an institution solely for the wealthiest farmers.

Simple statistical testing procedures can identify significant examples of exceptional chapters. For example, eight of the fifty-seven Grange indices surveyed suggested that a chapter was outside of the standard deviation either for average real estate value, average personal property value, or the number of active quarters. Only one chapter, Richwoods, was statistically unique from its neighbors in two of these three criteria. Three granges, Massainawa Valley, Mount Nebo, and Missinerva, stopped paying affiliation dues to the order months and sometimes years before the Grange faced a general defection in its ranks. These quarterly defaults generally resulted in an informal renunciation of the local affiliate by the state and national bodies. While the chapters often met several times after having their charters revoked, they invariably dissolved soon after. Since most requisition orders required the signature of a legitimate Grange master, delinquency almost always prevented offending members from availing themselves of the purchasing agency.

The three chapters all had one common attribute: their members

Table 4.1
Wealth of All Male Heads of Household, Grange and Non-Grange, Reporting Themselves to Be Farmers (listed in aggregate) and Township Non-Grangers

Description	N =	Declared Real Estate (RE) Value, 1870	Average RE Values	Declared Personal Property (PP) Value, 1870	Average PP Value
Grange Members	162	$852,970	$5,265	$211,548	$1,306
Non-Grange, Total	110	$711,240	$6,466	$197,971	$1,800
Non-Grange, Union Township	26	$133,470	$5,133	$41,221	$1,585
Non-Grange, Center Township	37	$242,550	$6,555	$45,450	$1,228
Non-Grange, Liberty Township	26	$153,295	$5,896	$36,440	$1,402
Non-Grange, Hamilton Township	21	$181,925	$8,663	$74,860	$3,565

were the most impoverished of the Delaware County Grange community. Only the personal wealth of four individual members prevented the chapters from falling below the standard deviation for the region. For example, in the Massainawa Valley Grange, which barely lasted two quarters, one member, Ambrose D. Hance, accounted for all but $7,350 of the $31,950 in aggregate real estate value credited to charter members. Discounting the wealth of Hance and the three other members of significant means (one from Mount Nebo and two from Missinerva) left the average at a paltry $2,149 in real estate and $668 in personal property. Many members fell well below these figures. For example, Mount Nebo accommodated three farm laborers and a lone, female domestic servant who, all four totaled together, claimed less than $600 in assets. Certainly the argument for consumer savings did little to support members who probably had little discretionary income.

Those chapters in existence statistically much longer than the others were operated by farmers of only moderate wealth. Planters in four chapters—the "No Name" (named for the No Name Creek running through Monroe Township), New Corner, Sharon, and Valley Granges—were neither notable nor needy. While Thompson Sharp of New Corner and M. J. Tuttle of "No Name" listed assets well above average, the remaining planters fell within the standard deviation for average wealth. Only Richwoods Grange exhibited economic qualities that might suggest Grange elitism. This chapter—one of the earliest to form and one of longest to maintain dues payments—was not formally read out of the order until 11 November 1883. Richwoods embraced many of Delaware County's most successful farm families (e.g., those of Josiah Cromer, Samuel Davis, Lambert Moffett, and Noah Bowers; also the Van Matre family). Still, Richwoods was an exception to the general pattern. By and large, most loyal Patrons were middle-rank farmers.

From these figures it appears that the rhetoric supporting collective purchasing activities was sustained by the material reality of early members. Local community and family persistence were supported through the order. Middling wealth, certainly not the poorest or richest, characterized most members who joined the Patrons at the time of the association making its most enthusiastic commitment to cooperative purchasing. The democratic and virtuous allocation of benefits derived by their efforts was a logical goal, considering the economic affinity of these farmers. Moreover, most were veterans of the stressful transition that the region's consumer marketplace underwent after the 1850s. Unlike their Southern brethren, Midwestern Grangers did represent the common homesteader and average farm family.

Yet regardless of their embodiment of the region, the rapid rise of the order and its Janus-faced approach to the market and the community blinded many members to some of the more mundane obstacles in their way. The need for more constructive coordination of local, state, and national policy was recognized by some but never addressed in any meaningful way as a significant barrier to their continued success. John Samuel, of the Missouri Grange, wrote to the Wisconsin purchasing agent, Joseph Osborn, that only a consolidated farm organization would provide "the magic touch of systemic business organization . . . [and] give the farmers movement the right direction." Indiana's Alpheus Tyner called for a meeting of the state agents of Ohio, Illinois, Missouri, Michigan, Kentucky, Kansas, and Wisconsin to join him in Indianapolis to accomplish this goal. These meetings were expected to give the order greater leverage with manufacturers through higher volumes and more powerful boycotts. Still, local and state representatives had a hard time convincing the national grange to devote much time to the problem.[57]

At a more practical level, state agents' business procedures often led to confusion and frustrations. Complaints about mundane issues such as the inept handling of mailed inquiries were common. The volume of mail often reached 125 letters per day, overwhelming the poorly staffed agents, who were required to process the orders and respond to queries about prices in time to suit the members' needs. More vexing was the fact that the state and local agents often kept very poor records of their transactions. While frequently audited by members, the agent for the Nettle Creek Grange voiced a familiar lament when he noted that his "foregoing [accounting] statement is only approximate. The bills for most of the goods are by some means mislaid. . . . I kept no accurate account [and] I cannot tell whether goods have held out weight and measure or not. (I commenced but lost some accounts and [another member] dealt a good deal of it out so it was utterly impossible to keep it correct)." Cheating and mail fraud were typical for many suppliers of the era, and Grangers came to view the prospect of sending away for goods with more caution than they had previously done. At a meeting of local purchasing agents of Illinois, on 15 September 1875, a state agent noted that his clients now "wished to see the goods before buying and put their hands on them before paying their cash," placing even more of a burden on the overworked and underpaid officials.[58]

The lack of serviceable retailing experience also harmed the Grange effort as it increasingly came into competition with private suppliers. As implied by these examples, Grangers were having difficulties maintaining their competitive position vis-à-vis the commercial marketplace. Both the Illinois and Indiana chapters expressed their need for greater commercial controls to be implemented at the national level. Most importantly, these agencies needed a sustained and adequate level of funding to vie successfully in the free market. By contrast, many state and national representatives fought the effort to create a commissioned sales office within the order. Possibly the thought of housing an agent within its midst was too much for leaders to accept. Regardless, few agencies were allowed to operate for profit and as a result many were run on the barest of margins. Much as independent agents like Isaac Greene battled for liquidity during the antebellum years, so too did the Grange need to establish funding systems by which they could predictably meet their customers needs. For the local Grange agency as with Greene, the slightest ripple in the funding stream between the consumer and the goods could spell disaster.[59]

The institutional rites of the Grange often proved to be troublesome. The most symbolic element of the order, its Masonic-like secrecy, rankled farmers who desired more open and direct access to goods. It seemed to many that the granges were seeking "private terms" at the expense of their neighbors. In defense of their institution's confidentiality, members argued "that the mere matter of making a few dollars by special terms with dealers is but a trifling matter as compared with the higher objects of the Order." The ritual secrecy of the order directly undermined the ideological crusade for the fair and open access to consumer goods. In a telling episode, Minnesota Grangers came down upon their state's purchasing agent "like a huge swarm of angry wasps" for what one Grange advocate termed "the dangerous policy of allowing all farmers equal rights in the advantages obtained by the order, after years of patient toil and the expenditures of thousands in money, a theory most fallacious on its face." A contributor to the *Prairie Farmer* with the pen name "Open Terms" exclaimed that such actions were sanctioned by Masonic-like secrecy and unwittingly made the purchasing agency less sensitive to the "extortionate prices to outsiders." At any rate, such vocal debates undermined the claims of the order that it represented a unified rural community.[60]

To make matters worse, in Illinois rumors spread that the state grange had clandestine plans to absorb the ISFA. One club member wrote to the *Prairie Farmer* condemning Grange secrecy, adding in a frustrated tone that the "whole country is alive to their interests, they can openly convene together, nominate, vote for and elect men, and take action against all that oppresses them without loosing their freedom as American citizens." Still, the farmer concluded, Grangers seemed to be secretly "pledged to do so and so" as a result of their Masonic-based structure.[61] Popular publications such as M. E. Gustin's *An Expose of the Grangers* and an article by Charles Francis Adam's in the *North American Review* saw even more insidious consequences from this confluence of institutional secrecy and mass cooperation. Gustin detected the makings of furtive class warfare. To his eye, the "Order has no respect for business men, mechanics, or the laboring poor . . . [and] has in view only its own aggrandizement and prosperity." Gustin held that farmers were "determined to drive out business men of every order, and take full possession of every branch of business." Calling for the dissolution of the Patrons of Husbandry, the author admonished its members and suggested they seek "forgiveness from God and humanity, through sincere repentance and a devoted exertion to atone for the many grievous wrongs that they have inflicted upon the people." The nationally eminent Adams called the order's various collective ventures a "wanton assault upon property." Grange leaders repudiated the insinuations about socialism in the order, and farm advocates responded strongly to Adams's public indictments. Ever ready for a fight, S. M. Smith wrote to Wisconsin's Joseph Osborn that "even a descendant of John Adams *can lie* when it will answer his purpose to do so. I wish it were possible for me to hear him and take notes. . . . I would like to *skin* him as I did [in debates with other critics of the movement]." Still, these censures dealt a blow to the foundation's claim that its efforts represented the broader interests of all Americans.[62]

Finally, Grange rhetoric often clashed with the reality of its members' expectations. In 1873, at the height of the shift throughout the Midwest from independent clubs to the Grange, Iowa State Master A. B. Smedley boldly proclaimed that "one mistake sometimes made, is in supposing that the saving of the money in buying and selling is the chief aim of the Order. Persons who take this view of the object and purposes of the Patrons, utterly fail to comprehend the scope and genius of the institution. Such persons will do better to turn their energies and thoughts in the direction of acquiring money OUTSIDE the gates of the Order." Yet, if anything, the promise of "pecuniary benefits" that was appended to the Grange fraternity was the driving force of the order's recent success. It was the tangible connection between consumer savings and the lofty rhetoric of producerism that made their efforts so representative of Midwestern commercial farmers. Separate the two components and neither are particularly unique to the region or era. Still, the rhetoric of the leadership and the complex, and often conflicting, goals of the members created volatile conditions in which the upstart rural institution was to grow.[63]

Smedley's comments are further magnified by the peculiar narrative of the Marion Grange No. 391, of Hamilton County, Iowa. As a people and a region, the farmers near Hook's Point in Hamilton County were fairly typical. Farmers first settled there in 1849, quickly turned to commercial corn and wheat production, participated in local fairs, discussed modern farming techniques through their clubs, and invested heavily in agricultural machinery. Meeting on 23 May 1872 "for the purpose of organizing a Grange," the charter members of Marion Grange were atypical only in that they joined the order well before the frenzy of 1873. Until March 1873, the minutes of their meetings discussed little more, or less, than social events such as picnics (purposely open to the general public), the lectures to be delivered on crop improvements, or the minutiae of Grange regalia and rituals.[64]

From early March 1873 until January 1874, however, Marion Grange went through what can only be called a Pauline conversion in their relationship with the order. It began innocuously enough with a growing involvement in the purchasing activities of the group. March 4 saw the first discussion on the collective buying of farm implements and sewing machines. One week later, the chapter authorized the spending of three dollars to purchase a Bible for the communal use of the chapter. By mid-April, information obtained through "circulars from various business men accompanied by price lists of various articles" and instructions "from J. D. Whitman, State Agent, relative to the purchase of farming implements" became almost the sole purpose of their regular meetings.[65] By summer, however, the mood had changed for the worse at Marion Grange. Two events seemingly sparked members' anger. The first was a mandate, initiated by the state grange executive committee and enforced by a new state agent, Spencer Day, to coordinate all local purchasing efforts through the central state office. Communal purchases were no longer to be left in the hands of the locally elected purchasing agent. The second event was the involvement in this reorganization of two men prominent in a neighboring town: W. W. Boak and John Day Hunter. According to a county history published in the 1980s, Boak was a local financier who had founded the First National Bank in Webster City in 1871. Hunter edited and owned the *Hamilton Daily*, also of Webster City, and had served in the Iowa House of Representatives as a Republican. The state grange purchasing directive brought these two men into close proximity with the Marion Grange, and as a result the local chapter renounced all of the order's purchasing activities.[66]

The source of the members' animosity remains hidden, but it is clear that their dislike and distrust of the sudden shift in purchasing practices revolved around Boak and Hunter. On 28 June 1873, the Marion secretary recorded that discussion concerned "a certain J. D. Hunter of Webster City"; it was believed that he had "been secretly admitted to affiliation in our Order as a Charter member of Union Grange [a nearby chapter] in a neighborhood distant from his place of residence." As a politician, and city dweller to boot, Hunter had no standing in the eyes of Marion Grange. He was "a newspaper editor and office holder, a professional partisan not 'interested in agriculture' except to 'thrust in his sickle to reap where others sow.'" Bank president Boak, who was also the Grange's deputy (second most senior official) for the county, was Hunter's benefactor; he had allowed Hunter access to the meetings despite the fact that the editor's "application for membership was rejected by [the neighboring] Webster City Grange within the past six months." The Marion Grange charged that "that the entrance of the said J. D. Hunter into our field of labor was through a gate designedly left unguarded by ones [i.e, Boak] whose sacred duty it was to keep it secure against enemies; and that his idle presence in the midst of our harvest preparations is not only suspicious, but is intolerably offensive and mischievous." In a unanimous resolution, the chapter called for the ouster of Hunter and the reprimand of Boak, who was said to be "inexcusably culpable. He has betrayed at a critical moment, in a manner that justifies the worst suspicions of his motives, the solemn and important trust we gave him to keep." No official action was ever taken against either man. Marion Grange was left to stew over its discomforts until the fall.[67]

When agent Day arrived in Webster City that November to try to coordinate the state purchasing activities, these latent tensions were released. Charles Whitaker and J. M. Greenwood, two charter members of Marion, attended the 22 November countywide caucus with about twenty-five other representatives from neighboring chapters. According to Whitaker and Greenwood, old hands well steeped in Grange ritual, Boak chaired the session "improperly . . . set[ting] a bad example of disorder." When Day took the floor to discuss the purchasing agency and the state grange's proposed plans to begin cooperative manufacturing, the Marion representatives saw something malevolent at work. The Marion secretary wrote:

> [Day's] work turned out to be only a thin cover for an opportunity to work up a stupendous project of fraud and rascality to which the State Grange is to be committed. . . . In order to have this scheme succeed as well as to cover up other frauds and irregularities practiced by our highest officers in the Order, it is necessary that a greater part if not all of the representatives to the coming session of the State Grange shall be men who will not thwart nor expose the schemes. It was plain to your committee that to secure these kind of representatives is the "special business" of this "Special Deputy" Day, and it was equally clear that he has already found fit tools to work with in our County. . . . Your committee are informed that other agents of the schemes at the head of the Order are industriously at work over the State to pack the body of representatives with the "right kind" of members.

For the Marion Grangers, greater coordination and structure from the top was as bad as, if not worse than, having the market retain control over their economic and political livelihood. The fact that it was all done under the guise of the order's democratic rule made the transformation only more galling to them.[68]

The rank-and-file of the chapter acted quickly to this perceived threat to their autonomy. On 3 January 1874, Whitaker worded a declaration for his fellow chapter members resolving that "Marion Grange is, and ought to be free and independent of the State and National Granges and that its connection with said Grange is and ought to be dissolved." The motion was tabled for two weeks, but meanwhile the declaration was forwarded to both the master of the state grange and to the *Webster City Index* for publication. Two weeks later, the motion was amended to include a sweeping indictment of the order. The "so-called" National Grange (*so-called* was the word used in the motion) was neither democratic nor virtuous but merely "a self constituted body of men, claiming and exercising autocratic powers of government over the members of the order, contrary to the true interests and the republican spirit of a free and independent class of people." The state grange officials, "though pretending to be a more popular body," were "characterized by the same autocratic organization and assumption of power, whose features are always obnoxious, and intolerably offensive to freedom and justice." The Marion Grange, once loyal Patrons, saw the order now as a "history of repeated wrongs, frauds, and insults, inflicted, upon it by those claiming and exercising the highest authority; and of insolvent assumptions, as well as high-handed usurpations." The Marion farmers now saw the Grange as harmful to their republican values. Although, notably, the chapter did not reject the goals of rural cooperation, they said that from their "experience and reflection" they still maintained "farmers can combine and perfect an organization for their benefit . . . which shall possesses fundamental laws more in harmony with the genius of our republican institutions and which can be maintained at a greatly diminished cost, in short, that farmers can get along better without than with the, at present, extravagant, pretentious, unprofitable, and viciously governed Order." The chapter voted in favor of the motion, seventeen to eleven. Ten months later, only one of the dissenters (the wife of a man who had voted in the affirmative) remained a member of the reconstituted local chapter.[69]

The now-independent Marion society now modeled itself on the Illinois State Farmers Association—which in retrospect is ironic, and even somewhat comical. Given Marion's obvious awkwardness with partisanship and "assumption[s] of power," the ISFA might not have been the best example for the Hamilton County farmers to follow. When they assembled for their next scheduled meeting, the secretary was quick to point out that the title of the chapter had changed to the Marion Grange No. 1 of the "Free Patrons of Husbandry." Formally read out of the old order in February, the chapter briefly returned to its more staid activities of lectures and picnics. By March, however, members began to melt away. Throughout the summer, the group tried to stem the flow by dropping dues and even planned recruiting trips to the Webster City Lyceum. In the record's final entries, for December, the Marion Grange finally abandoned its fraternalism and rechristened itself the Marion Township Farmer's Club. The association had lost its symmetry between the market and the community. It dissolved some time in early 1874. Soon, their neighbors still loyal to the Patrons of Husbandry would experience a similar sense of disappointment with the order.

At the commencement of the third annual session of the Iowa State Grange, in January 1873, the state master, Dudley Adams, boldly, and for the short term accurately, predicted the effect of the Grange's adoption of the Midwestern rural consumer ethos. Where once "middlemen laughed, manufacturers sneered, politicians stood aloof; our numbers were few; our voices were weak. Now middlemen fear, manufacturers court and politicians actually *love* us." Although, as Adams admitted, "our infancy has not been without the ills of early childhood," the Grange "learn[ed] to not hastily make radical changes, but with deliberation and candor consider well and always err on the side of safety." In the case of the Patrons of Husbandry, "safety" meant an embrace of both the market and communal values of Midwestern farmers. Furthermore, local planters were aware that their volition challenged the established economic structure. Most believed that this change was not revolutionary. In Wisconsin, preferring to call attention to the more pragmatic aims of the movement, the state agent, L. G. Kniffen, reassured suppliers in 1875 that it was "not our object to disturb existing relations in business, [only] to bring the Manufacturer and Consumer as near together as possible." One Champaign, Illinois, planter insisted that it was "not a question whether or not we dispense with this class of middle-men . . . but rather a division of profits, and to what extent they may be the arbiters of our financial operations. . . . This is the issue, and not that we propose to dispense with their services altogether."[70]

In order to do this, the Grange, by 1875, had codified four main tenets of a rural consumer ethos into its purchasing agency system. Unlike the efforts of the farmers' clubs, local granges went beyond the need for demand-based controls and incorporated the communal characteristics that many Midwesterners valued. In so doing, they created an institution loaded with the very paradoxes and promises that led to this rural consumer ideology in the first place. The rapid growth of the order indicates that they successfully expressed this unique agrarian ideology. Yet unexpected problems threatened the continued prosperity of the institution. A public position on the agency system was needed from the national grange to clarify the movement's goals, properly fund the purchasing agency, and press for greater reforms as visible evidence of the power of their unified beliefs. In the words of Illinois State Agent S. J. Frew, by 1875 the Grange was now "not in a situation to experiment with untried theories. We see discouragement pictured in the Granges all over the state, and the serious question presents itself . . . will we enter upon another year with no better plans than we now have?"[71]

Significantly, town merchants and agents who comprised the existing distribution network certainly were not blind to the movement and its attacks on their rural colleagues. Many firms, in fact, welcomed the potential for a newly consolidated agrarian consumer market. As noted above, the *Prairie Farmer* recognized that "scarcely a day" passed before their office and the consuming rural public received news of new suppliers promising easier access, cheaper prices, and more individual choices. To these suppliers, the logic of rural collective consumption held no significance. The journal's first mention of Montgomery Ward & Company in hindsight suggests the financial rewards available to those willing to address the rural marketplace.[72]

5

Town v. Country

Advertising and Consumer Patterns, 1865–1880

When Wisconsin Grangers opened their cooperative store in the town of Ripon in January 1878, founders and local farmers had just cause for optimism. In spite of recent setbacks to the national order, the region was a bastion of Patron activity and the state purchasing agency remained a uniquely successful Midwestern tradition. The town of Ripon and the editors at the principal newspaper, the *Free Press*, were generally in support of the goals of the Patrons of Husbandry. Further, the daily was an unabashed promoter of both new and existing retailing firms within the borough, devoting many columns to describe the variety of goods, terms of sale, and even the proprietor's personal history and ethics. There was every reason to believe that the arrival of the farmers' store would cultivate even more goodwill for the Grangers.

It was not to be. The frigid reception for the new venture was immediate, sustained, and intense. Editors of the *Free Press* briskly surmised: "We believe that in this move the gentlemen who are foremost think they are entirely right, and that they are encroaching upon the rights of no one, but they are simply mistaken." The paper went on to delineate the many supposed injustices of the new store. First, it asserted that there was "a degree of selfishness, or to use a farm expression, it looks a little hoggish" for the farmers to promote marketing reforms for consumer goods "and in turn say to the [local] retailer of clothes or ready-made clothing, 'we buy everything of the factory and have no use for you.'" Second, the paper noted, somewhat patronizingly, that Grangers had little or no knowledge of business and should therefore stay out of the retail trade. It was as if farmers had wandered accidentally into the consumer realm.

The *Free Press* further warned: "It seems so difficult to make the farmer understand that he today is better fixed than any class of traders, and that the farther he gets from his legitimate business, the worse it will be for him in the end." Writing as if they were privy to a cruel but constructive practical joke, the editors pontificated: "Still, it is better on all that they take a few lessons under that rigid old school master: experience." Discounting the years of seasoning that farmers had gained through the acquisition of capital goods, the paper concluded that "no man or set of men can be good farmers and good merchants at the same time. Either of the callings will afford a man plenty of business if he tends to it properly." The paper's village sensibilities took no notice of the intended benefits of communal purchasing. To them it seemed that the order's conflicting principles of cooperation and individual advantage were in many ways "a dangerous experiment of riding two horses, each going in different directions."[1]

Still, the greatest ire was reserved for what to the newspaper seemed to be the Patrons' conscious efforts to undermine the stability and growth of the town itself. According to the town's boosters, retailers already established in Ripon not only provided goods to the region but were "also busy in pushing the various enterprises in the place. Churches must be built, colleges founded, railroads encouraged, public highways thrown up, and a thousand and one things which were to benefit" the town. By contrast, the Grange store was an "injustice" to local boosters and a slap in the face of all who hoped to develop the region. The *Free Press* accused the outlying farm community of freeloading off the good nature of the town fathers, who had invested heavily and wisely with funds that "always made a big drain upon the purse of the merchant while that of the farmer were [*sic*] only lightly tapped." In a long and caustic summary, the booster newspaper claimed that,

> While this was going on, the farmer was unconsciously gaining in wealth by the enhancement of his property [due to] the railroads, factories, schools and colleges, [that] the mercantile people had labored so earnestly for, [such actions] had not only increased the value of these farms in the vicinity, but they had

likewise increased the price of all marketable commodities. To this state of things the farmers suddenly awoke, and found themselves well to-do. Few farmers today owe their financial success to their superior management, but more to the fact that they were here when the tide of wealth came in.

Clearly, the source of the anger and hurt expressed ran deeper than the added competition that a new shop (the town's twelfth general store) brought to Main Street. The Grange purchasing cooperative touched a raw nerve in this rural town.

The response by town businessmen is understandable. Villages and regional depots were highly dependent on farm-consumer dollars for their livelihood. The same economic, structural, and political forces that led farmers to turn to collective purchasing also took a toll on country towns. And village consumers, too, once suffered the deprivations of poorly stocked shops, a scarcity of cash and affordable credit, and the general inconvenience of the agent system. But while these factors may seem to have provided an opportunity for farmers and town dwellers to unite, to form an allied front in order to deflect the onrushing power of the great cities, village suppliers either would not or could not join in the consumer-based efforts of the Grange. In a very real sense, then, the rural consumer ethos that developed in the Midwest was relevant only to commercial farmers and their dispersed community, not to their town neighbors.

The reasons for many Midwestern towns not embracing the farmers' reforms were complex. Rural consumer reforms sought to benefit by new efficiencies of the marketplace that originated mainly in the largest cities. Ripon's commercial citizenry saw themselves less as provincial enemies of the farmers, more as competitors with the bigger suppliers of these great cities. To them, beneficial reform meant limiting the consumer choices that favored these central depots. Further, unlike planters who developed, via scientific farming, a mostly optimistic outlook regarding their ability to manage change, town leaders generally saw novelties such as the railroads and the vast sums of capital needed to create them as forces too extensive to command. One Springfield, Illinois, witness wrote, in 1869, that "a radical change [was] taking place in the relation of town and country in central Illinois, and I presume it to be common over the whole west and the entire country." While the farming community proved capable of "husband[ing] their time, and reduc[ing] their expenses" in the face of material challenges, rural towns were less elastic. They "have felt and will continue to feel the change. I believe there are today many houses, stores, and warehouses [bankrupted] in the principle towns of Central Illinois, than there were [formed] the whole six years from 1861 to 1867. I don't know any branch of business which has increased for these three years, but the business of banking." These fears consumed small-town merchants. Their focus remained on deflecting the blows delivered by the larger regional towns and cities, rather than in changing the agency of rural consumers.[2]

If the Midwestern economy was in a state of transition during the 1860s and 1870s, why did urban and small-town suppliers not work to embrace the potential revenues of the commercial patron? Recent urban and regional historians suggest that Chicago merchants, manufacturers, and financiers did just that, forging and controlling the consumer marketplace in the Great West. This argument hinges on three key actors. First, urban manufacturers transformed the city's exceptional access to rail transportation into a commanding market position.[3] Secondly, big-city agents captured the business of rural retailers by extending credit and creating a network of reliable business contacts. Finally, direct suppliers such as the mail-order firm of Montgomery Ward, started in 1872, completed the circuit by appealing directly to the rural consumer. Ward's catalog, according to William Cronon, "was only the purest expression" of Chicago's ability to capture the rural consumer marketplace.[4] This clear progression, from manufacturer to agents to catalogs, forms the backbone of the evidence supporting an urban-directed development of consumerism in the Midwest. According to this view, urban suppliers compelled rural consumers to change. In a sense, though no researchers have been so deterministic, once urban capitalists created the manufacturing and distribution scaffolding, it was only a matter of time before the farm community was forced to accept the modern retail economy.[5]

Timing is indeed critical to the question of consumer agency, for it approaches the very heart of whether Midwestern farmers had any control over the direction of change in their own consumer practices. It can hardly be denied that the structural and economic transformation of the transportation network, modern manufacturing and business control methods, and the concentration of venture capital following the war led to extremely dynamic market conditions. Without this infrastructure, all the purchasing cooperation in the world would not have changed the farmer's subordinate position within the distribution network. But to suggest that urban suppliers led farmers to this new relationship demands a reckoning with the vocal and highly visible demands made by commercial farmers between 1865 and 1880. Rural Midwesterners did everything short of stand on their farm machinery and shout, "We want to purchase directly from more efficient suppliers." Yet, oddly, given the notice paid to the Grange in most Midwestern periodicals, little narrative information is found in newspapers that might reflect how suppliers viewed this explosion of agrarian consumerism. Editorials and descriptions in most papers certainly allude to the existence of a "wholesale trade" market in the countryside. Yet, as in the case of Ripon, the response to farm activism was usually critical and always defensive. They focused on almost anything other than rural consumer desires.[6]

The key lies in finding a dialogue between town suppliers and farm consumers in the years after the Civil War. Were evidence to exist showing that the patron developed an active purchasing strategy, as in the case of rural Midwesterners, before the development of a modern, urban, consumer marketplace, it would lend support to the conclusion that planters had considerable volition. If, on the other hand, suppliers communicated this information to their clients, in essence showing them the new way, then a diagnosis of strong consumer agency would be significantly weakened. In many ways, the problem is a historiographical one. Sources are scarce for even the most indirect measurement of this relationship. Those that have been tapped, such as records from mail-order houses, agents, and manufacturers, are themselves predicated on the assumption that they are bringing new marketing techniques to the hinterland.

Advertisements offer a potential means by which to better gauge this relationship. As a primary source, ads have traditionally been underutilized for this time period. Yet at their core, commercials are a conversation between consumers and suppliers. Firms construct their ads in order to communicate with potential patrons. The response by consumers, in the form of sales, indicates their receptivity to such claims and promotions. Somewhere the Philadelphia department store mogul John Wannamaker remarked that half of his advertising budget was a pure waste—he just did not know which half. The importance was not the money wasted, but rather that advertisers had little control over what and how the customer perceived their ads. Similarly, as historical sources advertisements can provide crucial information about the changing relationship between the supplier and consumer. Few historians have used Gilded Age ads. Possibly the sheer volume of periodical advertisements preclude a systematic analysis. Quantitative methods, if used judiciously and cautiously, can effectively demonstrate the consumer agency demonstrated in these ads.[7]

A detailed analysis of the advertising trends in both small town and large city newspapers provides some clues to the possible intents of urban suppliers. In an examination of 4,117 advertisements from five regional periodicals, I identified the stated location of advertisers, the goods they wanted to sell, the type of firms that advertised in these publications, and the consumers that these ads targeted (see appendix 2). The newspaper ads are randomly culled from the *Chicago Tribune*, the *Milwaukee Daily News*, the *Indianapolis Journal*, the *Ripon Free Press*, and the *Oshkosh City Times* between 1863 and 1878.

The methodology and raw data from the analysis are described more fully in appendix 2; here, however, some important assumptions must be clarified. The first is the need to quantify at all. As noted above, traditional sources do not provide an adequate basis upon which to judge the central question of whether urban suppliers were steering farmers or not. Unfortunately, the ambiguous legacy of quantitative history, the statistical complexity, and the oftentimes overstated conclusions drawn from data create an inflated sense of hesitancy in using "manipulated" historical sources.[8] But given the prominence of the question, the aggressive arguments in support of urban agency, the dearth of traditional sources, and the validity of ads as an indicator of business trends, a quantitative approach seems justified.

Coding can also be problematic. Even with a strict methodology, the many decisions of how to categorize products, advertisers, and consumers are highly subjective. The coding for products and advertisers is consistent with how I have treated these terms throughout the text. More problematic are the consumer codes. These fell into four broad categories, each based on an assessment of the types of consumers most likely to be interested in the products. Identifying consumers assumes that advertisers were "targeting" their audience, but extreme caution was taken not to overstate the subtlety and precision of this market segmentation. Today, advertisers are fairly capable of making fine slices in the demographic pie of consumers. This was not so in the Gilded Age. Accordingly, these designations are broadly defined. Agents and manufacturers are fairly simple to deduce, given the types of products advertised. The category *none* is used for promotions that offered goods or services that were of interest to a nondescript audience. For example, taken from one single newspaper issue, no consumer was identified in ads for goods ranging from sheet music, paper hangings, brooms, clothing, coal, and most patent medicines. As a result, this is the most liberal of the four grades, possibly overstating the comprehensive intent of many advertisers but hopefully erring on the side of caution. Finally, *other* is used to designate unambiguous cases where ads are directed specifically toward "women" or "city gents," for example, within the text of their appeal.

Additional concerns lay outside of the methodology. For example, there were many other sources of advertising besides the local newspapers. Some, such as the agricultural press, were certainly more likely to concentrate their appeals to the rural consumer. Flyers, direct mail, and specific product catalogs were also in general circulation. While these forms of advertising were important, and increasingly subtle by the end of the century, by and large they rested on traditional methods of acquisition. Circulars were printed in great quantities and distributed in almost every conceivable manner. These announcements rarely varied in content and could no more be said to be an appeal to a certain audience than the flyers left today to clutter up bus stops, college campus bulletin boards, or public telephone booths. While most of the ads placed in the *Prairie Farmer* and other trade journals were intended for the rural community, a vast majority of these featured "name brand" agricultural machinery, were concerned with conveying performance information, and, largely due to their complexity, only rarely showed variation in ad content between issues. Although all are equally valid as advertisements, these sources do not get to the central question of rural or urban agency in the changing consumer marketplace. Newspapers, by contrast, were clearly resources shared by both communities.

Finally, it should be noted that contemporary advertisers were quite aware of the immediacy and emotional connection that could be generated through the dailies. While promotions in the first half of the nineteenth century were often "dreary, matter of fact reading . . . completely devoid of all the customer appeal of modern advertising," those following the war began to show some ingenuity. For example, one Oshkosh vendor placed an ad showing a herd of runaway steers trampling through town. The firm promised that they would go "through the grocery market with a rush—a regular bull team, one that can't be 'bucked off the bridge.' See how they (the bulls) come in, snorting, puffing and blowing! a regular jollification among the people!" Such vivid imagery caught the attention of consumers. Often tied to current events and regional moods of optimism or caution, promotions connected goods to the shifting ambience of everyday life. Newspapers, which once had relied solely on circulation revenue, began to bank on their advertising receipts.[9]

Midwestern newspapers made a point of calling to the attention of their clients the advertising advantages of their publications. The *Milwaukee Bulletin* reported that two thousand copies of the daily was circulated "at the hotels, private residences, theater, places of amusement, steamboat docks, railway depots, street car and railway trains, making it the best medium in the city for advertising." Many gave examples of successful advertising campaigns recently concluded by local businesses. Other publishers took the opposite tack with their patrons. The *Milwaukee Enterprise* gave a primer on "How to Dwarf a Town." The editors facetiously called on merchants to "Fail to advertise or in any way support your paper, so that folks abroad may not know whether any business is going on in that town or not." In either case, the message was the same: in order to reach consumer demand, businesses must advertise. As the *Oshkosh City Times* wrote, "the surest way of getting [sales was] by asking for it through the advertising and local columns of their papers."[10]

Chicago's role in the distribution network was pivotal. Before comparing all five Midwestern papers, a more detailed analysis of the *Chicago Tribune* can reveal if the advertisers in this bellwether paper were indeed seeking to address the needs of the hinterland. The *Tribune* was first published as a daily in 1847. Overshadowed by the more popular *Chicago Democrat* and *Chicago Daily Journal*, the *Tribune* remained a minor publication until 1855, when Charles Ray, J. C. Vaughn, and Joseph Medill acquired a controlling interest of the newspaper and committed it to the cause of the new Republican Party. With the success of the party and the editorial talents of Medill, the *Tribune*'s circulation grew until it emerged as one of the city's leading publications.[11]

The onset of war furthered the fortunes of the *Chicago Tribune*. In the broadest sense, armed conflict spurred the desire for all forms of printed information. News from the front, business opportunities to supply the army, and partisan politics filled all the dailies. The *Tribune* assumed the lead for the Republican cause in the West when, fearing the financial uncertainty of war, John Wentworth sold controlling interest of the *Chicago Democrat* to the *Tribune* on 24 July 1861. The extinction of their largest ideological rival was made more momentous when the Western News Company, a firm formed specifically to meet the growing demand for a high-volume newspaper distributor in the West, opened for business later that year. These windfalls led Medill to exhort ambitious

Chicagoans "to share in this general wartime prosperity, and to enlarge business, advertise in the *Tribune*. Our terms are below what they ought to be. Travel through the west anywhere and you will find the *Tribune*." By 1865 the paper was certainly regional in scope.[12]

The relevance of the *Tribune* to rural consumers should not be overlooked. While it was written and published in Chicago, a good number of its editorials, contributors, and feature articles concerned themselves with commercial agriculture. As was the custom, many articles from other publications, such as the *Prairie Farmer* and *American Agriculturalist*, were cited and reprinted, ostensibly to meet the relevant interests of their audience. Many rural scrapbooks and diaries contain references to, or clippings from, the *Chicago Tribune*. Typical was the star-crossed Marion Grange, who's "Worthy Lecturer" often "read from the *Chicago Tribune*" articles and editorials of particular importance. Probably the best evidence of the importance of the paper to the region's farmers is the number of notices posted in the paper having to do with unscrupulous agents, bankrupted manufacturers, and land sales relevant only to the rural hinterland.[13]

Chicago Tribune advertisers fell into four evenly divided categories: agents, manufacturers, retailers, and others. The most prevalent were (1) agents offering wholesaling services for a variety of goods; (2) local retailers and service professionals catering to the Chicago consumer. Combined, these two groups represented more than one-half of the advertisers identified in the study. Category 3, manufacturers, made up roughly 21 percent of the sample. Category 4—the remaining 22 percent of the *Tribune* advertisers—included auctioneers, educational institutions, publishers, and various forms of entertainment. As a comparison to other regional presses will demonstrate (again see appendix 2), the even distribution of providers reflects the city's diversity and economic opportunity.

A second important general characteristic of the ads was the type of product or service offered. The broad variety of goods advertised supports the notion that Chicago's distinctiveness and size had little bearing upon the nature of the advertisements.[14] The products promoted in the largest number were traditional consumer and business wares—exactly the goods mentioned by rural purchasing institutions as the type that they wanted to acquire. These include processed foods, clothing and other retail goods, machinery, bulk manufacturing supplies, agent and financial services, medical care, clothing, music and entertainment, patent medicines, printed materials, and transportation. The *Tribune* not only serviced a wide variety of clients, it also never overspecialized as a result of its wider circulation.

Being mindful not to read modern market segmentation into the sources, we find that a large portion of the advertisements failed to identify a "targeted" consumer. More than one-half of all ads gave no indication of their intended audience. Obviously, directing ads toward the general consumer was a supplier's best method to cast his message as broadly as possible. Still, the study shows that nearly one-third of the newspaper's advertisers did target agents and manufacturers. The appeals were fairly easy to differentiate from the other classes. For example, not many consumers had an interest in procuring 20,000 watches or 2,000 tons of coal. In one telling instance, the Chicago agency of William A. Butters & Company offered 400 dozen monkey wrenches to prospective remarketeers. This trading, removed from the direct needs of the average consumer, was typical of Chicago's singular place as the central city of the Great West. Advertisers unquestionably saw the paper as an influential medium by which to reach those seeking access to different points along the distribution network, not simply as retail customers.[15]

Given the vocal behavior of the rural consumers and the *Chicago Tribune*'s determined campaign into the hinterland via their expansion of circulation through the Western News Company, it is remarkable that almost no farm products, services, or bulked goods were advertised. It is easy to understand that many firms would not want to dedicate their primary appeal to the countryside (as Montgomery Ward did in their famous claim to be the "Original Grange Supply House"). But the fact that only 12 of the 1,875 ads specifically targeted farmers suggests that Chicago advertisers ignored the unique needs of rural patrons, at least until 1874. Even these few were mostly simple announcements of upcoming fairs and stock shows. Although ads targeting other specific audiences (such as city dwellers, men, or women) were also few in number, they still outnumbered promotions targeting farmers by more than thirteen to one. Magnifying this discrepancy, urban retailers already had a geographic advantage that erased much of the need to specifically solicit metropolitan patronage. It is often assumed that urban businesses and agents were reaching for consumers in the countryside during these years, but *Tribune* advertisements suggest quite the opposite.

Given the importance of the economic changes that took place in the Midwest and the nation between 1866 and 1874, tracking the promotional trends over time provides further clarity to the nature of Chicago print advertising. The stated location of *Tribune* advertisers shifted noticeably in favor of Chicago during these years. Nearly all advertisers included their name and address within the promotion. The city's increasing authority over its economic hinterland is best shown by comparing advertisers from Chicago with those from New York, Boston, and Philadelphia combined. Chicago advertisers consistently increased their representation during these eight years. For example, Eastern companies topped 7 percent of all ads in a single issue only once from 1870 to 1874, whereas they passed that number nine times between 1866 and 1870. To make this point in other words, Chicago-based advertisers grew from 76 percent of all ads in 1866 to more than 85 percent by 1874.

Neither the Chicago fire, the postwar depression, nor the paper's political positions seemed to have had any negative effect on this trend toward parochialism. The only noticeable deviation from the norm followed the Great Fire, when there was a rapid increase in the number of ads placed by all firms, regardless of location.[16] From an average of 74 ads per issue, the publication of 3 November 1871 had a total of 121 promotions, 100 of which were based in Chicago. In large part, this increase can be explained by the need to replace goods lost in the inferno, as well as an effort by local suppliers to affirm their survival to the public. For example, clothing wholesaler Clement, Morton & Company poignantly stated: "We ask neither discounts nor extensions from our creditors, and nothing from our debtors but prompt payment of bills at maturity." Displaying a credibility bestowed by tragedy, tin dealers K. & J. Frank Sturges & Company asked their patrons to "kindly send us our Statement of Account, mailed to you 1st this month, also a full statement of each bill you have received from us since that time, that we may know how we stand financially."[17]

The parochial trend supports the thesis that Chicago was increasingly the central city of the Great West, even though many of the more prominent Chicago-based manufacturers and retailers of the era were not actively advertising in the *Tribune*. Some larger firms (e.g., Field, Leiter, & Company, Matson & Company, and Carson, Pirie & Company) did promote some sales, but their presence was not representative of the top echelon. Local retailing giants McNeil & Higgens and W. M. Hoyt did not advertise in the *Tribune*. Regional manufacturing bellwethers Marsh Harvester, Kaestner Machines, the Scherzer Company, and Deering Harvester also were absent. Most likely, these suppliers, like Cyrus McCormick, still relied upon territorial agents to carry their message to the hinterland. In other words, Chicago's mastery over its Eastern rivals was not accompanied by, nor can it be explained by, an increased advertising emphasis of leading suppliers targeting rural consumers.

A simple regression analysis, such as that applied to the advertiser's location, can be used to explore other key attributes of the promotions. For example, three different types of advertisers display significant change over time. First, local retailers tended to increased their presence in the *Chicago Tribune*. Ranging, in the first year, from only 9 to 17 percent of the total number of ads, retailers comprised approximately one-third of the sample by 1874. Alternatively, agents and manufacturers exhibited a marked decrease in advertising presence, a fact that takes on greater significance when compared with the changing composition of the advertised products and the consumers specified.

Trends among the types of products offered correspond to these changes. General retail goods such as ready-made clothing, jewelry, fabrics, and notions rose from 10 to 16 percent. Goods classed as *other* increased even more dramatically, doubling from 16 to 33 percent of the sample.[18] Bulk manufacturing supplies and machinery fell in accordance with the drop in manufacturers placing ads in the *Tribune*. Interestingly, purveyors of patent medicines also showed a marked decrease. These suppliers were almost exclusively Eastern manufacturers who addressed the general consumer directly. However, in this case, an explanation of their precipitous fall (from 18 to only 9 percent) has to take into account that, while patent medicine ads became less numerous, very often they grew in size, usually occupying entire columns in the later issues.

The general reduction in advertisements that offered bulk goods implies that Chicago was moving away from, not toward, the basic tenets of the Grange effort, which promised to purchase large caches of merchandise for collective consumption. Rather, the promotions indicated that individual retail sales were becoming dominant. Not only were opportunities shrinking for farmers who wanted to contact agents and manufacturers directly, but the products that were advertised suggest an ever-increasing demand for fashionable, urbane goods that undermined the farmer's peculiar brand of consumer solidarity. In other words, it was an urban-consumer ethos, not the farm variety, that was sustained by these advertising trends.

The targeting of particular consumers was also in flux. While less dramatic than the other examples, this aspect of the period's ads confirmed the widespread trend away from agents and manufacturers and toward the general consumer. Although the number of "general" consumers did go down over time, this group was targeted in more than half of the ads by 1874. The *other* category (i.e., the targets of ads directed toward a gendered audience, for example, or consumers sought by use of the word *urban*) increased significantly in the later issues studied in the survey. The ads mirrored an attempt by retailers to fashion artificial definitions of community. Through this process, product usage was defined by the supplier and not controlled by the consumer. Again, no targeting of the rural patron was evident.

Combining these trends, several notable features of the city's consumer culture become apparent. One was that the earliest stages of product distribution, that from raw materials for manufacturers to bulked finished goods for agents, were being removed from the public consumer dialogue. *Tribune* readers were more likely to be aware of a new shoe store than to notice an opportunity to buy shoes in bulk quantities. Whether agents and middlemen relied more on private lines of communications, such as the city's board of trade or the secluded realm of the horizontally integrated corporation, is unclear from these sources. Agents clearly continued to buy wholesale, but their efforts were less likely to be made public through the *Tribune*'s advertisements.

Manufacturers, too, seemed to be increasingly dependent on markets that were not broadly cast to the general public. It was only in times of crisis, such as after the Great Fire, that agents and manufacturers scurried to place public notices and thereby reestablish these linkages. If agents and manufacturers were receding from popular view, then local retailers were filling the void. Advertisers, products, and consumers all reflected a trend toward the greater emphasis on retail sales in the *Tribune*'s ads. The change gave local consumers greater access to a larger variety of merchandise, but limited the appeal of the ads to those who had easy access to the store. Consumers traded their ability to choose the means of procuring those goods for a wider selection.

The changing nature of the Chicago consumer network suggests that the reduction in out-of-town competition and the rise of local retailing were linked. By the late 1860s, the city had been transformed from being a leading way station for goods into an important and final marketplace. Chicago was no longer simply sending goods from East to West, but was consuming a large portion of the traffic locally. At first glance, this transition appears to be a pivotal one in cementing the city's position of leadership in retail modernization, accompanied as it was by the growth of retail districts such as the popular State Street. Paradoxically, though, this image of dynamic retail leadership runs counter to the trends found in other regional papers. Ads from the more remote regions show that Chicago was, in fact, late at arriving at this stage of retail supremacy. Chicago advertisers were in all likelihood behind the curve because of that city's long-standing role as regional middleman. That made it highly improbable that Chicago advertisers would lead the region's consumer revolution during the Gilded Age.

A further topic that can be studied by an examination of *Tribune* ads is the statistical relationship between products offered, suppliers, and the consumers targeted in order to determine how Chicago advertisers addressed the changing consumer marketplace from 1866 to 1874. The key question here is: Did Chicago advertisers increasingly specialize their appeals to attract certain high-potential clients? Two specific analyses are important: the relationship between the advertiser and the product offered, and that between the products offered and the consumer targeted. Not surprisingly, the first inquiry indicates that products displayed a close correlation to the type of advertiser. For example, bulk processed metals, chemicals, and machinery were predominantly offered by manufacturers, rather than by agents or other providers. Likewise, two of three ads for patent medicines were furnished directly by the manufacturer, and fully 93 percent of professional services were offered directly by the provider. However, the reverse relationship does not hold. While one might expect certain groups to standardize around a single commodity, this was not so. Agents and others offered a wide variety of services, from bulk orders of shoes to the arranging of intercontinental travel. Specialization came to the products but not the businesses that made up the distribution network. In terms of rural consumption, Chicago providers were not working to fit the stated needs of consumers but rather were fashioning their businesses based on the goods that were available.

Following from this, a second examination can explore which products were targeted to address specific consumers. Again, not surprising given the other trends, most goods were not aimed at a definite consumer niche. Clothing, patent medicines, printed materials, medical services, entertainment, transportation, and other products were offered almost universally to the general, unspecified consumer. As Alfred C. Chandler, David Hounshell, Jackson Lears, and others have noted, these products represented goods and services from suppliers who were at the leading edge of business modernization.[19] Yet Chicago's national and regional prominence was gained by firms that sold bulk supplies and finished manufactured goods to rural retailers, and it was here that the Grange efforts sought allies in their struggle to supply their members. The data reveals that these suppliers' ads evidenced a close correlation between the product advertised and the intended consumer. Nearly four-fifths of the ads offering agent services were targeted to other agents and wholesalers. Those for bulk supplies were equally specific. As with regional retailers, it seems that Midwestern agents and manufacturers did not address their appeals to the vociferous consumer demand made by the farmers. The bulked goods available to Chicagoans were being targeted at agents and not the potential rural consumer. The city's wholesale marketplace was engaged in an active dialogue, but it was largely one limited to being between manufacturers, their agents, and traders within the city limits.

Several conclusions can be drawn from the above. First, the advertisements in the *Tribune* displayed a trend that moved away from the raw distribution of goods to a more nuanced, refined, and personalized consumer experience via retailers. These ads were placed by a wide range of suppliers and offered equally diverse products. But retail outlets were not what most rural consumers wanted. They demanded control over wholesale services that were not offered through the *Tribune*.

Second, Chicago providers significantly improved their competitive position in the consumer marketplace. The relative gains over their Eastern rivals provided Second City businessmen increased confidence to take even greater risks within their regional hinterland. But again, for rural consumers, this supremacy brought with it mixed blessings. While it was true that the city now offered more direct and less expensive access to goods than those that once originated in New York or Boston, Chicago providers were under less economic pressure to meet the demands of these isolated shoppers.

Third, the *Tribune* ads trended toward the newer, mass-produced consumer goods and away from access to the more traditional merchandise such as cloth, simple ready-made clothing, and bulked staples. The concurrent move toward nondescript, broadly cast messages aimed at the general consumer supported these new wares and was at direct odds with the collective purchasing strategies developed in the countryside. Further, given the vocal nature of agrarian protest, the rural clientele of the publication, and the pointed references to consumer issues by farmer and editor alike, the lack of *Tribune* advertisements targeting the farm consumer is striking.

Finally, urban agents, wholesalers, and manufacturers clearly used the *Tribune* to target some individual consumers and groups, supporting the notion that such segmentation was possible as early as 1874. However, the prospective patrons were predominantly people living within the area of the city's marketplace. In short, agents and manufacturers engaged in a strictly urban dialogue. Despite the Grange's bid to secure goods in large volumes, there is no indication in the paper that the existing distribution network responded to this increased demand. From the ads, it appears that suppliers were hardly the driving force behind Chicago's rising control over the rural hinterland.[20] It appears more likely that they acted merely to supply the newly acquired distribution network. While these transactions between wholesalers and retailers had lasting effects on the economy of the hinterland, they were not the central cause of the assimilation of rural consumers into the metropolitan marketplace.

More importantly, the story of the Chicago's changing internal consumer environment adds weight to the growing concerns expressed by small-town merchants. Provincial providers not only ignored consumer activities that failed to boost their local settlements—they attacked them. Further, the drive to promote retailers on Main Street led many to promote a distinctly urban material culture that was antithetical to the tenets of agrarian consumerism. A brief comparison of the Chicago advertisements with those of other regional markets adds some clarity to the interurban rivalries that passed in and around the changing rural consumer landscape.

A similar statistical analysis was completed for two urban centers, Indianapolis and Milwaukee (both of them large, but smaller than Chicago), and two small markets, Ripon, Wisconsin, and Oshkosh, Wisconsin. The two small towns ably represent the transformation affecting regional villages; the larger communities are typical of cities caught within the vise of modernizing consumer tastes and an expanding regional entrepôt such as Chicago. The 1,903 advertisements randomly selected from the *Indianapolis Journal*, the *Milwaukee Daily News*, the *Ripon Free Press*, and the *Oshkosh City Times* span the years of 1863 and 1878. They were examined with the same methodological concerns in mind as were described for the *Chicago Tribune* sample. Interestingly, the regional papers displayed nearly as many ads, averaging more than 61 promotions a day, as the *Tribune*, which averaged nearly 74 per issue.[21]

The products offered in the regional towns and cities remained consistent with the *Tribune* results. However, the types of advertisers differed markedly (table 5.1). *Tribune* advertisers reflected Chicago's unique market position: brokers and manufacturers advertised frequently. Also unlike in the secondary markets, in Chicago it seemed that an opportunity existed whereby farmers' unique demands might be met. By contrast, the distribution of the type of advertiser in the *Indianapolis Journal* and *Milwaukee Daily News* was similar to that in the smaller town journals. These regional papers were (unlike Chicago) dominated by local retailers. Significantly, the percentage of retail advertisers increases as the size of the town decreases. Farm cooperatives looking for suppliers found few allies in the advertisements of the regional publications. The retail consumer market was, if anything, more proprietary than that of Chicago.

A second noteworthy comparison was in regard to agents and manufacturers. Like retailers, the appearance of middlemen in this public consumer dialogue seemed tied to the relative size of the local economy. If local conditions were more diverse, as was the case in Chicago, Indianapolis, and Milwaukee, jobbers found the urban newspaper a profitable forum in which to do business. By contrast, the *Oshkosh City Times* and the *Ripon Free Press* were remarkable for their relative lack of advertisements by agencies. Moreover, in each of the markets outside of Chicago, local manufacturers were much more likely to advertise in the daily paper. Farmers scanning the local broadsheets found little to suggest that agents and wholesalers were out to assist them in buying direct. Rather, if planters wanted access to the largest suppliers and best prices, they needed to create these links on their own.[22]

The type of consumer in the ads also shows regional variation (table 5.2). Again, Chicago advertisers prove themselves to be distinct. In every regional paper except the *Chicago Tribune,* advertisements generally failed

Table 5.1
Type of Advertiser, Regional Newspapers, 1863–1878 (in percentages)

Type of Advertiser	*Regional Newspaper*				
	Chicago Tribune	*Ripon Free Press*	*Indianapolis Journal*	*Milwaukee Daily News*	*Oshkosh City Times*
Retailer	24.3	58.7	51.9	51.9	60.0
Manuf.	17.6	21.4	27.1	30.0	20.8
Agent	26.5	5.7	17.2	13.2	10.0
Other	16.3	14.2	3.8	4.8	9.2
N =	2,214	332	395	393	783

to identify a particular consumer for their product. These pitches, with a targeted consumer categorized as *none,* were broadly cast to all potential clients. The high percentage suggests that it was rare for small-town merchants to seek out any particular groups of consumers. Again, the demands of rural patrons were seemingly disregarded by advertisers. Whether by ignorance or design, farmers received scant attention from the Midwestern dailies. Only 41 of the 4,117 advertisements specifically addressed farmers. The *Chicago Tribune* accommodated 12 such ads. The smaller markets of Oshkosh and Ripon accounted for 24. The products offered in these ads included seed catalogs, corn huskers, "hog ringers," milling services, and agricultural machinery. In Milwaukee, the 4 farm advertisements announced regional distribution services such as granaries and depots offered by local commission merchants. The advertiser who placed the sole farmer-addressed ad in the *Indianapolis Journal* was not even a local supplier but came from the Pittsburgh Plow Company of Pennsylvania.[23]

A third general trend suggests that the relative location of advertisers in these Midwestern periodicals was relatively consistent (table 5.3). In both large and small markets, roughly four out of five advertisers were based in the same town as the newspaper. The category *other* refers to advertisers who were neither from the paper's home state nor from Chicago. The comparison hints that the smaller towns of Ripon and Oshkosh suffered more severely from predation by Chicago firms than the larger, more diverse economies of Indianapolis and Milwaukee, the physically closest market outside of Chicago. The in-state competition, primarily from Milwaukee, was also much larger than that faced by advertisers in

Table 5.2

Type of Consumer Targeted, Regional Newspapers, 1863–1878 (in percentages)

Type of Advertiser	*Regional Newspaper*				
	Chicago Tribune	*Ripon Free Press*	*Indianapolis Journal*	*Milwaukee Daily News*	*Oshkosh City Times*
None	53.2	88.6	99.2	96.9	95.7
Manuf.	7.7	0.6	0.3	0.0	0.4
Agent	23.8	3.9	0.3	0.5	2.0
Other	15.3	6.9	0.3	2.5	2.0
N=	2,214	332	395	393	783

Chicago, Indianapolis, and Milwaukee. Small-town retailers, struggling to retain their shrinking economic hinterlands, faced a greater challenge from these urban firms, and no doubt were less amenable to the purchasing arrangements of farmers.

Clearly the diversity of goods and the wide range of advertisers suggests a complexity to the distribution network. By 1873, and maybe a little sooner, the structure of a modern consumer marketplace was in place in the rural Midwest. This network was also increasingly dominated by Chicago businessmen who were gaining economic might just as rural consumers began to demand greater access to, and control over, an increased variety of goods. Chicago's growth certainly placed harsh economic pressures on neighboring towns and cities. Advertisers in Indianapolis, Milwaukee, Ripon, and Oshkosh seemed to concentrate their appeals to capture the local markets and limit poaching by Chicagoans. This bidding war no doubt created more than a little paranoia in suppliers. Advertisers were now on the defensive and eager to protect the local markets from all perceived threats, even those of sympathetic rural consumer cooperatives. Many concerned themselves not with meeting the stated needs of prospective clients, but rather in underbidding their cross-town rivals. Although farmers offered both subtle and overt indicators that they were unhappy with the established order—and were a ready market for perceptive entrepreneurs—small-town retailers showed no indication of being willing to change. The profusion of local advertisements that were broadly cast makes manifest that these merchants were unresponsive to the modern demands of their farming neighbors.

Table 5.3
Location of Advertiser, Regional Newspapers, 1863–1878 (in percentages)

Type of Advertiser	Regional Newspaper				
	Ripon Free Press	Chicago Tribune	Indianapolis Journal	Milwaukee Daily News	Oshkosh City Times
Hometown	68.7	80.5	79.2	79.1	84.3
Chicago	7.8	N/A	1.3	2.8	4.3
In-state	2.1	0.7	0.0	0.3	3.1
Other	22.3	18.7	19.5	17.8	8.3
N=	332	2,214	395	393	783

There were also more overt clues as to the intentions of small-town merchants toward their farm patrons. In 1923, Thorstein Veblen, who studied the evolving economic relationship between the Midwestern town and country between 1865 and 1900, maintained that the central function of small-town communities was to increase speculative property values. "Boosting" and "booming" local advantages became a full-time occupation for most investors and editors of indigenous newspapers. Taking control of their agricultural neighbors' economic participation in the marketplace became "a common understanding," said Veblen. "The traders as a body direct[ed] their collective efforts to getting what can be got out of the under-lying farm population." Merchants were not much concerned with the consumer inefficiencies of their decisions. Veblen concluded that "quite as a matter of course, the business of the town arrange[d] itself under such regulations and usages that it foots up a competition, not between business concerns, but between town and country, between traders and customers." In effect, rural towns formed local retail monopolies that exacted their profits largely from the pockets of farmers. Rather than fashioning a demand-based consumer ideology, retailers hoped to retain their traditional, supply-based authority over local merchandise markets.[24]

Veblen's economic analysis has not gone unchallenged. Critics noted that the monopolies were rarely absolute. But the fact remains that many small-town residents engaged in a barely concealed economic struggle with their farm neighbors from 1865 to 1880. Ironically, both communities shared many of the same sources of distress: market deflation, low prices, overinvestment in capital improvements, and factionalism about how to cut the local pie. But small-town citizens and suppliers reacted much differently as consumers. The same forces that led commercial farmers to forge a modern consumer ideology impelled many village residents to become more conservative in their approach to meeting these new and growing demands.[25]

Oshkosh and Ripon prove to be useful towns in which to demonstrate these anxieties. Both were well-established settlements, had prominent Grange activity, strong agricultural markets, and access to larger regional cities. Their urban retail markets were fairly diverse and can be connected to the advertisement patterns discussed above. In 1868, for example, the Oshkosh city directory boasted a population of 12,370 people, more than 2,100 dwellings, 220 merchants, and 101 manufacturers. And both Ripon and Oshkosh boosters voiced their belief that the commercial farmer's success was intricately linked to the success of the local town. Foreshadowing and reversing the themes of William Jennings Bryan's "Cross of Gold" speech, the *Ripon Free Press* argued that "it is more to the interest of the farmers in this section to have a city here than any other class. Blot out our mercantile houses and you blot out half the value of your farms and produce." In spite of such braggadocio, both towns were deeply dependent upon the consumer spending of rural patrons.[26]

Regional granges were quite active in both locales. In Oshkosh, reports on the Patrons of Husbandry were generally favorable. George Hyer, the editor of the *Oshkosh City Times*, served for a spell as the treasurer of the state grange, and other town notables also had close contact with the organization. Merchants from both towns understood the fundamental threat from Grange activity to be that farmers had "commenced a correspondence with some of the large manufacturing establishments, and learned that if they pay cash and give big orders, they will get articles very cheap." But the deep-seated tradition of boostering and a strong bias against the crudity of farm life proved insurmountable in fashioning a shared consumer philosophy.[27]

Farmers' changing attitudes toward access to goods was probably the greatest source of conflict. As both towns proudly pointed out, local retailing had mushroomed since the close of the Civil War. The fact that the Ripon Grange store was the town's twelfth general store, to say nothing of specialty shops, speaks volumes of the transformation that occurred within living memory of the region's consumer marketplace. When farmers proclaimed their desire to weed out what they believed to be superfluous establishments, they directly challenged one of the town's more visible measurements of progress. An article in the *Ripon Free Press* signed "Granger" rhapsodized: "What a benefit it would be to the commercial interests of Ripon if the city council had the power to issue license only to a legitimate number of merchants in each line." The writer envisioned "only six or seven" grocers with similar limits placed on other trades. Reflecting a core value of the Grange practice—democratic control over access to goods—which no doubt alarmed many developers, the farmer concluded: "If public sentiment could be worked up in such a way as to materially effect the demand for groceries, the council should take the matter under consideration and after mature deliberation decide how much 'lopping off' there should be." When, in the summer of 1879, many rural consumer reformers cheered the report of rising urban grocery failures in the region, the paper shot back: "Such sickly theoretical twaddle may do for people who have no bridges to build . . . but it is certainly below the basis on which fortunes can be risked or earned."[28]

Such backhanded recognition of the farmer's consumer opinions only increased with the rise of organized purchasing cooperatives. The editors were caught in the difficult position between defending town businesses, their source of advertising revenues, and the need not to offend their farm subscribers. In both town papers, editors deferred to the advertisers. Increasingly, farmers were presented as just "not getting" the scope or complexity of the problems. Sometimes this took the form of frivolous comments and portrayals of farm people, their fairs, and living habits. The newspapers often berated their farm acquaintances for lack of discrimination in purchasing preferences. One Oshkosh contributor described male farmers as simple, "round, stalwart, [and] comfortable animal[s]." Farm women, when they were not occupied "raising children and chickens, *ad infinitum*," were generally seen with "the same frowsy head [with which they] rose in the morning, darting hither and thither for what is wanted." It was suggested that progressive retailers not take their lead from such ill-bred consumers.[29]

In a more pointed critique, village reporters related how easily farmers fell prey to traveling salesmen and con artists. The primary tactic used by charlatans to fool the simple farmer was to invoke the Grange-like mantra that "the home merchant can not obtain goods as cheap as they, and that the rent of store and the hire of clerk, is paid for by the farmer." The "unsuspecting farmer" (a term by which farmers were often called) was usually indicted only for simple stupidity—an offense supposedly so common in the countryside that it was rated only as a misdemeanor. But others suggested that the farm population was often guilty of more serious crimes. The *Oshkosh City Times* moralized in regard to one such episode: "Act with honesty and do not consent to be a party to deception. Many frauds of the kind spoken of are successful, because the deceived party was willing to deceive others, if he could make money by so doing"; in any case, it was clear to all who could read that farmers not only lacked sophistication but basic business sense as well.[30]

Village residents certainly shared the farmers' own sharply critical view of territorial agents. Like the agriculturalists, their experiences with middlemen were at the heart of their views of proper consumer practice. However, unlike farmers, who generally saw the exclusive rights of the middlemen as an infringement upon their economic liberties, townspeople saw drummers simply as agents of external competitors. Their admonishments in the local papers were directed against consumers who falsely assumed that these salesman provided greater savings or better quality goods. Unconsciously mimicking the ways agents were reported to have duped their farm clients about town merchants, retailers claimed that the Chicago agents usually were "paid large salaries . . . their expenses enormous, and it is all paid by the parties who buy the goods that these fellows sell." Travel expenses, valises, and fine clothing were all extravagances that country patrons were "taxed to support" through inflated prices. In other words, it was the agents' custom of traveling to farm residences that was the central focus of their complaint. Town retailers were not, like the farmers, concerned that territorial jobbers were being granted exclusive retail monopolies by big-city suppliers.[31]

The rhetoric surrounding these attacks took on normative tones, especially when related to the farmer/agent contacts. In a front-page report, the *Ripon Free Press* told of "guerilla" tactics employed by agents of the Chicago-based Harper Brothers, a grocery dealer. Denying the right of individuals to choose their supplier, the paper reasoned that the trade with agents was justified only if it was first proved that "our merchants were swindling the farmers." The representatives were said to have spent "lots of money for hotel bills, livery, and whiskey" in a region noted for active prohibition, "and if they get wages *in addition* it would take mighty large sales to simply pay expenses." Undoubtedly, retailers believed it to be a foolish and expensive practice to meet the farmer at his home. Combining their disdain for drummers with a chastisement of the foolhardy farmers who patronized them, the contributor concluded that the Harper Brother agents "report that their sales in [the countryside] have been larger than in any place that they have visited. We regard this as about the worst compliment that could be paid our farmers." When farmers organized to meet the challenge presented by agents, neither the Ripon nor the Oshkosh communities rallied behind their efforts. Village voices stated that if farmers "but reflected a moment," the obvious result of their cooperatives "gives to [outside] manufacturers and speculators the control of the markets." The *Free Press* editorialized that if a local paper supported such enterprises as a Grange purchasing agency, "it ought not to get much encouragement from home merchants."[32]

Another key source of tension between town and farm consumers involved the intrusion of the larger markets of Milwaukee, Saint Louis, and especially Chicago. There were conflicting interpretations of the nature of the threat. Railroads in particular, it was said, had "equaliz[ed] prices at a rapid rate" between Chicago and its hinterland. A contributor to the *Cultivator and Country Gentleman* judged that "every mile added to the railroads of Illinois contributes to the growth of Chicago and St. Louis . . . it seems as if second and third rate towns suffered in the same proportion." Some farmers, although they feared the loss of individual control due to the rise of the central city, saw potential advantages in this transformation, but such a creative consumer response was not evident in small towns. Civic merchants were much more pessimistic and therefore more conservative in their reaction. While farmers took advantage of the "better prices and better opportunities" wrought by these changes, essayists were largely mute as to the options open to town retailers and their urban clients.[33]

Ripon and Oshkosh boosters were very parochial in their responses to the encroachment. Town residents raged that the "greater portion of the immense trade of central Wisconsin goes over Chicago roads, to Chicago markets, at Chicago rates, to receive Chicago prices. It is time Wisconsin looked a little to her own interests." Protectionism, they said, might retain many of their dwindling number of manufacturing jobs and thereby reduce the spiraling dependency upon the regional centers.[34]

Individual consumer demands were subsumed by the town boosters in favor of a communal rush for urban improvement. Veblen identified a "community" of promoters that was pressed to increase speculative property values. Village retailers claimed almost a natural right to exercise dominion over the consumer dollars of a locality. This claim superseded any conflicting consumer ideologies or even the modest pursuit of lower prices for similar goods through Chicago firms. The Ripon newspaper's editors thus concluded that big-city wholesalers who dealt directly with the public were "swindlers in one way or another." If they did not sell substandard goods, then certainly their "work [was] antagonistical to the interest of every home trader; they do not aid in keeping up a town, do not pay any taxes or sustain any schools; they do not patronize hotels and livery stables, but further than this they damage every trader in the city"; they deprived local merchants "the trade that naturally belongs to them." Towns claimed to be protecting communal solidarity against the raging economic individualism of farmers. That this view involved conflicting notions of social order was conveniently ignored.[35]

Oshkosh merchants echoed this approval of retail protectionism: the "greatest mistake made by a community, is in not patronizing home mechanics and home trade." The *City Times* related "five instances in the last two years in which we have declined to print Milwaukee and Chicago advertisements because we believed to do so would be injurious to business in Oshkosh." They had been "offered a fair price for the space," but any group that combined to "go abroad for their furniture, their boots and shoes, their dry goods, or other articles of luxury or necessity" was a betrayer to town solidarity. Many whined that "if our more wealthy people buy their more expensive supplies abroad, what encouragement is there for bringing costly supplies to this market?" The guarantee of cost savings to individuals was "not [a] good argument, even if true."[36]

Small-town merchants did not formulate new strategies based on the modernizing shifts in consumer demand; rather, they turned to sophisticated, and narcissistic, methods of generating artificial demand. We have already explored the origins of farmers' predilections for low-priced quality goods. During those same years, small-town consumers turned away from such communal norms and embraced competitive consumer concepts such as "fashion," "conspicuous consumption," and what T. J. Jackson Lears called the "therapeutic ethos" of goods.[37] While historians generally agree that the modern, urban, mass-consumer society was formed from 1865 to 1900, an understanding of the nature of this revolution has been problematic. Interpretations by Warran Susman and Christopher Lasch suggest that the pursuit for material goods has largely resulted in an ideological clash between "traditional" communal values, which resented change, and the various forces (ranging from radical socialism to reactionary Social Darwinism) that promulgated a faith in consumption.[38] In short, many saw the conflict as a contest between community and society, or the age-old debate between *Gemeinschaft* and *Gesellschaft* first forwarded by Ferdinand Tönnies in the nineteenth century.[39]

But this ideological reading of the process of consumption left only the determined impact of modernization as an explanation. As such, it results in a stark dichotomy between disciples of tradition and modernity. In reality, divergent consumer paths were taken by many different groups. Americans, particularly in the twentieth century, expressed beliefs about the role that consumerism played in their lives that were distinctive to their perceived group status.[40] The individual, as the entity that either embraces or rejects group affiliation, is the proper domain from which historians can profitably explore the consequences of the new mass market. Noting that the era was one that saw the "dawn of [consumer] self-consciousness," researchers have posited a number of reasonable interpretations to account for the rise in consumer activity.[41]

The most obvious example of the evolution of individual perception was the department store. William Leach and others have shown that the new emporiums, found from New York to San Francisco, coalesced the nebulous individual consumer ideologies through "refined" purchasing. The stores' peculiar concern with product presentation and ambiance made consumption a tangible, if exaggerated, experience. This consumer training altered the process of acquisition from a logical economic activity, as was suggested by farmers, to an emotional preference for selected goods. Merchandise was demonetized and buying became an end to itself as the means to achieve happiness. In this sense, individual consumers were molded by the process of urban consumption into communities of like-minded shoppers through these, obviously manipulated, trips through the store.[42]

The fixation with experiential consumption was evident in the descriptions of local department stores as recounted by Wisconsin newspapers. On slow news days, George Hyer of the *City Times* often gave subscribers descriptive tours of the many window displays of their town's largest firms. For example, the Dimmicks array was "a sight . . . with their endless variety of beautiful things. . . . Isn't that window a picture!" Often his fanfare was not needed. Once, as Hyer passed the firm of Bigger & Hills, he reported that he had merely become "one of the crowd that had gathered in front of the store in admiration of the magnificent display made in its windows." The array was set off by the novel "large panes of glass" and "filled in the most artistic manner with the fancy articles that give such charm to dress." The goods themselves came in "artistic patterns, [and] in all shades of color." Adding to the effect, the desirables were "beautifully lighted and shaded, by a jet of gas, thrown by reflectors in such a manner as to give the whole the appearance of a picture, useful and ornamental things displayed in the most tempting manner. We have seldom seen a better display." Hyer noted that these visceral reactions gave local consumers "an index to a store . . . in whose cases, are displayed the excellent goods of which such promise is given in the windows."[43]

The interior spaces of these bazaars were equally spectacular to the small-town consumer. Jacob Fowle's store in downtown Oshkosh offered shelves of luxury goods such as "prettily designed stone china ware, gold rimmed china sets . . . show cases of silver ware and of cutlery . . . and plated ware of every kind," all "fit for a palace." In Ripon, new stores that combined the colored glass and gaslights common to department stores inspired one observer to note that the merchandise "shine[s] like pure gold in the elegant new store. Their friends will enjoy these new premises, which they are invited to do." It is ironic—given the town merchants' view of big-city encroachment—that a favorable comparison to Chicago shopping styles was the highest compliment that could be paid to these presentations.[44]

The display windows and fine goods were not the only experiences available in small towns. Often, the activity of a store itself was enough to spark the imagination of patrons. For example, Biggers Dry Goods Emporium occupied a four-story building in downtown Oshkosh and employed eighteen clerks; seemingly they were perpetually busy with customers. A visit led one purchaser to exclaim that the "whole establishment is a 'bee hive' from top to bottom." Climbing the central staircase, which also allowed light into the lower floors, the patron observed that "to look down this hole in the floor, the moving mass of humanity on the first floor resemble a race of pygmies in size, coming and going." The activity of the store, combined with the allure of its displays, made department stores unique in their propagation of an enlivening consumer experience. Although retailers increasingly invested their energies in displays of luxury, style, and sophistication, they were fighting an uphill battle: the largest cities set standards for glamour that exceeded the reach of smaller operators.[45]

Nevertheless, village and small-town patrons had shifted away from the rational and collective consumer goals of commercial farmers. When one Illinois farmer wrote about the wide range of consumer goods, he noted that the greatest challenge was the fight to check the "propensity to gratify pride—an expensive article in a new country." By contrast, when the Boston Store opened in Ripon in December 1878, consumers expected, according to the proprietors, a "thoroughly assorted stock," carrying "all the novelties of the season," and available "at all time." Questions about the cost of carrying all this variety to meet individual tastes—cost that certainly was passed along to the community—were never asked.[46]

Although town purchasers were as distressed as the farmers were by the contraction of currency and the depression of 1873, their response as shoppers was vastly different. While farmers sought means of creating efficiencies within the distribution network, urban citizens were told in a newspaper editorial to accept the fact that "the moment you purchase . . . you personally owe [the merchant] for not only the original material, but you owe for all the labor necessary to produce the article as well as the cost of transporting it from an eastern market." The only real modification to urban consumers's access to goods was the development of the "one-price" system. The Biggers emporium was lauded for marking all goods "in plain figures, and there being only *one price*, it does not take long to make a trade. This feature alone should recommend the establishment, as it stops all dickering." Instead of collectively bargaining for lower prices, small-town buyers became solitary "bargain hunters," much as today many spend time finding low-cost, used goods at garage sales, flea markets, and thrift stores. Oshkosh merchants derisively dismissed such consumers, noting that the bargain hunter's "various losing investments in battered silverware, cracked china, and trashy stuff" eventually "cured [him] of his salesroom folly, but seldom of his self-conceit and greed, and thus only changes the scene of his bargain hunting and its *modus operandi*." Rather than cede control over pricing to the town merchants, the odd discount-seeker "flatters himself that he can make his dollars go farther than his neighbors. He is always endeavoring to buy under the market price; and men when they see him, are in self-defense obliged to raise the valuation of their wares that they may reduce it to gratify [this] idiosyncrasy."[47]

Clearly, village consumers, charmed by the dynamism of the local department store and unable to maintain a unified front, were no more likely to support the tenets of rural consumerism than were town merchants. They may have shared similar economic misfortunes, such as tight credit and a general downturn in regional markets, but their purchasing practices suggest that they had polar interpretations of individual consumption. While farmers based this capacity on personal fiscal savings and a greater control over the availability of goods, town dwellers relied on the experiences of shopping to provide their lives with a larger meaning. In fact, by the turn of the century, many Americans would come to define their sense of belonging by the goods that they consumed. Small-town residents, not having the same purchasing experiences as farmers, failed to join with their rural cousins in support of a unified consumer ethos.

When J. M. Little addressed the Ripon Grange on 8 January 1881, his farm allies had already seen the collapse of their local store, the disintegration of their national movement, and the rejection of their cause by town consumers. Still, Little's tart criticism of "capital aggregated and central-ized" and its stultifying effects on "those who buy and carry" goods sug-gested that he and his audience adhered to the original ideological goals of the order. In the preceding years, he reasoned, farmers had "gained some information" about those who either ignored or fought their cause and had found a new appreciation for their own unique perspective on the problems of the Midwest. What they saw of urban consumerism no doubt justified a redoubling of their efforts. By the 1880s, small towns had little defense against the invasion by retail chain stores, big-city department stores, and mail-order firms. Steeped in a tradition of experiential con-sumerism, small-town patrons slowly shifted their allegiances to firms that were better able to provide the therapeutic benefits demanded of them. Oshkosh and Ripon merchants who played by the rules established by big-city merchants found that they had been dealt a losing hand. Aided by professional advertising campaigns, larger retailers perfected the system of consumer manipulation begun in the 1870s.[48]

During these years, Midwestern farmers found that they were with-out allies in their effort to perfect a consumer-controlled purchasing sys-tem. As Little would say later: "The farmers of this nation are on trial before the world. The question is to be settled now, whether we are com-petent to do business." Their work, however, was now contained wholly within the institution of the Patrons of Husbandry.

6

A Battle of Standards

*The Renunciation of the
Rural Consumer Ethos by the
Patrons of Husbandry, 1875–1882*

In February 1874, at the seventh annual meeting of the National Grange of the Patrons of Husbandry, the national master, Dudley Adams, invited the assembled leadership to give their full attention to the question of rural consumption. Adams noted that many farmers had "given this one point more thought and attention than perhaps any other," resulting in an independent purchasing-agency system throughout much of the Midwest. But while "satisfactory progress has been made . . . we are as yet only on the threshold of this great work." To advance it further, the grange asked the standing Executive Committee on Business Plans and Agencies to conceive a national strategy to coordinate regional activities. The committee duly reported later that the system, as it existed locally, suffered from "want of cash, the efforts of antagonistic interests, lack of confidence, and probably more than all these, the failure to effect combined co-ordinated action." The committee proposed a novel and seemingly straightforward solution to unite the disparate state plans: the national grange would organize, fund, and promote regional mail-order supply houses, based in New York, Chicago, and New Orleans, to provide members a full array of discounted consumer goods.[1]

While ambitious, these purchasing strategies were rooted in the basic ideology of the Grange movement. Balancing individual consumer desires and the need for fair access to goods by the entire rural community, the order followed the axiom that "successful results of general welfare can be secured only by general effort." The prosperity of the grassroots purchasing-agency system from 1867 to 1875 gave farmers confidence that "combined co-ordinated action" at the national level would maximize individual benefits while providing a truly communal alternative to the established distribution system.[2]

By the end of the decade, however, many Midwestern states' purchasing efforts were in a shambles. Rather than create independent organs by which farmers could control access to goods, members met in Chicago on 8 October 1879 to investigate how to educate Patrons "in the ways of doing business in the city of Chicago." It seems that Grangers no longer hoped to direct purchases through their institution; they were content to allow suppliers to regain control over the terms and conditions of consumption. Whereas they once led the movement, Midwestern state granges now followed the more radical and heavy-handed management of the national body.[3]

The cause of this ideological retrenchment was complex and goes to the heart of the problem created by the institutional control over such a grassroots phenomenon. Beginning in 1875 and lasting until the close of the decade, the Grange faced a general desertion from its ranks that almost destroyed the order. Participation plummeted from 858,000 in 1875 to about 124,000 in 1880. Most of these losses occurred in the Midwest. Illinois alone fell from 676 to fewer than 100 subordinate chapters statewide. It was during these years of institutional decline that the purchasing-agency system also failed in the region. The links between falling membership and the agency are not clear, however. For example, while the state master's address at the 1876 meeting of the Wisconsin Grange focused on the numerical losses to the order, the state agent, L. G. Kniffen, reported a rapidly increasing business volume. If there was not a direct correlation between falling membership and the success of the agency, then the actions taken by the leaders of the state and national grange were paramount in understanding why such a popular service failed to sustain itself.[4]

The historiography of the Grange generally agrees on the root causes of the failure of the purchasing arm. Most historians have claimed that the efforts lacked central guidance and business experience or were undercapitalized. Still, in light of the basic desire of many farmers to construct a purchasing agency, the question of what role the national leadership played in the bureau's collapse requires examination. Historians have so far focused on the changes that led to the institutional survival of the Grange, not the agencies unwittingly destroyed in that process. Thomas Allan Woods's account, *Knights of the Plow: Oliver H. Kelley and the Republican Origins of the Grange,* makes the convincing argument that, beginning in 1875, "radical" leadership wanted the Grange to focus on the social agenda originally proposed by founder Kelley. These members openly clashed with those who were more hesitant to abandon the burgeoning purchasing department. The confrontation over the intent of the business activities resulted in a coordinated effort to return to the "true" purpose of the order. Central to this change was rural consumerism.[5]

Woods's thesis of an ideological coup d'état stands up in terms of the various consumer strategies discussed by the Grange. The debate surrounding the purchasing agency demonstrated the national order's intent regarding the role of rural consumption in the union. By examining the theories that buttress the leaders' disagreement with the purchasing-agency concept, our understanding of the various consumer options can be freed from the limiting institutional focus of the order. The following analysis focuses on the state grange in Wisconsin (where a purchasing agency existed the longest) and the leaders of the national grange: the object of the analysis is to discover whether it was the actions by the leaders of the order or the underlying consumer ideology of Grange members that caused the downfall of the purchasing system.

The purchasing-agency system, or what came to be known as the "granger style" by competing retailers, was both revolutionary and evolutionary. This technique was based on the dedication of Midwestern farmers to the demand-driven access to goods, the progressive reform of the distribution system, a communal justification of purchasing activities, and a democratic and virtuous application of the economic benefits derived from their efforts. This ideology overturned the traditional supply-based distribution process and placed consumer demand at the apex of the new consumer economy. This novel approach, if fully implemented, blurred traditional geographic, occupational, and gendered distinctions. In other words, attributes such as rural and urban, farm or nonfarm, and even male or female became less important than an individual's distinction as cooperative consumer. Importantly, these efforts were not intended to overturn the capitalist economic order but rather to assert a greater appreciation for farmers' purchasing power. Still, the circulation of these beliefs was insurgent enough to bring down the charge of socialism upon the Grange by those who opposed their consumer efforts.[6]

The agency was also enmeshed with the traditional buying customs of generations of Midwestern farmers. Bulk sales and purchases, interaction with territorial agents, the need for large amounts of cash and credit, and the communal evaluation of capital goods all gave their current consumer practices deep roots in their prairie experiences. The Patrons of Husbandry obtained much of its organizational legitimacy from the time-honored practices of local farmers' clubs and horticultural societies. As a result of this heritage, regional Grange "stores" varied greatly, depending on earlier purchasing activity. For example, as in the case of Ripon, Wisconsin, outlets could be open to the general public, thus competing directly with other stores. Low cost was their chief draw. Other local stores were only for members who had bought stock in the enterprise. Members bought goods at retail (nondiscounted) prices and then received an annual dividend based on the profits. The loosest structure was an informal, and usually secret, agreement with local, non-Grange retailers who simply concentrated Grange-member purchases and passed along a predetermined discount at the point of sale. The role of the state agent was to coordinate the activities and purchases of these stores. In these ways, the purchasing agency was both a new and a conventional application of rural consumerism.

Yet, despite these advantages, after 1874 the state agencies often struggled to remain solvent. For example, sales through the Illinois state agency fell to a trickle by 1876. Farmers were lured by the unscrupulous pricing tactics of retail competitors and the state agent, S. J. Frew, lamented "that the present dime was . . . better than the future dollar" to many farm consumers. Additionally, the proximity of urban suppliers in Indianapolis, Saint Louis, and Chicago made this betrayal all the more common. In a letter to Wisconsin Granger Joseph Osborn, R. M. Guy, of Bloomington, commented that Illinois members "have so many other ways into this state besides coming through Chicago that they will not do business" with the state agent. Agent Frew reported annual sales of only $4,049.38 at the December 1875 meeting of the state grange. It seems questionable whether the Illinois State Grange actually had a viable purchasing agency by this date, compared with its neighbors: the Wisconsin State Grange sold more than $6,000 in the month of December alone, and $38,149.39 for the year, and the Indiana State Grange had annual sales of more than $58,000. Without national supervision, the Illinois state agency looked as if it was condemned to become an unused and ridiculed department, reliant on the same competitors that the purchasing-agency concept was originally formulated to surmount. As late as 1881, the Wisconsin State Grange held up their neighbor's efforts as "an office doing strictly a commission business, and keeping no goods on hand."[7]

In neighboring Indiana, Patrons also faced stiff competition from the many regional supply houses. Using a theme later echoed by national leaders, Indiana State Grange executives feared that the potential failure of the agency carried with it an implied threat to the order itself. The state master, Henley James, commented that "some of the state granges [chapters in the state] have bankrupted their treasuries, by attempting to carry an intricate and expensive business at the expense of the State Grange." He contended that the purchasing agency must be "self-sustaining to be successful, and the expense of such enterprise must be derived from the profits growing out of the business." It was "both unwise and hazardous . . . to assume financial responsibility on account of any business enterprise of any character whatever."[8]

Despite strong sales, the Indiana agency demonstrated a profound need for fiscal stability by early 1876. Agent Alpheus Tyner reported that the department had incurred a deficit through "a combination of circumstances . . . unavoidable upon our part." He asked the state officials to consider "some plan for the better protection of the interests of the agency." Contrary to State Master James, Tyner urged that "a business fund be provided for, separate and independent from the regular revenues now derived from the fees and dues, and that this fund be raised upon a mutual basis." The response by state leaders was clear and absolute. The special committee to oversee the bureau demanded "the present system of the State Agency be discontinued" and its assets liquidated. The motion was passed by the assembly and the task was given over to the executive committee in January 1876.[9]

Without a doubt, the purchasing activities of Midwestern state granges suffered dearly from operational problems such as a lack of business experience, rising competition, and an unreliable source of funding. Routinely, Grange purchasing agents were ill-equipped to contend with the huge volumes of mail, large quantities of diverse goods, and often poorly kept records that the transactions generated. Yet this lack of experience was not a problem in itself until the order was faced with competition for farmers' dollars by the large urban supply houses in Chicago, Saint Louis, and Milwaukee.[10]

In the early years of the movement, access to Chicago wholesalers was actually encouraged by Grange leaders. The *Prairie Farmer* gave numerous examples of subordinates that did business through Chicago: one of them "bought something near $1,000 worth of goods, which have given the best of satisfaction . . . being just what they were recommended." The periodical often evaluated local firms: "Z. M. Hall, the first grocer of Chicago to attempt direct dealings with Grangers, was mentioned in the highest terms"; the "wholesale grocery house of Roe Brothers . . . [was] unexceptional [sic] in all respects"; and "Montgomery, Ward & Co. . . . [was] of considerable business tact, and bearing a reputation for honesty and promptness."[11]

Only later did state agents recognize the threat to Grange-sponsored departments from the private sector. Thomas Wilcock, the secretary for the La Valle Grange in Wisconsin, wrote to Osborn that "members generally feel that we shall have to give up the State Agent and fall back on direct trade with Chicago Houses." In 1876, Wisconsin's agent, Kniffen, observed that he was "compelled to decline to fill orders of this character, and the majority of Granges continued to send their orders to such 'Grange Supply' houses as would give them satisfactory terms."[12]

Matters were made worse by underfunding: state agents had difficulty in securing reliable operating capital with which they might obtain prices comparable to those of the larger wholesalers. Often obliged to use their personal lines of credit, agents were loath to seek out greater volume purchases due to the risk of insolvency. Just as Alpheus Tyner hoped to secure an endowment for his ill-fated Indiana agency, an "implement fund" was often created through a special assessment of the state's members. One agent felt that such a fund would make "every member of the order . . . feel that he has an interest in [the agency] and the success of the business." Unfortunately for this development, the lax collection of the levy by officials made the fund woefully inadequate. Kniffen noted the institutional limits of the Grange in enforcing this communal consumer ethos: "Do not say that the Grange is a failure. It is a grand success. . . . The failure, so far as there is any, is in the men—in the material composing the Grange, not the Grange principles. . . . A Grange society organized purely from selfish motives and personal agreement can never succeed." The farmer's traditional dislike of commission agents worked against many of these Grange-sponsored businessmen. Hesitancy of the membership to pay competitive salaries, provide adequate operational funds, and allow legitimate profits to pass along to the middleman worked against the order's larger goals.[13]

While not directly related to purchasing options, the diverse social agenda of the order lessened the concentration that was applied to these operational complexities. The demise of the Marion Grange (see chapter 4) was an extreme example of how the purchasing activities often worked counter to the social purposes of the order. Moreover, the complex agenda pursued by state and local chapters lessened their ability to coordinate purchasing activities. Chapters were working to create a department of agriculture, establish state agricultural colleges and experimental stations, free rural mail delivery, and parcel post, as well as "many other [programs] of lesser importance or too numerous to mention." Participation by women and children also broadened the pursuits of the order. As one Wisconsin chapter noted, it was "hard for parents to leave children below [the age of fourteen] home alone, so a Juvenile Grange was organized for them, under the guidance of a Matron. Thus the whole family can come to our meetings and the youngsters receive great training and enjoyment." Picnics, parades, dances, Fourth of July and Christmas celebrations, and Grange ritual, while legitimate pursuits of this social union, also competed with the time and energy available for the purchasing effort.[14]

On top of these social digressions were the tensions caused by incessant conflict between local and centralized authority. Midwestern farmers resisted the push by state and national leaders to enhance centralization. One clear example of this trend was the sudden and unsanctioned formation of county "Pamona" granges and county councils that sought to redirect power toward local Patrons. Thomas A. Woods discovered that "although the councils were not authorized under the national constitution, members found that they were essential to pool the orders of county subordinate granges." The independent purchasing activities of the subordinates were in step with this trend. In 1873 and 1874, the Champaign County Pamona Grange found that they were capable of negotiating discounts for clothing and general merchandise on their own. State leaders had to contend with these hierarchical tensions in providing the state agency with a suitable implement fund. Wisconsin executive committee member H. D. Hitt reported that while "it is thought by some of the brethren that [the implement fund] had better be left to our county organizations . . . on full consideration I am satisfied that the central power in this department should rest in your Executive Committee. From them an inexpensive and simple channel may be devised through which this business may be carried into the county organizations."[15]

A good example of these opposing and often paradoxical local stances was the Nettle Creek Grange, of Dalton, Indiana. The members believed that the formation of a Grange store was essential to their order, but the various local communities argued over the actual placement of the depot. One organizer lamented "we have conferred with Little Creek Grange but did not receive much encouragement, some members promise to take stock if it is located at Dalton, some would take stock only if certain persons could manage it, &c." While the locals debated the physical site, two regional wholesalers attempted to pick off hesitant Grangers by offering slight discounts on their merchandise. Patrons ultimately rejected these offers, basing themselves instead on the supporting tenets of rural consumerism: communal action and individual, demand-driven consumption. One member reported: "After mature deliberation we give it as our opinion that members of the order will not be benefitted by making a contract with either of [the wholesalers] because each [on the committee] have a preference as to which place to trade . . . & because we believe we can by clubbing together make purchases on better terms than we could with either." In the end, Little Creek set up its local store to defend the members' rights as consumers, "because neither of the above persons kept goods that will give persons a chance to have a choice of goods and one frequently could not obtain what they wished."[16]

Clearly, by 1875 the Grange-sponsored purchasing-agency policy was at a crossroads. While the issues facing the department were thorny, the rationale for collective consumer practices remained sound. The demand for a delicate balance between market individualism and communal solidarity was credible because of the widespread belief in the principles of the rural consumer ethos. The fact that a great number of purchasing agencies had been generated, well before the national grange even attempted to lend a centralized, institutional equilibrium, testifies to the potential of this grassroots conception. The plan for regional supply houses in Chicago, New York, and New Orleans was a workable one, had the national grange showed as much agility as its local affiliates.[17]

Adams's call to action in 1874 indicated that the national grange indeed intended to respond to the need for "combined co-ordinated action." Yet by the end of that year, plans formulated to meet these wants showed that national and state leaders were headed in opposite directions. Terms like *radical* and *conservative* are probably too strong to use in this context, but they can be used to describe the split in the Grange as a whole in goals and leadership during this critical year. The "conservative" purchasing strategies, supported primarily by local officials and state representatives, called for greater promotion of regional, commercially based supply houses: they wanted to see the Grange do more to provide financial benefits to commercial farmers. These "conservatives" were small capitalists—men not seeking to remove themselves from the market but rather to find better ways to profit by their knowledge of the trade. They built on a broader conservative tradition within the organization that promoted the Grange as merely (to use Kelley's words) "[an] auxiliary to the Department of Agriculture." By contrast, national leaders (Kelley, Daniel A. Robertson, F. M. McDowell, and others) favored more ideological, or "radical," plans for collective purchases. True consumer cooperation according to this view needed to be evaluated not on the savings to individual Patrons but rather as to how it benefitted the farmers' class consciousness. The sudden decrease in national membership after 1875 undoubtedly heightened the stakes. The need for a system that was safe (i.e., fiscally sound) and that sustained active membership in the order became foremost in the minds of both camps. Even the executive committee's 1874 report (cited in the introduction) recognized that the agency concept would further erode membership if not treated delicately. The radicals used this opportunity to realign the consumer strategy of the Grange fundamentally.[18]

The radicals believed that the best and "truest" form of cooperative purchasing was a system commonly called the Rochdale Plan. The Rochdale Equitable Pioneers Society was founded in 1843 by twenty-eight weavers in the Lancashire, England, town of Rochdale. It quickly spread throughout Britain. Using ideas popularized by Robert Owen, "co-op" members pooled their funds to purchase goods and services. The goods were sold to them at market prices and the profits were reinvested in the society. Dividends, based on the volume of a member's purchases, were issued either annually or quarterly.

The Plan, as it was known, gained supporters throughout the industrialized world and first appeared in the discussions of the order in 1869. William H. Burnham, a Wisconsin Granger and close supporter of founder Kelley, was one of the system's earliest advocates. In the December 1869 issue of the *Minnesota Monthly,* a Grange publication, Burnham gave the first evidence that radical leaders saw consumption as a way to further the cause of solidarity. But with the phenomenal growth of the organization and the regional flavor of consumer cooperation, it was not until the crisis in 1875 that the national grange gave the program much serious consideration. The "Report on Co-Operation," issued by the national grange the following year, concluded that the "more thoroughly we investigate and understand what is known as the Rochdale Plan, so fully tested and matured throughout England, the more we are convinced that it is the safest and best system of co-operation which can be devised to secure, in business matters, 'the greatest good to the greatest number.'"[19]

Despite such praise, the executive committee report expressed doubts about the applicability of the Rochdale concept in the rural United States. While successful in England and in some regions in the U.S. East, the panel questioned "whether or not the conditions for their success exists, to any great extent, among the members of our Order." The prerequisite for the Rochdale cooperative was proximity to "large manufacturing establishments" where "a numerous working population is compacted." Noting that this scenario was exactly contrary to the conditions existing in much of the agricultural Midwest, it was noted, with some understatement, that "some modification . . . will ultimately be identified" to adapt the existing Midwest system to the Rochdale principles.[20]

The Rochdale proposal was a significant departure from the Grange purchasing-agency concept. Rather than refashioning rural consumer experiences into a working consensus for use in uniting a state or national organization, the plan capitulated to the members' incipient longing for local autonomy. The Plan involved a concept much like that used earlier by the farmers' clubs: the requirement of stock membership in the Rochdale societies discontinued the need for a centralized implement fund. While this erased an irritating problem for many state granges, it further limited the movements' stated goal of helping all farmers to acquire goods more cheaply and easily. Some Rochdale stores were open to all consumers, but the benefits derived were contained locally. Combined with the fact that the Rochdale Plan needed some fairly nonrural conditions in order to survive, the policy in fact ignored many of the smaller communities that did not have access to local manufacturers or a concentration of urban laborers. The Iowa state master recognized as much when he told his members of the decisions made by the national grange to turn to the Rochdale Plan: benefits from the new plan would be paid to those willing to invest ten dollars in one of the 2,500 shares in an Iowa state store. The state agent's report granted that Iowa farmers "have not received pecuniary benefit commensurate with the strength and ability of the Order in the state"; farmers were concerned that under the new system only a small number of depots would be founded near the largest towns and cities. The report restated that the agency's primary mission was to operate "so that its benefits may be enjoyed by every patron in the state."[21]

Further—unlike the proposal for centralized supply depots in Chicago, New York, or New Orleans—the new plan did little to address the abuses of the distribution network that were at the heart of the movement. In other words, rather than all Midwestern farmers benefitting by the collective funding and amassed orders of a centralized purchasing agency, farmers in one locality only would capitalize on the limited purchasing activities of stockholding members of a Rochdale-type society. The former rewarded small, independent capitalist farmers with collective consumerism, regardless of whether the local chapter convened; whereas the latter, the Plan type, assured the solvency of the local stores and the viability of the national grange but did not have much concern over the general, regional, fate of commercial farmers.

Backers of the new plan had no reservations about problems of implementation and proximity to local centers. The national grange master, John T. Jones, proclaimed that the Rochdale Plan alone offered a "deep philosophy, pure morality, lofty virtue, and genuine religion, that underlies cooperative life. . . . The material, moral, social and intellectual influences are in near connection with each other." And others were even more direct in their support of the plan. The Rochdale system was said to be the only "practical application of true co-operation." According to the plan boosters, the state and local agencies in their present form were cooperative in name only. What these Plan supporters overlooked was that Midwesterners came to cooperative purchasing primarily as a means to better compete within the shifting capitalist economy. The social benefits were important, yet ancillary. The national grange voiced its position that it did "not approve [of this] existing system, if system it be." While agreeing to support the regional plans temporarily, "our efforts should be to convince the most arrogant as well as the humblest Patron that self must be forgotten for the benefit of the many. . . . We have much to undo that has been incorrectly done."[22]

In their effort to "undo" the existing structure, the national grange vilified the purchasing agency's role in regulating rural participation in the broader, capitalist marketplace. By November 1875, the national hierarchy was agreed that agencies had fallen far short of the benefits that "could be realized under a more perfect and uniform system." They believed that the discounts were only marginally greater than those obtainable from the usual commission merchants. The national grange proclaimed the purchasing agency, which was the founding principle of the association at the grassroots level in 1867, "false in theory, unjust to our members." Under this system, national leaders said, "instead of building up our Order, we are building up commission merchants under our auspices." In one of the last acts of its November session, the national body voted, eight to thirty-five, against the resolution providing state agencies with regional control centers in New York, Chicago, and New Orleans. The purchasing-agency system, as defined by local rural consumers, was never again considered by the national grange as a viable alternative to the Rochdale Plan.[23]

The actions of the national grange might not have been so destructive to many of the state agencies had they remained simple resolutions or speeches. The national grange, however, published and promoted an unprecedented series of pamphlets in order to weaken existing purchasing strategies. Three pamphlets in particular, issued in early 1876, led the attack. In one, Master John T. Jones proposed an international fraternal and economic union through the Rochdale Plan "by which the farmers of America and the co-operators of Great Britain, and perhaps eventually of other countries, may begin a more direct international trade, to handle at least a portion of the products of their farm and factories." A second suggested that this cooperative confederation would allow for a kinder and more "mutual system of trade, or manufacture, as distinguished from the competitive system of either."[24]

Grange founder Kelley wrote the most popular pamphlet of the three. Priced at five cents, Kelley's bulletin explained how "true cooperation" differed from the more mercantile pursuits of the purchasing agency in that it "invest[s] the profits in favor of those who purchase." Furthermore, the Rochdale policy of retail pricing did not foster complaints from urban competitors; the wholesale practices of the agency, on the other hand, gave "no substantial evidence of profit, but an invariable creation of prejudice throughout the mercantile community." Taken together, and isolated from the realities of most farmers, these pamphlets demonstrate how Grange leaders fell prey to simplistic economic theory: "True" cooperation, under the guise of the Rochdale Plan, may have fostered greater fraternalism than the purchasing agency, but it sacrificed the economic individualism that was at the heart of their (capitalist) membership.[25]

The pivotal operational changes proposed by Jones, Kelley, and others to the existing system revolved around the allocation of profits. Midwestern subordinates had already shown that they were hesitant to fund the delivery vehicle of consumer goods through depots and storerooms (see above); now the Rochdale Plan would demand that these consumers first underwrite the local implement fund then wait for dividends to accrue before pocketing the dividend on their purchases. The national master, Adams, justified the policy of retaining consumer profit to fund the Rochdale societies:

> The system which our grange agencies started upon of giving the profit on each transaction to the purchaser, by not adding ordinary trade profits, is one whose whole scale of advantage begins and ends in this single act; there is no intercourse amongst members, nor is there any object to be attained, or any idea promulgated beyond that of getting goods—at cost price. If this be the only object, it is equally answered whether the advantage be given in each separate transaction, or in the form of dividends at the end of a quarter or half year, while the latter places at the disposal of the agency funds for the extension of business.

In other words, the Rochdale concept demanded a greater investment by consumers and lent less assistance to individual solvency than the existing system.[26]

The Rochdale Plan also escalated a promise of benefits to rural consumers. The pamphlets, by basing themselves on the assumption that farmers would allow their savings to be reinvested in the operating fund of the local society, could describe an upward cycle of readily available cash to be used by members. Consequently, the promise of a global union of consumers that participated in the Rochdale society led to heightened expectations. The logic played off of Midwesterners' traditional biases and paranoia against middlemen of all sorts. Advocates of the rival approach—the purchasing-agency concept that focused on achieving economies of scale—defended the use of a modicum of agents, and even advocated the creation of additional ones (like the state agent). As noted earlier, one Illinois farmer succinctly stated this in 1873: "We are not unwilling to support a sufficient number of middle men to do the business, but we do not want such a host of barnacles sticking to our ship." The Rochdale Plan's promise to sail in a ship without barnacles was in fact a reworked utopian-socialist dream of sheltering consumers from the squalls and eddies of market capitalism.[27]

If the rapid collapse of the Illinois, Iowa, and Indiana purchasing agencies hints at causes other than the directional changes of the national leadership, then the slow death of the Wisconsin purchasing agency more clearly points to such forces. The Wisconsin State Grange successfully operated under the purchasing-agency concept until 1882, surely aided in its longevity by the state's relative isolation. Removed from the constant pressures of urban suppliers, the state agency was able to operate profitably throughout the decade; while suffering from localism and underfunding, it did not succumb to these forces. The proceedings of the state grange demonstrate how the competing consumer philosophies clashed as the agency was buffeted by operational and institutional changes. The battles fought by Wisconsin Patrons dedicated to returning the order to its "founding" social principles were representative of those at the national level.

The Wisconsin State Grange was organized in Ripon on 10 December 1872. For four months, H. E. Huxley held two positions: he was both the state secretary and the purchasing agent. At that time, Huxley resigned as agent and the body elected Osborn, who was from Oshkosh, in his place. Osborn, who was also chairman of the executive committee, was central to the development and leadership of the agency from 1873 until 1875. He helped create the insurgent subordinate "county councils," which provided local funding for purchasing activities, and actively promoted the growth of the order; for example he addressed three hundred prospective members at Ripon in 1873, and shepherded legislation through the State of Wisconsin government to support Grange purchasing activities. Osborn was state grange master in 1876: he resigned from leadership in 1877.

Osborn's fraternalism was not limited to the Grange. An active member of the Sovereigns of Industry, which he joined in 1874, he worked to form cooperatives based on the "industrial interests of society." He wanted to unite these workers with rural "producers"—members of the Grange. His correspondence with the Sovereigns' secretary, J. C. Abbott, and business secretary, J. L. Sands, indicate that Osborn planned to undertake "nothing less than the revolution of the Commerce of the Country—a pretty big job." This activism was transferred to his duties with the state grange. He was particularly passionate in his efforts to disrupt the territorial agents and the manufacturers who depended on them. To Osborn, these agents were "so well established, so extensive, and so strongly entrenched upon the wants of our people as to have rendered themselves almost a necessity, as well to the manufacturers as to the

farmers." More than any other factor, his desire to see the total eradica-
tion of these drummers fueled his radical vision of rural consumerism.[28]

At the second annual session of the state grange, Osborn explained
his conception of a purchasing agency for the order. Noting that the existing agency "may be considered as preparatory," the state agent suggested
that Wisconsin move aggressively to form collectives based on economic
class. Osborn recounted his state's early and bitter disputes with local suppliers, concluding that "to-day there is no misunderstanding the fact that
[farmers and manufacturers] cannot be reconciled with one another."[29]
Osborn's idealism is evident in the goals he saw for this new consumer
bureau. His proposed union with the Sovereigns of Industry was to start
nothing less than a revolution in U.S. business practices. Osborn was
"seiz[ed] with eager joy and exultation [by] the long looked for means of
relief, the ranks of mechanical labor are to-day marching in the footsteps
of agricultural labor and the very air resounds with the tread of marshalled
hosts everywhere." In January 1875, Osborn assembled and edited the
Bulletin, a monthly publication that he would manage throughout his
years with the state grange. By July, the periodical, available by subscription to Grangers, was the primary forum for speeches by leading members
of the Sovereigns, tracts on "true" cooperation, and numerous, spirited
editorials impelling the order to do battle with U.S. suppliers.[30]

Osborn represented the earnest revolutionary fervor and fraternal intent of the Patrons. His political activism, as aide to Governor W. R. Taylor and later with the Greenback Party, was transferred to the Grange,
where he sought to form a "movement culture" very similar to the one
S. O. Daws achieved with the Alliance in 1886. Yet Osborn wrote to
colleagues of his frustration with the Grange. This disappointment, coupled with his desires for cooperation and rapid change, made Osborn the
perfect emissary for the national grange's "radical" swing toward the
Rochdale Plan and the outright rejection of the more malleable and
market-based purchasing agency.[31]

L. G. Kniffen acted as Osborn's ideological opposite in his resolute
support for this "traditional" purchasing-agency concept. Biographical
data on Kniffen is scant, but from grange records it is clear that he was
both a farmer and businessman from the town of Tomah in Monroe
County, Wisconsin. He was the elected representative for his community
at the state sessions. Kniffen was appointed state purchasing agent upon
the sudden death of Adelmorn Sherman in June 1875. Voted into the

post the following year, Kniffen held the elected office until he was forced from the order in 1890. His business experience apparently was extensive. He declared that he had "over fifteen years as a manufacturer, and devoted much time to handling a large corps of agents, I know the pro and con of selling goods." This training gave him an exacting manner when dealing with the purchasing agency. His articles in Osborn's state-grange *Bulletin* reflected a strong belief in the "laws of commercial relations." Patrons could benefit from these principles, but only through the collective power of the agency. As agent, Kniffen demanded that expenses be paid promptly, circulars and other advertisements be used to promote business, and that his column in the *Bulletin* be devoted to boosting trade. Agent Kniffen frequently visited the subordinates in order to promote the purchasing-agency concept. He was most pleased by the fact that "the granges always patronize us after we visit them," rather than from any increase in social fraternalism ancillary to his mission.[32]

Most significantly, Kniffen's level-headed administration kept the agency solvent when other states suffered from mismanagement and neglect. For example, Kniffen was the driving force behind the early use of national grange funds to support the state agency. Additionally, he lectured his peers in the Wisconsin State Grange about the necessity of promoting and maintaining the state implement fund. Kniffen's belief in a reasoned and moral approach to the agency was revealed in an article published in May 1875:

> When we entered upon this position we laid aside our individualism. We have no pet plan to promulgate. In every business transaction we endeavor to act for the individual Patron, the same as he would act for himself, standing in our place keeping in mind our duty to the whole Order. . . . It is a fact that we have been so long in the habit of judging commercial institutions and stores by the glitter and tinsel they display in their shop windows, and magnifying men by the office or position they hold, that we have become like moths flickering around the light of a candle, and occasionally get singed. Should not the Grange teach Patrons the true value of implements and merchandise?

These and other examples suggest that Kniffen believed in the purchasing-agency concept as it was originally conceived: a subtle combination of community and individualism, of cooperation and capitalism. Kniffen represented an agency that reflected the conflicting aspects of rural life, not one that demanded adherence to a doctrine intended to avoid these tensions.[33]

By all appearances, Kniffen and Osborn should have been closely allied. Both were representative of their managerial brethren in that they were white, native-born, middle-aged males with middling to above-average economic prospects (much like the leading elites in the Georgia State Grange as described by Steven Hahn). Further, Osborn and Kniffen both had extensive retail experience, in Oshkosh and Tomah, respectively. Although Osborn's political affiliations indicate that he was more partisan than his successor, Kniffen on occasion voiced his belief that the public ballot was sometimes preferable to the often cloistered protest of the order. Their similarities notwithstanding, they held unequivocally opposing views on the purchasing-agency issue: the established purchasing-agency system versus the Rochdale Plan.[34]

The clash between Kniffen and Osborn did not occur at a personal level, but only in their different approaches to the role of the state agency. In correspondence, the two were cordial, and they cooperated frequently. True, there was an attack on the agent by his aide, who wrote to Osborn: "There is something about Kniffen in [the purchasing agency] I don't like. . . . I see mischief in his eye and danger in his actions. . . . Keep your eye on the purchasing agency there is blood there. . . . if you let Kniffen beat you I shall again have the unpleasantness of knowing that it is your own fault. Caution and grit is about which is wanted." But Osborn publicly defended his successor against most complaints. It was not until the pressures, such as decreasing membership, competition, and rising localism, began to multiply that the two split in their general support for the agency. There is no need here to invent an unnecessarily stark dichotomy in order to better understand the past: in this instance, Kniffen and Osborn did indeed offer antithetical goals for a single institution.[35]

In 1876, Osborn demonstrated his frustration with the purchasing-agency concept by turning to the Rochdale Plan. In a letter to Huxley (the state's first agent), Osborn decried the agency for involving the grange with hated manufacturers and other "outside parties, to a degree which interferes with that absolute freedom of control which . . . is imperative in our affairs." To another Granger, H. D. Hitt, he flatly stated: "I do not like the commission business inside of the Grange." By April 1876, Osborn actively promoted the replacement policy advocated by the national grange. He often specified Kelley's "little pamphlet on Cooperation" as a vital tool to educate local consumers. Osborn favored the philosophy of "true cooperation," as defined in the Rochdale Plan, over the more mundane state agency when instructing subordinates.[36]

Kniffen's defense of the agency was utilitarian. At the 1876 annual session, he noted that the funding policies of the agencies in the Midwest were the key source of concern. Citing as exemplar the loan secured from the national grange, Kniffen recounted the "great advantage which the very moderate sum of money placed at his disposal has been to the agency." Appealing to members of the Wisconsin assembly, he added: "It is of paramount importance that this agency, already successfully established, should receive your fostering care." In response to the intense call for change, based largely on the utopian promises of a global union, Kniffen wrote in the *Bulletin* in July 1877 that while the grange could "look for the coming of a financial savior [it] must not expect some Moses to lead us out of our financial wilderness of debt. We must save ourselves by laboring earnestly, economizing frugally, and voting intelligently." The purchasing agency in Wisconsin survived the era of institutional reconstruction largely due to Kniffen's fiscal conservatism and business experience.[37]

Notions of "true cooperation" and the "false theory" of the current purchasing agency were, however, gaining in popular currency. The pamphlet campaign of the national grange led the way, and in Wisconsin, the *Bulletin,* under Osborn's direction, subtly increased its attacks on the purchasing-agency concept. In September 1877, an editorial spelled out the "Distinction Between Joint-Stockism and Co-Operation." Joint-stockism, or independent stock companies formed by local, usually well-to-do, farmers, fostered only individualism motivated by profit. On the other hand, true cooperation in the form of the Rochdale Plan lifted members "above the murky atmosphere of false pretenses, of personal aims and selfish cares . . . into a purer air, bright with the vision of the true, the just, and the good." Given the goals of the current purchasing agency to aid the bottom line of commercial farmers, only the most forgiving reader could fail to lump the existing system in with the stock companies.[38]

Wisconsin reformers called for change in several ways. Osborn pressed the grange to merge their agency with that of the Sovereigns of Industry and turn toward their unique cooperative ethos. Others, such as State Master H. C. Sherman, echoed the sentiments of national grange leaders who recommended the complete discontinuance of the department. He effused that the Rochdale Plan was a sure panacea for debt among our farmers; as a sure cure for strikes and mobs; as the harbinger of peace and plenty among all classes of laborers. Hundreds, and I may say thousands of men are in possession of a home today in England, Scotland, and Wales, who never put the sum of one dollar directly to the purchase of that home, simply permitting the profits on the household necessities to be applied to the purchase or building of the same. Fathers, mothers, and children, weep with joy and sing loud hallelujahs in praise of co-operation. What is good for England's poor, hard-worked, half-paid sons of toil, surely ought to be good for America's hard-worked, doubly-taxed, interest-eaten, agent-ridden, monopoly-bound farmers.

Sherman's florid prose presented a vivid comparison if seen against the stark savings of the existing agency. Yet a more somber development for advocates of the purchasing-agency concept was the move to withdraw the implement fund from Kniffen's use. Thomas Wilcock, now master of the La Valle Grange, led the call for the restitution of funds for their use in forming local Rochdale societies.[39]

Kniffen was able to defend the state agency from these attacks, but the Wisconsin State Grange was irrecoverably split on the issue after 1877. Kniffen argued that the "innumerable little Grange stores" allied to the agency concept were "almost invariably prosperous and profitable." Stripped to only the barest essentials in order to provide services locally, these "stores [were] safe from all competition . . . [because the] more opposition hurled against them, the greater the reduction in prices to defeat them, the more their customers benefitted by a general reduction in cost of supplies." It is important to note that the reduction of prices and increased access to a greater variety of goods were often seen as signs of success by the agency. While this ability to purchase goods selectively—today at the grange store, tomorrow at a traditional provider—severely undermined the solvency of many state purchasing agencies, it is consistent with the more conservative, original intention of the cooperative movement. Kniffen maintained that the purchasing-agency concept was never based on abstract rules, nor did it rely on the "recommend[ation] or advoca[cy] to any extent by Grange authority . . . [but] have come naturally into existence as the necessity of the hour."

By contrast, each Rochdale store had to turn a consistent profit in order to pay dividends on the large, up-front cost to its stockholders.

Often, Rochdale stores focused on only a few products that were habitually desired by the farm community. Unable to benefit by the collective effects of a coordinated purchasing strategy, which could harmonize many
of the local idiosyncracies of supply and demand, Rochdale societies were
subject to isolated marketing tactics aimed at destabilizing the individual
outlets. Kniffen warned that competing firms might "sell groceries at cost
leaving the Grange store no margin of profit whatever at competing
prices." Kniffen concluded that "with less capital than is necessary or less
experience and ability available, it would appear that the little store in
connection with the Grange had better be adhered to."[40]

Kniffen's arguments carried the day, but clear lines had been drawn
between state leaders. Most obvious was the departure of Osborn from
the grange hierarchy. After his proposition to unite with the Sovereigns
through the Rochdale Plan failed, Osborn resigned from the executive
committee. He then led a group of prominent Grangers, including Huxley, in forming an independent "Industrial and Provident Society" in alliance with local Sovereigns. Ironically, by this time the radical leadership
at national level was also either gone or in eclipse. Still, the damage had
been done.[41]

Between 1879 and 1882, Kniffen faced a constant assault on his
agency by members who favored the Rochdale Plan. These Grangers, unable to malign Kniffen's reliable accounting practices, forced repeated resolutions to the floor demanding the return of the implement fund. Seeing
Kniffen as an obstacle to reform, they tried a series of procedural maneu-
vers to make the state-agency post an appointed position, tenured for only
one year, rather than an elected one with no limitation on length of service. Again and again, Kniffen publicly defended his position using the
"logic" of market capitalism and the need for concentration of assets (i.e.,
keeping the implement fund). He avowed that "business is only business
the world over, and it is not different whether under Grange auspices, private firms, corporations, or co-operations." To Kniffen, the "foundation"
of the U.S. economy "rests on this basis: capital, responsibility, and confidence." Accordingly, stores with "limited capital, and limited responsibility, must necessarily be a limited operator. Our successful grange
operations are those that have not been backed by limited capital, but by a
lien on the honor, capital, and full responsibility of parties contracting for
goods." Kniffen's repeated annual reelection as state agent suggests that
his views most clearly reflected the majority opinion of the Wisconsin
rank-and-file.[42]

By 1882, however, the oppositional tactics successfully undermined the state agency through lost membership and financial support. As locals were instructed to open Rochdale societies, they withdrew their support of the general implement fund. In 1879, in an effort to disarm opponents of their most effective weapon, Kniffen proposed that the agency be made fiscally self-sufficient by giving it a small commission on sales, but in 1881 a deficit at the bureau opened the way for opponents to dissolve the agency. Kniffen reacted sharply to the "personal onslaught" on his stricken bureau. Having been exonerated from blame by the executive committee, Kniffen held that the charges against the agency "had no foundation—in fact were made only for effect." But the attacks proved to be effective. The following year the implement fund was returned to the regional agents (elected Grange officials at local levels who handled the paperwork) and Kniffen was left only a nominal reservoir with which to keep his office operational.[43]

Kniffen lingered as state agent until 1890, but the agency concept never again approached the level of the 1870s. Without independent funding, the agency merely created an additional layer of bureaucracy and overhead for farmers seeking bulk purchases. Further, by the 1880s, urban supply houses had fully exploited the delays in the application of the purchasing-agency concept by the grange. Kniffen's departure from the order was as ignominious as that of the agency concept: in 1890, Kniffen sued the Wisconsin State Grange, claiming to have been cheated of $2,500 for goods alleged to have been delivered by the order, and in 1897 the case, which was heard by the state supreme court, was settled against him. Henceforth, Wisconsin Grangers were referred to Luis Losse, a private supplier in Milwaukee, to provide for their needs.[44]

Kniffen proved to be a resolute defender of the agency because he understood that it was based on the deeply held convictions of many rural consumers. At the 1882 annual session, he spoke of his hope that "future laborers in this work may unearth the mouldy records of this State Grange and review this, our early labor, with interest and curiosity. Our works will live when we are all passed away and forgotten." Yet what remained after the agency had passed into oblivion was a region dominated by commercial farmers seeking better access to the consumer marketplace. While farmers were not immune to the allure of a cooperative "vision of the true, the just, and the good," they demanded low prices and easy access as the essential precondition of local participation. Critics may charge that these pragmatists were too simplistic, demanding low costs through cooperative purchases while asking for high prices as individual suppliers of raw materials. In my view, however, their unique experiences gave farmers an early insight into the properties of modern mass consumption and rapid distribution that validated the efforts of the purchasing agency. At that time, it was possible for a well-organized consumer group to gain control over the distribution and pricing of many mass-produced goods.[45]

The failure by the national grange was due largely to its drive for ideological purity over "pecuniary benefit." Although Midwestern purchasing agencies had proven to be extremely versatile, the forced march of "true cooperation" drove from their ranks those most interested in participating in the new consumer economy. The paucity of primary sources makes it tempting to conclude that falling membership alone scared Grange leaders into the fateful decision that sealed the agency's doom. Yet Osborn's actions in Wisconsin suggests just the opposite—that the ideological movement had deep roots in many of the leading members. Unfortunately for their hopes, their fashionable doctrines failed to account for the wide range of rural consumer needs.

But the failure to fashion "combined co-ordinated action" was not due entirely to a loss of faith. Without adequate funding and accounting procedures, a hierarchical and efficient agency was beyond the experience of these small capitalists. Even experienced managers such as Kniffen had difficulties in maintaining liquidity and customer loyalty in the small markets of Wisconsin. Only the development of large corporations made such internal integration possible, and even·then it occurred by trial and error. For example, Montgomery Ward was not even a dominant regional supplier when his firm catapulted to the lead of the mail-order industry. Many of his larger competitors fell from view simply as a result of the caprice of the marketplace. Given their divided leadership and chronic underfunding, the failure of the Grange endeavors was predictable.

The formation of a collective consumer strategy by rural Midwesterners was, from 1869 until 1882, largely contained within the Patrons' purchasing agency. The failure of Grange efforts was not an indictment against the order, but simply the result of a conflict between the endemic desire for goods by members and the intended goals of the parent institution. Organizers of the Grange were plain in their proposed use of the agency to attract members to their social union. The rapid growth of both the grange and its consumer departments attested to the wisdom of this policy.

But Grange officials were soon faced with the costs of such a strategy. The intended universal benefits and autonomous operation of the purchasing agency ran counter to the fraternal goals of the order. Furthermore, by 1876, the mounting requirements for money and administration were seen, through the prism of a rapidly declining membership, as a danger to the very existence of the grange. The "radical" swing toward the Rochdale Plan was a legitimate response by the national and state bodies to return the order to its cooperative ideological roots. The resulting collapse of the state and local agencies, seen in this light, is neither an indication of the failure of the grange nor evidence of an inadequacy of rural Midwesterners to articulate a clear plan of action to realize their consumer desires.

Rural consumers had based their actions on the communal experience of farm life. The common need for implements, distance from suppliers, interaction with territorial agents, the education gained at the fairs, and knowledge of the distribution network led to a grassroots effort to form a communal policy. The grange formed in the Midwest concurrently with these desires and became the vessel in which these hopes were contained. The failure of the purchasing-agency concept left an inefficient and redundant marketing arm within the order. As they had before, rural Americans now turned to alternative means by which to satisfy their continuing consumer wants. The reciprocal relationship between these farmers and the urban supply houses became the new nexus for the rural consumer vision.

7 Mail Order

*The Commercialization of the Rural
Consumer Ethos, 1873–1906*

The mail-order firm of Montgomery Ward & Company began inauspiciously. The *Chicago Tribune* headlined on 8 November 1873: "Grangers, Beware! Don't Patronize 'Montgomery, Ward & Co.' They Are Dead-Beats." The editors warned that still "another attempt at swindling has come to light . . . and the parties specially aimed at by the project are no less important a body than the Grangers." The "swindling firm" had in fact used, in various forms of promotional material, the catchy phrase "Grangers Supplied by the Cheapest Cash House in America," a motto that would be only slightly modified over the next thirty years.[1]

The suspicions of the *Tribune* (a paper that, it will be recalled from chapter 4, had carried few advertisements addressed to the countryside) were raised not by the demands made by farmers for an urban supplier but rather by the list of "Utopian" prices for more than two hundred articles. The paper was not to be fooled by the company's scheming claims, noting astutely that "the firm boast[s] that they 'make no display;' in fact they keep altogether retired from the public gaze, and are only to be reached through correspondence sent to a certain box in the Post Office." The absurdity of the process (for what self-respecting consumer would forego the experience of shopping in the great emporiums?) was astounding to the editors. The firm claimed "to make purchases . . . of all kinds of merchandise they do not keep . . . [and] employ no agents. There is probably only one man, and he wants to have all the money the gulls send him for himself. He gets all the letters, with 10 cents enclosed for sample, the occasional sums sent to make purchases on commission, and all of the remittances for the trash sent to his dupes, if, in fact, anything at all is sent." The *Tribune* then detailed how they thought the scheme was run, concluding both cynically and sarcastically that Ward will ultimately prosper "until wealth brings renown, and finally, he becomes the successful candidate for aldermanic or higher honors on the ticket of a bummer party."

Although the attack was not grounded in any investigative reporting, an editorial of this ilk had a direct affect on rural consumers. Even though the *Tribune*'s and other regional papers' advertisers did not directly address the purchasing needs of the farm public, rural readers were certainly searching the dailies for suppliers from whom they could get goods more cheaply and with greater control than by current methods. On 8 November, the same day as the Ward editorial, the Marion Grange of Hamilton County, Iowa, read into its meeting minutes an earlier article by *Tribune* editors that similarly castigated "the swindling operations of the Union Furnishing Company." Midwestern farmers were not only acutely aware of the need for reliable urban supply houses but were also highly exacting in the qualities they demanded from such firms before they would patronize them. Only recently have historians examined this rural agency in the formation of urban mail-order firms. Hal Barron relates that the tensions that arose from Ward's entry into the market were primarily based on "rural sensibilities," and that the "attitudes toward mail-order buying became a referendum on the meanings and the place of the local community in American rural society." Unlike earlier accounts, which suggest that the progressive and determined expansion of urban culture drove modern consumerism into the countryside, Barron suggests that Ward's fantastic growth was due to its responsiveness to the existing consumer demands of rural Midwesterners.[2]

Fortunately for Ward, on Christmas Eve, less than two months after the slandering of his firm, the *Tribune* gave his enterprise an unexpected gift. The paper retracted its editorial. The *Tribune* admitted that its conclusions were "grossly unjust, and not warranted by the real facts" and that Ward's concern was "a bona fide firm, composed of respectable persons and doing a perfectly legitimate business in a perfectly legitimate manner." Describing their practice of large, cash purchases, the rapid dissemination of a wide variety of merchandise directly into the hands of rural consumers by means of express and freight shipments, the lack of retail overhead, and the use of a liberal return policy (whereby the consumer is in no "way obliged or compelled to take the goods, or pay therefor, except for his own volition"), the journalists conclude: "It is difficult to see how any person can be swindled or imposed upon by business thus transacted." In many ways the event served to introduce the *Tribune* and its readers to modern rural consumerism.[3]

This tale of urban editors being astonished by the marketing genius of Aaron Montgomery Ward—on a par with the *Tribune*'s infamous "Dewey Defeats Truman" gaff—has become folklore in accounts of modern rural consumer practices. The mistaken impression given by a partial reading of the paper's honest admission of error is that Ward's venture, so well known to succeeding generations, was so unconventional that even experienced urban consumers were blind to its potential. To many trying to understand this exchange, the sudden appearance of these remarkable business practices suggested that an urban supplier had finally discovered, like Prometheus returning from heaven, how to integrate the stubborn rural consumer into the modern mass-consumer society. The unquestionable result of this fusion was progress: the advancement of U.S. business, the material refinement of the farm population. By 1947, the Grolier Club of New York City, a society for bibliophiles, included the Ward catalog as one of the one hundred most influential books published before 1900. They reasoned that "no idea ever mushroomed so far from a small beginning or had so profound an influence on the economics of a continent as the concept, original to America, of direct selling by mail for cash, the mail order catalog has been perhaps the greatest single influence in increasing the standard of American middle-class living."[4]

The establishment's breadth and rapid growth also came to represent twentieth-century American enterprise and opportunity at its best. Teddy Roosevelt merged this domestic conceit with dreams of imperial cultural hegemony when he related to Chicago's Union League Club his experiences in Africa. The former president recalled: "Coming down the Nile—a most interesting journey, for I came out of an absolutely immemorable past, out of a perfectly wild and naked savagery, degree by degree—until I got down to the complete civilization of the seaport at the mouth of the Nile." Roosevelt stopped at a mission station, though "still within the domains of savagery," and was stunned to find "that they fitted themselves with whatever they needed from a catalogue sent them by a Chicago business house." Amazed that in a location "where, excepting the missionaries, there was not anyone who had a rag of clothing on . . . the two things that struck me most about it was the enterprise of the house that sent it there, and the fact that they made good so absolutely what they said in the catalogue that the missionary could afford to buy it on trust with a certainty that what he bought would come there." The Rev. Elbert L. McCreery, head of the American Mission in Sudan, confirmed to representatives from Wards that "the bed Mr. Roosevelt slept on, the food on his table, the furniture, bed clothing, even the house over his head were [all] bought from Montgomery Ward & Co., and shipped to the coast of Africa."[5]

Logically, in later years as a means to promote its contemporary sales, the firm propagated the myth that it alone had solved the vexing problems of affordable consumer goods for many rural patrons. In an 1895 poem titled "Here! I want it!" penned to the rhythm of Longfellow's "Hiawatha," the company portrayed itself as the savior of the poor and underprivileged:

> *Times hard and cash not plenty;*
> *Clothes worn and cupboards scanty.*
> *We must try and save and pinch and*
> *Go without much that is needful.*
> *Thus the hard times cry uplifted,*
> *carried far throughout the nation,*
> *Reached the ears of those we speak of—*
> *Of Montgomery Ward & Comp'ny.*

Two years later, the mail-order house claimed that Gilded Age farmers came to see "that *our way* is the right way, and now our way is their way, and everyone is pleased with our prices and the way we treat them." All around, people were convinced that the catalog business begun by Ward in 1872 was a novel, urban-centered solution to the problems of rural consumers.[6]

The reality of Ward's success and growth was much more complicated. While it cannot be denied that Ward and his partner and brother-in-law George R. Thorne gambled their personal savings on the practice of a mail-order supply house attuned to the needs of rural consumers, the underlying tenets of this operation had deep roots in the established consumer customs of Midwestern farmers. Concluding its Yuletide article, the *Tribune* explained to its urban audience that this "plan of doing business was [initially] suggested by the growing combinations of farmers and Grangers, to deal directly with first houses." Further, "manufacturers have already made arrangements in many cases to deal through agents with Granges or Clubs, at wholesale prices." Ward's venture merely offered the "same arrangement, but extend[ed] the advantage to all persons, clubs, or individuals."[7]

The idea of rural consumerism stoked the drive by farmers to join the Grange and form purchasing agencies. The failure of institutional support for these efforts allowed private concerns such as Montgomery Ward access to this powerful economic authority. The success of the Ward firm, and later of Sears, Roebuck & Company, is visible evidence that the basic tenets of the purchasing agency were viable, given a proper "combined co-ordinated action."

More troublesome was the consequence of commercialization on the founding principles that defined rural consumerism. Private control added a new wrinkle to an already paradoxical relationship between the individual and the collective in consumer practices. The convention professed the primacy of consumer demand, as generated by communal desires and mores, and in the Grange elected men such as L. G. Kniffen acted as ideological sentinels by checking the excessive growth of individualism or communalism in the purchasing agency. Would Ward, the "watchdog of the lakefront," prove to be as vigilant in defense of these beliefs as he was of Chicago's shoreline? What about those who would follow Ward? What about the forces unleashed through competition for finite consumer dollars?

By 1873, urban suppliers were pliable to the stated demands of rural consumers. Suffering from a general economic malaise and the coordinated efforts of the Grange, many wholesalers looked for ways to cooperate with farmers in order that they might satisfy their specific consumer needs. In Chicago, businesses such as Ward's provided all manner of merchandise along terms very similar to those of the Grange purchasing agencies. For example, three days after the *Tribune* apology, the *Prairie Farmer* announced that the new firm of Dickinson & Co., "well-known wholesale dealers of this city [Chicago]," had announced that they were "ready to deal direct with Granges and Clubs. It looks as though it will not be very long before every respectable house in Chicago will fall in line with the new order of things."[8]

Regional Grange agents such as Kniffen, S. J. Frew, and Alpheus Tyner all commented on the dampening effect that these urban houses were having on state grange purchasing departments. Ward was only a secondary player in the earliest period of this new market. Chicago-based Z. M. Hall & Company was the firm most often cited as a supplier of granges and farmers' clubs. In a series of articles titled "The Business Feature of It," the *Prairie Farmer* noted a clear preference by purchasing agents to deal with Hall. In one issue alone, the periodical published letters from eight separate granges that mentioned "the name of Z. M. Hall, the first grocer of Chicago to attempt direct dealings with Grangers . . . in the highest terms."[9]

To understand the tremendous growth of Ward's venture, one must know the history of its founder. Born 17 February 1844, in Chatham, New Jersey, Ward moved with his family to Niles, Michigan, via the Erie Canal, in 1852. Aaron left his Niles job in a barrel-stave factory to pursue retail sales in neighboring Saint Joseph. Ward wrote in his diary: "Within nine months I was engaged as a salesman in a general country store at the princely salary of $6 per month and board." Young Ward quickly rose to the level of head clerk, then general manager, earning up to $100 per month before he left for Chicago at the close of the Civil War.[10]

Ward unquestionably had a strong sense of rural community from his time in Michigan. The official Montgomery Ward corporate publication *Forward* noted in 1928 that its founder "maintained a practice of visiting Niles every Christmas until the death of his mother and remained in close touch with the little city long after he was established in Chicago." Further, Ward "provid[ed] liberally" for local residents who became destitute or found themselves without a means of support. While in Saint Joseph, Ward met and became friends with fellow retail clerk George R. Thorne, with whom he maintained a lifelong business relationship. *Forward* had clear reasons to stress the founder's simple roots and deep rural connections, but there is no doubt that Ward's link to the Midwestern countryside were extensive and influential.[11]

Upon arriving in Chicago, Ward bounded from firm to firm endeavoring to make his fortune. He clerked at Field, Palmer, & Leiter from 1865 to 1866, then for two years worked as a traveling agent, filling orders from country retailers for several Chicago wholesalers. In 1870, working for the Saint Louis firm of Walter M. Smith & Company, he saw much of the southern Midwest. The next year, Ward returned to Chicago for good when he hired on at C. W. & E. Partridge & Company (later the

Boston Store and then Hillmans), a wholesaler and retailer of dry goods, notions, and carpets on State Street, near the corner of Washington Street. Thorne, who also migrated to the big city after the war, entered retail trade in partnership with his father-in-law, Merritt D. Cobb, just north of the Chicago River. In their 1876 catalog, Ward and Thorne wrote that "one of the firm was brought up on a farm, and when of age went into a country store and served there in different capacities for fifteen years. The other served twelve years in a country store, and ten years as a buyer for some of the largest wholesale houses in Chicago and St. Louis. We think our experience has been sufficient to enable us to know our business."[12]

Ward remained close to his Michigan friend. When he decided to start his own wholesale endeavor in 1871, he approached Thorne as a prospective partner. Despite his friend's refusal, by the fall Ward was able to scrape together enough money on his own to acquire a small stock of goods and print a price list. The inventory, brochures, and seemingly Ward's dream went up in smoke with most of the rest of the city in October. Remarkably, Ward allowed his assets to burn while he aided Partridge & Company in the salvage of their goods from the inferno. Still, he was not deterred—resilience that reflected Ward's personal energy, the obvious business potential in the country, and the city's natural advantages in providing for this trade. In his next start up, Ward successfully made partners of two associates at C. W. & E. Partridge, George S. Drake, a cashier, and Robert Caufield, an entry clerk. The three gathered $1,600 in capital (roughly the same amount needed to begin commercial farming operations in the Midwest) and rented a small shipping room on North Clark Street. They published their first price list in 1872 and began anew.

An interesting yet (because of the lack of sources) purely speculative narrative arises from the timing of events following the fire. Ward first joined the Partridge firm in 1871. As an experienced, senior agent, Ward surely desired to advance to being a partner. That he tried to save Partridge's stock during the blaze, rather than his own, suggests that his investment in his own goods was less than the value he placed on his relationship to Partridge. The following year, however, C. W. & E. Partridge reorganized under the name of the Boston Store and gave a large interest of the new firm to a twenty-year-old Buffalo native named Charles Netcher. Netcher had worked for Partridge since the age of twelve as a bundle carrier; he later acquired control of the firm. After the promotion of Netcher, Ward departed to start his own venture.

Whatever the details are in that part of Ward's story, 1872 proved eventful in the development of his future business. First, Thorne, who had invested in a lumber business after the fire claimed his grocery, lost almost everything to a corrupt business partner. When Drake and Caufield, who showed little stomach for the risks associated with a start-up company, withdrew from the firm, Ward again offered his old acquaintance a stake in the business. This time Thorne accepted, buying a one-third share of the firm. A second key event occurred in February, when Ward married Thorne's sister-in-law, Elizabeth Cobb. The connection to the Cobb family was fateful: Ward was (probably) obliged to employ Merritt and Nathan Cobb, Elizabeth's father and brother, as Thorne had done at his store and lumber yard. It is equally probable that the Cobbs joined Ward at the same time as Thorne. Significantly, Elizabeth's uncle Jerome Cobb took an active interest in the promotion of what had now become a family business. This Cobb was the state purchasing agent for the Michigan State Grange and he directed Ward's firm toward the growing demand of Patrons in Illinois and other neighboring states.

The sources are unclear on the direct links between Cobb's and Ward's relationship with Grange buyers. Part of this can be attributed to the fact that by the time Ward had achieved his renown, much of the attention focused on the man himself as a "Captain of Industry" rather than as an opportunist whose ship had come in. Moreover, by the late 1880s the order's prestige had fallen precipitously. Being the "Official Grange Supply House" meant less by this time than being the "Original" Chicago supplier to the countryside. Most of the internal documents of the company were destroyed by order of corporate president Sewell Avery during his tenure from 1932 to 1955. Yet indirect evidence suggests a close link between Cobb's influence and Ward's early actions. An internal company document from the secretary to the "General Attorney," dated 28 June 1938 remarked that the Grange affiliation of the firm "probably" started in early 1872, but that it was "strange that there should be so much mystery about the date of the origin of the business." In spring 1872, immediately following his marriage, Ward made his first overture at gaining Grange patronage when he spoke at mass rally and picnic in Bloomington, Illinois. The son of the McLean County Grange master, Leo Dillon, recalled that "Mr. Ward . . . said if this Grange would canvass McLean County & Get $300 worth of purchases he would entertain the Patrons [for] 2 nights in Chicago & all expenses paid." Dillon's father responded favorably and quickly "appointed a committee who canvassed the county, [while] he canvass[ed] Normal Township, he also sold over $300 and he took [thirteen-year-old Leo] with him to Chicago which was my first visit to Chicago."[13]

What was more certainly influential was the vocal support lent by Jerome Cobb to his nephew's new firm. A lengthy testimonial letter by Cobb, acting in his official capacity as the Michigan State Grange purchasing agent, was prominently appended to Ward's earliest catalogs. It was unusual for the order to provide such an executive blessing. Most Grange officials remained mute in these early years in favoring specific firms. Cobb's testimonial noted, somewhat deceptively, that "having a little spare time in Chicago I called on Montgomery Ward & Co. . . . for the purpose of learning more of their extent and manner of doing business with our Order." He found his relative's company "occupying commodious but not expensive quarters, with ample room for doing an extensive business, and with a very complete assortment of such goods as come within the range of farmers' wants." Further, a "careful examination of their books and business" (made possible no doubt through his close ties with the founders) enabled Cobb to laud the "system" that pervaded every department. While he admitted that he had "known the gentlemen of this firm for some years," he assured his readers that "with me, the 'good of the Order' [was] the object of first and vital importance." Cobb's conclusion is most instructive. The purchasing agent urged farm patronage of the Chicago firm only until the time that they could control their own consumption through the combined coordinated actions of the Grange. In 1873, the Patrons were riding a wave of optimism over the potential for their collective strategies. Ward's appeal to the Grange showed a clear deference to these hopes. Cobb was pointed that "in our attempt to inaugurate a better system, [the grange was] compelled to apply the convincing argument of ordering supplies, for a time," to private firms "where we can obtain [goods] at wholesale rates for cash." Unquestionably, the Granger was supporting the underlying concepts of Ward's endeavor, not his company per se.[14]

Cobb's countenance had its intended effect. As long as the order continued to evince credible efforts at displacing these private suppliers, much of the rural consuming public remained true to the vision of the Grange-sustained purchasing-agency system. For example, while the *Prairie Farmer* championed Ward as a man of "considerable business tact, and bearing a reputation for honesty and promptness," they flatly stated that they "do not recommend the firm, [but] are only stating what we learn and believe about them. In general, we caution Granges and Clubs against these specious schemes and offers." They held that the Grange purchasing agent, "whose competency and honesty are above question," were the proper contacts for "these organizations to tie to." By the first quarter of 1876, as the national grange turned away from its own centralized purchasing operations, Ward's catalogs still relied on passionate endorsements by prominent leaders such as Dudley Adams, Oliver Kelley, Illinois state agent S. J. Frew, and Wisconsin's H. E. Huxley. One local grange organizer, John P. Jones, of Benson, Illinois, reflected the tremendous confidence instilled in farmers by these official commendations. Jones requested additional catalogs for his Grange affiliates, for of late he was "besieged by dozens of men, since the receipt of your goods, for your Catalogs, and I have but one left."[15]

From the time of his marriage and formal association with Thorne and the Cobb family in 1872 until the dissolution of the national grange purchasing strategy in 1876, Ward firmly hitched his enterprise to the institution of the Grange. Far from being a pragmatic, urban solution to the problems of rural consumers, Montgomery Ward & Company was a logical extension of the Grange efforts, which were in turn based on the tenets of rural consumerism. As with their organizational focus on rural patrons, this ideological indebtedness can also be traced to the concerns that had been voiced by farmers for the better part of thirty years. The rural consumer ethos was transplanted onto the pages of the Ward catalogs for all to see.

Consumer beliefs such as those expressed by Midwestern farmers often sound like platitudes when set in the corporate arena. While it is tempting for modern, more cynical readers to disregard these maxims as superficial pandering to egotistical consumers, in the context of this early date they should be accorded greater respect. Throughout the 1870s, Grange activity created palpable strife between the various social and economic elements of the region. As we saw happening in Ripon, Wisconsin, cooperative stores and their related ideological precepts alienated many urban patrons and upset traditional distribution patterns. By forcefully stating their allegiance to the popular adages of the rural philosophy, the Ward firm assumed enemies where none need exist. These "illogical" economic actions substantiate the claim that farmers' purchasing beliefs were the bedrock upon which Ward's mail-order business was based.

Most discernible was the central role that consumer demand played in the shaping of Ward's policies. The catalog was structured in such a way as to present merchandise as a means of meeting customer expectations; it was not simply an aggregation of random advertisements. Beginning in 1875, Montgomery Ward committed itself to a series of procedures intended to ensure that their patrons' wishes always guided corporate behavior. Most notably was the money-back guarantee that allowed dissatisfied shoppers to return goods deemed unacceptable. While the policy was probably copied by Ward from the guarantee pioneered in 1866 by Marshall Field, Potter Palmer, and Levi Z. Leiter (during which time Ward clerked for that firm), Ward's commitment went beyond this earlier policy.[16]

The need for strict guarantees by the Chicago firm is often overblown in analyses of rural consumerism. While assurances and return policies were important, they were only one component in a broader commitment by Ward to respect the wishes of his consumers as to type of goods presented in the catalogs, the terms of sale, and the ease of obtaining those wares. Although Ward specified certain restrictions on sales and shipping, these strategies were always presented with clear explanations as to how they gave the consumer greater benefits from the various aspects of the sale. Policies were constructed to meet the consumer demand for lower costs, greater variety, and a better utilization of railroad shipping rates.

By the release of catalog no. 17 on 15 August 1876, the company had perfected this pivotal focus on the consumer. Through their "experience of past years" with rural patrons, the firm publicly committed to increase the variety of merchandise displayed in their directory and to give more descriptive information of each item. Ward intended to make the biannual document "more complete and comprehensible . . . [by] add[ing] several useful lines of goods to our present quotations, and in every way endeavor to meet the wants and merit the esteem of our extensive trade." Sometimes missed in an examination of these early Ward catalogs is their sparse promotional tactics. Although not just randomly thrown together, in many catalogs the products were simply listed by category, providing the name, quantity, and price of an item. The resemblance to a modern telephone directory is more than coincidental: both publications seek to provide the knowledgeable customer with just the information that is needed to complete the business in hand. In other ways, too, consumer demand directed Ward's actions. For example, in 1876 the firm discontinued its profitable trade in alcohol at the behest of its rural patrons. Unlike its urban-market colleagues, the mail-order house was in the business of meeting consumer needs, not shaping them.[17]

Ward clearly viewed his firm as an overdue reform of the established distribution system. Rather than abiding by conventional practices, the first Ward catalog related how the firm, like the Grange purchasing-agency system, overturned ensconced business protocols. Ward paid no rent for retail premises, employed no "high-priced [retail] salesmen to sell our goods," sold nothing on "six-months" time, and did not use middlemen to distribute his wares. More tellingly, unlike the crass consumer manipulations employed by urban retailers (e.g., exotic lighting and crafty advertising schemes), Ward promised his clientele that he would eschew all fakery in favor of simple business efficiency. Catalog no. 12, issued in fall 1874, implored farmers to be convinced that "we are a house of mushroom[ing] existence!"

> No grand gift enterprise! No lottery scheme!! No false Inducements!!! We simply ask you to trade with us, and pay for what you buy only. It is not customary for people to work without pay. When you see a lavish display of printers' in calling attention a "Grange Annual Distribution!" "Extra Grand Offer!!" "Goods Given Away!!!" etc. etc. BEWARE!!!!

Two years later, Ward summarized the firm's square dealings: "Our motto has been, and shall continue to be, value for value."[18]

But most importantly, Ward's catalogs reflected the farmers' belief that the process of consumption was in essence a balance between individual and communal needs achieved through the application of civic virtue. As late as 1895, when Ward finally and voluntarily removed himself from active leadership of his colossus, the firm emphasized its conviction that consumers "don't owe any [supplier] a living." The company communicated its primary goal of creating an unwritten social contract, or trust, between rural consumers and the urban supply house, whereby each party was granted both rights and responsibilities.[19] For their part, farmers were expected to extend to the Ward establishment a level of credibility that they had rarely accorded retailers. Ward explained that he needed his clients to perform certain duties in new and specified ways in order for the whole operation to be a success. Early catalogs suggested that skeptics attempt a small trial order in order to verify the company's claims. Ward, removed by many miles from his mail-order patrons, assured them that "distance counts for nothing except time." All the supplier asked was that customers write their "name and address *Plain*. We can read anything else."[20]

In fact, rural patrons were also expected to be trusting with their money. Ward was forthright in explaining the firm's particular practice of gaining profit through the use of strictly cash sales. Their object was to "close the transaction at the first entry, hence, be sure and send enough; if you send too much we will refund the balance at once." While the firm did prepay shipping charges and allow granges COD express shipments for their goods, Ward asked that chapters regularly submit updated lists of officially sanctioned members. Further, in the fall 1874 catalog Ward wrote: "This being an affair of honor, and a place wherein we put our trust in the honesty of the Granger, we hope we shall never be called upon to refuse shipment in this way because of the risk of non-payment." Ward kept a "blacklist" of unprincipled granges "and unless remittance are made without unnecessary delay, we shall be obliged to place [others] on this list as being too slow, and refuse to ship them goods." This was clearly a formality—an administrative method by which Ward could control the number of authorized shipments—but it indicates that the firm placed farmers' cooperative actions squarely at the center of its marketing plans.[21]

For its part, Montgomery Ward "pledged . . . faith" to "the people" and promised to supply them "with the necessaries of life, and sell them everything they used at wholesale prices, whether they bought in large quantities or small." Catalogs said that while the cash-only policy might lose some sales, the company was committed to the practice because of its obligation to support the wishes of its clientele. One catalog asked: "Hasn't your experience in this life proven to you the truth of the old saying that 'the Lord helped those who help themselves?'" Ward recognized that as "every mother and father owes it as a duty, not only to themselves, but to those they love so well, to make that dollar go as far as they can," so too would his company strive to make the "almighty dollar" as valuable as possible to rural consumers. Ward further justified the cash-only policy by warning of the dangers of "the credit business" that "almost without exception . . . will lead to the financial ruin of any man." Credit sales, Ward suggested, so common among town retailers, may provide temporary respite for strapped rural consumers, but "time never ceases to roll along —the note becomes due." Then after the farmer fails to meet growing financial obligations, his "mortgage is foreclosed, and you find yourself and family driven from home. It will be no use then to think of what might have been done. It's too late!" The Chicago company pledged: "Our system of doing business will keep you out of debt."[22]

The Ward company underwrote consumer confidence through its return policy and promised not to resort to spurious advertising schemes. Facing growing competition in the 1880s from firms that did not respect rural consumer ethics, Ward reminded his patrons that "we never have, nor never shall, make a practice of advertising goods at less than cost to catch orders, and then say 'out at present' when orders are received." And he warned: "There are houses that do this. *Look out for them.* They are sure to 'get back at you' in some other way." Ward drew attention to his fidelity to agrarian consumerism as a marketing strategy—a competitive advantage found in no other enterprise and a key reason for farmers to shop only with him.[23]

The reciprocal relationship between supply house and Midwestern farmer, based on these complementary, moral obligations, was central to the company's eventual success. Only nine years after Ward first aligned his enterprise to the tenets of rural consumerism, his firm boasted that it was "the only house that ever made a success in selling direct to the consumers, Why? Because they gave 36 inches to the yard, 16 oz. to the pound, and never misrepresented their goods." The catalogs were visible proof of Ward's commitment to providing farmers with the greatest amount of useful product information on a large variety of goods at the lowest market prices. The establishment openly chided rural patrons who failed to abide by their mutual social contract: "The Buyers Guide is just what the name indicates. It tells you the RIGHT PRICE of nearly everything; IF YOU PAY MORE YOU'RE THE ONE TO BLAME. It opens to you the markets of the world, and affords you all the advantages in buying that are enjoyed by the residents of the largest cities."[24]

Montgomery Ward's voluntary assault on urban retailing practices reflected the firm's commitment to its farm clientele. The first broadsheet in 1872 confirmed Ward's devotion to providing rural consumers greater control over their purchasing decisions. By 1898, a Ward advertising executive let it be known that this public battle with retailers and middlemen was one of the most popular characteristics of the catalog titan in the eyes of many farmers. It certainly proved to be profitable. The executive noted: Ward's "best advertising return comes from our catalogues, but one of the best mediums is the talk of retail dealers. They run us down, our goods and our methods. This comes to the ears of our customers, who know what the retailer says isn't true. The result is, the retailer antagonizes his customer by lying about us, and very naturally that customer comes to us."[25] One visitor to Ward's Chicago operation in 1906, Samuel Kaufman, of Thayer, Missouri, recounted how local merchants alienated their rural clientele through their attacks on Ward's. Their action "only inclined to make converts for such houses as yours." Kaufman cited the local Thayer newspaper as being indicative of a growing bias against rural culture when it stated that "it was not the city or town people who patronize mail order houses for they are too intelligent; but it is mainly the farmers, who are more ignorant, who do not know better than to work against their own interest, and in the interest of the home merchants." Kaufman, a Grange purchasing agent, was unwilling to accept such prejudice. He countered that although farmers might "get beat" by local retailers, they were "sufficiently intelligent to quit dealing with the beating party, and know enough to keep on dealing with them just as long as we think we gain by ordering." In mounting an offensive on urban retailers, Ward was in harmony with such rural consumer beliefs.[26]

For such reasons, then, Ward felt justified in presenting his operation as the "Store of All the People." He dedicated his venture to the principles of demand-based consumer control, the efficient and progressive reform of the established distribution network, and to a virtuous and interactive social contract with the rural community of consumers. Ward's attention to rural ideology sustained the rapid, continual, and notable growth of his firm. From their original investment of approximately twenty-four hundred dollars, Ward and Thorne saw their concern earn more than one million dollars in sales by 1887. Between 1886 and 1889 alone, the company received more than three million letters and express-mailed more than eight hundred thousand parcels. Freight shipments, which were not totaled, required three to five "double trucks" every day of the year to haul the goods to the train depot. In 1889, the partnership became a corporation, listing more than a half million dollars in assets.[27]

Ward liked to tell an anecdote that illustrated the growing reputation of the firm. A New York supplier of goods asked for a cash advance to cover a particularly large order. Sensing the manufacturer's mistrust, and since he "did not have a lot of money lying idle," Ward decided to secure a short-term loan to get the funds needed to reassure his Eastern partner supplier. Ward recalled that "Mr. Thorne put on his Prince Albert coat and silk hat and went down to the First National Bank, where we have always done the largest percent of our banking." Thorne spelled out his business case to the local financier and, rather than ask for the relatively small sum needed to cover the manufacturer's expenses, asked instead to borrow the princely sum of $100,000 to send "to this concern, telling them we were glad to be of service to them." The banker was willing to go along with the fun, thinking that "it was a pretty good thing to put over," and the check was soon forwarded to New York City. A letter "accompanied it stating how sorry we were to learn that they were in financial difficulties and, as it was very important to us to have our merchandise shipped on time, we were sending this check which they could put to our credit and charge against it, and if this was not sufficient we would be glad to do something further for them, as we had a very kindly feeling toward them." After four days, the check was returned, along with the manufacturer's apology. "This was my story of high finance," Ward would say. "It was one of the happiest moments of my life when I could take $100,000 back to the bank and say 'We don't need it.'"[28]

Ward's catalog matched this capital expansion. The catalog grew from a single sheet in 1874 to 238 pages by 1882 and more than 1,000 pages by the turn of the century. The diversity of products expanded apace, from 163 items in the earliest catalogs to more than 8,000 by 1882. The catalogs chart accompanying growth in physical plant. Beginning in a single room, the concern expanded to two whole floors by 1875, three stories and a basement one year later, and finally seven floors, with various adjacent warehouses, when the firm moved to Michigan Avenue in 1887—into the Tower Building, which still stands today. The structure, which was patterned after the Campanile in Venice, led architect Frank Lloyd Wright to sniff contemptuously that "Montgomery Ward presents us with a nondescript Florentine Palace with a grand campanile for a 'Farmer Grocer.'"[29]

More telling than the firm's physical and fiscal development was the fidelity that many Midwestern farmers demonstrated to the concern. Stories abound of customer loyalty that stretched decades, a fealty that could be explained only by Ward's commitment to the farmers' purchasing cause. For example, E. J. Nicholson, of Ross Station, Indiana, traded with the mail-order house for twenty-eight years and "averaged a trip to the store each month during that time." Nicholson reported that everything he consumed "with the exception of a few groceries . . . [was] supplied by this firm." He even deposited the commissions he earned from the sale of his produce with the company's cashier, taking the Ward's check for any balance due after paying for his purchases. To Nicholson this was an added bonus: he could return home "without any fear of being robbed or of losing his funds." Even Grange purchasing agents such as the above-mentioned Kaufman were so pleased with Ward's commitment to rural patrons that they "now [did] as much missionary work for Montgomery Ward & Co. as the next best man."[30]

Grange activist Henry Griswold exemplified how farmers dedicated to the community principles of the Patrons of Husbandry responded to Ward's efforts. From 1889 to 1904, Griswold maintained a log of his purchases from all suppliers. During these years, Griswold transacted business with Ward no fewer than thirty-four times, spending more than $657. His long-term loyalty to the "Original Grange Supply House" was evident. For example, despite sending a small trial order to Sears, Roebuck, $3.34 for a pair of pants in August 1895, he never again used Ward's crosstown rival. More importantly, after a neighbor was "humbugged in the goods bought of" an agent for Harper Brothers, a grocery dealer in Chicago, Griswold sent all but one subsequent order to Montgomery Ward. Clearly a special relationship existed between Midwestern Grangers and this responsive urban supplier.[31]

Ward's success must be attributed to the firm's adoption of the rural consumer ideology, rather than an urban-formulated strategy, so commonly identified in the historiography. As early as 1876, Ward's admitted that it was already an "undisputed fact that all consumers, whether Patrons or not, have been benefitted, which fact must redound to the credit of the Patrons alone." Ward responded to these collective purchasing efforts much as the Grange had for the past decade. He encouraged their vision, pleading "do not be selfish, but remember that you are doing your Christian duty by helping your neighbors as well as yourselves; if you hold fast together the day will soon come when every manufacturer in the land will consider how he can best place his wares before you at the least possible price." This was a full and intense expression of the consumer ideology: born of the common experiences of Midwestern commercial farmers, codified during the turmoil of the Grange experience, and popularized through the Ward catalogs.[32]

Inevitably, success and expansion brought challenges to the management of Ward's concern. The firm's response to these trials indicates that the corporate leadership was not immune to the temptations of abandoning these rural roots. By 1895, not only Ward but Thorne, too—both of them steeped in the rural consumer traditions—were leaving the daily operations to a younger generation of men who did not share their formative experiences. Anecdotal evidence suggests that Thorne's sons, who assumed command of the firm, greatly lacked for the "common touch" that had so wisely guided the founders in their early policy decisions.[33] Yet generational indiscretions cannot explain all of the Ward company's growing estrangement from its clientele. For example, it was during Ward's and Thorne's tenure, in 1879 and 1880, that the firm briefly experimented with retail operations, in Milwaukee, and even the employment of territorial agents "in every town throughout the Western States and Territories to sell our goods." When the establishment retreated from these policies in 1882, it was due not to a guilty sense of lost mission, but rather to the fiscal failure of both schemes. Clearly, something was prompting Ward to extend beyond the bounds of the consumer practices proscribed within the company's association with rural patrons.[34]

The clearest source of change in the operational practices at Montgomery Ward was the rising competition from other mail-order houses. One survey indicated that by 1899 farmers were being contacted by no fewer than ninety-eight mail-order houses across the country. While Ward remained in a dominant market position, Sears, Roebuck had made significant inroads into its traditional consumer base. General manager William Thorne noted that competition with Sears "has made old and less expensive methods unattractive to the buyer, with the result that we are obliged to have a larger and more attractive catalog, more specials, more and better circulars, and are also obliged to follow up all applicants to get satisfactory results." Competitive pressures were building for Ward either to discard its traditional approach to customer satisfaction or lose market share.[35]

Richard Sears, born in Stewartville, Minnesota, on 7 December 1863, had no such obligations to established rural sponsors when he formed his "Supply House" thirty years later. But what Sears lacked in market connections, he made up for in salesmanship. He parlayed a surplus watch consignment, shipped to the train depot where he worked as a telegraph operator in 1886, into a mail-order watch business. Three years later he sold it for $100,000. Sears's success was due primarily to his innate ability to craft enticing, if sensational, sales promotions. Julius Rosenwald and Otto Doering applied organizational and inventory management to Sears's broadly cast marketing, leading to the brilliant success of their venture.[36]

Richard Sears did have connection to farm consumers. His having come from rural Minnesota gave him a critical eye toward useful goods and instilled in him a driving passion to lower costs. Sears knew that servicing the farm patron could be highly lucrative. In 1890, when visited in Minneapolis by his long-time associate Fred Biffar, Sears slammed his hand down on a copy of the Montgomery Ward catalog and exclaimed: "That's the game I want to get into—the biggest game in the United States today!" His firm proved to be highly receptive to rural needs, scoring a string of successes in the early twentieth century in supplying farmers with a variety of goods at low prices. For example, when Sears pioneered a line of inexpensive cream separators in 1907, the company booked more that $1 million in business in the first six months alone.[37]

But Sears's prosperity generally emanated from his firm's focus on pleasing the individual consumer without regard for communal conventions. He aggressively pressed advertising campaigns that were based on the maxim "Send No Money." But the claim made by company historians Louis Asher and Edith Heal that "until Richard Sears came along, no one tried to overcome the farmers' doubt and fears [about sending away]" is certainly not true. His predecessor Ward had demanded mutual responsibility on the part of supplier and purchaser; he tried to cut out all expensive and unnecessary frills in promoting goods while the farmer sent payments immediately to keep expensive credit charges at a minimum. Sears's policy largely ignored these anxieties over debt. He dared individuals to use consumption as a means to create their own community based on the products' various uses, and not to conform to existing standards of merchandise evaluation. Asher, who was also a Sears advertising manager, reported that the "Send No Money" campaign was ended in spring 1902 after "the story had ceased to be sensational to the millions who had already read it and who had been educated to the use of [their] catalog."[38]

Sears was deeply involved in the development of catchy slogans, promotions, and ad copy to sell his goods. He had, according to one Sears executive, an "extraordinary faculty" for the pitch, and often "dictate[d] without pause or hesitation, describing the goods in great detail, punching home the sale with every conceivable argument for buying. Once down, the copy was seldom changed." In newspaper and trade advertisements, Sears boldly added lines such as "Sears, Roebuck & Co. are thoroughly reliable—Editor" on the margins of his text. Moreover, the firm expanded the line of goods sold to include a host of seemingly questionable products, including contraceptive devices and patent medicines that could at best be described as hopeful and at worst as larceny. The famed "Giant Power Heidelberg Electric Belt," selling for eighteen dollars in 1902, applied shocks to male genitals through five electrodes, in order, said the catalog, to correct "weakness, disease or debilitated condition of the sexual organ from any cause whatsoever." The company guaranteed that the product "absolutely doubles the sexual force and power" of the user while restoring "heath and strength, vigor, manliness, and happiness." To Richard Sears, the "guarantee" was simply an extension of his willingness to take business risks. If a consumer was willing to admit that the benefits that he had bought into were not apparent, possibly due to some failing of his own, well then, Sears would gladly cut him a check. By contrast, the mutual responsibilities between supplier and consumer spelled out in Ward's guarantees were much closer to a social compact: both parties were working to support a larger goal of trust, community, and honesty.[39]

Montgomery Ward initially defended its traditional practice of educating rather than persuading rural consumers through its ads and catalogs. An article in a leading advertising journal praised the firm for "printed salesmanship of a very high order. In a field distinguished for sensation, appeal to the imagination and emotions, overstatement and questionable advertising tricks, the house has relied upon common sense arguments alone, using hard headed logic and backing up its advertising statements with technical information, diagrams, definitions of trade terms and comparisons of reliable merchandise with unreliable." In contrast to Sears's embellished commercials, Ward's "straightforward talk, giving an argument in a terse and plain manner, gets better results that a more 'flowery' style." But the rapid success of Sears casts doubt on this analysis. Matching its Chicago rival for scope of catalog, guarantee, and use of the city's advantageous transportation facilities, the younger company used its aggressive marketing ploys to earn more than $48 million in annual sales by 1906. That year, Sears publicly offered to forfeit $10,000 to charity if anyone could prove that the combined sales of any five mail-order houses (including Wards) exceeded the sales of his concern.[40]

The catalogs published between 1894 and 1906 offer the best examples of the differences between the two firms. Especially apparent is the dissimilarity in appeal to individual and communal purchasing conventions. By 1893, Ward had begun to shift subtly away from its close association with the Grange consumer ideology and toward quality products. Ward's 1875 circular rarely mentioned quality, focusing instead on universally low-cost and iron-clad guarantees; yet by 1894 listings almost invariably featured quality over price. By 1904 the catalog's introduction stated:

It seems unnecessary to say anything about the prices printed in this catalogue, but there are so many shoddy adulterated or generally worthless goods offered for sale nowadays, that we feel compelled to ask our customers to always consider the quality of an article when comparing our prices with those of any other firm, and remember that we refuse absolutely to handle any but the best grades of merchandise.

Don't believe that we are undersold just because other firms sometimes make lower prices on certain articles. It looks bad for us, we will admit, but nine times out of ten an inferior article—poor stuff that we refuse to handle at any price—is shipped.

In the next catalog, Ward's somewhat defensively stressed that its prices were structured to be low "365 days in the year" and not as the result of "one-time bargain offerings" intended to drive quick sales. It was here that Sears was able to use his exciting ad copy to differentiate his goods from those of his more venerable rival. Three catalog products, in particular, highlight the struggle between Ward's quality and Sears's marketing: bicycles, sewing machines, and patent medicines.[41]

Bicycles were prominent items in both firms' promotions. Each firm issued a special catalog featuring its unique line of "wheels." Ward's 1895 *Bicycles and Cycling Sundries, Catalogue M* and the Sears *Bicycle Announcement* of 1898 provide examples. Since the Sears catalog played off of the Ward circular, it is enlightening to review Ward's method of advertising first. Ward focused on established quality, standard "terms and conditions," and colorless sales copy. They proudly reminded their readers that they were "pioneers in the bicycle business and a sore thorn in the side of high priced dealers." Through sober management they would "enable thousands of our customers who have long contemplated purchasing a bicycle to do so." As with their other catalog products, Ward's bicycles could not be ordered "cash on delivery." Their top-of-the-line model, the Hawthorne Safety, retailed at $65.00; the cheapest sold for $45.00. More copy was devoted to describing the extensive terms and conditions of sale for the Hawthorne models than was used to describe the bike itself. Excluding a dry inventory of "specifications," ranging from bearings to wheels, the Hawthorne was hailed only as "strictly high grade" and "the equal of any $100.00 Cycle on the market."[42]

Sears's strategy was to underprice the competition, meet their terms and conditions, and then use advertising copy to sway those who were tempted to doubt the Ward claim of superior quality. On price, Sears was unquestionably the leader. Their top model, the Acme Queen and the King, sold for $35.00; their cheapest was a mere $13.95. Sears gave no mention of their history as pioneers, but noted that "our million customers in every state" know them to be "the Cheapest Supply House on Earth." Sears gave an explanation for why their prices were so low, thereby addressing one of the chief criticisms against their product line: quality. Citing production control, large contracts, and the fact that their "business [was] not confined to Bicycles alone . . . hence we do not have to look to the profits on bicycles alone to defray our expenses," they argued that quality was not sacrificed for the sake of price. Quality was assured for all bicycles—that is, for all but one, the Cincinnatus.[43]

The advertising copy for the Cincinnatus demonstrates the cunning Sears sales technique. The firm baldly claimed that "the fact is, this bicycle is worthless." The Sears Cincinnatus model was included in the catalog ostensibly to warn patrons of the "scheme trade" in poor quality goods by other firms. Even if the reader had not yet fathomed Sears's subtle, further intentions regarding the Cincinnatus, two things are evident from the catalog: First, Sears reinforced their role as an honest broker by openly describing why the Cincinnatus was a poor-quality product. For example, they admitted that "Quality and Durability is Sacrificed for Price and Appearance. Notwithstanding, we tell you just what the bicycle is." In the description of the bike, Sears professed that "we sell them for what they are" and do not pretend to pass poor quality off on unsuspecting consumers. Second, on a separate page from the Cincinnatus, Sears suggested that one "can Make Big Money Selling Our Bicycles." Sears openly offered a "worthless" bike "sold by others at $18.00 to $25.00 and by many at even more"—and in a nearby part of the catalog, suggested the resale opportunities that their bicycles afforded (this contrasted with Montgomery Ward, who had a policy, rarely enforced, never to allow agents to mark up and resell their goods). Alongside several other lines, notably the Acme Crown, selling for $22.50, Sears wondered aloud: "Don't you think you can sell it for $35.00? Do you think you could ride it a week before some one would admire it? Just tell them you can get them one like it for $35.00, and it will be sold. You sell it the day you get it for $12.50 profit . . . you will be surprised the money you can make taking bicycle orders."

Sears offered terms and conditions for their bikes similar to Ward's: one-year guarantee and cash discounts; yet they differed significantly on descriptive copy. Where Ward's best bicycle was "the equal . . . of any $100.00 Cycle," Sears had "The Most Perfect Bicycle Ever Made." Furthermore, the Sears ladies' Acme Queen was shown with four pages of descriptive text, two views of the bicycle, and extensive use of printed graphics such as underlining, bold type, borders, and icons.

A brief qualitative comparison of the descriptions used for Sears's Acme Queen and Ward's Hawthorne Safety further illustrates this difference. Ward's wheels were described simply as "28 inches"; Sears effused: "We believe we furnish the strongest, best built and most perfect bicycle wheel used." Ward wheel hubs were "carefully tempered and accurately ground"; Sears's were "turned from bar steel, highly polished and finished, and are fitted with the latest improved ball retaining device, such as you will not find on the cheap wheels." Finally, the older firm's bicycles were finished in a pedestrian "black enamel, hand rubbed and polished"; Sears promised: "Our Acme Queen is given the highest and finest finish put on any bicycle. It is enameled in four coats, baked on by the manufacturer's patent process, and comes in coach green, royal blue, maroon, vermillion and black. It is handsomely decorated with transfer and line striping." Only a strong-willed consumer could resist the glib stylishness of the Sears, Roebuck approach.

But it is a final example of Sears's marketing assault that shows them at their most subtle. It applied only to those patrons who had both catalogs in their homes. Within the text, Sears noted to unwary consumers that "if you do not know this [Cincinnatus to be a bad bike] you may pay $18.00, $20.00 or even $30.00 or $40.00 . . . to small advertising firms, auction houses, cheap department stores, newspaper premiums, etc." Even a cursory comparison between this and Ward's catalogs, hardly an "unknown house," reveals that the Cincinnatus looks remarkably similar to the upscale Hawthorne Safety. While such images may have been fleeting, Sears's bicycle advertising suggested that they followed a radically different marketing path than their Chicago rivals.[44]

Sewing machines offer similar evidence of difference. In the 1902 Sears, Roebuck *Consumer Guide* and the 1904 Montgomery Ward *Catalogue No. 73* we can see a complete inventory of the techniques used by both firms during this period. Sewing machines were one of the most popular products ever sold via the Sears catalog: they shipped more than 100,000 machines in 1902 alone. They claimed that "even our competitors will have to admit that we are the largest dealer in sewing machines in America." Using an approach similar to their later (1906) challenge, Sears professed that they sold as many machines as their four closest competitors combined.[45]

In terms and conditions of sale for sewing machines, Sears and Ward were not dissimilar. The Sears 1902 line consisted of six models, ranging from $10.45 to $23.95. Ward, too, offered six designs, priced from $13.50 to $23.95. Both firms manufactured their own machines, or assigned others to manufacture models specifically for their use. Each offered a three-month, money-back trial for those who purchased a machine with cash. Ward offered a five-to-ten-year unconditional guarantee on their machines; Sears promised a twenty-year guarantee, but nowhere in the sales copy gave details of this pledge.[46]

Sears, unlike Ward, sprinkled advertising copy throughout the administrative sections. The way they used testimonials and word-of-mouth advertising suggests that Sears hoped to use all available copy space to promote sales. For example, sandwiched between the description of prices, features, and ordering procedures, Sears invited readers to "ask your neighbors about our sewing machines, for the best proof of quality is the actual test. There are some of our sewing machines in your town, in your neighborhood. Possibly a friend, a relative, maybe your next door neighbor, has one of our machines." Then in italics: "*Ask them how much they feel they have saved by using their sewing machine from us. All we ask is that you make this little investigation before buying a sewing machine from your dealer at home or ordering one elsewhere.*" The active involvement of the reader in the copy is a recurring Sears theme—one not found in the Ward catalogs.[47]

A comparison of the two distributors' least-expensive and most-expensive models again illustrates the advertising schemes used. As entry-level models, Sears had the New Queen, Ward had the Amazon. The pricing information greatly favored Sears. Listed at $10.45, the New Queen offered "all the up to date points" needed on a sewing machine. But in comparing the Sears model with the Ward Amazon, it is important to note that Sears charged separately the $0.70 for attachments, whereas Ward included attachments in their advertised price of $13.50. This made the Ward product appear to be significantly more expensive. The Ward copy honestly explained that "in our former catalogue we quoted this machine without attachments. . . . Our reason for making this change is that . . . nearly every purchaser . . . desires a complete outfit so that every kind of work can be successfully handled." Recognizing that they were in a price war for the low-end market, Ward's compared their product with

"$15.00 to $18.00 . . . machines which, from any standpoint, are of no better value." A casual observer, of course, looking at both catalogs, would conclude that Sears's lowest price was $3.05 (or 22 percent) cheaper than Ward's price.[48]

The sales copy showed characteristics similar to the bicycle descriptions. The Ward catalog highlighted the technical achievements of their sewing machines. They described the "needle bar" as "covered and protected by a handsome nickel plated cap, which insure cleanliness of the bearings, and does away with the unpleasant rapid movement of the upper end of the needle bar above the face plate." The machines also had "anti-friction ball bearings." Sears gave little space to technical descriptions, preferring to focus on the attractiveness of the machine as furniture and its popularity "in your neighborhood." Invoking reader involvement, Sears showed two views of their machine, one with it open for sewing and one with it closed—a piece of furniture.[49]

The copy for the most-expensive models, Sears's Minnesota and Ward's Damascus, mirrored that for the less-expensive machines. Ward's list price again included the set of attachments. In this case, the Damascus appeared to be more expensive, although if adjusted for attachments the price of $23.95 was the same as that for the Minnesota. Ward in this case did dress up their prose, but they kept such stilted descriptions as "the drive wheel and pitman connection are on roller bearings which make it run as easily as any of the other styles. The head . . . has the eccentric action, absolutely positive feed motion, independent take-up, automatic tension liberator, together with all other valuable improvements found on any other good machine." Sears highlighted the beauty, pleasure, and ease to be found in operating the "Finest Sewing Machine Cabinet made." They suggested that those interested in the technical description of the "head, mechanical construction, attachments, etc., etc." turn to other pages. This time using three views, Sears chose to involve viewers rather than educate them.[50]

The Montgomery Ward catalog examined above was issued two years after the Sears offering yet still lagged in merchandising savvy. While price difference was in reality very small, if not nonexistent, Sears presented their product as the least-cost alternative. Whereas Ward's copy was filled with technical information, Sears used pictures, active descriptions of operation, and repeated references to personal prestige, and it is probable that the latter approach weighed equally, and perhaps more, on the average purchaser's mind when assessing importance. The Sears copy offered a product appealing to both the technically erudite and the visceral buyer.

In a comparison of patent-medicine selling, the difference in catalog-marketing style can be seen even more clearly. There was a complete split in approach. In *Among Ourselves*, Montgomery Ward described their "drug division" as "wholly without solicitation . . . a real pharmacy or apothecary shop. It is not a depot for nostrums." Sears placed no such limits on the marketing efforts of their drug department. The catalogs analyzed here were the Sears drug catalogs for 1897 and 1903 the Ward circulars for 1894 and 1902. Ward's earlier effort ran to ninety-four pages, listing every kind of medicinal product from "Acids, Drugs, and Chemicals" to "Plasters, Cotton, and Gauzes." In line-by-line listings reminiscent of the telephone-directory style of the early Grange price lists, Ward provided simple price and quantity information only. The sole bit of marketing came on the back page of the circular, mildly suggesting to readers: "Anticipate your needs . . . keep a supply of medicine in the house because when you want it you will not have time to get it. You cannot afford to take any risk."[51]

The Sears catalog in 1897 was quite different. Where Ward offered one page of limited descriptions on patent medicines, Sears displayed dozens. Ward's Bromo-Caffeine was "an almost certain remedy" for headaches, indigestion, hangovers, and the symptoms of "neurasthenia"; and "Dr. Chaise's Nerve and Brain Pills . . . *WILL CURE YOU* if you feel generally miserable or suffer with a thousand and one indescribable bad feelings." The Sears products claimed to cure obesity, lethargy, tobacco or alcohol addiction, baby coughs, and the common cold. They had catchy titles such as Pink Pills for Pale People, Dr. Pasteur's Microbe Killer, Neutralizing Cordial, and Dr. Beaumont's Pennyroyal Female Pills. Not only was the catalog's advertising copy markedly more colorful than Ward's: what really evinced a difference was the space devoted to such plugs and the pictures that were used to confirm the products' efficacy. For example, where Ward provided a small picture of the bottle to help spur the sales of Ayer's Hair Vigor at $0.68 a jar, Sears offered Princess Tonic Hair Restorer, a comparable product at $0.57 a bottle, using a picture of a woman with flowing hair and the claim that it was "not an experiment, not an untried, unknown advertisement for sale" but rather a cure as guaranteed as their bicycles or sewing machines.[52]

Sears continued to issue catalogs with such spurious claims throughout the era. Ward's 1902 circular demonstrated their refusal to copy the more free-wheeling style of the competition. However, the back page of the 1902 catalog makes clear that Ward, well aware of the competition's tactics, intended to reassert their advantages;

> *Don't be Stampeded* by the "Lowest Prices on Earth," "world beating bargains," . . . All is not gold that glitters. Price and quality go hand in hand. . . . We know all the tricks of the trade, but we have no desire to be tricky. . . . We have been in business 30 years—upright, honest business treating our customers as we ourselves would like to be treated. . . . They know us and know that we want the trade of their children when our children are in command of this business. *Our Word is Sufficient.*

The pointed reference to the Sears motto and then the retreat into touting their pioneering history suggests that by 1902 Ward recognized that the upstart company had surpassed the old master.[53]

On the back page of Ward's 1903 "Price List of Groceries," the distributor reaffirmed their business goals. "*As Progressive Merchants:* We recognize the worth of the proper study of mankind. We believe that a careful study of men and women, their needs, tastes, points of view and habits of thought and life, is essential to the success of a great house such as ours." Their catalogs reflected the Granger and Progressive view that businesses, such as mail-order houses, existed to provide the people a service, such as distribution, to meet these scientifically "studied" needs. Historians of advertising have shown, however, that the modern consumer age was being ushered in contemporaneously to these Progressive ideals.[54]

Ward's implied claim to have made a "careful study" of their customers begs several questions. We have already seen that the advertising techniques in the catalogs differed. What, specifically, was different? And did the new approach reflect a challenge to rural consumerism? In the examples studied above, the Sears catalog bombarded readers with more illustrations and diagrams than their competitor. Asher, the company historian of Sears, wrote to his boss that their "simple, plain, [and] easily read" descriptions coupled with vibrant imagery sold "double to four times . . . that our usual advertising write-ups sold." Historians like Neil Harris have suggested that the compressed imagery of pictures was an important element of the new advertising age. The publication of periodicals in the late 1880s that increasingly relied on this graphic style (*Cosmopolitan, McClure's, Ladies' Home Journal*) and their instant success heralded the new advertising method. Sears, in its catalogs, was clearly more willing to rely on pictures to deliver their message than was Montgomery Ward.[55]

A second difference was that Sears was among the first to deliberately, consciously create demand for products. From the descriptions of the three commodities examined above, the copy styles of Sears and Ward were in sharp contrast. David Potter once proposed that the attempt to generate consumer desire was a key component of the modern advertising age. This "reason why" advertising suggested a change to the buyer's life from the purchase of the product. For example, the quality of a bicycle became less important than the image projected by that bicycle through its color, price, or features. Ad copy moved away from the product and toward the intended affects. In 1905 Montgomery Ward and Company admitted that they hoped to "eliminate the enthusiasm" of their buyers in writing the description of various articles. Sears, Roebuck demonstrated no such restraint, and probably garnered additional market share for their stance.[56]

A third technique further differentiated Sears from Ward. As noted by T. J. Jackson Lears, modern advertisers attempted to involve the reader emotionally. Much like "reason why" advertising, this method hoped to gratify the psychological needs of many Americans for meaning and attachment in their lives. For example, Sears's bicycles suggested life as a profitable dealer and distributer; owning one of their sewing machines made one a community leader; a patient was reformed through the use of their medicines. In each example, Sears showed how their product would make a change in the consumer's life. Ward's ads offered none of this. Roland Marchand shows that beginning in the 1920s this trend came to be the central tenet of modern advertising. Campaigns presented life "as it should be" through the use of specific products. Rather than using their own, preexisting notions of community to direct their purchasing decisions, consumers were increasingly being persuaded to "join" sects of individuals who were similarly swayed by these compelling images.[57]

These changes were significant to the Midwestern population: the development of modern advertising obstructed many of the goals of the rural consumer ethos. Most immediately, suppliers such as the mail-order firms became guardians over the coveted goods displayed in their ads. Rather than providing efficient access to the merchandise demanded by a unified clientele, wholesalers acted simply as large retailers, persuading individuals to take membership in a community of style and conspicuous consumption. Paradoxically, the use of the guarantee only aided in this transformation of demand-based control because it enabled shoppers to experiment more freely with newer and more exotic goods.

Rather than continue the grassroots reform of the distribution network, the modern mail-order houses were active participants in the practices that captured their customer base. Much like the picture windows and colored lights employed by urban retailers, Sears and Ward fashioned their catalogs into portable facsimiles of these consumer enticements. A modern critique of the catalogs by a Montgomery Ward executive supports this point of view. He noted that with their new custom of placing colored prints on both front and back pages, "like the stores that have two fronts, the new catalog now has two sets of 'show windows,' two sets of 'front covers.' This gives opportunity for better display of more major lines. Everything's up front now, nothing in the back part of the store."[58]

The very nature of "reason why" advertising and demand creation reconstructed the needs of the individual in ways that were antithetical to communal experiences. The historiography is brimming with studies that indicate that modern advertising took advantage of the profound economic and social changes at the turn of the century to promote products. Most notably, the use of brand names, even for the most mundane and indeterminate goods, soared in the last decade of the nineteenth century.[59]

Farmers were not immune to the allure of these pitches. A study commissioned in 1899 by an advertising manager, R. S. Thain, of the farm journals *Farm, Field and Fireside* and the *National Rural*, polled more than two thousand planters, predominantly in the rural Midwest. Thain expected to find that his readers were swayed by the spots placed in his publication (a natural position for a man responsible for selling space); what surprised him was the extent of the phenomenon. Thain confessed that "the showing in many instances has proven a surprise [even] to us. We were quite confident that our subscribers were liberal buyers of the best, both of necessities and the luxuries of life, but now we have proven beyond the controversy that this is true."[60]

Thain's study confirms two facts about rural buying patterns at the turn of the century. The first was that farmers were still active consumers of all manner of wares. While traditional and basic goods, such as reapers and flour, for example, were in great demand, luxury items were also bought with regularity. More than one-half of the respondents owned either a piano or organ and one-quarter owned bicycles. Moreover, 96 percent of those surveyed reported that they had purchased a sewing machine; and the 2,143 respondents reported that they owned 2,668 watches.

The second fact confirmed by Thain's poll is that, by the turn of the century, farmers seemed to be greatly affected by the new product advertising. Brand loyalty for even the most insipid merchandise was already well-established. For example, while 147 brands of hand soap were mentioned, 4 varieties (Ivory, Kirk's, Lennox, and "Grandpa's Tar" soap) commanded more that two-thirds of the market. The manufacturers of Gold Dust, a washing compound for general cleaning around the farm, found that after three years of advertising in farm journals, they had captured more than one-quarter of the market. Similar examples can be found for scouring soaps, baking powder, and stove polishes, prompting Thain to remark that the "results of judicious advertising are very apparent here. Sixty-seven kinds of Stove Polish, named by 1,988 of our subscribers, and yet two kinds advertised in our columns control over eighty-five per cent of the trade."[61]

Comparisons of selected catalogs reveal that Montgomery Ward slowly changed its advertising style to meet this modernizing trend. Ward himself gave the last defense of the older practice upon his retirement. He wrote in 1895 that "if a person, through either ignorance or poor judgement, desires to invest in shoddy, second rate merchandise, it becomes the duty of my firm to protect him. . . . I cannot sanction my firm catering to their trade, and much as I dislike to lose a customer, I know that in the end they will see the folly of their methods and in time will restore their patronage to my firm." Yet soon after Ward's departure, company managers piloted the firm toward the brighter beacon of new-style advertising. Twentieth-century catalogs prided themselves on jettisoning the "time honored practice of opening the book with a 'President's Letter' and a lot of institutional ballyhoo."[62]

Much of this "institutional ballyhoo" was devoted to responding to the rural communal concerns discussed in this chapter. One chronicler of the Ward corporation described how the firm's catalogs also turned to the "full pages illustrated in color, displaying last-minute styles" made familiar by Sears. Ward's further allowed consumers to buy on credit and discarded the "old fetishes of art typography and printing" in favor of the more flowery style used by Sears. In short, the author observed, "the public witness[ed] a new mail order era" by these changes "and seem[ed] to like it."[63]

At the seventh annual conference of Montgomery Ward executives in November 1928, the firm's research department noted the changes that had taken place over preceding decades. They asked: "Has our buying public . . . been educated to the point where they no longer regard price and serviceability as the outstanding points? Are they inclined to buy more to gratify their desire for style and novelty? If the trend is in this direction, what must be our future catalogue policy?" Sears's relative success in "educating" rural patrons and the conversion by Ward to their rival's more aggressive marketing style suggest that this repudiation of the traditional farm purchasing patterns was met with equanimity in the farm population.[64]

The advertising methods that emerged at the end of the nineteenth century interacted with a well-defined and active belief in community by a firm's fundamental constituency. Through the Grange, farmers briefly balanced the needs of the many with the economic freedom of the individual. Through the mail-order houses, these patrons hoped to continue this symmetrical relationship. Yet the progression from Ward's first Grange-sponsored catalog in 1873 to the huge, corporate competition between his firm and that of Sears illustrated that this harmony was destroyed along the way. By the turn of the century, the catalog giants openly pandered to the needs of individual consumers without an apparent need to defer to communal sensibilities. Cut off from their cooperative moorings, individual rural consumers were susceptible to all of the dazzling manipulations that the new ads offered. Orchestrated to appeal to this public "weightlessness" (to use Jackson Lears's word) advertisers refashioned the notions of community to include the use of their products.

The commercialization of rural consumerism progressed along three tracks. First, Ward had relied upon his rural clientele for the organizational and intellectual foundations of his firm. Second, the grand success of his venture liberated him from the need to appeal to all of the tenets of agrarian consumerism—most notably, that of individual consumer accountability to a larger, like-minded population. Finally, as Sears gained market-supremacy over their more-seasoned rival, the advertising styles of the mail-order firms showed significant, if subtle, changes to content and style.

The intertwined evolution of Montgomery Ward and the rural consumer ethos is a rare opportunity whereby historians can gauge the potential for individual alienation caused by modern mass consumption. Men such as Henry Griswold (see above and chapter 4) must have been disillusioned by these developments. As a long-time commercial farmer, founding member of the Social Grange in White Hall, Illinois, and loyal client of Montgomery Ward, Griswold saw his community's efforts at establishing customer controls over the access to goods crushed as the new century dawned.

Conclusion

The computer revolution of the 1980s and 1990s has fundamentally altered the way many Americans now communicate. Via the Internet, the World Wide Web, and a host of networking sites, individuals with the technical skills and resources can access an expanding array of information and merchandise. A beneficiary of this movement, Microsoft Corporation's Bill Gates, wrote that this connectivity will fundamentally alter the way citizens purchase goods. In a recent article, James Fallows observed that Gates's "position implied that imperfections and inefficiencies of the market . . . will virtually disappear . . . when we are all wired. Total communications will give us . . . 'friction-free capitalism,' in which nothing will stand between willing buyers and sellers making the best possible deal."[1]

Historical comparisons are often anachronistic and misleading, yet the similarity between Gates's forecast and that made by rural consumers in the nineteenth century is more than coincidental. In the Gilded Age, technologies led to greater and more abundant consumer goods accessed through new and easier methods. These changes made it possible for Americans to reevaluate their association with material goods. As a result, rural patrons expressed a well-articulated vision of their desired position within the modern consumer culture.

Rural Midwesterners were able to take advantage of this opportunity because of their unique economic experiences as commercial farmers. From around 1840 to 1873, purchasing decisions were central to the practice of scientific farming. Agricultural journals and fairs reinforced the important role of consumption in farm life. The tremendous growth in the market brought about by the Civil War and the critical experiences of this conflict further linked this population to materialism. The economic collapse of 1873 coalesced this education into a shared consumer vision that was expressed through farmers' clubs and the Grange.

Territorial agents, as a class of businessmen, provided the mechanism by which this shift was realized. Independent agents and wholesalers pressed small-town merchants to adopt a new conception of their stores, increased the involvement by manufacturers in the wider distribution of their goods, and related to others along the distribution network the transportation limitations of the region. Agents circulated news of credit and market conditions in an effort to stabilize the consumer economy. All of these were attempts to lower the risk that agents assumed in order to get goods into the hands of rural consumers. As a result, wholesalers empowered farmers by providing them with meaningful consumer options. By 1861, escalating competitive pressures and the increased availability and awareness of goods ended the opportunity for rural merchants to maintain local monopolies. Supply gave way to demand as the governing force in the consumer economy. By diluting and decentralizing this business force, agents democratized the control over mass consumption.

The rural consumer ethos forged by farmers was an assertive policy that reflected the unique character of this Midwestern population. Codified by the purchasing agency of the Patrons of Husbandry, agrarian consumerism was lifted from the prairie soil and applied to the sweeping changes that were taking place following the war. As such, it contained the very paradoxes and prejudices that are associated with such grassroots efforts. While farmers wanted their consumer demands met by suppliers, they were less concerned about the mechanisms used to achieve this goal. Communal solidarity was employed as a recruiting tool for many rural cooperatives, yet sating individual wants proved to be more critical to the ultimate success of these operations. This Janus-faced disposition—as individual commercial farmer and as a member of the rural community— was never fully addressed by the farmers' consumer ideal.[2]

By contrast, urban and small-town consumers expressed much less concern about the control over modern merchandising. The experience of shopping was the focus of consumption in both small and large

Midwestern towns. Their consumer ethos, if it existed at all, was almost wholly individualistic. The lone voice of concern coming from towns in the heartland were from those who feared the retail competition from large urban centers such as Chicago and Saint Louis. Small-town advertisements addressed an undifferentiated and largely neglected retail audience, not one concerned about the direction and control of modern consumerism. Aided by professional advertising campaigns and the growing size of local retailers, small-town consumers placed themselves at the disposal of the expanding distribution system.

Chicago retailers did not reach out to address this rural vision. While farmers clearly articulated a new demand-driven consumer ideology through the purchasing agency of local granges, their urban neighbors supported a distinctly opposing viewpoint. The *Chicago Tribune*'s focus on local retailing, agents, and manufacturers meshed with the emerging urban consumer culture as exemplified in the department stores of all Midwestern towns. During these years, Midwestern farmers found that they were without allies in their effort to perfect a consumer-controlled purchasing system.

The Patrons of Husbandry proved unable to manage the operational complexities or balance the ideological tensions of the rural consumer ethos. The institution was founded as a fraternal association, yet its growth was based on its application of this individualistic economic ideal. From 1873 to the end of the decade, the state and national bodies deliberated the relative strengths of the various options. Falling membership convinced many that the order needed to retrench its economic policy around the more stable and communal Rochdale Plan. The resulting collapse of the Grange's state and local agencies, seen in this light, is neither an indication of the failure of the Grange nor of an inadequacy by rural Midwesterners to articulate a clear plan of action to realize their consumer desires. The failure of the purchasing-agency concept left an inefficient and redundant marketing arm within the Grange. Rural Americans turned to the private sector to satisfy their continuing consumer wants.

Rural consumerism was rapidly integrated into these market forces. The mail-order firm of Montgomery Ward & Company, from their inception in 1873, was closely linked to the rural ideology and buying patterns developed at the grassroots and later forcefully demonstrated through the Patrons of Husbandry. Aaron Ward's marketing genius was not in developing a new and unique method by which urban suppliers could capture this farm population, but rather in his compliance with the manifest demands of these Americans. However, his bold success drew competition that was not rooted in these practices. In particular, the new business started in 1893 by Richard Warren Sears employed the latest marketing and advertising ploys in an effort to convert these patrons over to the new, individualistic doctrine of consumption. Sears's modernization changed the industry, and by the turn of the century even Ward's firm was forced to follow in this new direction. Commercial pressures on consumption negated communal mores demanding control over the access to high-quality goods. In its place, a doctrine emerged that was devoted to uncompromising individualism, style over substance, and the perceived exclusivity of the various wares consumed.

Modern advertising was the lever used by twentieth-century suppliers to overturn the traditional and shared beliefs—customs that treated the process of consumption with skepticism and circumspection—of many rural consumers. As promoters created new necessities of modern living, from having fresh breath to wearing a three-button blazer, the general public lost its ability to direct the supply-and-demand relationship. Further, as more and more firms yielded to this recent marketing style, the distribution network became less and less pliable to internal reforms. Finally, notions of virtue and responsibility—which for decades had informed the farmers' purchasing decisions—melted away as suppliers increasingly catered to the individual needs of their patrons.

As with the historiography of rural unrest, this rural consumer angst adds a poignant backdrop to the broad syntheses of the era. As many have noted, the expanding middle class in the United States experienced a loss of cultural control during the Progressive Era. The consumer experience of rural Midwesterners must be considered a central cause of this detachment. In their pioneering study of Muncie, Indiana, Helen and Robert S. Lynd confirmed that, by 1924, modern consumerism acted like a cancer on rural communal values. The institutionalization of buying transformed even the very essence of what it meant to be middle-class in rural America. Rejecting notions of freedom, virtue, and even democracy, the Lynds showed how the children of Indiana's farmers now worked to obtain and spend money rather than to advance their society. More insidiously, modern consumerism left nothing to replace the traditional ideology upon which it fed. Shoppers could only buy more goods, being promised that Brand X would reinfuse meaning into their lives. The resulting confusion in the minds of many only fueled the growth of modern advertising, as shoppers sought information and reassurance.[3]

The defeat of rural consumerism—promulgated by a large section of white, native-born farmers in America's heartland—indicates the strong grip that modern materialism holds over the cultural practices of the United States. Midwestern farmers expressed their purchasing preferences and acted to see them executed. Unfortunately, the institutions employed for this purpose proved incapable of sustaining a subtle balance between community and the individual. These tensions, first demonstrated by Midwestern farmers, remain at the heart of our modern consumer culture today.

APPENDIX 1

Delaware County Granges

As with many other states, the Indiana State Grange recorded grange formation sequentially based on the date of charter and payment of first dues. Granges recorded with lower numbers, like Richwoods No. 68, were formed earlier than those with higher numbers, such as Stringtown No. 399. The state kept two types of permanent records. The first was the charter document, indicating who formed the chapter; the second was of active dues payments for members. Using these charter records, I first tallied the county of origin for granges formed between December 1869 (the first entry) and October 1873. The later date is well within the phase of booming growth that characterized the rapid rise of the order.

These records show the distribution of grange creation described in the text: two broad corridors—one from the center of the state to the northwest, the other from the center of the state due east. Of the counties outside these corridors, only two—Vermillion County (11 chapters) and Bartholomew County (8 chapters)— developed more than three chapters during the period studied. The northwest quadrant included the counties of Lake (8), Porter (15), Jasper (27), Pulaski (9), Newton (15), Benton (18), White (22), Cass (4), Carrroll (13), Tippecanoe (23), and Boone (5). The west-central region included Tipton (15), Grant (37), Blackford (10), Madison (11), Delaware (19), Randolph (12), Hancock (6), and Henry (7).

Delaware County was chosen as representative of a region due to its average Grange activity, location within one of these zones, and for not adjoining either Cook County, Illinois (i.e., Chicago) or Marion County, Indiana (i.e., Indianapolis). The significant town of Muncie, located within Delaware County, added to my decision to use this region in large part because it added additional marketing and purchasing options for commercial farmers.

From the dues records, I noted the location, name, and number of the grange, the first date of dues payment, the total number of quarters of active dues payment, and the names of the men and women who chartered the granges (table 1). In 1873, there were 759 active number of dues-paying members in Delaware County.

Charter members were also indicated in the state records. These individuals are a subset of the total dues-paying members. In 1873, 435 of the 759 dues-paying members were listed as founders of the Delaware granges (table 2). Tracking them in the 1870 federal census, I was able to locate 257, or 59.1 percent of the charter members. The census of 1870 is famous for its spotty and inaccurate reporting, but as a relative guide for wealth it can be useful. I used the *History of Delaware County, Indiana* (Chicago: Kingman Bros., 1881) to substantiate some of the claims of residency and wealth. For the minimum years of Indiana residency, I recorded the age, in 1870, of the youngest child reportedly born in Indiana, and added three years: 185, or 72.0 percent of the sample, recorded at least one child born in the state. For those who were childless or who had their last child before settling in the region, I dated their first residency as 1870. Real estate and personal property values were self-assessed by the respondents. Clearly, the specific values of each family can be questioned, but a rough estimate is possible

Table 1
Early Granges with Dues-Paying Members, to October 1873,
Delaware County, Indiana

Grange Name, Number	*# Male Dues-Payers*	*# Female Dues-Payers*	*First Dues Paid*	*Active Qtrs. Dues Payments*
Richwoods, 68	58	11	3/12/73	19
"No Name," 125	12	10	4/23/73	17
Center, 128	27	7	5/1/73	13
Hamilton, 148	21	11	5/24/73	10
Union, 149	21	11	5/12/73	14
Sharon, 153	57	34	6/1/73	20
Smithfield, 174	18	7	6/4/73	11
Missinerva, 193	48	25	6/11/73	9
Eaton, 216	36	15	6/23/73	12
Valley, 244	35	21	6/12/73	20
Mount Pleasant, 265	16	9	7/26/73	14
Mount Olive, 353	22	11	8/29/73	21
Stringtown, 399	10	6	9/11/73	11
Washington, 273	53	25	7/28/73	14
New Corner, 294	47	18	8/7/73	22
Massinnewa, 326	27	9	8/22/73	12
Massainawa Valley, 329	21	14	8/25/73	2
Mount Nebo, 406	25	15	9/23/73	5
Pleasant Ridge, 514	30	16	10/23/73	12
Totals	584	275		258
Averages	30.7	14.5		13.5

using these figures. Accordingly, I totaled the real estate (RE) and personal property (PP) figures for each "head of household." I thus found that 162, or 37.2 percent of the charters, were listed as property holders. For women and children listed as dependents, no number was assigned or recorded.

The standard deviation is the average distance between numbers in a list and their mean. A small deviation suggests a uniform set of figures. The mean, or average, and standard deviation for the number of active quarters, real estate value, and personal property value were computed for the charter members listed as head of household (table 3). By subtracting the standard deviation from the mean and comparing this figure with the numbers reported and calculated above, it is possible to show Delaware County assemblies that were statistically unique from the group (table 4).

Table 2

Comparison of Real Estate Value, Personal Property Value, and the Number of Active Quarters for Charter Members (CM) in Delaware County, Indiana

Grange Name, Number	Township	Residency	N =	Total RE Value	Total PP Value	Avg. RE Value	Avg. PP Value
Richwoods, 68	Salem	25.5	14	$164,770	$30,454	$11,769	$2,175
"No Name," 125	Monroe	23.7	9	32,400	7,485	3,600	831
Center, 128	Center	19.2	9	47,500	16,300	5,277	1,811
Hamilton, 148	Center	15.1	7	55,000	18,900	7,857	2,700
Union, 149	Hamilton	23.3	3	10,900	2,400	3,633	800
Sharon, 153	Center	16.0	11	60,650	12,115	5,513	1,101
Smithfield, 174	Liberty	6.6	7	78,820	19,155	11,260	2,736
Missinerva, 193	Liberty	17.1	10	49,100	7,890	4,910	789
Eaton, 216	Union	18.4	11	67,260	16,148	6,114	1,468
Valley, 244	Center	23.2	9	44,620	11,008	4,957	1,223
Mount Pleasant, 265	Liberty	15.6	7	20,100	6,499	2,871	928
Mount Olive, 353	Center	16.0	13	52,300	12,820	4,023	986
Stringtown, 399	Center	20.2	5	9,000	1,000	1,800	200
Washington, 273	Washington	21.4	7	20,000	7,560	2,857	1,080
New Corner, 294	Washington	19.9	10	34,800	11,804	3,480	1,180
Massinnewa, 326	Washington	21.3	6	32,000	8,410	5,333	1,402
Massainawa Valley, 329	Niles	9.8	5	31,950	6,600	6,390	1,320
Mount Nebo, 406	Mt. Pleasant	20.3	10	24,200	7,500	2,420	750
Pleasant Ridge, 514	Mt. Pleasant	26.4	9	17,600	7,500	1,955	833
Total		20.1 (avg.)	162	$852,970	$211,548	$5,265	$1,306

Finally, a simple random sample was drawn from the 1870 U.S. census for non-Grange, male, heads of household reporting themselves as farmers in Delaware County. Using the same methods as those described above, the real estate and personal property figures were tallied for heads of household and then averaged (table 5).

Table 3
Means and Standard Deviations for Grange Heads of Household

Average number of active quarters	13.47 months
Standard deviation from the average number of active quarters	5.24 months
Average real estate value	$5,265
Standard deviation from the average real estate value	$2,780
Average personal property value	$1,306
Standard deviation from the average personal property value	$662

Table 4
Statistically Significant Deviations from Averages (italicized)

Grange Name, Number	Active Qtrs.	Avg. RE Value	Avg. PP Value
"No Name," 125	*17*	$3,600	$831
Sharon, 153	*20*	5,513	1,101
Missinerva, 193	9	4,910	789
Valley, 244	20	4,957	1,223
Mount Olive, 353	*21*	4,023	986
Richwoods, 68	17	*11,769*	*2,175*
New Corner, 294	*22*	3,480	1,180
Massainawa Valley, 329	*2*	6,390	1,320
Mount Nebo, 406	5	*2,420*	750

Table 5
Wealth of All Male Heads of Household, Non-Grange,
Reporting Themselves to Be Farmers (listed by township and aggregate)
and Charter Grange Members (in aggregate, italicized)

Description	N =	Declared Real Estate (RE) Value, 1870	Average RE Values	Declared Personal Property (PP) Value, 1870	Average PP Value
Non-Grange, Union Township	26	$133,470	$5,133	$41,221	$1,585
Non-Grange, Center Township	37	242,550	6,555	45,450	1,228
Non-Grange, Liberty Township	26	153,295	5,896	36,440	1,402
Non-Grange, Hamilton Township	21	181,925	8,663	74,860	3,565
Non-Grange, total	110	711,240	6,466	197,971	1,800
Grange Members	*162*	*$852,970*	*$5,265*	*$211,548*	*$1,306*

APPENDIX 2
Advertisements

The database is a collection of all advertisements from sixty-one randomly selected issues between 1863 and 1878 of the *Chicago Tribune* (1866–74; 30 issues; 2,214 ads), the *Indianapolis Journal* (1870–74; 6 issues; 395 ads), the *Milwaukee Daily News* (1863–69; 7 issues; 393 ads), the *Oshkosh City Times* (1868–77; 12 issues; 783 ads) and the *Ripon Free Press* (1874–78; 6 issues; 332 ads). A total of 4,117 ads were cataloged, using codes to describe the advertiser, product, "targeted" audience, and the location of the advertiser.

Coding for the type of advertiser fell into five categories (table 1). "Agents, Jobbers, and Wholesalers" comprised a class that used the ads to describe their distribution of bulked goods and services. A second class, "Manufacturers, Publishers, and Patent-medicine Manufacturers," offered products directly from their warehouse to the consumer. Except for the medical suppliers, these, too, generally offered only bulked goods. A third class, "Retailers, Service Providers, and Medical or Legal Professionals," distinguishes advertisers who directly addressed the consumer about merchandise. The category *Other* includes providers of less tangible services; for example, educational institutions, fraternal associations, auctioneers, theater halls, concert halls, lotteries, and other forms of entertainment. The *None* category (to be distinguished from *Other*) includes those whose ads did not seek a consumer, per se: their ads are public notices announcing bankruptcy, dissolution of partnerships, government auctions, and so forth. Some ads, offering convict labor or the services of a "Magnetic Doctress and Clairvoyant," are beyond conventional categorization: fortunately, few such ads were evident in the other regional papers studied here, and given their lack of participation in the consumer "dialog" of newspaper advertisements, I dropped them from consideration in the analysis of Indianapolis, Milwaukee, Oshkosh, and Ripon.

Coding for the various products in the ads was made difficult in large part because of the diversity of goods. In my examination of the *Chicago Tribune*, I began with twenty-five separate codes that soon became too finely conceived to be of much use in an analysis of broader tendencies in consumer culture. Recoding resulted in the formation nine general types of products (table 2). Given my focus on the relationship between Chicago advertisers, the rural consumer, and the products offered, I did not code the products from the regional papers. Again, a code for *None* was created to deal with the ads that provided general information

Table 1

Type of Advertiser, Regional Newspapers, 1863–1878 (in percentages)

Type of Advertiser	Regional Newspaper				
	Ripon	Chicago	Ind.	Milw.	Oshkosh
Retailer	58.7	24.3	51.9	51.9	60.0
Manuf.	21.4	17.6	27.1	30.0	20.8
Agent	5.7	26.5	17.2	13.2	10.0
Other	14.2	16.3	3.8	4.8	9.2
None	N/A	15.3	N/A	N/A	N/A
N =	332	2,214	395	393	783

Table 2

Products Advertised in the *Chicago Tribune*, 1866–1874

Product advertised	N =	Percent
Agent and financial services	267	15.53
Machinery, supplies for business use, bulk processed goods	253	14.72
Agricultural machinery and supplies	17	0.99
Bulked raw agricultural goods (e.g., produce, meats, lumber)	105	6.11
Professional and personal services	182	10.59
Mass-produced retail goods (e.g., clothing, shoes, notions)	204	11.87
"Home" goods (e.g., sewing machines, furniture, carpets, musical instruments, artwork)	163	9.48
Patent medicines	171	9.95
Other (e.g., alcohol, real estate, printed materials, educational services, entertainment)	357	20.77
Total	1,719	99.99

and notices, such as government auctions, notification of relocation, partner dissolution, and bankruptcy.

Targeting of audiences is a modern concept, and I was hesitant to label it as such for nineteenth-century advertisements. The familiarity with targeting by contemporary readers, a cautious use of classifications, and the reality of crude targeting in many ads convinced me of the applicability of this code. Again, five general categories were created (table 3). *None* refers to the vast majority of ads in which the assignment of a specific audience would be insupportable. By and large, ads without a specific target were for goods that could be consumed by anyone. By contrast, the distinctions *manufacturer* and *agent* were determined by the types and quantities of goods and services offered. I am aware that the distinctions made are subjective; I based them on the style and substance of the ads. The appearance and wording of the ads were such that they suggested an intended audience. For example, "manufacturers" were targeted by products such as industrial boring tools, steam engines, boilers, industrial scales, machinery, and bulk metals and chemicals. "Agents" were sought to deal with bulked grains, flour, "wholesale wool," army-surplus clothing and "mess beef," and other items that were simply too large for ordinary purchasers (500,000 barrels of pork, lard, and whiskey, or 10,000 pounds of black tea). The "others" were an aggregate of consumers such as women, men, farmers, hobbyists, and those seeking information on urban entertainment. In Chicago, this category was the largest, reflecting the diversity of the city's consumer offerings and suggests that targeting was indeed practiced as early as the 1870s. For example, patent medicines and medical practices offered "treatments" for sexually transmitted diseases, abortion, and advice on how to be a "better lover" that were clearly specific to sex. Men's and women's fashions and "Ladies" schools were also common. As noted in chapter 5, farmers were also singled out in twelve of the *Tribune*'s many promotions.

Finally, in some ads the stated location of advertisers was the most clearly distinguishable characteristic. Most advertisers, thankfully, included some indication

Table 3
Type of Consumer Targeted in Regional Newspapers, 1863–1878 (in percentages)

Type of Consumer	Regional Newspaper				
	Ripon Free Press	Chicago Tribune	Indianapolis Journal	Milwaukee Daily News	Oshkosh City Times
None	88.6	53.2	99.2	96.9	95.7
Manufacturer	0.6	7.7	0.3	0.0	0.4
Agent	3.9	23.8	0.3	0.5	2.0
Other	6.9	15.3	0.3	2.5	2.0
N =	332	2,214	395	393	783

of how consumers might contact them. For the study, I identified four classifications: the hometown of the newspaper; Chicago; other locations within the state of the newspaper; and those other than these (table 4).

Cross-tabulations simultaneously classify codes based on two sets of variables. In tables 5, 6, 7, and 8, I have provided percentages (rather than raw numbers) for

Table 4
Location of Advertiser, Regional Newspapers, 1863–1878 (in percentages)

Advertiser Location	Regional Newspaper				
	Ripon	Chicago	Ind.	Milw.	Oshkosh
Hometown	68.7	80.5	79.2	79.1	84.3
Chicago	7.8	N/A	1.3	2.8	4.3
In-state	2.1	0.7	0.0	0.3	3.1
Other	22.3	18.7	19.5	17.8	8.3
N =	332	2,214	395	393	783

Table 5
Type of Advertiser and Products Offered, *Chicago Tribune*, 1866–1874 (in percentages; read horizontally)

Products Offered	Agents	Manuf.	Retail	N=
Business machinery and supplies	31.7	60.6	7.7	208
Agent and financial services	57.2	4.9	37.9	203
Professional and personal services	3.6	3.0	93.4	168
Mass-produced retail goods	27.9	21.2	50.9	165
Patent medicines	22.6	67.2	10.2	137
Other	26.7	24.6	48.7	232

Table 6
Type of Advertiser and Products Offered, *Chicago Tribune*, 1866–1874 (in percentages; read vertically)

Products Offered	Agents	Manuf.	Retail
Business machinery and supplies	20.2	38.8	3.5
Agent and financial services	35.5	3.1	16.7
Professional and personal services	1.8	1.5	34.1
Mass-produced retail goods	14.1	10.8	18.2
Patent medicines	9.5	28.3	3.0
Other	18.9	17.5	24.5
N=	327	325	461

these values. The tables have to be read either vertically or horizontally, as indicated.

Table 9 provides a cross-tabulation between the targeted consumer and the stated location of the advertiser in the *Indianapolis Journal*, the *Milwaukee Daily News*, the *Oshkosh City Times*, and the *Ripon Free Press*.

Table 7
Products Offered and Targeted Consumer, *Chicago Tribune*, 1866–1874
(in percentages; read horizontally)

Products Offered	None	Agents	Manuf.	Other	N =
Business machinery and supplies	24.8	23.6	48.4	3.2	250
Agent and financial services	18.3	78.6	1.1	1.9	262
Professional and personal services	91.0	4.8	2.4	1.8	167
Mass-produced retail goods	65.2	26.6	0.0	8.2	158
Patent medicines	97.4	0.9	0.9	0.9	155
Other	78.3	9.6	1.6	10.5	313

Table 8
Products Offered and Targeted Consumer, *Chicago Tribune*, 1866–1874
(in percentages; read vertically)

Products Offered	None	Agents	Manuf.	Other
Business machinery and supplies	8.1	17.0	90.3	12.7
Agent and financial services	6.3	59.5	2.2	7.9
Professional and personal services	19.9	2.3	3.0	4.8
Mass-produced retail goods	13.5	12.1	0.0	20.6
Patent medicines	19.9	0.2	0.7	1.6
Other	32.1	8.6	3.7	52.4
N=	762	346	134	63

Table 9
Comparison of Advertiser Location and the Consumer Targeted, Regional Newspapers, 1863–1878 (in percentages)

Advertiser Location	Consumer Targeted				
	None	Agents	Manuf.	Other	N =
Hometown	97.2	0.5	<0.1	2.2	1509
Other	88.6	5.6	1.3	4.3	394

Finally, table 10 lists the issue date, the number, and the percentages for the stated location of *Tribune* advertisers.

Table 10
Advertiser Location Showing Time Spread, *Chicago Tribune*, 1866–1874

Date	Chicago N / % of Issue	Other N / % of Issue
02–09–66	58 / 76.5	18 /23.5
06–05–66	69 / 66.3	35 / 32.7
08–17–66	66 / 75.8	21 / 24.2
11–05–66	39 / 75.0	13 / 25.0
02–02–67	83 / 88.3	11 / 11.7
06–18–67	71 / 76.3	21 / 23.7
08–17–67	57 / 75.0	19 / 25.0
11–07–67	47 / 85.7	8 / 14.3
02–20–68	46 / 71.8	18 / 28.2
06–26–68	55 / 82.1	12 / 17.9
08–05–68	48 / 70.6	20 / 29.4
11–22–68	67 / 91.7	6 / 8.3
02–06–69	53 / 76.8	16 / 23.2
06–11–69	64 / 84.2	12 / 15.8
11–15–69	54 / 87.1	8 / 12.9
02–11–70	37 / 74.0	13 / 26.0
06–05–70	114/ 92.7	9 / 7.3
11–29–70	45 / 85.0	8 / 15.0
02–14–71	30 / 65.2	16 / 34.8
06–03–71	55 / 70.5	23 / 29.5
11–03–71	100/ 82.6	21 / 17.4
02–22–72	74 / 81.3	17 / 18.7
06–10–72	65 / 84.2	12 / 15.8
11–19–72	55 / 88.7	7 / 11.3
02–17–73	37 / 80.4	9 / 19.6
06–10–73	69 / 81.1	16 / 18.9
11–13–73	48 / 90.5	5 / 9.5
02–02–74	45 / 83.3	9 / 16.7
06–24–74	79 / 79.0	21 / 21.0
11–10–74	52 / 86.7	8 / 13.3
Total	1,782	

NOTES

Abbreviations

AA   *American Agriculturalist*

AHC   American Heritage Center, Laramie, Wyoming

CHS   Chicago Historical Society, Chicago, Illinois

CT   *Chicago Tribune*

ISHL   Illinois State Historical Library, Springfield, Illinois

InSL   Indiana State Library, Indianapolis, Indiana

PF   *Prairie Farmer*

SHSI   State Historical Society of Iowa, Iowa City, Iowa

SHSW State Historical Society of Wisconsin, Madison, Wisconsin

Introduction

1. For additional examples dealing with this paradox between definitions of market economy, moral economy, and rural America, see Winifred Barr Rothenberg, *From Market-Place to Market Economy: The Transformation of Rural Massachusetts, 1750–1850* (Chicago: University of Chicago Press, 1992), 7–23; Joyce Appleby, "Commercial Farming and the 'Agrarian Myth' in the Early Republic," *Journal of American History* 68 (March 1982): 833–49; Norman Pollack, *The Populist Response to Industrial America* (Cambridge: Harvard University Press, 1962), 11. See also Walter T. K. Nugent, *The Tolerant Populists: Kansas Populism and Nativism* (Chicago: University of Chicago Press, 1963), 231–43; Bruce Palmer, *"Man Over Money": The Southern Populist Critique of Northern Capitalism* (Chapel Hill: University of North Carolina, 1980), 199–221; Steven Hahn, introduction to *The Roots of Southern Populism: Yeoman Farmers and the Transformation of the Georgia Upcountry, 1850–1890* (New York: Oxford University Press, 1983); and Ann Mayhew, "A Reappraisal of the Causes of Farm Protest in the United States, 1870–1900," *Journal of Economic History* 32 (June 1972): 465–75. I found a useful analysis in studying the role of ideology in Barbara Jeanne Fields, "Slavery, Race, and Ideology in the United States of America," *New Left Review* (May–June 1991): 95–118.

2. The institutional history of the Grange has mirrored the increasing hesitancy on the part of historians to take organizational rhetoric at face value. For example, Solon Buck followed the lead of Grange advocates when he found the order to be wholly an economic phenomenon based on the very "yeoman myth" attacked by Hofstadter and others. Accordingly, the Patrons were often castigated as the perfect example of what the Alliance was not: backward looking, illogical, and conservative. See Buck, *The Granger Movement: A Study of Agriculture Organization and Its Political,*

Economic, and Social Manifestations, 1870–1880 (New Haven: Yale University Press, 1913), chap. 1; and Buck, *The Agrarian Crusade: A Chronicle of the Farmer in Politics* (New Haven: Yale University Press, 1920). By contrast, a movement to revise the history of the Patrons of Husbandry, led by Dennis S. Nordin, has shown that many of the grassroots members had vastly different reasons for "crossing the gate." See Nordin, *Rich Harvest: A History of the Grange, 1867–1900* (Jackson: University Press of Mississippi, 1974); and, esp., Thomas Allan Woods, *Knights of the Plow: Oliver H. Kelley and the Republican Origins of the Grange* (Ames: University of Iowa Press, 1992).

3. For similar discussion of the focus on farmers, see Danbom, *Born in the Country: A History of Rural America* (Baltimore: Johns Hopkins University Press, 1995), xi; or Hal S. Barron, *Mixed Harvest: The Second Great Transformation in the Rural North, 1870–1930* (Chapel Hill: University of North Carolina Press, 1997), xi–xii, 7–16.

4. Peter S. Onuf, *Statehood and Union: A History of the Northwest Ordinance* (Bloomington: Indiana University Press, 1987).

5. Hamlin Garland, *A Son of the Middle Border* [1917] (New York: Penguin, 1995), 85.

6. For Turner, a Midwesterner steeped in regional and class bias, see Andrew R. L. Cayton and Peter S. Onuf, eds., *The Midwest and the Nation: Rethinking the History of an American Region* (Bloomington: Indiana University Press, 1990), passim and 125–26.

7. Allan G. Bogue, *From Prairie to Corn Belt: Farming on the Illinois and Iowa Prairies in the 19th Century* (Chicago: University of Chicago Press, 1963); Cayton and Onuf, *Midwest and Nation;* John Mack Faragher, *Sugar Creek: Life on the Illinois Prairie* (New Haven: Yale University Press, 1986). In large part, these authors are highlighted because of their influence on my interpretation of the Middle West, not because others have lesser claim to an authoritative understanding of the region. For more in a diverse and impressive field, see James R. Shortridge, *The Middle West: Its Meaning in American Culture* (Lawrence: University of Kansas Press, 1989) David C. Klingaman and Richard K. Vedder, eds., *Essays on the Economy of the Old Northwest* (Athens: Ohio University Press, 1987); James H. Madison, ed., *Heartland: Comparative Histories of the Midwestern States* (Bloomington: Indiana University Press, 1988); and Susan E. Gray, *The Yankee West: Community Life in the Michigan Frontier* (Chapel Hill: University of North Carolina Press, 1996).

8. Barron, *Mixed Harvest*, 12. For other broad perspectives of Northern agriculture, see Barron, *Those Who Stayed Behind: Rural Society in Nineteenth-Century New England* (New York: Cambridge University Press, 1984); Jeremy Atack and Fred Bateman, *To Their Own Soil: Agriculture in the Antebellum North* (Ames: Iowa State University Press, 1987); Gilbert C. Fite, "The Pioneer Farmer: A View over Three Centuries," *Agricultural History* 50 (January 1976): 275–89; Paul Wallace Gates, *The Farmer's Age: Agriculture 1815–1860*, vol. 3 of *The Economic History of the United States* (New York: Harper & Row, 1960); Fred A. Shannon, *The Farmer's Last Frontier: Agriculture, 1860–1897* (New York: Farrar & Reinhart, 1945), 123–47; and Clarence H. Danhof, *Change in Agriculture: The Northern United States, 1820–1870* (Cambridge: Harvard University Press, 1969).

Introduction

1. Henry David Thoreau, *Walden, or, Life in the Woods and On the Duty of Civil Disobedience* (New York: Harper & Row, 1965), 25.

2. For Puritan-republican values, see Warren Susman, *Culture as History: The Transformation of American Society in the Twentieth Century* (New York: Pantheon, 1984).

3. Garland, *Son of the Middle Border,* 142, 293.

4. For Jeffersonian idealism, see Thomas Jefferson, *Notes on the State of Virginia* (Chapel Hill: University of North Carolina Press, 1996); and Merrill Peterson, *The Jeffersonian Image in the American Mind* (New York: Oxford University Press, 1960). While Veblen eschewed Christian morality, he viewed conspicuous consumption in evolutionary terms that belied a distinctive progressive and positivist sensibility. Daniel Horowitz noted that Veblen saw consumerism as spreading the destructive, "savage qualities" of acquisition within American society. See Horowitz, *The Morality of Spending: Attitudes toward the Consumer Society in America, 1875–1940* (Baltimore: Johns Hopkins University Press, 1985), 40. See also Morton G. White, *Social Thought in America: The Revolt Against Formalism* (New York: Viking, 1952).

5. For examples of gendered clothing, cosmetics, and jewelry, see Edward Bellamy, *Equality* (New York: Appleton, 1897), 43–47, 129; for fashion and luxury, ibid., 181. See also Bellamy, *Looking Backward: 2000–1887* [1888] (Boston: Bedford Books, St. Martin's, 1995), 78–82. For more on Bellamy and other like-minded authors, see Carl Guarneri, *The Utopian Alternative: Fourierism in Nineteenth-Century America* (Ithaca: Cornell University Press, 1992); and David Montgomery, *Beyond Equality: Labor and the Radical Republicans, 1862–1872* (New York: Vintage, Knopf, 1968). For his treatment of farmers and their role in the final revolution, see Bellamy, *Equality,* 240–42, 310–11, 324–25.

6. The quotations are from two issues of *Agricultural Advertising,* both printed in February 1902, cited in Ray Lewis White, ed., *Sherwood Anderson's Early Writings* (Kent, Ohio: Kent State University Press, 1989), 9, 12. Anderson was of course attempting to promote advertising in his employer's publication, so such claims about the strength of the rural retail economy are not surprising. A salient point remains: for a long time, few advertisers recognized that farmers were active consumers of a large number of retail goods.

7. For recent work on modern consumer culture and its effect on the larger American populations, see Jackson Lears, *Fables of Abundance: A Cultural History of Advertising in America* (New York: Basic, 1995), 9–13, 18–133; William Leach, introduction to *Land of Desire: Merchants, Power, and the Rise of a New American Culture* (New York: Pantheon, 1993); James D. Norris, *Advertising and the Transformation of American Society, 1865–1920* (New York: Greenwood, 1990), chap. 1; Pamela Walker Laird, *Advertising Progress: American Business and the Rise of Consumer Marketing* (Baltimore: Johns Hopkins University Press, 1998); and Richard L. McCormick, "Public Life in Industrial America, 1877–1917," in Eric Foner, ed., *The New American History* (Philadelphia: Temple University Press, 1990), 93–117. Also useful are Lendol Calder, *Financing the American Dream: A Cultural History of Consumer Credit* (Princeton: Princeton University Press, 1999); Leigh Eric Schmidt, *Consumer*

Rites: The Buying and Selling of American Holidays (Princeton: Princeton University Press, 1995); Susman, *Culture as History;* Robert H. Wiebe, *The Search For Order, 1877–1920* (New York: Hill & Wang, 1967); David Potter, *People of Plenty: Economic Abundance and the American Character* (Chicago: University of Chicago Press, 1954); and Daniel Boorstin, *The Americans: The Democratic Experience* (New York: Random House, 1973). For recent accounts of modern advertising, see also Roland Marchand, *Advertising the American Dream: Making Way for Modernity, 1920–1940* (Berkeley: University of California Press, 1985); and Daniel Pope, *The Making of Modern Advertising* (New York: Basic, 1983). For a useful overview of consumerism, see David Blanke, "A Selected Bibliographic Essay: Consumer Culture during the Gilded and Progressive Eras," for H-SHGAPE and archived on the H-Net home page http://www.h-net.msu.edu/~shgape/bibs/consumer.html.

8. Samuel P. Hays, *The Response to Industrialism, 1885–1914* (Chicago: University of Chicago Press, 1961); Wiebe, *Search for Order;* Carl Degler, ed., *The Age of Economic Revolution, 1876–1900* (Glenview, Ill.: Scott, Foresman, 1977); Alfred Chandler Jr., *The Visible Hand: The Managerial Revolution in American Business* (Cambridge: Belknap/Harvard University Press, 1977); David A. Hounshell, *From the American System to Mass Production, 1800–1932* (Baltimore: John Hopkins University Press, 1984); Olivier Zunz, *Making America Corporate, 1870–1920* (Chicago: University of Chicago Press, 1990); Timothy B. Spears, *One Hundred Years on the Road: The Travelling Salesman in American Culture* (New Haven, Conn.: Yale University Press, 1995). For the emergence of brand-name products and national consumers, see Susan Strasser, *Satisfaction Guaranteed: The Making of the American Mass Market* (New York: Pantheon, 1989); and Richard S. Tedlow, *New and Improved: The Story of Mass Marketing in America* (New York: Basic, 1990). The works of Christopher Clark, Winifred Barr Rothenberg, Carole Shammus, and T. H. Breen contend that modern consumerism was forming throughout the Atlantic community as early as the 1750s but certainly lacked the widespread structural support needed to expand into the rural hinterland.

9. All three have been lauded for their use of consumer culture to expand our understanding of traditional historical subjects. Andrew Heinze is most positive about how materialism can be managed by a small population. His work demonstrates how immigrant Jews used consumerism to assimilate rapidly into mainstream society while maintaining their own cultural identity. Lizabeth Cohen demonstrates how modern materialism lowered ethnic and neighborhood barriers between Chicago laborers and aided in the transformation to New Deal pan-unionism. Dana Frank focuses on the limits of consumer cooperation during the Seattle labor strike of 1919. Heinze, *Adapting to Abundance: Jewish Immigrants, Mass Consumption, and the Search for American Identity* (New York: Columbia University Press, 1990); Cohen, *Making A New Deal: Industrial Workers in Chicago, 1919–1939* (New York: Cambridge University Press, 1990); and Frank, *Purchasing Power: Consumer Organizing, Gender, and the Seattle Labor Movement, 1919–1929* (New York: Cambridge University Press, 1994). For an earlier effort that in many ways set the pattern for these works, see Roy Rosenzweig, *Eight Hours for What We Will: Workers and Leisure in an Industrial City, 1870–1920* (New York: Cambridge University Press, 1983).

10. David B. Dandom, *Born in the Country: A History of Rural America* (Balti-

more: Johns Hopkins University Press, 1995), 134. Many earlier studies remain absolutely vital to understanding the political and economic challenges that faced nineteenth-century farmers; see Bogue, *From Prairie to Corn Belt*; Gates, *The Farmer's Age*; Gilbert C. Fite, *The Farmers's Frontier, 1865–1890* (New York: Holt, Rinehard & Winston, 1966); Shannon, *Farmer's Last Frontier*, 123–47; and of course Walter Prescott Webb, *The Great Plains* (Boston: Ginn, 1931).

11. Danbom, *Born in the Country*, xi. For a selection of the New Rural History, see David B. Danbom, *The Resisted Revolution: Urban America and the Industrialization of Agriculture* (Ames: Iowa State University Press, 1979); Hal S. Barron, "Rediscovering the Majority: The New Rural History of the Nineteenth-Century North," *Historical Methods* 19 (fall 1986): 142–52; Faragher, *Sugar Creek*; Allan Kulikoff, "The Transition to Capitalism in Rural America," *William and Mary Quarterly*, 3rd ser., 46 (July 1989): 120–45; Kulikoff, *The Agrarian Origins of American Capitalism* (Charlottesville: University Press of Virginia, 1992), 1–59; and Kulikoff, "Households and Markets: Toward a New Synthesis of American Agrarian History," *William and Mary Quarterly*, 3rd ser., 50 (April 1993): 342–55.

12. William Cronon, *Nature's Metropolis: Chicago and the Great West* (Chicago: Norton, 1991); Barron, *Mixed Harvest*.

13. Donald B. Dodd, comp., *Historical Statistics of the States of the United States: Two Centuries of the Census, 1790–1990* (Westport, Conn: Greenwood, 1993), 157–58.

14. Cayton and Onuf, *Midwest and Nation*, 25, 35. Barron, *Those Who Stayed Behind*; Rothenberg, *From Market-Place to Market Economy*; Christopher Clark, *The Roots of Rural Capitalism: Western Massachusetts, 1780–1860* (Ithaca: Cornell University Press, 1990).

15. Clark, *Roots of Rural Capitalism*; Winifred Barr Rothenberg, *From Market-Place to Market Economy*; Carole Shammus, *The Pre-Industrial Consumer in England and America* (Oxford: Clarendon, 1990); and T. H. Breen, "Narrative of a Commercial Life," *William and Mary Quarterly*, 3rd ser., 50 (July 1993): 471–501.

16. Studies of the Farmers Alliance and Populism are diverse. I have used Lawrence Goodwyn, *Democratic Promise: The Populist Movement in America* (New York: Oxford University Press, 1976); Robert C. McMath Jr., *American Populism: A Social History, 1877–1898* (New York: Hill & Wang, 1993); James Turner, "Understanding the Populists," *Journal of American History* 67 (September 1980): 354–73; Martin Ridge, "Populism Redux, John D. Hicks and *The Populist Revolt*," *Reviews in American History* 13 no. 1 (1985): 142–54.

17. All too often these popular presentations either gloss over the complexities of farm life (e.g., Jeanne Jordan and Steven Ascher, *Troublesome Creek: A Midwestern* [Artistic License/Forensic Films, 1996]) or focus on the dysfunctions of the rural family (e.g., Jane Smiley, *A Thousand Acres: A Novel* [New York: Fawcett Columbine, 1991]).

Chapter 1. Buying the Farm

1. Letters of William Clark (Bloomington, Ill.) to Calvin Goudy (Taylorville, Ill.), recollecting life in early Bear Creek, Illinois, dated 10 August 1874, in William Clark, letters, ISHL. For other hardships, see also Thomas Church, MSS, "Autobiography,"

76–78, ISHL, and reminiscence of Mrs. Matthew Maze, n.d., in Tipton County, Indiana, misc. records, InSL. An acre measures approximately 43,560 square feet, or the equivalent of a square with sides measuring a little more than 208 feet. For those who need a more relevant yardstick, the infield at Yankee Stadium is approximately one-quarter of an acre.

2. Harriet Bonebright-Closz, *Reminiscences of Newcastle, Iowa, 1848: A History of the Founding of Webster City, Iowa* (Des Moines: Historical Department of Iowa, 1921), 169; letters of Clark to Goudy, 10 August 1874, in Clark, letters.

3. Unlike studies that expound urban and technical determinism in the development of the region's crop structure, these new efforts suggest that, for example, the effects from railroads, the Chicago Board of Trade, and expanding cities all worked in conjunction with the rational choices made by farmers. For the study cited and ancillary supporting information, see Mary Eschelbach Gregson, "Rural Response to Increased Demand: Crop Choice in the Midwest, 1860–1880," *Journal of Economic History* 53, no. 2 (1993): 332–45; and Jeremy Atack and Fred Bateman, "Self-Sufficiency and the Marketable Surplus in the Rural North, 1860," *Agricultural History* 58 (July 1984): 296–313. Köhler's quote is in Frederick Troutman, ed. and trans., "Eight Weeks on a St. Clair County Farm," *Journal of Illinois State Historical Society* (1982): 176–77.

4. For the stove story, see Bonebright-Closz, *Reminiscences*, 169. For the old-timer tale, see E. F. Wells, "Old Times in Illinois," *Illinois State Historical Society Journal* 5, no. 2 (1912): 192–93.

5. For two outstanding studies that demonstrate how rural Americans attempted to balance, rather than choose between, community and the marketplace, see Jane Marie Pederson, *Between Memory and Reality: Family and Community in Rural Wisconsin, 1870–1970* (Madison: University of Wisconsin Press, 1992); and Woods, *Knights of the Plow*. The works dealing with producerism as a unifying historical concept are too extensive to list. A good place to begin is Sean Willentz, "Against Exceptionalism: Class, Consciousness, and the American Labor Movement, 1790–1920," *International Labor and Working Class History* 26 (fall 1984): 1–24; Palmer, *"Man Over Money,"* 9–19; Paul E. Johnson, *A Shopkeeper's Millennium: Society and Revivals in Rochester, New York, 1815–1837* (New York: Hill & Wang, 1978), 15–36; and Eric Foner, *Free Soil, Free Labor, Free Men: The Ideology of the Republican Party before the Civil War* (New York: Oxford University Press, 1970), 11–39. See also Sean Willentz, "Society, Politics, and the Market Revolution, 1815–1848," in Eric Foner, ed., *The New American History* (Philadelphia: Temple University Press, 1990), 51–73.

6. For statistics, see David C. Klingaman and Richard K. Vedder, eds., *Essays in Nineteenth Century Economic History: The Old Northwest* (Athens: Ohio University Press, 1975), ix–x; also Cayton and Onuf, *Midwest and Nation*, 25; and Allan G. Bogue, "An Agricultural Empire," in *The Oxford History of the American West* (New York: Oxford University Press, 1994), 275–313. For the citation, see *The History of Appanoose County, Iowa . . . Its Cities, Towns &c. . . .* (Chicago: Western Historical Company, 1878), 368.

7. Several studies suggest that this process was already in place elsewhere as farmers came to deal with the capitalist market: see Winifred Barr Rothenberg, *From Market-Place to Market Economy: The Transformation of Rural Massachusetts,*

1750–1850 (Chicago: University of Chicago Press, 1992); Clark, *Roots of Rural Capitalism;* Appleby, "Commercial Farming," 833–49.

8. *New England Farmer* (December 1855): 554. Donald R. Adams Jr. shows that one such consequence of Eastern uncertainty with the Midwest was the Panic of 1837, quite possibly caused by capitalists' failure to provide suitable capital reserves for Western banks: Adams, "The Role of Banks in the Economic Development of the Old Northwest," in Klingaman and Vedder, *Essays—Economic History,* 240–41.

9. Richard K. Vedder and Lowell E. Gallaway, "Migration and the Old Northwest," in Klingaman and Vedder, *Essays—Economic History,* 161; see also R. Carlyle Buley, *The Old Northwest: Pioneer Period, 1815–1840* (Bloomington: Indiana University Press, 1950).

10. For Eastern promotion of migration to the Midwest, see Foner, *Free Soil,* 27–28. The most influential works relating to my interpretation include Kathleen Neils Conzen, *Immigrant Milwaukee: Accommodation and Community in a Frontier City* (Cambridge: Harvard University Press, 1976); Conzen, *Making Their Own America: Assimilation Theory and the German Peasant Pioneer* (New York: Berg, 1990); Jon Gjerde, *The Minds of the West: Ethnocultural Evolution in the Rural Middle West, 1830–1917* (Chapel Hill: University of North Carolina Press, 1997); and Robert C. Ostergren, *A Community Transplanted: The Trans-Atlantic Experience of a Swedish Immigrant Settlement in the Upper Middle West, 1835–1915* (Madison: University of Wisconsin Press, 1988).

11. Richard White, *The Middle Ground: Indians, Empires, and Republics in the Great Lakes Regions, 1650–1850* (New York: Cambridge University Press, 1991). For Southern migration to the region, see Juliet E. K. Walker, "Entrepreneurial Ventures in the Origins of Nineteenth-Century Agricultural Towns: Pike County, 1823–1880," *Journal of the Illinois State Historical Society* 78, no. 1 (1985): 45–64.

12. Bogue, *From Prairie to Corn Belt,* 285.

13. "Susan Short May, Story of Her Early Life in Illinois," *Illinois State Historical Society Journal* 6, no. 1 (1913): 120; Barron, *Those Who Stayed Behind,* 108–10.

14. "Susan Short May," 123; Christiana Holmes Tillson, *A Woman's Story of Pioneer Illinois* (Chicago: Lakeside/Donnelley, 1919), 81–82.

15. For Stone, see *Illinois State Historical Society Journal* 3, no. 4 (1911): 89; "Ancestry and Recollections of Mrs. John Young, Rochelle, Illinois," *Illinois State Historical Society Journal* 6, no. 2 (1913): 239; Tillson. *A Woman's Story,* 123; Elizabeth Krynski and Kimberly Little, eds., "Hannah's Letters: The Story of a Wisconsin Pioneer Family, 1856–1864," *Wisconsin Magazine of History* 74, no. 4 (1991): 281.

16. See Foner, *Free Soil,* 48–50. For a good overview of the growing sectional conflict in the Midwest, see Cayton and Onuf, *Midwest and Nation,* 89–92. For quotes, see *History of Buchanan County, Iowa, with Illustrations and Biographical Sketches* (Cleveland: Williams Bros., 1881), 88–89.

17. Vedder and Gallaway, "Migration and the Old Northwest," 162–64, 170, 174.

18. William N. Parker, "From Northwest to Midwest: Social Bases of a Regional History," in Klingaman and Vedder, *Essays—Economic History,* 16.

19. Garland, *Son of the Middle Border,* 101. A good example to cite is that of claim clubs—probably the earliest and least-studied Midwestern institution of the antebellum

years. Formed in the early 1840s throughout the region, claim clubs provided a form of legal protection against claim jumping and used social intimidation to protect the economic rights of squatters and other early arrivals. See Bogue, *From Prairie to Corn Belt*, 32–38.

20. Vedder and Gallaway, "Migration and the Old Northwest," 166; for accounts of immigration to the Middle West, see Gjerde, *Minds of the West*; Conzen, *Making Their Own America*; Ostergren, *A Community Transplanted*; Walter D. Kamphoefner, *Transplanted Westfalians: Chain Migration from Germany to a Rural Midwestern Community* (Princeton: Princeton University Press, 1987); and Linda Schelbitzki Pickle, *Contented among Strangers: Rural German-Speaking Women and Their Families in the Nineteenth-Century Midwest* (Urbana: University of Illinois Press, 1996).

21. Immigrants were less likely to migrate than the native-born, but generally this, too, fell away by the second generation. See Bogue, *From Prairie to Corn Belt*, 26; Faragher, *Sugar Creek*.

22. One example was the shared hesitancy of Yankees and Danes to settle on the prairie, whereas Germans and native-born Southerners proved more willing to trek into the interior, which entailed moving away from the comfort of the river systems. See Bogue, *From Prairie to Corn Belt*, 47–56.

23. Many leading Republicans such as William Seward and later the party itself embraced foreigners in the West for their rejection of slavery, the easing of labor burdens, and for continuing capitalist farming in the West. See Eric Foner, *Free Soil*, 234–36; Gjerde, *Minds of the West*, 283–317. Michael F. Holt, "The Politics of Impatience: The Origins of Know-Nothingism," *Journal of American History* 55 (1973): 309–31; Paul Kleppner, *The Cross of Culture: A Social Analysis of Midwestern Politics, 1850–1890* (New York: Free Press, 1970); Richard J. Jensen, *The Winning of the Midwest: Social and Political Conflict, 1888–1896* (Chicago: University of Chicago Press, 1971).

24. Vedder and Gallaway, "Migration and the Old Northwest," 168.

25. Bogue, *From Prairie to Corn Belt*, 23–24; Edward H. Rastatter, "Nineteenth Century Public Land Policy: The Case of the Speculator," in Klingaman and Vedder, *Essays—Economic History*, 135.

26. For Jeffersonian idealism, see Jefferson, *Notes on the State of Virginia;* and Peterson, *The Jeffersonian Image*.

27. For an outstanding recent contribution to this fruitful debate, see Sally Ann McMurry, *Transforming Rural Life: Dairying Families and Agricultural Change, 1820–1885* (Baltimore: Johns Hopkins University Press, 1995).

28. See Allan Kulikoff, *The Agrarian Origins of American Capitalism* (Charlottesville: University Press of Virginia, 1992), 1–59; Kulikoff, "Households and Markets: Toward a New Synthesis of American Agrarian History," *William and Mary Quarterly*, 3rd ser., 50, no. 2 (1993): 342–55; and Michael Merrill, "Cash Is Good to Eat: Self-Sufficiency and Exchange in the Rural Economy of the United States," *Radical History Review* 3 (1977): 42–71.

29. For the best example of such incremental change, see Clark, *Roots of Rural Capitalism*.

30. Cayton and Onuf, *Midwest and Nation*, 35. This statement would apply to the vast majority of diaries and account books surveyed for this book. Of course, those

keeping an account book (i.e., taking the time to write down their expenses) are also more likely to be in support of scientific farming principles.

31. For quote and costs, see Jeremy Atack, "Farm and Farm-Making Costs Revisited," *Agricultural History* 56 (October 1956): 676. For additional works on start-up expenses, see Clarence Danhof, "Farm-Making Costs and the Safety Valve: 1850–1860," *Journal of Political Economy* 49 (June 1941): 317–59; Danhof, *Change in Agriculture: The Northern United States, 1820–1870* (Cambridge: Harvard University Press, 1969); Atack and Bateman, "Self-Sufficiency and the Marketable Surplus," 296–313; Robert E. Ankli, "Horses vs. Tractors of the Corn Belt," *Agricultural History* 54 (January 1980): 134–48; and Homer E. Socolofsky, "Success and Failure in Nebraska Homesteading," *Agricultural History* 42, no. 2 (1968): 103–9.

32. Roger L. Ransom, "Public Canal Investment and the Opening of the Old Northwest," in Klingaman and Vedder, *Essays—Economic History*, 249. See also John Denis Haeger, *The Investment Frontier: New York Businessmen and the Economic Development of the Old Northwest* (Albany: State University of New York Press, 1981); Jeffrey S. Adler, *Yankee Merchants and the Making of the Urban West: The Rise and Fall of Antebellum St. Louis* (Cambridge: Cambridge University Press, 1991). Bogue, *From Prairie to Corn Belt*, 173–79.

33. For accounts of Sullivant or Alexander, see the *Wisconsin Farmer* (March 1866): 93; *Chicago Evening Post*, 11 January 1871, 2; and *Chicago Evening Post*, 2 November 1870. For similar accounts, see *PF*, 14 February 1856; and *Country Gentleman* (Albany, N.Y.) 8, no. 6, 25 December 1856. For an example of itinerant Midwesterners seeking the market returns, see Mark E. Nackman and Darryl K. Paton, "Recollections of an Illinois Woman," *Western Illinois Regional Studies* 1, no. 1 (1978): 27–44. For economic egalitarianism in the Midwest, see Jeremy Atack and Fred Bateman, "The 'Egalitarian Ideal' and the Distribution of Wealth in the Northern Agricultural Community: A Backward Look," *Review of Economics and Statistics* 63 (February 1981): 124–29; and Atack and Bateman, "Egalitarianism, Inequality, and Age: The Rural North in 1860," *Journal of Economic History* 41 (March 1981): 85–93.

34. To make a current comparison, most would agree that our bellwether technologies—computers, software, and telecommunications—were in their awkward youth thirty years ago. Still, in the 1970s many could foresee the rapid growth of the sundry applications for these tools. The same cannot be said for the rural Midwest in 1850.

35. Bonebright-Closz, *Reminiscences*, 18.

36. Bogue, *From Prairie to Corn Belt*, 70–73; Hiram M. Drache, *Legacy of the Land: Agriculture's Story to the Present* (Danville, Ill.: Interstate Publishers, 1996), 112–13.

37. Drache, *Legacy of the Land*, 113–15. Weeding and mowing, too, were constant tasks for wheat crops (less so for corn) and until the 1850s the farm family had little option but to hoe and mow by hand. Mechanized weeders and mowers provided productivity benefits but were more important in encouraging many farmers to weed their fields for the first time.

38. Bogue, *From Prairie to Corn Belt*, 164; Drache, *Legacy of the Land*, 105, 110–11; Bogue, *From Prairie to Corn Belt*, 164; R. Douglas Hurt, "Out of the Cradle:

The Reaper Revolution," *Timeline* 3 (October 1986): 38–51; Thomas D. Isern, *Bull Threshers and Bindlestaffs: Harvesting and Threshing on the North American Plains* (Lawrence: University Press of Kansas, 1990).

39. Bogue, *From Prairie to Corn Belt*, 164; Isern, *Bull Threshers and Bindlestaffs*, 8.

40. Robert E. Gallman, "The Agricultural Sector and the Pace of Economic Growth: U.S. Experience in the Nineteenth Century," in Klingaman and Vedder, *Essays—Economic History*, 37, 55–56; for statistics, see Bogue, "Agricultural Empire," 296.

41. Allan Kulikoff, "The Transition to Capitalism in Rural America," *William and Mary Quarterly* 46 (July 1989): 139. Deborah Fink, *Open Country, Iowa: Rural Women, Tradition, and Change* (Albany: State University of New York Press, 1986); Garland, *Son of the Middle Border*, 126.

42. Glenda Riley, ed., "The Morse Family Letters: A New Home in Iowa, 1856–1862," *Annals of Iowa* 45 (winter 1980): 220–21, 225.

43. Gates, *The Farmer's Age*, 338, 339–58. For regional specialization, see George F. Lemmer, "Early Agricultural Editors and Their Farm Philosophies," *Agricultural History* 31, no. 4 (1957): 3–22. For numbers, see Gates, *The Farmer's Age*, 343. For other leading accounts, see Richard T. Farrell, "Advice to Farmers: The Content of Agricultural Newspapers, 1860–1910," *Agricultural History* 51 (January 1977): 209–16; Richard W. Abbott, "The Agricultural Press Views the Yeoman: 1819–1859," *Agricultural History* 42 (January 1968): 35–48; and Jack W. Van Derhoof, "Eastern and Mid-Western Agricultural Journalism, 1860–1900." Ph.D. diss., Columbia University, June 1951.

Chapter 2: Breaking the Prairie and Taming the Market

1. Lears suggests that much of the "magic" of shopping has been lost due to modernity. His interpretation shows how ads created a "symbolic universe" for American consumers that led them away from a more traditional relationship with the material world to one that was individualistic, rational, and oriented toward personal efficiency. According to this view, modern consumerism did not displace the traditional concerns of materialism—self-control and producerism—as much as it altered the understanding of these principles; Lears, *Fables of Abundance*, 1, 3, passim.

2. "Memoirs of Mary D. Bradford," *Wisconsin Magazine of History* 14 (1930–31): 3–37. *Illinois State Historical Society Journal* 6, no. 1 (1913); "Susan Short May," 119–28. Riley, "Morse Family Letters," 212–27. See also Mark E. Nackman and Darryl K. Paton, "Recollections of an Illinois Woman," *Western Illinois Regional Studies* 1, no. 1 (1978): 27–44; Christiana Holmes Tillson, *A Woman's Story of Pioneer Illinois*, Milo Milton Quaife, ed. (Chicago: Lakeside/Donnelley, 1919), 98.

3. C. Thurston Chase, *Chase Western Rural Handbooks*, no. 2, *The Useful and the Ornamental: Western Manual of Practical Rural Affairs, for the Farm and Home: About Hedges, Evergreens, Forest Planting and Flowers* (Chicago: Griggs, 1860), vi. For "plunder," see Tillson, *A Woman's Story of Pioneer Illinois*, 47.

4. *Chase Western Rural Handbooks*, no. 2., vii.

5. Bogue, *From Prairie to Corn Belt*, 146, 203; *History of Buchanan County, Iowa, with Illustrations and Biographical Sketches* (Cleveland: Williams Bros., 1881), 89.

6. *PF*, 15 August 1852, 352.

7. Charles B. Fulton, *History of Jefferson County, Iowa: A Record of Settlement,*

Organization, Progress, and Achievement (Chicago: Clarke Publishing, 1914), 256. *AA* (New York) 16 (August 1857): 185. Margaret Beattie Bogue, "Patterns from the Sod: Land Use and Tenure in the Grand Prairie, 1850–1900," Ph.D. diss., Cornell University, 1955, 120; appears as an article in the ISHL collection.

8. *PF*, 15 August 1852, 352.

9. *Chase Western Rural Handbooks*, no. 2, vii.

10. Gates, *The Farmer's Age*, 338; see also pages 339–58. For regional specialization (largely after 1825), see Lemmer, "Early Agricultural Editors," 3–22. For numbers, see Gates, *The Farmer's Age*, 343. For other leading accounts, see Richard T. Farrell, "Advice to Farmers: The Content of Agricultural Newspapers, 1860–1910," *Agricultural History* 51 (January 1977): 209–16; Abbott, "Agricultural Press," 35–48; and Van Derhoof, "Agricultural Journalism."

11. Van Derhoof, "Agricultural Journalism," 172.

12. Donald R. Murphy, "The Centennial of a Farm Paper," *Palimpsest* 37, no. 9 (1956): 449–59.

13. Asa Abbot, Diaries, Scrapbooks, ISHL.

14. For quote, see Van Derhoof, "Agricultural Journalism," 35. For demagoguery and the rise of the yeoman myth, see Abbott, "Agricultural Press," 35–48.

15. The literature regarding crop specialization is vast and not of central importance here. For an introduction to the topic, see Bogue, *From Prairie to Corn Belt*, 148–68; Gates, *The Farmer's Age;* and Douglass C. North, *The Economic Growth of the United States, 1790–1860* (New York: Norton, 1961), 135–55. The literature on technological specialization and innovation is likewise immense; for an example, see Gould Colman, "Innovation and Diffusion in Agriculture," *Agricultural History* 42 (July 1968): 173–87; Atack, "Farm and Farm-Making Costs Revisited," 663–76; and Atack and Bateman, "Self-Sufficiency and the Marketable Surplus," 296–313.

16. For Sullivant, see *Wisconsin Farmer* (March 1866): 93. For reference to small farms in Illinois, see *AA* 16 (November 1857): 252; for Wilcox letter to implement dealers Drury, Hayner & Co., 8 April 1868, see Drury, Hayner & Co., correspondence, 1867–1868, ISHL.

17. Willis Boughton, MS "Drover Days," ISHL, 110–12. Boughton recounted that "when the harvester was in operation, it took six good binders to 'keep up with the machine.'" The machine's "rounds" of the sixty-acre wheat field were nearly a mile in circumference. To maximize worker productivity, owners placed their laborers at "stations" on the machine's route. Much as in a batting order in baseball, the first station could expect to work sooner and in a day's work would take part in more "rounds." Boughton's men recognized this and obliged him to let them decide the order of the work schedule. The crew actually gambled for the last station, "for to wait might mean a long rest." For an additional perspective on these traveling gangs of laborers, see Peter H. and Jo Ann Argersinger, "The Machine Breakers: Farmworkers and Social Change in the Rural Midwest of the 1870s," *Agricultural History* 58 (July 1984): 393–410. Laborers were a rare commodity in many rural communities. One traveler to Illinois in 1851 noted that "help is hard to find and costly at harvest, when every farmer has plenty [to reap]. . . . Here, unlike Germany, there are no professional farm laborers." In Troutman, "Eight Weeks," 172.

18. Garland, *Son of the Middle Border*, 42. Boughton, "Drover Days," 110–12. An important book dealing with the changing perceptions of the role of "productive"

work by women, in this case seen through vernacular housing designs, is Sally Ann Mc-
Murray, *Families and Farmhouses in Nineteenth-Century America: Vernacular Design
and Social Change* (New York: Oxford University Press, 1988).

19. James Sanders, ed., "'Times Hard but Grit Good,' Lydia Moxley's 1877
Diary," *Annals of Iowa* 47 (1984): 286–87. Letter of 7 July from Catherine to her husband, in Gilbert Ethan Durin, papers, ISHL.

20. *Chase Western Rural Handbooks,* no. 2, 42–43. See also Ruth Schwartz
Cowan, *More Work for Mother: The Ironies of Household Technology from the Open
Hearth to the Microwave* (New York: Basic, 1983); and McMurray, *Families and Farm-
houses.*

21. Garland, *Son of the Middle Border,* 294. For women's work on the farm, see
Deborah Fink, *Open Country Iowa;* Stephanie Coontz, *The Social Origins of Private
Life: A History of American Families, 1600–1900* (London: Verso, 1988); Glenda
Riley, *The Female Frontier: A Comparative View of Women on the Prairies and the
Plains* (Lawrence: University Press of Kansas, 1988); and Faragher, *Sugar Creek.*

22. "Ancestry and Recollections of Mrs. John Young, Rochelle, Illinois," *Illinois
State Historical Society Journal* 6, no. 2 (1913): 239.

23. See Ruth Schwartz Cowan, *More Work For Mother;* McMurray, *Families and
Farmhouses;* Virginia K. Bartlett, *Keeping House: Women's Lives in Western Pennsylva-
nia, 1790–1850* (Pittsburgh: Historical Society of Western Pennsylvania, University of
Pittsburgh Press, 1994).

24. Glenda Riley, ed., "The Memoirs of Matilda Peitzke Paul," *Palimpsest* 57, no.
2 (1976): 59. Letter to to Sarah Springer Davidson, 29 January 1865, Davidson-
Springer family, papers, 1846–1934, ISHL. Christina Ann Rook, Journals, ISHL.
Rook's text also provides good examples of the types of chores commonly associated
with farm work.

25. For productivity figures, see Lucy Eldersveld Murphy, "Her Own Boss: Busi-
nesswomen and Separate Spheres in the Midwest, 1850–1880," *Illinois Historical
Journal* 80, no. 3 (1987): 155–76. For White's letters, dated 25 September and 12
November 1871 and 7 January 1872, see Tyner-White family, papers, 1862–1881,
InSL. Such accounts are common in farm women's records; see also Davidson-
Springer family, papers, esp. letter to Sarah Springer Davidson, 29 January 1865.

26. Bartlett, *Keeping House,* 33; Christiana Holmes Tillson, *A Woman's Story of
Pioneer Illinois,* 150.

27. For various varieties of "coffee" (e.g., one containing barley corn and acorns),
see Heitmann, Tildy Keist, Composition Books, 8, ISHL. Bonebright-Closz, *Reminiscences,* 170–73.

28. *PF,* 19 June 1875. "The Diary of Anna R. Morrison, Wife of Isaac L. Morrison, 1840–1841," *Illinois State Historical Society Journal* 7, no. 1 (1914): 39; Murphy,
"Her Own Boss," 174.

29. *AA* 23 (January 1864): 5. One farm woman's diary included a newspaper
clipping headlined "Too Much Extravagance: Why Men Are Afraid to Marry the Girls
of To-day" (n.p., n.d.). The text describes a wife who is not frugal in the purchase of
consumer goods such as ribbons, but it makes no mention of capital goods. In Tyner-
White family, papers, 1862–1881, InSL.

30. Sanders, "Times Hard," 270–90; see also Sarah Ann Davidson, diary and let-

ters, 1846–1934, ISHL; Mary E. Pasco, diary, 1883–1886, SHSW; and Sarah Browne-Armstrong Adamson, Diaries, 1818–1834, 1834–1851, SHSI.

31. For Neth and Hahn, see Wava G. Haney and Jane B. Knowles, eds., *Women and Farming: Changing Roles, Changing Structures* (Boulder, Colo.: Westview, 1988); Pederson, *Between Memory and Reality;* Tillson, *A Woman's Story of Pioneer Illinois,* 103–4.

32. For the quote and costs, see Atack, "Farm and Farm-Making Costs," 676 and 663–76. For additional works on start-up expenses, see Clarence Danhof, "Farm-Making Costs and the Safety Valve: 1850–1860," *Journal of Political Economy* 49 (June 1941): 317–59; Danhof, *Change in Agriculture;* Atack and Bateman, "Self-Sufficiency and the Marketable Surplus," 296–313; Robert E. Ankli, "Horses vs. Tractors," 134–48; and Homer E. Socolofsky, "Success and Failure in Nebraska Homesteading," *Agricultural History* 42, no. 2 (1968): 103–9.

33. Generally, only total crop failure or the death of the sole adult male could "wipe out" a commercial farmer. Robert Higgs, *The Transformation of the American Economy, 1865–1914: An Essay in Interpretation* (New York: Wiley, 1971), 99; Zunz, *Making America Corporate,* 156. For economic equality, see also Atack and Bateman, "Egalitarian Ideal," 124–29; and Atack and Bateman, "Egalitarianism, Inequality, and Age," 85–93.

34. For agents, see Zunz, *Making America Corporate,* 157–63; for the quote, see *Chicago Evening Journal,* 26 February 1856. See also *PF,* 30 October 1869.

35. See *The Greenwood Encyclopedia of American Institutions* (New York, 1986), s.v. "farmers' organizations" (Lowell K. Dyson); and John A. Oostendorp, "The Co-operative Movement in the Patrons of Husbandry in Iowa, 1870–1878," M.A. thesis, University of Iowa, 1949, 5–35.

36. Robert J. Woodruff, M.D., *An Address Delivered Before the Agricultural Society of Bureau County . . . March 27, 1856, by Robert J. Woodruff, M.D., President . . .* (Princeton, Ill.: Printed for the society, Pine & Lemar, 1856), 3. For Wisconsin, see *Oshkosh City Times,* 6 April 1870 and 11 January 1871. In Champaign County, Illinois, the first agricultural society was formed in 1852; four years later there were at least fifty-five on record; see *Transactions of the Illinois State Agricultural Society, 1856,* vol. 2; and *Emery's Journal of Agriculture* 1 (January 1858): 18. Bogue, *From Prairie to Corn Belt,* 210.

37. Report by John A. Kennicott in *Transactions of the Illinois State Agricultural Society, 1856–7,* vol. 2 (Chicago: 1858); *PF,* 15 August 1852, 352.

38. Wayne Caldwell Neely, *The Agricultural Fair* (New York: AMS, 1967), 83–85. For Blakely's letter, see *Emery's Journal of Agriculture* 1 (January 1858): 18. For attendance during the war, see *Transactions of the Illinois State Agricultural Society, 1861–4,* vol. 5, 34–5. Leslie Prosterman, *Ordinary Life, Festival Days: Aesthetics in the Midwestern County Fair* (Washington: Smithsonian Institution Press, 199); David C. Jones, *Midways, Judges, and Smooth-Tongued Fakirs: The Illustrated Story of County Fairs in the Prairie West* (Saskatoon, Saskatchewan: Western Producer, 1983); Warren J. Gates, "Modernization as a Function of an Agricultural Fair: The Great Grangers' Picnic Exhibition at William's Grove, Pennsylvania, 1873–1919," *Agricultural History* 58 (July 1984): 262–79.

39. Entry for 10 September 1868 in Mary J. Lane, Journal, 21 May 1868–4 July

1869, ISHL. For the self-worth quotation, see *PF,* 2 September 1871, 274; see also Neely, *Agricultural Fair,* 89, 168–69. Also cited, *Emery's Journal of Agriculture* 1 (January 1858): 18. Boughton, "Drover Days," 257–64.

40. Garland, *Son of the Middle Border,* 135. For holidays, see Boughton, "Drover Days," 257–64. For recollections of Henry A. Griswold as he attended the Illinois State Fair in Jacksonville from 10 September to 13 September 1868, see Griswold family, papers, 1814–1943, Box 1: Diaries, ISHL. For Davenport fair, see 10 September 1868 in Lane, Journal, 21 May 1868–4 July 1869. For races, see *History of Buchanan County, Iowa, with Illustrations and Biographical Sketches* (Cleveland: Williams Bros., 1881), 90. For baseball, see *Oshkosh City Times,* 14 September 1869. Reformers were wholly unsuccessful: the races remained one of the most popular elements of the state fairs. For the indictment of nonagrarian activities, see *PF,* 19 September 1868, 89.

41. *PF,* 17 October 1868, 122. For the "Art" quote, see 9 September 1868 in Lane, Journal, 21 May 1868–4 July 1869. For Springfield fair, see James Caird, *Prairie Farming in America, with Notes by the Way on Canada and the United States* (London: Longman, Brown, Green, Longmans, & Roberts, 1859), 56. For Illinois State Fair, *PF,* 3 October 1868, 106. For the lack of "abundant" goods, see *Genesee Farmer* 13, no. 11 (1852): 350.

42. *Indiana State Trial of Agricultural Implements* (Indianapolis: Indiana State Board of Agriculture, 1872), 5.

43. Circular issued by William B. Young Plows, c. 1866, *Farmer's Friend,* CHS. For perceived role of premiums, see opening address of William H. Van Epps, *Illinois State Agricultural Society at the Illinois State Fair* (Decatur, Ill.: 1864), 3, CHS.

44. McSherry to agents Drury, Hayner & Co., 17 September 1867—see Drury, Hayner, correspondence. For Deere, see *PF,* 3 October 1868, 106.

45. For two examples of this request, see the *PF,* June 1853, 242; and ibid., 4 July 1868. For advertisers, see, for example, the *Illinois State Agricultural Society, Premium List, 1861,* CHS; and the Indiana State Board of Agriculture, *Indiana State Trial of Agricultural Implements, Indianapolis, Indiana, June 10, 1872,* ISL. Editorial by R. H. Holder, Bloomington officer of the ISAS, in ISAS, *Premium List, 1861,* 183, CHS. For similar discussions, see *PF,* 3 October 1868, 105.

46. See ISAS Premium List, 1861, 193, CHS. For Deere, see *PF,* 3 October 1868, 106.

47. McCormick agent E. C. Beardsley, cited in Zunz, *Making America Corporate,* 157.

48. Fulton, *History of Jefferson County,* 256, 261.

49. Ibid., 265.

50. For low premiums, see Emma Perkins Howell, diaries, box 3: misc. papers, ISHL. For example of premiums, see *History of Buchanan County, Iowa,* 87–88, 90; For Winslow, see *History of Jasper County, Iowa,* 441.

51. Fulton, *History of Jefferson County,* 263–64.

52. Henry Adams, *The Education of Henry Adams: An Autobiography* (Boston: Houghton Mifflin, 1971), 106.

53. For economic policy during the war, see Philip Shaw Paludan, *"A People's Contest": The Union and Civil War, 1861–1865* (New York: Harper & Row, 1988), 127–50. See also Ralph L. Andreano, ed., *Economic Impact of the American Civil War,*

2nd ed. (Cambridge, Mass.: Schenkman, 1967); and Harold M. Hyman, *A More Perfect Union: The Impact of the Civil War and Reconstruction on the Constitution* (Boston: Houghton Mifflin, 1975).

54. See General J. H. Vajen, Civil War MSS, InSL.

55. For Davis records, see letters dated 22, 23, 24, and 31 May 1861, in Jefferson Columbus Davis, papers 1826–1873, InSL.

56. For Vajen quote, see letter to H. S. Holman, Congressional Investigating Committee, dated 17 March 1862, in Vajen, Civil War MSS, InSL. For his work in relation to the region, see *Marion Co. (Ind.) Daily Sentinel*, 3 September 1862.

57. See letter dated 7 November 1861, from James Vanderbilt to his mother in Paducah, Ky., in James Cornelius Vanderbilt, Civil War letters, 1861–1864, InSL. For Illinois, see letter dated 10 July 1861, from A. S. Hatch in camp at Macon City, Missouri, to Cousin Madison Hatch, Griggsville, Pike County, Illinois, in Hatch and Fessenden families, papers, 1844–1882, ISHL. For the "parade" of goods, see letter dated 28 September 1862 from Bush at Camp Morton, Indiana, to Molly Bush in Andrew Bush, papers, 1862–1865, InSL.

58. For nourishment, see letters dated 17 November 1861, 22 October 1862, and 20 January 1863; for clothing and other goods, including, pants, woolen shirts, shoes, socks, drawers, plug tobacco, jackets, butter, flour, and ham, all bought at the army commissary, see account of commissary store, October 1864, and letter dated 3 January 1864 in Bush, papers, 1862–1865, InSL. For the second example, see letter dated 7 November 1861, in Vanderbilt, Civil War letters.

59. For the quote, see letter dated 10 July 1861, in Vanderbilt, Civil War letters.

60. For Pankhurst letter, dated 3 December 1863, see Alexander, Howell, & Co., business corr., 1865–1876, ISHL. For commissary pledge, see accounts, dated October 1864, in Bush, papers, 1862–1865, InSL.

61. For Cornell Sewing Machines and other examples, see ISAS, Premium List, 1861, 191, 193, 195, CHS.

62. "Ancestry and Recollections of Mrs. John Young, Rochelle, Illinois," *Illinois State Historical Society Journal* 6, no. 2 (1913): 235–41, 240.

63. Louisa Jane Phifer, "Letters from an Illinois Farm, 1864–1865," *Journal of the Illinois State Historical Society* 66, no. 4 (1973): 387–403.

64. For the quote, see *Ninth Annual Exhibition of the Illinois State Agricultural Society . . . Chicago . . . September, 1861* (Springfield: Steam Press of Chas. A. Lamphier, 1861), 37–38. As noted above, the country and state fairs did not stop promoting commercial agriculture during the war, see ISAS Transactions, 1861–64, vol. 5 (Springfield: 1865), 34–35.

65. See letter from O. P. Morton to Vajen, 15 July 1861, in Vajen, Civil War MSS, InSL. Vajen noted that most goods were bought for cash, thereby further inflating local and national markets. McCole letter dated 12 January 1862, in George M. McCole, papers, InSL. For greenbacks, see Walter T. K. Nugent, *Money and American Society, 1865–1880* (New York: Free Press, 1968), passim.

66. For Gates's letter, dated 9 June 1862, see Alexander, Howell, business corr. See also Chicago merchant and landlord Thomas Church Jr., *Autobiography, 1834–1868*, 58, ISHL. *PF,* 27 November 1869, 385.

67. For cash accounts and the $2,000 purchase by V. R. Price, 28 August 1865,

see J. B. Jolly and Lewis Mayo, cash book, 1860–70, ISHL. The use of account books as representative source material could vex some scholars. True, it is difficult to argue that local conditions, type of consumer, regional influence, and other contingencies do not make each ledger unique to its time and place. I defend my use of them on two grounds: First, that such business information and similar materials have been used in the past by historians; for example, see Winifred Barr Rothenberg, *From Market-Place to Market Economy: The Transformation of Rural Massachusetts, 1750–1850* (Chicago: University of Chicago Press, 1992), chap. 3. Second, the fact that merchants kept these documents suggests that they, too, were looking for ways to better understand their businesses and their customers' consumer practices. Although it is impossible to argue that these documents and later business sources definitively describe rural consumer practices, the facts they contain lend significant credence to the other data.

68. *PF,* 27 November 1869, 385.

69. For Western migration, see article in the *Cultivator and Country Gentleman* 33 (11 February 1869): 114. The quote is from idem, vol. 35 (7 July 1870): 420.

70. See Rendigs Fels, *American Business Cycles, 1865–1897* (Chapel Hill: University of North Carolina Press, 1959), 221. For an excellent overview of the process of monetary constriction in this era, see Walter T. K. Nugent, *Money and American Society,* chap. 9.

71. Many works deal with rural unrest. For the most important works on this region and period, see Allan G. Bogue, *Money and Interest: The Farm Mortgage on the Middle Border* (Ithaca: Cornell University Press, 1955); Bogue, *From Prairie to Corn Belt;* Paul Wallace Gates, "Land Policy and Tenancy in the Prairie States," *Journal of Economic History* 1 (May 1941): 60–82; Gates, *The Farmer's Age: Agriculture 1815–1860,* vol. 3 of *The Economic History of the United States* (New York: Harper & Row, 1960); Gates, *Landlords and Tenants on the Prairie Frontier* (Ithaca: Cornell University Press, 1973); Fred A. Shannon, *American Farmers' Movement* (Princeton, N.J.: Van Nostrand, 1957); Shannon, *Farmer's Last Frontier;* Jeffrey Ostler, *Prairie Populism and the Fate of Agrarian Radicalism* (Lawrence: University Press of Kansas, 1993); and McMath, *American Populism.*

72. For the development of producer rhetoric and the currency issue, see Nugent, *Money and American Society,* 15, 28, 139. Nugent notes that up until 1873 farmers lacked a clear group awareness. It was this issue, therefore, that most directly aided in the expression of rural unrest throughout the remainder of the century. *CT,* 23 August 1873, 8.

73. See *Oshkosh City Times,* 22 September 1869, 1. For an example of rural consumers and money scarcity, see Maria Bennett letter dated 19 December 1869, in Bennett-Carter family, papers, 1836–1942, "Robert S. Carter" folder, ISHL.

74. Data taken from Griswold's account books. See Griswold family, papers, 1814–1943, box 4: account books, bank books, etc., ISHL. For a second example of the stifling effects that limited currency had on farming, see Joseph W. Dalrymple, papers, 1858–1891, InSL.

75. See letters dated 8 January 1867, 7 February 1867, and 3 September 1868 in John Kirk, Letterbooks, 1852–1871, CHS. For a second example, see letter from agent J. M. Wilcox, dated 8 April 1868, in Drury, Hayner, corr.

76. William Schneider, papers, 1850–1902, "Account Books, 1866–1871," InSL.

77. Letter dated 4 October 1869, in Bennett-Carter, papers, InSL. For Stowman's accounts, see Charles W. Stowman, Account Books, 1851–1907, InSL.

78. In 1867, as noted by Stowman, the Peru House came under the control of D. J. Nicoles. Whether some other connection between Stowman and Nicoles may have been the source of the change in the fiscal relationship is unknown. However, Nicoles does appear in other accounts, both before and after this date, and the facts suggest that this relationship was strong and experienced no major shifts throughout the years in question.

79. Clark's spending can be found in Adeline Clark, diaries, 1851–1911, ISHL. In 1867 she recorded $136.49 in "table" expenses, $406.63 in "incidentals." In 1871, no records were kept on table receipts, but she spent only $198.47 on incidentals (a figure that included a $147.80 "Chicago Spree"). By 1878 this number climbed well beyond its earlier amount to roughly $876.26 in incidentals. For Richardson, see letter dated 8 May 1868 in Drury, Hayner, corr.

80. *Oshkosh City Times,* 22 September 1868. White letter dated 16 March 1870 in Tyner-White family, papers, InSL. *PF,* 27 November 1869.

81. For Applegate, see Bartholomew Applegate, daybook, 1874–77, InSL. This example is from July to November 1875. For another example of farmers entering into debt to avoid losing capital investments, see letter dated 8 May 1868 from farmer Thomas B. Richardson, Chesterfield, Macoupin County, Illinois, to Walter A. Wood, in Drury, Hayner, business corr., ISHL.

82. See William Schneider, papers, InSL. For additional information, see Charles W. Stowman, account books, 1851–1907, InSL. Stowman's accounts show that his firm extended six loans in 1869 for $2,107.80, seven loans in 1870 for $3,600.00, and twelve loans in 1872 (1871 was unavailable) for $5,030.

83. See Zunz, *Making America Corporate,* 154–56. For the Welch account, see *PF,* 1 August 1868, 36. For timeliness, see *Cultivator and Country Gentleman* 33 (20 May 1869): 394.

84. *Oshkosh City Times,* 23 March 1869; *CT,* 23 August 1873, 8. See also Spears, *One Hundred Years on the Road.*

85. *AA* 21 (July 1862): 203. Creighton quoted in ISFA, *Proceedings . . . Second Annual Meeting . . . Decatur, 1873 . . .* (Chicago: Southard, 1874), 68. For the account of overconsumption in Jo Daviess County, Illinois, see *PF,* 19 December 1868, 193. The Wheeler poem is in the *PF,* 25 September 1869, 309.

Chapter 3: The Men in the Middle

1. Harmon dealt in commercial scales over a wide area. His and his associates' dealings with agents and retailers in the Illinois towns of Ottawa, Galesburg, Springfield, Peoria, Rock Island, Galena, and Peru and the Wisconsin towns of Fond du Lac, Portage City, Janesville, Kenosha, and Oshkosh were only a part of his business. He had other lines of trade with retailers in many additional places. See Harmon family, papers, box 164, folder 17, "Scales accounts of agents, 1856," CHS.

2. Donald L. Miller, *City of the Century: The Epic of Chicago and the Making of America* (New York: Simon & Schuster, 1996), 66–88. Just as farmers tried to conserve tradition as they expanded staple-crop agriculture, undoubtedly so too did Charles Harmon allow communal and social factors to enter into his business calculations. For

example, Charles refused to deal in the profitable trade of firearms, imploring Isaac, who had arranged for the transport of a cannon, "not [to] consign the 'instrument of death' to me. I have [considerable] scruples about having anything to do with it—if I should pay the charges that will be the end of it." "Considerable" is the best rendering I can make given the poor condition of the letter in the original. Harmon to his brother, 26 June 1847, in Harmon family, papers, vol. 8, letter books, 1846–48; 1848–49, CHS.

3. Harmon to his brother, J. D. Harmon, 8 November 1848, in Harmon family, papers, vol. 8. A second example, similar in style and tone can be found in the accounts of Chicago agent Osborn Keith. See Edson Keith to Osborn Keith, 18 August 1863 in Keith family, papers, CHS. For the second citation, see letter of Harmon to J. D. Harmon, 13 October 1848, in Harmon family, papers, vol. 8.

4. As several recent historians have noted, the story of the urban middleman is the near antithesis of Frederick Jackson Turner: city markets supporting the establishment of commercial agriculture. Turner concluded that cities and markets predictably flowed from the pioneers' tepid efforts to peddle their surplus crops; these more current assertions suggest that the concentrated urban market, internal improvements (especially rail), financial links, and geography were much more vital contingent factors in the development of the Midwest. See Miller, *City of the Century*, 60; and Cayton and Onuf, *Midwest and Nation*. For the early market economy of the region, see William Cronon, *Nature's Metropolis*, 55–309. More pointedly, Timothy Mahoney shows how regional towns like Saint Louis became economic hubs largely based on their agent activities. Mahoney writes: "To establish a role within the regional system of trade and to connect local progress to regional mechanisms of urban development became the agreed upon strategy for success. To survive and prosper, a town had to rise above the web of local trade." See Mahoney, *River Towns in the Great West: The Structure of Provincial Urbanization in the American Midwest, 1820–1870* (New York: Cambridge University Press, 1990), 210–15. Also useful is Lewis E. Atherton, *The Pioneer Merchant in Mid-America* (University of Missouri Studies 14, 1, no. 2, April 1939; reprint, New York: DeCapo, 1969), chap. 1.

5. Spears, *One Hundred Years on the Road*, xi. Spears explores the cultural meaning of salesmanship in the United States. He sees agents as providing a "connecting link" between rural consumers and urban suppliers that ultimately was incorporated into mainstream American business. He argues that "the extensive and distributive role of commercial traveling brought an essentially urban-based market culture into small-town, rural America, threatening well-established notions of economic self-rule and domestic ideology. Relationships between antebellum wholesalers and storekeepers laid the foundation for the urban/rural thoroughfare but hardly prepared other Americans for the appearance—some might say intrusion—of whole armies of traveling salesmen." Ibid., 54, 60–61. The more traditional and widely known works are also valuable: see Atherton, *Pioneer Merchant*, 11, 32, 82; Chandler, *Visible Hand*, 27–28, chap. 7, esp. 208–23; and esp. Glenn Porter and Harold C. Livesay, *Merchants and Manufacturers: Studies in the Changing Structure of Nineteenth-Century Marketing* (Baltimore: Johns Hopkins University Press, 1971), 22–36.

6. Boughton, "Drover Days," 60.

7. Guengerich also used his surplus funds to extend small loans, at interest, to neighbors. See Samuel D. Guengerich, diaries, 1866, 1868–69, 1873, SHSI.

8. The first citation is from Atherton, *Pioneer Merchant*, 45; the second is from Caird, *Prairie Farming in America*, 69. For the "goods life" quote, see Thomas Schlereth, *Victorian America: Transformations of Everyday Life, 1876–1915* (New York: Harper-Collins, 1991).

9. Garland, *Son of the Middle Border*, 74. *Chase Western Rural Handbooks*, no. 2, 40–41. *PF*, 29 May 1875.

10. For narrative, see "Reminiscences of Pendleton" (1927) by Benjamin Rogers and I. Price Rinewalt, typescript in Madison County, Miscellaneous Records, InSL; and the *Pendleton Republican*, 27 February 1896.

11. Bartlett, *Keeping House*, 55–56, 76. Bonebright-Closz, *Reminiscences*, 129. For additional comments about peddlers, see Tildy Keist Heitmann, composition books, ISHL.

12. In Boughton, "Drover Days."

13. This store was in Petersburg, Menard County, near Springfield, Illinois. Recollection of the store was written in 1860 by John Bennett, in "Autobiography of John Bennett," Bennett-Carter family, papers, 1836–1942, ISHL. For early store conditions and use of contents as collateral, see *History of Appanoose County*, 361–62. For bonding, see *History of Benton County, Iowa*, 330.

14. Christiana Holmes Tillson, edited by Milo Milton Quaife, *A Woman's Story of Pioneer Illinois* (Chicago: Lakeside/Donnelley, 1919), 124. For the Waterloo store, see John C. Hartman, ed., *History of Black Hawk County Iowa and Its People*, vol. 1 (Chicago: Clarke Publishing, 1915), 116.

15. Isaac D. Harmon, daybook, Naperville, 1837–11, CHS. The brothers all participated in the store and shared in doing the accounts.

16. For Clayes, see Harmon, papers, vol. 7, sales ledger, H. G. Loomis, April 1, 1837–40, CHS. For lawsuits, see Isaac D. Harmon, daybook, Naperville, 1837–41, CHS.

17. Harmon, papers, vol. 7, sales ledger, H. G. Loomis, April 1, 1837–40, CHS.

18. Letter from Peter Wheelock Jr. to Fairbanks Scale Company, 2 June 1849 in E[rasmus]. & T[haddeus]. Fairbanks & Co., records, 1838–1853, ISHL; for example of monthly receipts with Fairbanks, see Charles L. Harmon, Account Books, box 163, folder 15, "Invoices," CHS.

19. Isaac D. Harmon, daybook, 1837–41, CHS.

20. James Taylor Dunn, *The St. Croix: Midwest Border River* (New York: Holt, Rinehart & Winston, 1965), 16–18, 37, 78–81.

21. All of these men were involved in a drawn-out legal battle over the rights of the mill and an aligned copper mine, but this issue is secondary to that raised by their relationship to rural consumption. For more on the legal battles and citation, see Dunn, *St. Croix*, 78–98; and Caleb Cushing, papers, SHSW. Cushing served as U.S. attorney general under Franklin Pierce and was eventually nominated to the Massachusetts State Supreme Court.

22. Dunn, *St. Croix*, 78–81, 86–87. Investors were tied up in court from 1851 until 1857, placing little capital in the hands of locals by which they might fund expansion projects.

23. Contributions to the national economy by these types of agent activities are recorded in the historiography. Most of the major works agree that agents affected the region's economy in three main areas: they fueled local economic growth by providing access to relatively easy credit; they highlighted the need for better shipping services; and they were harbingers of new business concepts (e.g., cost accounting and inventory management) that revolutionized the American economy in the postbellum years. See below for a more complete explanation of each.

24. For bills of lading, including "16 trunks merchandise," see Cheever & Co., Saint Louis, to Perkins, 7 July 1847, in Cushing, papers, 1849–70, SHSW. Letter from Perkins & Co. to Cheever, 19 March 1848 (which included such essential items as "3 dozen red flannel shirts . . . 4 dozen hickory [shirts?] . . . 2 doz. silk handkerchiefs; fine linen."), ibid.

25. Most agents had to order their wares a full year ahead of their expected liquidation in the hinterland. This timing was pivotal in the long-term success of a firm. See Mahoney, *River Towns,* 167–71. Letter from Greene to Perkins, 28 May 1849, in Cushing, papers, 1849–70. Greene was not the only regional agent to fail as a result of the Saint Croix development plan. Mineralogist George W. Brownell aided Cushing and others in securing two mineral permits. Yet in a letter to Cushing dated 22 August 1848, he lamented the loss of more than $3,261 due him by Rantoul and Perkins. See letter, ibid. For history of the Saint Croix region, see Dunn, *St. Croix,* 52. Most of the correspondence between Cheever and Co. and Hamlet Perkins is in Greene's characteristic handwriting. His letter to Perkins, cited above, is signed by Greene. Other letters, attributed in this chapter to Greene, are sometimes signed "Cheever & Co.," but remain distinctively comparable to those signed by Greene.

26. Greene to Perkins, 30 August 1847, Cushing, papers; the second citation is from Judith Keith, in Barre, Vermont, to her brother Osborn Keith, in Chicago, on 21 March 1858, in Keith family, papers. Other examples abound describing the stress related to maintaining liquidity in this difficult business environment. See letter from Ellen White to Sarah Tyner, 10 October 1871, in Tyner-White family, papers, or John Kirk, letter books, 1852–1871, CHS. For the effect of this stress on one agent's relations in his family, see Charles L. Harmon to his brother Edwin, 13 October 1848, in Harmon family, papers, vol. 8.

27. Adler, *Yankee Merchants,* 67, 71–82. Adler states that "Western capital shortages, for example, presented few problems for Yankee entrepreneurs." Ibid., 77.

28. Mahoney, *River Towns,* 121–28.

29. 23 October 1857, cited in Mahoney, *River Towns,* 168.

30. Isaac Greene to Hamlet Perkins, 25 October 1847, in Cushing, papers, SHSW. A second example shows how one Philadelphia supplier asked an agent actually to take over a retail shop that was unsuccessfully operated by the man's son. See S. L. Smith to Charles L. Harmon, 7 May 1841, in Harmon family, papers, box 163, Harmon papers folder, 1847–51, invoices, 1841–48, CHS.

31. Harmon himself noted that his office in Chicago suffered from a lack of space. See letter from Harmon to his partner, Horatio Loomis, 21 August 1847, in Harmon family, papers, vol. 8.

32. The list of "trimmings" included paper, "blacking," two qualities of sugar and molasses, "java coffee," brandy, table condiments, and pickles. Harmon probably took

to using the word *trimmings* due to his relationship with hardware merchants, but letters—such as this one—indicate that he also used it to mean dry goods, coffee, and other scarce items. Letter of Charles L. Harmon to brother Edwin R. Harmon, 9 April 1847, in Harmon family, papers, vol. 8.

33. Joseph Bowren to Hamlet Perkins, 10 January 1847; and B. H. Cheever & Co. to Perkins, 25 August 1847, in Cushing, papers, SHSW. Additional goods from Boston included 61 barrels of beans, 240 barrels of pork, and a collar for a circular saw. See B. H. Cheever & Co. to Perkins & Co., 11 October 1847, ibid. The second letter from Franklin Steel to Perkins, 3 December 1847, ibid. Letter from G. S. Howell to Maxwell Howell, 28 August 1870, Howell papers, box 3, ISHL.

34. In addition to the items mentioned above, Greene forwarded other luxury goods (e.g., brass clocks) that were in high demand in the interior. See letter from Isaac Greene to Hamlet Perkins, 25 October 1847, in Cushing, papers.

35. Thomas Bennett to his father, John Bennett, 2 September 1855, in Bennett-Carter family, papers, ISHL.

36. Isaac Greene to Hamlet Perkins, 8 October 1847 and 25 October 1847, in Cushing, papers; for other comments on "fair" compensation, see Charles L. Harmon to Edwin Harmon, 9 April 1847, in Harmon family, papers, vol. 8.

37. Greene to Perkins, 6 September 1847 and 25 September 1847, in Cushing, papers.

38. Greene to Perkins, 25 September 1847 in Cushing, papers.

39. Chicago Agent John Kirk to Youngstown Manufacturing Co., 18 March 1867, in John Kirk, letter books, 1852–1871, CHS.

40. Harmon to Smith & Wilkins, 8 September 1846, in Harmon family, papers, vol. 8.

41. Harmon to Smith & Wilkins, 7 April 1847, in Harmon family, papers, vol. 8.

42. Harmon to Smith & Wilkins, 7 June 1848, ibid. For examples of Harmon's efforts to get the glass manufacturer to supply him with more product, see letters dated 8 September 1847, 30 September 1847, and 6 October 1847, ibid.

43. Harmon to A. J. Dunham & Co., 10 February 1847, in Harmon family, papers, vol. 8.

44. Harmon to A. J. Dunham & Co., 27 August 1846, and Harmon to his brother Edwin, 9 June 1847, ibid.

45. See Atherton, *Pioneer Merchants,* 82. For poor facilities, see H. Robert Grant, "Frontier and Western Transportation," In *American Frontier and Western Issues: A Historiographical Review,* ed. Roger L. Nichols (New York: Greenwood, 1986), 89–109; and George Rogers Taylor, *The Transportation Revolution: 1815–1860* (New York: Rinehart, 1951).

46. Edson Keith to Osborn Keith, 16 December 1855, in Keith family, papers.

47. For the example dealing with the railroads, see Peter Wheelock Jr. to Fairbanks [Scales] & Co., 16 June 1849 in E[rasmus] & T[haddeus] Fairbanks & Co., records. See also the *Cultivator and Country Gentleman* 13 (January 1869): 54; this issue noted that in Illinois "it is being demonstrated that while railroads greatly stimulate and increase production, they stimulate and increase consumption at a very greater rate." For lake transport, see Chicago agent William Blair to retailer Alexander, Howell & Co., 24 September 1855 in Alexander, Howell, business corr. For canals, see agent

John Mayers to Milo Custer, 20 June 1848, in Milo Custer, papers, 1830–1925, ISHL; and Charles L. Harmon to Holton & Goodall, 29 April 1847, in Harmon family, papers, vol. 8. For roads, see Charles L. Harmon to Smith & Wilkins, 15 December 1847 and Harmon to Wood & Sheldon, ibid.

48. In Fairbanks, records. See also discussion of early (1852) access to Wisconsin's hinterland in *Oshkosh City Times,* 28 March 1868; for later references to the effects of good rail transportation in relation to Chicago, ibid., 17 November 1868. Nowhere was this relationship between access to ready transportation and manufactured goods more apparent than in the boomtown of San Francisco. A "Letter Sheet of Prices, Prepared Expressly for the Daily Alta California, San Francisco, June 14, 1851" gives a review of the general market conditions in a town regularly supplied by ocean transports: "The market is altogether overstocked. That has been shipped during the last year, more than equal to one case for every resident of California . . . nothing but a very decided falling off in shipments will relieve the difficulty."

49. Harmon to Wood & Sheldon, 23 September 1846 and 26 March 1847, in Harmon family, papers, vol. 8.

50. Letter dated 6 December 1868 in Drury, Hayner, corr.

51. For his letter to Perkins regarding the various duties of an agent, see Cheever & Co. to Perkins & Co., 4 August 1847, in Cushing, papers, SHSW. For his letter providing pilots, see 11 September 1847, ibid.

52. Harmon to Wood & Sheldon, 18 January 1847, in Harmon family, papers, vol. 8.

53. See letters from Boston firm of Collander Rogers & Co. to Alexander, Howell & Co., 21 September 1855, and Troy, New York stove manufacturer Fuller Warren & Co. to Alexander, Howell & Co., 8 February 1860 in Alexander, Howell, business corr. See also letter from Kensington Iron & Nail Works, Pittsburgh, Lloyd & Black, to Alexander, Howell & Co., 11 June 1861, ibid. For examples of evaluating and often discounting paper, see Charles L. Harmon to Wood & Sheldon, 9 June 1847, stating that "there is a great scarcity of money here and exchange abundant at par on Buffalo & 1/2 to 1/4 on N.Y." in Harmon family, papers, vol. 8.

54. Harmon to D. O. Dickinson, 6 August 1848, in Harmon family, papers, vol. 8. William Blair to Alexander, Howell & Co., 4 May 1861, in Alexander, Howell, business corr.

55. Dated 16 May 1861, in Alexander, Howell, business corr. See also Charles L. Harmon to Wood & Sheldon, 9 June 1847, in Harmon family, papers, vol. 8. Edson Keith to brother Osborn Keith, 10 August 1858, in Keith family, papers.

56. First quotation from letter from Edson Keith to his mother, 19 June 1856—describing his travels throughout Portage City, Kenosha, Racine, Milwaukee, Sheboygan, Manitowoc, Two Rivers, and Green Bay, Wisconsin—the second from letter from Edson to Osborn Keith, 18 June 1856, in Keith family, papers.

57. For "shorts" citation, see Edson Keith to Osborn Keith, 7 December 1855, in Keith family, papers.

58. Edson Keith to Osborn Keith, 6 February 1859, in Keith family, papers, CHS. Isaac Harmon to Charles L. Harmon, 25 January 1848, in Harmon family, papers, vol. 8.

59. See letters from Collander, Rogers & Co., 21 September 1855; from Fuller

Warren & Co., 8 February 1860; and from William Blair & Co., 12 April 1871, in Alexander, Howell, business corr.

60. For a few examples of merchants who were not supplied with credit, see Charles Harmon to E. T. Fairbanks & Co., 30 March 1848 and 9 April 1848, in Harmon family, papers, vol. 8.

61. Many letters served to merge both credit and market information; see for example Harmon to E. T. Fairbanks & Co., 30 March 1858 and 9 April 1858, ibid. Also see general correspondence of Harmon in the summer of 1860, in Harmon family, papers, vol. 26, letter books, 1860, CHS.

62. For citations and other examples, see Charles L. Harmon to Wood & Sheldon, 23 September 1846; to Smith & Wilkins, 10 November 1846 and 18 December 1846; to Holton & Goodhall, 29 August 1846; to E. & T. Fairbanks & Co., 9 April 1858; and to his brother Edwin, 9 June 1847—all in Harmon family, papers, vol. 8.

63. Ellson Keith to Osborn Keith, 17 August 1858, in Keith family, papers.

64. For oysters, see Charles L. Harmon to James A. Bennet, 28 October 1846; for candles, see Harmon to his brother, 30 October 1846, in Harmon family, papers, vol. 8.

65. For credit reporting, see James D. Norris, *R. G. Dun & Co., 1841–1900: The Development of Credit-Reporting in the Nineteenth Century* (Westport, Conn.: Greenwood, 1978). For the *Chicago Tribune*'s effort in establishing market data and the geographic rivalries between the Western News Company—formed by the *Tribune* in 1865—and the New York–based American News Company, see J. Seymour Curry, *Chicago: Its History and Its Builders: A Century of Marvelous Growth*, vol. 2 (Chicago: Clarke, 1912), 201–3.

66. These goods included mustard, ground pepper, ginger, raisins, starch, "java coffee," and quality tea. See Charles L. Harmon to Wood & Sheldon, 8 August 1847, in Harmon family, papers, vol. 8.

67. Along with other examples, given in this chapter, see the development of Hartford City, Indiana. Again, there is a progression from local monopoly to competitive retailer from 1857 to 1863. See William F. Jones, papers, 1827–1890, InSL.

68. Harmon's transformation from a "traditional" multi-product agent to a "wholesale grocer and commission merchant" is typical of many urban middlemen. To see this transition, including the change to a cash-only business, see letters beginning 1 May 1860, in Harmon family, papers, vol. 26.

Chapter 4: An All-Consuming Vision

1. For the news account, see *Oshkosh City Times*, 12 February 1873.

2. The chapter discontinued its affiliation with the National Patrons of Husbandry in 1914. Diary entry dated 4 March 1874, in Griswold family, papers, ISHL. See also White Hall Social Grange No. 1308, treasurer's [receipts and disbursements], 1874–1914. ISHS.

3. Two other useful terms, *democratic coordination* of the marketplace and the *republican origins* of the Grange are incorporated within the phrase *rural consumer ethos*. Keillor's use of *democratic coordination* was run in opposition to Alfred Chandler's *administrative coordination*. Thomas Woods's use of the word *republicanism* ably describes the communal ideology of the Grange. Other popular terms, such as Daniel

Boorstin's *community of consumers,* fail to develop the conflicting nature of the underlying themes of community and individualism described in this chapter.

    4. For Iowa, see Mildred Thorne, "The Grange in Iowa," *Iowa Journal of History*
47 (October 1949): 289–324. For similar contractions throughout the region, see
Thomas Allan Woods, *Knights of the Plow: Oliver H. Kelley and the Republican Origins
of the Grange* (Ames: University of Iowa Press, 1992), 79. For notions of farmers as
"chronic revolutionaries," see Stanley B. Parsons, *The Populist Context: Rural Versus
Urban Power on a Great Plains Frontier* (Westport, Conn.: Greenwood Press, 1973);
and Norman Pollack, *The Populist Response to Industrial America* (Cambridge: Harvard University Press, 1962), 1–12. The debate over the economic and social causes
of conflict from 1865 to 1900 is almost as old as the profession of U.S. history. In recent years, these two motives took on decidedly conflicting postures following the
publication of E. P. Thompson's *The Making of the English Working Class.* Thompson
popularized the belief that a "moral economy" regulated economic exchange in the
premodern world; social mores rather than market pressures such as supply and demand determined economic behavior. Yet, even before Thompson introduced the
nomenclature, historians had already bifurcated the understanding of the causes of unrest between economic and social factors. See E. P. Thompson, *The Making of the English Working Class* (London: Gollancz, 1980); and Thompson, "The Moral Economy
of the English Crowd in the Eighteenth Century," *Past and Present* 50 (1971):
76–136. For predominantly economic explanations, such as the role played by debt
and market restrictions, see Walter T. K. Nugent, *Money and American Society,
1865–1880* (New York: Free Press, 1968); Stanley B. Parsons, *The Populist Context:
Rural versus Urban Power on a Great Plains Frontier* (Westport, Conn.: Greenwood,
1973); Fred A. Shannon, *American Farmers' Movement* (Princeton, N.J.: Van Nostrand, 1957); Robert P. Sharkey, *Money, Class, and Party* (Baltimore: John Hopkins
University Press, 1959); Robert Klepper, "The Economic Basis for Agrarian Protest
Movements in the United States, 1870–1900," Ph.D. diss., University of Chicago,
1973; Robert A. McGuire, "Economic Causes of Late Nineteenth-Century Agrarian
Unrest: New Evidence," *Journal of Economic History* (December 1981): 835–52; and
esp. John D. Hicks, *The Populist Revolt: A History of the Farmers' Alliance and the
People's Party* (Lincoln: University of Nebraska Press, 1961). For social causes of
changes, such as anxiety over change and the communal fear of economic effects, see
Richard Hofstadter, *The Age of Reform: From Bryan to F.D.R.* (New York: Knopf,
1955); Steven Hahn, *The Roots of Southern Populism: Yeoman Farmers and the Transformation of the Georgia Upcountry, 1850–1890* (New York: Oxford University Press,
1983); and Bruce Palmer, *"Man Over Money": The Southern Populist Critique of Northern Capitalism* (Chapel Hill: University of North Carolina, 1980).

    5. For the citation, see Cronon, *Nature's Metropolis,* 340. For market participa-
tion and development, see Ann Mayhew, "A Reappraisal of the Causes of Farm
Protest," 469; and Mahoney, *River Towns in the Great West,* 16–54. For ancillary supporting information, see Mary Eschelbach Gregson, "Rural Response to Increased Demand: Crop Choice in the Midwest, 1860–1880," *Journal of Economic History* 53, no.
2 (June 1993): 332–45; and Jeremy Atack and Fred Bateman, "Self-Sufficiency and
the Marketable Surplus in the Rural North, 1860," *Agricultural History* 58 (July
1984): 296–313; for the "logic of capital," see Cronon, *Nature's Metropolis,* 310–40.

    6. For effects of winner-take-all political system on third parties, see Peter H. Arg-

ersinger, *The Limits of Agrarian Radicalism: Western Populism and American Politics* (Lawrence: University Press of Kansas, 1995), 102, passim. Palmer served as a Democratic (antebellum) state representative, Republican governor, Liberal Republican Party official, Democratic (postbellum) U.S. senator, and presidential candidate for the "Gold Democrats." See Robert P. Howard, *Mostly Good and Competent Men: Illinois Governors, 1818–1988* (Springfield: Sangamon State University and Illinois State Historical Society, 1988). For fusion parties, see Goodwyn, *Democratic Promise*, 430–32; for earlier efforts such as the Illinois Independent Party, see John H. Keiser, *Building for the Centuries: Illinois, 1865–1898*, vol. 4 of *The Sesquicentennial History of Illinois* (Urbana: University of Illinois Press, 1977), 72–115; in Wisconsin, see Miller, *Railroads and the Granger Laws*, 140–60. For a contemporary, Northern view of the Democratic Party, see letter dated 3 September 1868 from John Kirk to James A. Parsons, in John Kirk, letter books, 1852–71, CHS. The rhetoric of producerism and yeomanry, common to this time, has been shown to resonate mainly with the ideologies of the individual journal editors and not the broader farm population. See Richard W. Abbott, "The Agricultural Press Views the Yeoman: 1819–1859," *Agricultural History* 42 (January 1968): 35–48. For more on journals and their editors' views, see Paul Wallace Gates, *The Farmer's Age: Agriculture 1815–1860*, vol. 3 of *The Economic History of the United States* (New York: Harper & Row, 1960), 338–58; George F. Lemmer, "Early Agricultural Editors and Their Farm Philosophies," *Agricultural History* 31, no. 4 (1957): 3–22; Richard T. Farrell, "Advice to Farmers: The Content of Agricultural Newspapers, 1860–1910," *Agricultural History* 51, no. 1 (1977): 209–16; and Jack W. Van Derhoof, "Agricultural Journalism."

7. Pederson, *Between Memory and Reality*, 60–91.

8. Sally McMurry, *Transforming Rural Life: Dairying Families and Agricultural Change, 1820–1885* (Baltimore: Johns Hopkins University Press, 1995); see also Hal Barron, *Those Who Stayed Behind*.

9. For the figures on the rise of the Grange, see *Greenwood Encyclopedia*, "farmers' organizations"; Buck, *The Granger Movement*, 60–73.

10. *The History of Appanoose County, Iowa* (Chicago: Western Historical, 1878), 398.

11. For a concise treatment of Goldschmidt, see Stephen Jay Gould, *The Flamingo's Smile: Reflections in Natural History* (New York, Norton, 1985), 371–73. The early historiography of the Grange focused exclusively on Patron leaders and their efforts to maintain the institution. As a result, initial researchers missed much of the more relevant aspects of what grassroots members actually attempted to do through their local chapters. The greatest misconception was the notion, promulgated by Solon Buck, that the national body actually provided farmers with their first direct experience with the distribution of goods and an awareness of the various consumer options open to them. While other claims pertaining to the national grange were often valid, the focus on the institutional success and failure shrouded the genuinely revolutionary character expressed by farmers and their local associations from 1865 to 1875. For the rigorous institutional focus, see Solon J. Buck, *The Agrarian Crusade: A Chronicle of the Farmer in Politics* (New Haven: Yale University Press, 1920), 71; see also Buck, *The Granger Movement*, chap. 2. Even recent works that have gone a long way toward reclaiming the Grange as a social institution have shown the effects of Buck's earlier thesis. In an otherwise excellent article, Roy Scott wrote that it was the national body

that "roused" farmers from their "apathy" rather than the body being an expression derived from it; Roy V. Scott, "Grangerism in Champaign County, Illinois, 1873–1877," *Mid-America* 43 (July 1961): 139. The best works on the Grange are the most recent, which focus on the order's social program: see Dennis S. Nordin, *Rich Harvest: A History of the Grange, 1867–1900* (Jackson: University Press of Mississippi, 1974); William D. Barns, "Oliver Hudson Kelley and the Genesis of the Grange: A Reappraisal," *Agricultural History* 41 (July 1967): 229–42; Woods, *Knights of the Plow;* and Margaret K. Andersen, "Agrarian Union: The Grange in the Midwest, 1870–1900," Ph.D. diss., Northwestern University, December 1989.

12. For an analysis of utopian societies, see Ronald Walters, *American Reformers, 1815–1860* (New York: Wang & Hill, 1978), 39–75. For contemporary discussions of the movement in the mid nineteenth century, see E. B. Bassett, *The Model Town; or, The Right and Progressive Organization of Industry for the Production of Material and Moral Wealth* (Cambridge, Mass.: Printed for the author, 1869).

13. For example, see C. R. Hoffer, "Co-operation as a Culture Pattern within a Community," *Rural Sociology* 3, no. 2 (1938): 153–58; Hoffer, "Services of Rural Trade Centers," *Social Forces* 10 (October 1931): 66–75; and Steven James Keillor, "Democratic Coordination in the Marketplace," chap. 6, 526. See below for a discussion concerning the formation of granges in Delaware County, Indiana.

14. For Clinton County, Illinois, see the *PF,* 4 July 1844, 181. For the first quote, see *Transactions of the Illinois State Agricultural Society* 1 (January 1862): 21. For club membership, see Buck, *The Granger Movement,* 74; and *Cultivator and Country Gentleman* (19 January 1860): 49.

15. Ann Mayhew makes the point that farmers reacted against the roads only *after* they found themselves in a vulnerable market position; i.e., when they had to pay precious cash or credit. This need for money was the critical factor that led most farmers to cite railroads for heavy-handedness. See Mayhew, "A Reappraisal of the Causes of Farm Protest in the United States, 1870–1900," 469. For lost respect by manufacturers, see *PF,* 25 October 1873, 339.

16. For boycott by planters, see comments made at 1872 Farmers' Convention, Kewanee, Illinois, recorded in the *PF,* 25 January 1873, 25. See also *PF,* 8 March 1873, 73, 75. The citation regarding DeKalb Grange is in the *Chicago Times,* 28 May 1873, 3. *Greenwood Encyclopedia,* "farmers' organizations."

17. *PF,* 25 October, 1873, 339.

18. For Hall, see Isaac and Benjamin B. Beeson, papers, 1870–1897, box 11, folder 4: Circulars and Advertisements, 1873–78, ISL. For others, see *PF,* 1 November 1873, 348.

19. For example of discounts, see *Chicago Times,* 17 September 1873, 7. For Iowa Grange, see *Report of Proceedings of the Fifth Annual Session of the Iowa State Grange,* 18. For $2,000 figure and ISFA slogan, see "Mr. Gorham," of Fulton, Illinois, in ISFA, *Proceedings* (1873), 18. For formation of the ISFA, see *Greenwood Encyclopedia,* "farmers' organizations"; the *Joliet Signal,* 20 January 1874, 4; *PF,* 30 October 1869, 353.

20. The association published the purchasing activities of farmers' clubs in Fulton County, Bureau County, and those of "a large number of other delegates, [who gave] their experience in the advantages gained by co-operation in the purchasing of their

supplies and in disposing of their products." See 3 May 1873, 13 May 1873, and 13 December 1873, in Elk Prairie Farmers' Club (Elkville, Ill.) minutes, 1873–74, ISHL. For association members, see ISFA, *Proceedings* (1873), 1–2, 18. For communal cost savings, citing a Grange store in Sedalia, Missouri, see John G. Wells, *The Grange Illustrated; or Patron's Hand-Book in the Interests of the Patrons of Husbandry* (New York: Grange Publishing, 1874), 172.

21. For family stability in the prairie, see John Mack Faragher, "Open Country Community: Sugar Creek, Illinois, 1820–1850," in Steven Hahn and Jonathan Prude, eds., *The Countryside in the Age of Capitalist Transformation: Essays in the Social History of Rural America* (Chapel Hill: University of North Carolina Press, 1985), 233–58; for visiting patterns, see Jane Marie Pedersen, "The Country Visitor: Patterns of Hospitality in Rural Wisconsin, 1880–1925," *Agricultural History* 58 (July 1984): 347–64. For quote of Mercer County, Illinois, farmer, see *CT*, 15 September 1873, 4. For Smedley, *Proceedings*, Fourth Annual Session, Iowa State Grange, 9.

22. *Past and Present of Hardin County Iowa* (Indianapolis: Bowen, 1911), 360. Fulton, *History of Jefferson County*, 388.

23. Citation from the *Western Farmer*, 14 June 1873, in the *Oshkosh City Times*, 18 June 1873. For second quote, see *PF*, 25 October 1873, 339.

24. For a skillful overview of "progressivism," see David P. Thelan, introduction to *The New Citizenship: Origins of Progressivism in Wisconsin, 1885–1900* (Columbia: University of Missouri Press, 1972). Remarkably, Grange efforts were involved in all three of the historiographical "camps" defined by Thelan: progressivism rooted in the class and status of a social group; that based on national interest groups by professional associations; and the progressivism of national elites hoping to suppress competing groups. For the citation, see *CT*, 23 August 1873, 8. For consumer focus, see Thelan, *The New Citizen*, 2; Mayhew, "A Reappraisal of the Causes of Farm Protest," 467–69.

25. For "oily" agents, see *PF*, 25 October 1873, 339. For other comments on exclusive territorial agencies, see *Oshkosh City Times*, 23 July 1873. For effects of lowered prices, see letter from J. Andrews of Rockford, Illinois, in *PF*, 25 February 1871, 57. For communal cost savings, citing a store in Sedalia, Missouri, see Wells, *The Grange Illustrated*, 172. For Illinois activist, James Creighton, see *Proceedings . . . Second Annual Meeting . . . Illinois State Farmers' Convention, Decatur . . . 1873 . . .* (Chicago: Southard, 1874), 5. See also *Oshkosh City Times*, 14 January 1874.

26. Whitman goes on to add an indictment against the patent laws, a bête noir of rural reformers, "they being the real foster mothers of some of the most oppressing monopolies of the present day." *Proceedings . . . Fourth Annual Session, Iowa State Grange* (Des Moines: Homestead and Western Farm, 1873), 19.

27. Ibid. and *Proceedings . . . Fifth Annual Session . . .* (Des Moines: Patron's Helper, 1874), 20.

28. *Proceedings . . . Fifth Annual Session*, 19–20.

29. Johnson's focus was on the "Burnt Over District" of western New York in the 1820s and 1830s. Many of these individuals were the parents of the Illinois, Indiana, and Wisconsin farmers detailed in this work. See Paul E. Johnson, *A Shopkeeper's Millennium: Society and Revivals in Rochester, New York, 1815–1837* (New York: Hill & Wang, 1978), 136–41.

30. Stressing virtue and democracy, farmers expressed their beliefs in a manner

that was much less radical than many antebellum republican movements. For antebellum agrarian radicalism, see Ronald P. Formisano and William G. Shade, "The Concept of Agrarian Radicalism," *Mid-America* 52, no. 1 (1970): 3–30; and Woods, introduction to *Knights of the Plow*. For Beeson, see Isaac and Benjamin B., papers, 1870–1897, box 11, folder 9, InSL. For a similar stance, see *Chicago Times,* 28 May 1873, 3.

31. For text of speech, see Isaac and Benjamin B., papers, 1870–1897, box 11, folder 9, InSL; for letter, see *PF,* 1 February 1873, 35.

32. *Proceedings . . . Second Annual Meeting of the Illinois State Farmers' Convention, 1873,* 70; *Proceedings, Fourth Annual Session, Iowa State Grange, 1873,* 10.

33. The central role of consumption in the ideology of large groups is not a new concept. This subtle yet powerful organizing force makes up the core of several very important works in U.S. urban history. See Roy Rosenzweig, *Eight Hours For What We Will: Workers and Leisure in an Industrial City, 1870–1920* (New York: Cambridge University Press, 1983); Lizebeth Cohen, *Making a New Deal: Industrial Workers in Chicago, 1919–1939* (New York: Cambridge University Press, 1990); Dana Frank, *Purchasing Power: Consumer Organizing, Gender, and the Seattle Labor Movement, 1919–1929* (New York: Cambridge University Press, 1994); and Andrew Heinze, *Adapting to Abundance: Jewish Immigrants, Mass Consumption, and the Search for American Identity* (New York: Columbia University Press, 1990).

34. For the utilitarian nature of the clubs, see *PF,* 4 March 1871, 65. For personal improvements, see remarks of M. L. Dunlap of the Savoy Farmers' Club, Champaign County, Illinois, in ISFA, *Proceedings* (1873), 19. For manufacturer quote, see *PF,* 9 November 1873, 355.

35. For the first quote, see *Oshkosh City Times,* 22 September 1868. For the second, see ISFA, *Proceedings* (1874), 5.

36. For Wisconsin efforts, see Gerald LeRoy Prescott, "Yeoman, Entrepreneurs, and Gentry: A Comparative Study of Three Wisconsin Agricultural Organizations, 1873–1893," Ph. D. diss. University of Wisconsin, 1968, 58–78, 107–54; and Miller, *Railroads and the Granger Laws,* 91, 140–60, 166. For Illinois and Indiana, see Buck, *The Granger Movement,* chap. 3, 98; *Greenwood Encyclopedia,* "farmers' organizations"; *Chicago Evening Journal,* 24 December 1873, 1. For a critical, contemporary review of this fusion, see *CT,* 30 January 1877, 4.

37. For Smith citation, see *PF,* 1 November 1873, 346. For meeting, related to Wisconsin Granger Joseph Osborn by his friend William Orlidge, in letter dated 16 September 1875, see Joseph H. Osborn, papers, 1873–1877, SHSW.

38. For dangers, see *PF,* 5 March 1873, 105. Similar warnings were issued from Wisconsin farmers: see *Oshkosh City Times,* 30 April 1873. For second quote, see *Chicago Evening Journal,* 24 December 1873, 1. In Wisconsin, Patrons feared that such active politics would affect the very newspapers that they chose to publicize their movement. See *Oshkosh City Times,* 23 July 1873, and 30 July 1873.

39. This fundamental fracture between clubs and granges over the political participation of their institutions made cooperation in pursuit of purchasing strategies extremely difficult. Only at the local level did they succeed in achieving discounts from regional suppliers from their merged efforts. In Ford County, Illinois, 108 Grangers and 30 club members purchased nearly $1,000 worth of family supplies, saving 30 per-

cent over "what the same class of goods formerly cost." Members were "so well satisfied with [their] purchases that [they] concluded to order a small stock of staple articles
to be kept constantly on hand for the benefit of the members of both." Communities
in Rockford, Kewanee, and elsewhere paralleled these activities. For the quote, see *PF,*
13 December 1873, 395. For other examples, see *PF,* 6 January 1872, 4; 26 October
1872, 337; 22 February 1873, 59; *Chicago Times,* 22 May 1873, 3 and March 2,
1875, in Winnebago County minutes, ISHL. For "forced existence," see *PF,* 24 February 1872, 60. See also ibid., 12 October 1872, 326. D. Wyatt Aiken, *The Grange; Its
Origins, Progress, and Educational Purposes* (Philadelphia: Wagenseller. 1884), 26–27.
For examples of Smith's effect on local Grangers, see *PF,* 5 March 1873, 105; 19
March 1873, 123; 30 August 1873, 275–76.

   40. For first quote, see *Ripon Free Press,* 1 September 1875. For second quote, see
Wells, *Patrons' Hand-Book,* 163.

   41. *PF,* 3 January 1874, 1.

   42. For information on Kelley, see Oliver H. Kelley, *Origins and Progress of the
Order of the Patrons of Husbandry in the United States: A History from 1866 to 1873*
(Philadelphia: Waganseller, 1875); and Woods, *Knights of the Plow.*

   43. For citation, see *CT,* 13 October 1873, 7.

   44. For letter, dated July 12, 1868, written from Itasca, Minnesota, see Kelley,
Origins and Progress, 112–13. For protection, ibid., 113–14; and *PF,* 18 July 1868, 20.

   45. Oliver H. Kelley, *Origins and Progress of the Order of the Patrons of Husbandry
in the United States: A History from 1866 to 1873* (Philadelphia: Waganseller, 1875),
112–13, 180.

   46. For Minnesota experience, see Kelley, *Origins and Progress,* 183–86.

   47. For Indiana citation, dated January 26, 1875, see Indiana State Grange, executive committee minutes, Indiana State, Patrons of Husbandry, 1874–93, InSL. For
second quote, *CT,* 7 March 1874, 5.

   48. For bond contract and clerks, see executive committee minutes, Indiana State
Grange, 28 January 1875, InSL; for establishment of a depot, see "Report of Special
Committee on establishing a depot for the distribution of merchandise," Wisconsin
State Grange, *Proceedings . . . State Grange of Wisconsin, Second Annual Session . . .
1874* (Oshkosh: Times Printing, 1874), 15–18. See also the Champaign Grange No.
621, records, 1873–77, 7 October 1873, University of Illinois, Champaign-Urbana;
and ibid., 19 August 1874; *Oshkosh City Times,* 13 March 1872, 4; and grange minutes
dated 5 March 1874 in Beeson, papers, box 11, folder 1: 1870–75, InSL.

   49. For questioning of the need for a variety, see *Oshkosh City Times,* 12 March
1873; for musical instruments, ibid., 28 January 1874, 1. For Grange author, see
Wells, *Patrons' Hand-Book,* 171. For Osborn letter from James Cassidy, 19 March
1873, see Osborn, papers, 1873–77, SHSW.

   50. See *PF,* 25 October 1873, 339. For national grange perspective, see Wells,
Patrons' Hand-Book, 172, 175.

   51. For "tidal wave," see letter to J. G. Kingbury & Co., 8 March 1874, in Beeson, papers, box 11, folder 1: 1870–75, InSL. For role of purchasing agency, see *PF,* 6
December 1873, 388; 12 December 1873, 395–96; and 3 January 1874, 4. For the
figures on the rise of the Grange, see *Greenwood Encyclopedia,* "farmers' organizations"; Buck, *The Granger Movement,* 60–73. For national sales figures, see *Ripon Free*

Press, 25 November 1875. For social advantages to the larger community, see *PF,* 11 January 1873, 11; 1 February 1873, 35; 25 February 1873, 57; and 29 November 1873, 377. See also ISFA, *Proceedings* (1874), 70; and executive committee, Wisconsin State Grange, *Bulletin,* July 1877, SHSW.

52. For the Southern Grange, see Hahn, *Roots of Southern Populism,* 222–23.

53. *History of Delaware County, Indiana with Illustrations and Biographical Sketches of Some of its Prominent Men and Pioneers* (Chicago: Kingman Bros., 1881) 61–62, 241, 245.

54. Ibid., 297.

55. Ibid., 64.

56. Appendix 1 addresses sources, methodology, and the problems associated with the federal census of 1870. In brief, I argue that the real-estate and personal-property values assigned in the enumeration offer a crude but *relative* guide by which to compare Grange and non-Grange farmers in Delaware County.

57. See letter of John Samuel, Grange No. 222, Saint Louis, Missouri, to Joseph Osborn, 23 January 1874, in Osborn, papers, box 1, folder: 1855–74, SHSW. For second citation, see Tyner letter to L. G. Kniffen, 29 July 1875, in Osborn, papers, 1873–1877. See also Jeannette E. Yates, *History of Fifty Years in Illinois State Grange, Prepared for the Golden Jubilee . . . 1921,* SHSW.

58. For examples of inept mail handling, see Erastus Brown to Joseph Osborn, 14 July 1875, in Osborn, papers; and letters from Alpheus Tyner to Isaac Beeson, 27 April 1876, and 2 May 1876, in Beeson, papers, InSL. For examples of the overloaded agency, see April 1875 and March 1877 in executive committee, Wisconsin State Grange, *Bulletin,* SHSW. For record keeping, see the "Account of the transactions of the agent of the Nettle Creek Grange No. 735 during the year 1876," in Beeson, papers, InSL. In another account, 10 December 1876, when auditing the books of the Indiana State Grange, State Secretary C. C. Post noted that while the ledgers balanced, the agent's books were "in the form of notes of the value of which I will not now express an opinion." In Indiana State Grange, executive committee minutes, InSL. For examination of goods, see the Winnebago Pamona Grange, minutes, ISHL.

59. For debates over commission agency, see *Proceedings, Iowa State Grange* (1874), 19, 24. See *Ripon Free Press,* 23 December 1875. For a state implement fund, see Wisconsin State Grange, *Proceedings* (1874), 5–8. For requests for funding to national grange, see National Grange, *Proceedings . . . Ninth Session . . .* (Louisville: Morton, 1875), 20. While most loans were made in order to provide for the manufacture of agricultural implements, many states used the funds for their purchasing activities; see Wisconsin State Grange, *Proceedings* (1876), 9.

60. For Minnesota, see *Oshkosh City Times,* 29 October 1873. For "Open Terms" see *PF,* 21 June 1873, 195. For "trifling matter," offered by a farmer from Lovington, Illinois, ibid., 26 July 1873, 235.

61. *PF,* 6 September 1873, 283. See also issues for 21 June, 1873, 195; 26 July, 1873, 235; and 9 November, 1873, 355. The secrecy surrounding grange purchasing activities often was at the behest of the manufacturers who granted them discounts. The suppliers feared loss of business from nonmembers who were not eligible for the savings. See Osborn circular, 20 June 1873, in Osborn, papers, SHSW; and Wisconsin State Grange, *Confidential Price List, 1874* (Oshkosh: Fernandez & O'Bryan, 1874),

SHSW. For traditional fears of conspiracy and group secrecy, see David H. Bennett, *The Party of Fear: From Nativist Movements to the New Right in American History* (Chapel Hill: University of North Carolina Press, 1988).

62. M. E. Gustin, *An Expose of the Grangers: Containing the Opening and Closing Ceremonies of a Granger's Lodge; the Ceremonies of Initiation, and the Eight Degrees of the Order. Being an accurate description of one of the Greatest Monopolies of the Age* (Dayton, Ohio: Christian Publishing Association, 1875), 56–57, 70–72. Charles F. Adams Jr., "The Granger Movement," *North American Review* 120 (April 1875), 395. For a reply, see letter from S. M. Smith, 16 September 1875, to Osborn, in Osborn, papers, 1873–77 (Oshkosh Public Museum; copy at SHSW). See also two interesting exchanges regarding socialism in the farm community, *PF,* 3 January 1874, 1; and *Oshkosh City Times,* 17 January 1872.

63. *Proceedings, Fourth Annual Session, Iowa State Grange, 1873,* 10.

64. Iowa State Grange, minutes, Marion Grange No. 391, Hamilton Co., Iowa, 1872–1874, SHSI, 1–60.

65. Ibid., 64, 65, 72–73.

66. *History of Hamilton County, Iowa,* vol. 1 (Dallas: Curtis Media, 1986), 84, 307, 495.

67. Minutes, Marion Grange No. 391, SHSI, 90.

68. Ibid., 117–19.

69. Ibid., 148–50.

70. For Adams, see *Abstract of the Proceedings of the National and State Granges for the Year 1872: Including Receipts and Expenditures of Both* (Des Moines: Iowa Homestead Steam Print, 1873), 17. For Kniffen, see circular, c. 1875 in Osborn, papers, 1873–1877. For Champaign farmer, see ISFA, *Proceedings* (1873), 18. See also *PF,* 22 November 1873, 371.

71. For Frew quote, see Illinois State Grange, *Proceedings . . . Third Annual Session . . . 1875* (Chicago: Fish, 1875), 24.

72. *PF,* 1 November 1873, 348.

Chapter 5: Town v. Country

1. For the debate surrounding the grange store, including support for the grange, see *Ripon Free Press,* 17 January and 7 February 1878.

2. *Cultivator and Country Gentleman* (24 June 1869): 494.

3. Probably the best example of this was Cyrus McCormick's reaper works, called by William Cronon a "case study in the growth of Chicago industry and the sale of manufactured goods to hinterland customers." Cronon, *Nature's Metropolis,* 313. While I am critical of Cronon's overall conclusions regarding rural agency, the text remains a seminal work on the region and it has still untapped potential for new interpretations. I am greatly indebted to his work for raising many of the questions that are at the heart of my study.

4. Cronon, *Nature's Metropolis,* 339.

5. For a more nuanced appreciation of rural/urban consumer interactions, see Barron, *Mixed Harvest,* 155–91.

6. See *Oshkosh City Times,* 11 May 1870; 14 June 1871; 11 December 1872; and *Ripon Free Press,* 18 September 1879.

7. Much has been written on the subject of advertising and consumption, but most of it remains closely linked to urban populations. The most complete works on advertising and consumption are David Morris Potter, *People of Plenty: Economic Abundance and the American Character* (Chicago: University of Chicago Press, 1954); Stuart Ewen, *Captains of Consciousness: Advertising and the Social Roots of the Consumer Culture* (New York: McGraw-Hill, 1976); Richard Wightman Fox and T. J. Jackson Lears, eds., *The Culture of Consumption: Critical Essays in American History, 1880–1980* (New York: Pantheon, 1983); Daniel Pope, *The Making of Modern Advertising* (New York: Basic, 1983); Stephen R. Fox, *The Mirror Makers: A History of American Advertising and Its Creators* (New York: Morrow, 1984); Roland Marchand, *Advertising the American Dream: Making Way For Modernity, 1920–1940* (Berkeley: University of California Press, 1985); Richard S. Tedlow, *New and Improved: The Story of Mass Marketing in America* (New York: Basic Books, 1990); Susan Strasser, *Satisfaction Guaranteed: The Making of the American Mass Market* (New York: Pantheon, 1989); James D. Norris, *Advertising and the Transformation of American Society, 1865–1920* (New York: Greenwood, 1990); William Leach, *Land of Desire*; and T. J. Jackson Lears, *Fables of Abundance: A Cultural History of Advertising in America* (New York: Basic, 1994).

8. For a relevant discussion of historical paradigms and schema, see Thomas L. Haskell, *Objectivity Is Not Neutrality: Explanatory Schemes in History* (Baltimore: Johns Hopkins University Press, 1998), 1–24.

9. For first citation, see Lewis E. Atherton, *The Pioneer Merchant in Mid-America* (New York: DeCapo, 1969), 125. For the ad, see *Oshkosh City Times*, 25 January 1871.

10. *Milwaukee Bulletin*, 11 August 1866. For examples of successful campaigns, see *Ripon Free Press*, 9 January 1879. *Milwaukee Enterprise*, 12 April 1873. For citation, see *Oshkosh City Times*, 29 December 1868.

11. For more on the relationship between newspapers (including Horace Greeley's *New York Tribune* and John Wentworth's *Chicago Democrat*) and the new Republican Party, see Eric Foner, *Free Soil, Free Labor, Free Men: The Ideology of the Republican Party before the Civil War* (New York: Oxford University Press, 1970), passim; for the *CT* and the Republican Party, see Lloyd Wendt, *The Chicago Tribune: The Rise of a Great American Newspaper* (Chicago: Rand, McNally, 1979), 3–25.

12. For the geographic rivalries between the Western News Company and the New York–based American News Company, as well as Medill's role in the formation of the Western Associated Press (1865), see J. Seymour Curry, *Chicago: Its History and Its Builders: A Century of Marvelous Growth*, vol. 2 (Chicago: Clarke, 1912), 201–3. For Medill quote, see Wendt, 168.

13. Minutes, Marion Grange No. 391, SHSI, 90.

14. Each category provides evidence of "expected results," with no startling deviations. By this I mean that agents, manufacturers, and patent-medicine ads are commonly seen in the newspapers of this time and are well represented in the secondary literature on the subject.

15. Agents were targeted consumers by "describing themselves" within the ads, as seen in spots such as those placed by F. Lester, who advertised "2,000 tons of coal," see *CT*, 22 November 1868, 1; or the firm of Stark & Allen, who promoted the sales of

20,000 "damaged watches," see *CT*, 3 November 1871, 1. A common indicator that the ads were intended for remarketeers was the claim made by, for example, the wholesale clothing firm of Hamlin, Hale & Co., that "our buyers for the several departments have purchased at auction and of the manufacturers, liberally, at low prices, and we are prepared to fill orders and to supply the trade." See *CT*, 19 November 1872, 5.

16. The ads do demonstrate a remarkable seasonal pattern—one that appears to wane as the years pass. For example, in seven out of ten instances, when Eastern firms evidenced an increase over expected results in the number of ads, it was during the cold weather months of November and February. It seems to make sense that Chicago firms would dominate the market at such times (due to difficult shipping conditions, suspended grain markets, etc.), but this was not so.

17. A common request by businesses after the fire was for their customers to notify them on the state of their accounts. This sentiment was echoed by piano dealer W. W. Kimball, who asked "all persons who have rented or leased pianos [to] please call and report"; see *CT*, 3 November 1871, 4. For the quote in text, ibid., 2. For Sturges & Co., see Dixon Retail Hardware Store, papers, 1854–76, ISHL.

18. "Other" goods includes a grab bag of items: alcohol, tobacco, religious goods, unusual ads (e.g., response to slander), consumer clubs, multiple products, residential property, printed information, educational services, live plants, fuels, theater, concerts. skating, lotteries, dancing, and circuses.

19. See Wiebe, *Search for Order*; Alfred Chandler, *The Visible Hand, The Managerial Revolution in American Business*; David A. Hounshell, *From the American System to Mass Production, 1800–1932* (Baltimore: John Hopkins University Press, 1984); and T. J. Jackson Lears, *No Place of Grace: Anti-Modernism and the Transformation of American Culture, 1880–1920* (New York: Pantheon, 1981).

20. For a particularly aggressive critique of Cronon's work, see Peter A. Coclanis's article *"Urbs in Horto"* in *Reviews in American History* 20 (1992): 14–20.

21. While each locale had unique economic traditions, both were symbolic of the developing rural/urban conflicts of the era. By 1865, both locations had diversified and had traditional commercial economies that relied heavily upon the patronage of the local farmers. Ripon, noted as the founding location of the Republican Party in 1854, was settled initially by farming families dedicated to the phalanx principles of Charles Fourier. Oshkosh was organized around more conventional commercial precepts, focusing on the harvesting of the white-pine forests indigenous to Wisconsin. In 1868, Oshkosh alone boasted more than 2,100 residences, 220 "buildings occupied for the sale of goods," and more than 100 factories. For more on both towns, see Larry Gara, *A Short History of Wisconsin* (Madison: State Historical Society of Wisconsin, 1962), 62, 85, 102, 143, 164, 169–70. See also *Oshkosh City Times*, 18 February 1868; 25 February 1868; 31 March 1868; and 28 August 1868.

22. The *other* category is less clearly distinguished. In Ripon, for example, a large number of these advertisers were associated with the local college. In sum, the *other* category in the big city reflects a larger diversity in the economy, whereas this is not a valid conclusion for the smaller markets. Unfortunately, this is a problem that cannot be fully explored using this coding method.

23. *Indianapolis Journal,* 13 October 1870.

24. See Thorstein Veblen, "The Country Town," *Freeman* (11 July 1923): 417–20; and (18 July 1923): 440–43. For more on Veblen, see Paul T. Homan, *Contemporary Economic Thought* (New York: Harper & Bros., 1928), 107–92.

25. For refutation of Veblen, see Lewis E. Atherton, *Main Street on the Middle Border* (Bloomington: Indiana University Press, 1954), 49–57.

26. *Oshkosh City Times,* 6 April 1869 and 31 March 1868; for quote, see *Ripon Free Press,* 18 September 1879. On 21 August 1872, the *City Times* reported two national banks; one savings bank; eight dry-goods houses, two of them wholesale; two wholesale houses of hardware; eight dealers in hardware; thirty grocery and provision stores, three of them wholesale; two crockery stores; eight drug stores; three music stores; five book and stationary stores; eight boot and shoe stores; one wholesale oil, paint, and glass store; six watch and jewelry stores; two wholesale liquor dealers; eight dealers in flour-grain; seven clothing stores; two hat and cap stores; five fancy dry-good and millinery stores; seven furniture stores; three for brick and lime; two for leather and shoes; three for agricultural implements; three grain elevators; and three commission merchants.

27. *Oshkosh City Times,* 17 January 1872, 13 March 1872, 20 March 1872. *Ripon Free Press,* 17 January 1878.

28. *Ripon Free Press,* 15 May 1879, 21 August 1879.

29. *Oshkosh City Times,* 10 December 1867.

30. *Ripon Free Press,* 19 August 1875; *Oshkosh City Times,* 23 March 1869.

31. *Ripon Free Press,* 9 January 1879.

32. For Harper Brothers, see *Ripon Free Press,* 11 September 1879 and 18 September 1879. For cooperatives, see *Oshkosh City Times,* 22 September 1868; *Ripon Free Press,* 20 January 1876.

33. *Cultivator and Country Gentleman* 35 (2 November 1870): 708.

34. See *Oshkosh City Times,* 17 November 1868; an article in support of Prairie du Chien river improvements. See also *Oshkosh City Times,* 12 January 1869. For Milwaukee complaints, see *Ripon Free Press,* 26 August 1875. For lost manufacturing opportunities, see *Oshkosh City Times,* 29 October 1867.

35. *Ripon Free Press,* 26 August 1875.

36. *Oshkosh City Times,* 6 April 1869. For denial of ad space, see 26 May 1877.

37. For the economic and social changes underpinning this movement, see Samuel P. Hays, *The Response to Industrialism, 1885–1914* (Chicago: University of Chicago Press, 1957), 4, 13, 54, chap. 7; for technology, transportation, and new "system building" by businesses, see Alfred Chandler Jr., *The Visible Hand: The Managerial Revolution in American Business* (Cambridge, Mass.: Belknap/Harvard University Press, 1977), 122–43, 147–67, 175, chap. 7. For an understanding of other social and psychological changes wrought, see Wiebe, *Search for Order,* 111–63.

38. See Warren I. Susman, *Culture as History: The Transformation of American Society in the Twentieth Century* (New York: Pantheon, 1973); and Christopher Lasch, *True and Only Heaven: Progress and Its Critics* (New York: Norton, 1991). For an overview of the many consumer ideologies, see Lears, *No Place of Grace,* 1–47. For a socialist interpretation of consumption, see Karl Marx's theories as presented in Patrick Brantlinger, *Bread and Circuses: Theories of Mass Culture and Social Decay* (Ithaca: Cornell University Press, 1983), 82–183; and Gary Cross, *Time and Money: The Making of Consumer Culture* (New York: Routledge, 1993), 16–45. See also Edward Bel-

lamy, *Equality* (Upper Saddle River, N.J.: Gregg, 1968), iii–iv, 31–61. For a liberal perspective, circulated by Thorstein Veblen, Simon Patten, and James Bates Clark, see Morton G. White, *Social Thought in America: The Revolt Against Formalism* (New York: Viking, 1952), passim; James T. Kloppenberg, "In Retrospect: Morton White's Social Thought in America," *Reviews in American History* 15 (September 1987): 507–19; and Paul T. Homan, *Contemporary Economic Thought* (New York: Harper & Bros., 1928), 15–103, 107–92. For conservatives such as William Graham Sumner, see Robert G. McCloskey, *American Conservatism in the Age of Enterprise: A Study of William Graham Sumner, Stephan J. Field, and Andrew Carnegie* (New York: Harper & Row, 1964), chap. 2, passim. For a sociological perspective, which includes Emile Durkheim, the "Chicago School," and Robert and Helen Lynd, see Hugh Dalziel Duncan, *Symbols and Social Theory* (New York: Oxford University Press, 1969), xx, 147–54, 284, 285, chap. 12; Robert E. Park and E. W. Burgess, *Introduction to the Science of Sociology*, 3rd ed., revised (Chicago: University of Chicago Press, 1969), 443–44, 482–88, 978; R. E. Parks, E. W. Burgess, and R. D. McKenzie, *The City* [1925] (reprint, Chicago: University of Chicago Press, 1967), 37–38; Albert J. Reiss Jr., *Louis Wirth: On Cities and Social Life, Selected Papers* (Chicago: University of Chicago Press, 1964), xx, 26; Robert S. Lynd and Helen M. Lynd, introduction to *Middletown: A Study of American Culture* (New York: Harcourt, Brace, Jovanovich, 1956), and 87, 81–82, 158. See also Richard Wightman Fox, "Epitaph For Middletown: Robert S. Lynd and the Analysis of Consumer Culture," in Fox and Lears, *Culture of Consumption*, 125–26, 130–34. For a longer, yet still limited historiographical essay, see David Blanke, "A Selected Bibliographic Essay: Consumer Culture during the Gilded and Progressive Eras," at http://www.h-net.msu.edu/~shgape/bibs/consumer.html.

39. For good reviews of the problems of this ideological focus and the perceptions of irreconcilable conflicts between the camps, see Gary Cross, *Time and Money: The Making of Consumer Culture* (New York: Routledge), 1–45; Daniel Horowitz, introduction to *The Morality of Spending: Attitudes toward the Consumer Society in America, 1875–1940* (Baltimore: John Hopkins University Press, 1985), xii; and Daniel Miller, *Material Culture and Mass Consumption* (Oxford: Blackwood, 1987), 3–18, part 3. For an excellent recent work dealing with the cultural ambiguities of consumer debt, see Lendol Calder, *Financing the American Dream: A Cultural History of Consumer Credit* (Princeton: Princeton University Press, 1999).

40. Most tellingly, class stratifications offered a variety of interpretive frameworks. See Andrew Heinze, *Adapting to Abundance: Jewish Immigrants, Mass Consumption, and the Search for American Identity* (New York: Columbia University Press, 1990); Lizabeth Cohen, *Making A New Deal: Industrial Workers in Chicago, 1919–1939* (New York: Cambridge University Press, 1990), 99, chap. 3; Gunther Barth, *City People: The Rise of Modern City Culture in Nineteenth Century America* (New York: Oxford University Press, 1980), chap. 3; Lears, *No Place of Grace*, 300, 62–67, 100, 206, passim.; Elaine S. Abelson, *When Ladies Go A-Thieving: Middle-Class Shoplifters in the Victorian Department Store* (New York: Oxford University Press, 1989), chap. 1; W. Hamish Fraser, *The Coming of the Mass Market, 1850–1914* (London: MacMillan, 1981); and Dana Frank, *Purchasing Power: Consumer Organizing, Gender, and the Seattle Labor Movement, 1919–1929* (New York: Cambridge University Press, 1994).

41. For the "dawn of self-consciousness," see Neil Harris, introduction to *The*

Land of Contrasts, 1880–1901, ed. Neil Harris (New York: Braziller, 1970), 1. For "consumer lifestyle," see Grant McCracken, *Culture and Consumption: New Approaches to the Symbolic Character of Consumer Goods and Activities* (Bloomington: Indiana University Press, 1988), 27; this pattern was demonstrated earlier in Europe—see Rosalind Williams, *Dream Worlds: Mass Consumption in Late Nineteenth-Century France* (Berkeley: University of California Press, 1982), 1–15; and Thomas Richards, *The Commodity Culture of Victorian England: Advertising and Spectacle, 1851–1914* (Stanford: Stanford University Press, 1990), chaps. 1 and 2. For the mythical "therapeutic" effect from consumption, see Lears, *No Place of Grace,* 42–58. For the propagation of these self-defining myths, see Martin V. Martel and George J. McCall, "Reality-Orientation and the Pleasure Principle: A Study of American Mass-Periodical Fiction, 1890–1955," in *People, Society, and Mass Communications,* Lewis Anthony Dexter and David Manning White, eds. (New York: Free Press, 1964), 317–19, and Christopher P. Wilson, "The Rhetoric of Consumption," in Fox and Lears, *Culture of Consumption,* 39–64.

42. See William Leach, *Land of Desire: Merchants, Power, and the Rise of a New American Culture* (New York: Pantheon, 1993); and Abelson, introduction to *When Ladies Go A–Thieving,* and chaps. 1, 2, and 3.

43. *Oshkosh City Times,* 15 December 1868; and 11 May 1870.

44. For Fowle's store, see *Oshkosh City Times,* 21 July 1868; for Ripon, see *Ripon Free Press,* 26 October 1882. For Chicago references, see *Oshkosh City Times,* 14 June 1871, 11 December 1872.

45. For Biggers, see *Oshkosh City Times,* 11 December, 1872.

46. *AA,* July 1862, 203; *Ripon Free Press,* 6 February 1879.

47. *Ripon Free Press,* 23 April 1876. *Oshkosh City Times,* 11 December 1872. The Palace Store and Hart's Dry Goods Palace also turned to one-price shopping. See *Oshkosh City Times,* 26 April 1871. For "Bargain-Hunters," *Oshkosh City Times,* 26 November 1867.

48. *Ripon Free Press,* 13 January 1881.

Chapter 6: A Battle of Standards

1. For Adams, see National Grange, *Proceedings . . . Seventh Session . . .* (New York: Green, 1874), 13–14. For report of committee, see National Grange, *Proceedings . . . Eighth Session* (Claremont, N.H.: Claremont Manufacturing, 1875), 23–26.

2. For Wisconsin Grange motto, see circular to granges from Joseph Osborn, Oshkosh, 2 January 1874, in Joseph H. Osborn, papers, 1855–90, folder 1855–74, SHSW.

3. For Chicago meeting, see Indiana State Grange, *Proceedings, Seventh Annual Session . . .* (Indianapolis: Indiana Farmer, 1879), 44. See, for example, a letter from R. S. Thompson, publisher of the *Live Patron,* of Springfield, Ohio, to Benjamin Beeson, December 2, 1879, in which Thompson demanded that discounted consumer goods were available only to subscribers of the magazine: "If anyone else wants any of these articles let them subscribe for the [Live] *Patron* first, then they can get them at the same terms." In Beeson, papers, folder 3: 1878–97, InSL.

4. For numbers, see *Greenwood Encyclopedia,* "farmers' organizations"; Morton Rothstein, "Farmer Movements and Organizations: Numbers, Gains, Losses." *Agricultural History* 62 (June 1988): 169; Roy V. Scott, "Grangerism in Champaign

County, Illinois, 1873–1877." *Mid-America* 43 (July 1961): 162–63. For Wisconsin, see Wisconsin State Grange, *Proceedings* (1876), 6–10, 39–45.

5. For examples of problems facing the purchasing movement, see Colston Estley Warne, introduction to *The Consumers' Co-Operative Movement in Illinois* (Chicago: University of Chicago Press, 1926), and chap. 1. For leading works on the Grange and a discussion of purchasing activities, see Dennis S. Nordin, *Rich Harvest: A History of the Grange, 1867–1900* (Jackson: University Press of Mississippi, 1974); William D. Barns, "Oliver Hudson Kelley and the Genesis of the Grange: A Reappraisal," *Agricultural History* 41 (July 1967): 229–42; Woods, *Knights of the Plow;* Douglass R. Hurt, "The Ohio Grange, 1870–1900," *Northwest Ohio Quarterly* 53 (December 1981): 19–32; and Margaret K. Andersen, "Agrarian Union: The Grange in the Midwest, 1870–1900," Ph.D. diss., Northwestern University, December 1989.

6. For "granger style," see purchasing agent's department, in executive committee, Wisconsin State Grange, *Bulletin*, July, 1875. For charge of socialism, see Charles F. Adams Jr., "The Granger Movement," *North American Review* 120 (April 1875): 395. See also *PF*, 3 January 1874, 1; and *Oshkosh City Times*, 17 January 1872.

7. For Frew, see Illinois State Grange, *Proceedings, Third Annual Session, 1875* (Chicago: Fish, 1875), 19; for Guy to Osborn, dated March 18, 1876, see Osborn, papers, SHSW. For Illinois numbers, see Illinois State Grange, *Proceedings* (1875), 31; for Wisconsin, see Wisconsin State Grange, *Proceedings, Fourth Annual Meeting, 1876* (Milwaukee: Sentinel, 1876), 15; for Indiana, see Indiana State Grange, *Proceedings, Sixth Annual Session . . .* (Muncie: Hoosier Patron Steam Printing, 1876), 17. For quote from the executive committee report, Wisconsin State Grange, *Proceedings, Ninth Annual Meeting, of the Wisconsin State Grange, 1881* (Milwaukee: Trayser, 1881), 36.

8. The state master noted that competition was rife "growing chiefly out of location, and facilities of trade." See Indiana State Grange, *Proceedings* (1876), 5–6.

9. Tyner quote, ibid., 17–18. For committee response, ibid., 21–22. See also "Business Circular to the Granges Office of the Indiana Farmer," 7 January 1877, in Isaac and Benjamin B. Beeson, papers, 1870–97, box 1, InSL.

10. For examples of inept mail handling, see Erastus Brown to Joseph Osborn, 14 July 1875, in Osborn, papers; and letters from Alpheus Tyner to Isaac Beeson, April 27, 1876 and May 2, 1876, in Beeson, papers, InSL. For examples of the overloaded agency, see April 1875 and March 1877, executive committee, Wisconsin State Grange, *Bulletin*, SHSW. For record keeping, see the "Account of the transactions of the agent of the Nettle Creek Grange No. 735 during the year 1876," in Beeson, papers, InSL. In another account, 10 December 1876, when auditing the books of the Indiana State Grange, the state secretary, C. C. Post, noted that, while the ledgers balanced, the agent's books were "in the form of notes of the value of which I will not now express an opinion." In Indiana State Grange, executive committee minutes, InSL. For examination of goods, see the Winnebago Pamona Grange, minutes, ISHL.

11. For Montgomery, Ward & Company (the firm included a comma in the founder's name at this time for unexplained reasons), see *PF*, 1 November 1873, 348; for Hall and Roe Brothers, ibid., 13 December 1873, 395.

12. See Wilcock to Osborn, 2 August 1875, in Osborn, papers, 1873–1877. For Kniffen, see Wisconsin State Grange, *Proceedings* (1876), 41–42.

13. For the first quote, see Indiana State Grange, *Proceedings* (1876), 18. In one

year, only one in eight subordinates paid their dues to the implement fund. See Wisconsin State Grange, *Proceedings* (1876). For Kniffen, see executive committee, Wisconsin State Grange, *Bulletin,* September 1879, SHSW.

14. South Greenville Grange No. 225 in Greenville, *Records, 1873–1973* (microfilm edition, 1979), SHSW. For other social functions, see "Circular No. 3 for Sovereigns of Industry," in Osborn, papers, 1873–77.

15. Woods, *Knights of the Plow,* 160. For Pamona formations, see Champaign County Pamona Grange, *Proceedings, August 2, 1873–August 1, 1877,* Illinois Historical Survey Collections, University of Illinois, Champaign-Urbana; and the Big Spring Grange, treasurer's book, 1874–76, October 17, 1874, in Jonathan Turley, papers, 1875–85, InSL. For county councils, see Wisconsin State Grange, *Proceedings . . . Second Annual Session . . .* (Oshkosh: Times Printing, 1874), 50–51; and Wisconsin State Grange, *Confidential Circular* [c. 1875], SHSW. Hitt noted that "in fact, I have had some sympathy with this idea [of local control] myself." For his comments, see Wisconsin State Grange, *Proceedings . . . Third Annual Session . . . 1875* (Neenah, Wisc.: Boyton & Cunningham, 1875), 34. Pamonas and county councils were also more likely to deal directly with independent wholesalers. See 19 December 1873 and 16 January 1874 in Champaign County Pamona Grange, *Proceedings, August 2, 1873–August 1, 1877.*

16. For Nettle Creek Grange in Dalton, Wayne County, Indiana, see Beeson, papers, InSL; for the quote, ibid., see box 11, folder 9, n.d.

17. The need for competent managers at these imaginary clearing houses was not an insurmountable obstacle. While the retail skills of the average farmer were often overmatched, even at the local level, there did exist competent businessmen within and affiliated with the Grange who had the acumen to run such an operation successfully. See, for example, L. G. Kniffen in the following discussion.

18. My treatment varies in some ways, particularly for "conservatives," from Woods. For treatment of rival camps, see Woods, *Knights of the Plow,* 35, 95–96, 149.

19. For Burnham, see Woods, *Knights of the Plow,* 127–29. See executive committee, Wisconsin State Grange, *Bulletin,* September 1878, SHSW; Cerny, "Cooperation in the Midwest," 204; for the quote, see National Grange, *Proceedings . . . Tenth Session . . . 1876* (Louisville: Morton, 1876), 144.

20. National Grange, *Proceedings* (1875), 35.

21. *Proceedings . . . Sixth Annual Session . . . Iowa State Grange* (Des Moines: Patron's Helper, 1875), 6, 12, 45–46.

22. For the Jones quote, see National Grange, *Proceedings . . . Tenth Session . . . 1876* (Louisville: Morton, 1876), 7–8. For the second quote, ibid., 110–11. Ironically, while the national grange met in Chicago, busily undoing the purchasing-agency system, they accepted an invitation from Montgomery Ward and Company to visit their store and inspect the stock; ibid., 93.

23. National Grange, *Proceedings* (1875), 21; for the vote, ibid., 166–67.

24. National Grange, *Grange Co-Operation: A Pamphlet Containing Circular Letters Issued to the Patrons of Husbandry July 14, 1876* (Louisville, Ky.: Morton, 1876); *Rules for Patrons' Co-operative Associations of the Order of Patrons of Husbandry, and the Directing for Organizing Such Associations* (Louisville, Ky.: National Grange, 1876); and *Co-operation: Europe and the Grange. Address by J. W. A. Wright,*

of Borden, Cal., Who was Commissioned by the National Grange to Visit Europe in the Interest of American Farmers (n.p., 1876).

25. For Jones, see National Grange, *Grange Co-Operation,* 3–4; for second example, authored by J. W. A. Wright, see *Grange Co-Operation,* 1–3; for Kelley, see National Grange, *Rules for Co-operative Associations,* 4–7.

26. For Samuel E. Adams, see National Grange, *Proceedings . . . Eleventh Session . . . 1877* (Louisville, Ky.: Morton, 1878), 9.

27. In one example, used by Kelley, an original $100 investment saved $10 on purchases. The following year, Kelley assumed that $110 was available, which would produce an $11 profit, thus producing $121 for the following year, and so on. See National Grange, *Rules for Co-operative Associations,* 6. For the "barnacles" citation, see ISFA, *Proceedings* (1873), 18.

28. The "nothing less" quote appears in a letter from Sands to Osborn dated 28 November 1874, in Osborn, papers, 1873–77. For the "so well established" quote, see Wisconsin State Grange, *Confidential Circular,* n.d. [c. 1875]. See other letters that support these sentiments dated 23 February 1874, 24 February 1874, and 17 March 1874; all SHSW; see also Wisconsin State Grange, *Proceedings* (1874), 51–52.

29. Wisconsin State Grange, *Proceedings* (1874), 49–52.

30. For example, see January 1875, July 1875, and December 1875 in executive committee, Wisconsin State Grange, *Bulletin* SHSW.

31. For example, see letters dated 29 January 1876 and 17 March 1876 in Osborn letter book, 1876, 13 January 1876–5 March 1877, SHSW. For Osborn's frustrations, see letter to Osborn from J. C. Abbott, 23 February 1874; and circular for Weed Sewing Machines, 20 June 1873, both in Osborn, papers, 1873–77; and Wisconsin State Grange, *Proceedings* (1874), 49–59.

32. For Kniffen experience, see Wisconsin State Grange Circular, c. 1875, in Osborn, papers, 1873–77. For article cited, see executive committee, Wisconsin State Grange, *Bulletin,* September 1875, SHSW. For grange visits, see Kniffen to Osborn, 2 June 1875 and 9 June 1875, in Osborn, papers, 1873–77. See also letter dated 9 June 1875.

33. For Kniffen's use of the implement fund, see Wisconsin State Grange, *Proceedings* (1876), 8. For May article, see executive committee, Wisconsin State Grange, *Bulletin,* May 1875. In addition, Kniffen also expressed his beliefs that the purchasing agency take an active role in the consumer exhibitions at state and county fairs; he even promulgated the need for product guarantees and return policies. All of this corresponds with the fact that the purchasing agency was intended as an expression of consumer experience and not something cobbled together to insure the survival of the Patrons of Husbandry. For members' consumer individualism, see Beeson, papers, box 11, folder 9, n.d., InSL; for fairs, see executive committee, Wisconsin State Grange, *Bulletin,* March, September, and December 1875, SHSW; for guarantees, etc., see Wisconsin State Grange, *Proceedings* (1876), 68–69.

34. For Georgia experiences, see Hahn, *Roots of Southern Populism,* 220–25. For demographics of Wisconsin State Grange, see Gerald L. Prescott, "Wisconsin Farm Leaders in the Gilded Age," *Agricultural History* 44, no, 2 (1970): 183–99.

35. In a letter from aide William Orlidge to Osborn, dated 28 July 1875. Orlidge's credibility can be questioned when he wrote letters like one to Osborn that

ended "Devil! Devil! I am not so far gone as that, no wonder you thought me crazy or perhaps drunk." See Osborn, papers, 1873–77.

36. See letter dated 17 March 1876 in Osborn, letter book, 1876, 13 January 1876–5 March 1877, SHSW. For Huxley letter, see 29 January 1876, ibid., SHSW. For his reference to Kelley's book, see letter to H. F. Clark, a local grange master, ibid., SHSW.

37. Wisconsin State Grange, *Proceedings* (1876), 9. Executive committee, Wisconsin State Grange, *Bulletin,* July 1877, SHSW.

38. Executive committee, Wisconsin State Grange, *Bulletin,* September 1877.

39. For Osborn, see Wisconsin State Grange, *Proceedings* (1877), 51–52. For Sherman, see Wisconsin State Grange, *Proceedings* (1878), 10. For Sherman, ibid., 14; For Wilcock, ibid., 67–68.

40. For Kniffen's defense of the communal benefits of the agency, see Wisconsin State Grange, *Proceedings* (1878), 28–30. For article, see executive committee, Wisconsin State Grange, *Bulletin,* March 1878, SHSW.

41. See articles of association for the Winnebago County Industrial and Provident Society, 5 April 1877, in Osborn, papers, 1855–90, folder: 1875–77, SHSW. For Osborn's resignation, see Cerny, "Cooperation in the Midwest"; and Marquart, *Wisconsin's Agricultural Heritage,* 13–17.

42. Wisconsin State Grange, *Proceedings . . . Seventh Annual Meeting . . . 1879* (Milwaukee: Sentinel, 1879), 41–42.

43. For the executive committee, see Wisconsin State Grange, *Proceedings . . . Ninth Annual Meeting . . . 1881* (Milwaukee: Trayser Bros., 1881), 35–36; for Kniffen quote, ibid., 38–40. For return of funds, see Committee on Appeals and Complaints, Wisconsin State Grange, *Proceedings . . . Eleventh Annual Meeting . . . 1882* (Milwaukee: Trayser Bros., 1883).

44. Kniffen was forced to sell eighty acres of property to meet the judgment. Marquart, *Wisconsin's Agricultural Heritage,* 20. See also Wisconsin State Grange, *Proceedings . . . Nineteenth Annual Meeting . . . 1890* (Neenah, Wisc.: Gazette Steam Print, 1891), 16–17.

45. Wisconsin State Grange, *Proceedings* (1882), 35.

Chapter 7: Mail Order

1. Quotations from the *Chicago Tribune,* both above and in the next paragraph, are from the issue of 8 November 1873, page 3. The pointed reference to their Grange readers suggests that, at least by 1873, the *Tribune* believed that their publication was widely circulated and read by Midwestern farmers. The comma in "Montgomery, Ward & Co." appears in the original version.

2. See 8 November 1873, minutes, Marion Grange No. 391, SHSI. Most notable in the historiography are Daniel Boorstin, "Ward's Catalog," *Chicago History* 2 (spring-summer 1973): 142–52; Boorstin, *The Americans: The Democratic Experience* (New York: Random House, 1973), 121–24; Cronon, *Nature's Metropolis,* 333–35; Barron, *Mixed Harvest,* 155–91; Cecil C. Hoge Sr., *The First Hundred Years Are the Toughest: What We Can Learn from the Century of Competition between Sears and Wards* (Berkeley: Ten-Speed, 1988), 2–11.

3. *CT*, 24 December 1873.

4. For the Grolier Club, see Montgomery Ward, collection no. 8008–87–01–30, box 45, folder "Catalog History" AHC.

5. For Roosevelt's speech, made on 22 February 1911, see Montgomery Ward, 8008–87–01–30, box 13, folder "Manuscript, Alfred Lief" AHC, 67; and Montgomery Ward & Co., *The History and Progress of Montgomery Ward & Co., "The Oldest Mail Order House," The Romance of the Golden Rule and Some Interesting Facts About the Mail Order Business* (Chicago: Montgomery Ward, 1925), 35. For McCreery, ibid., 36.

6. For poem, see *Flyer No. 58, Fall and Winter 1895*, in Montgomery Ward, 8008–87–01–30, box 1, folder "Advertisements" AHC. For second quote (my italics), see Montgomery Ward, *Our Silver Anniversary: Being a Brief and Concise History of the Mail Order or Catalogue Business, Which Was Invented by Us a Quarter of a Century Ago* (Chicago: Montgomery Ward, 1897), in Montgomery Ward, 8008–87–01–30, box 27, folder "Newspaper and Magazine Clippings, 1849–1959," AHC.

7. *CT*, 24 December 1873.

8. *PF*, 27 December 1873, 412. For problems with urban supply houses, see Illinois State Grange, *Proceedings . . . Third Annual Session . . . 1875* (Chicago: Fish, 1875), 19; Wisconsin State Grange, *Proceedings, Fourth Annual Meeting, 1876* (Milwaukee: Sentinel, 1876), 15; Indiana State Grange, *Proceedings, Sixth Annual Session* (Muncie, Ind.: Hoosier Patron Steam Printing House, 1876), 17; and Wisconsin State Grange, *Proceedings, Ninth Annual Meeting, 1881* (Milwaukee: Trayser Bros., 1881), 36.

9. *PF*, 13 December 1873, 395. For other references to Hall, ibid., see 1 March 1873; 26 April 1873; and 1 November 1873. By comparison, Montgomery Ward was first mentioned in this influential periodical only on 27 September 1873. For the flyer from Hall distributed to regional granges, dated 13 April 1874, see box 11, folder 4: "Circulars and Advertisements, 1873–1878" in Isaac and Benjamin B. Beeson, papers, 1870–97, InSL.

10. Ward's diary, cited in several secondary works, has not been found (I made a thorough, but unsuccessful, search for it myself). For Ward's early accounts, see Alfred Leif manuscript in Montgomery Ward, 8008–87–01–30, box 2, folder "Biographical File: Aaron Montgomery Ward," AHC.

11. *Forward* (July–August 1928), 4.

12. Montgomery Ward, 8008–87–01–30, box 2, folder "Biographical File: Aaron Montgomery Ward," AHC. For the quote, see *Catalogue No. 14, Wholesale, Fall and Winter 1875–1876*, 5.

13. Letter from Leo A. Dillon, of Severn, Maryland, 24 June 1889, in Montgomery Ward, 8008–87–01–30, box 4, folder 1 "Correspondence, 1889–1969," AHC; see also Montgomery Ward, 8008–87–01–30, box 13, folder "Manuscript, Alfred Lief" 13, AHC. Internal document from F. W. Jameson (secretary) to Charles Fullerton, general attorney, 28 June 1938, in Montgomery Ward, 8008–87–01–30, box 4, folder 1 "Correspondence, 1889–1969" AHC. See Montgomery Ward, 8008–87–01–30, box 46, folder "Subject File: A Century of Service" AHC (one employee notes, herein, that the company archives were meager as "most of which were cleaned out in the Sewell Avery sweep in the 1940s"). For more on Avery, see Frank

M. Kleiler, "The World War II Battles of Montgomery Ward," *Chicago History* 5, no. 1 (1976): 19–27.

14. For Cobb's and other, much shorter, testimonials, see *Catalogue No. 13, Spring and Summer, 1875* (1875), 59–63.

15. *PF,* 1 November 1873, 348. For renowned leaders, see *Catalogue No. 15, Winter and Spring, 1876,* 150. For Jones's letter, dated 20 June 1874, see Montgomery Ward, *Catalogue No. 13.* (1875), 59–63.

16. The first money-back guarantee was issued in the 1875 catalog; the guarantee continued from then on. See *Catalogue No. 13, Spring and Summer, 1875* (1875), inside front cover.

17. For this false assumption, see Daniel Boorstin, "Ward's Catalog," *Chicago History* 2 (spring–summer 1973): 143–44, where he states that "only the creation [by Ward] of vast new communities of consumers could fully exploit the peculiarly American opportunities," when in fact these communities already existed. For citation, see Montgomery Ward, *Catalogue No. 15, Winter and Spring, 1876* (1876), inside cover. For retraction of alcohol sales, see Grolier Club announcement, in Montgomery Ward, 8008–87–01–30, box 45, folder "Catalog History," AHC.

18. For early policies, see *Catalogue No. 10* (Chicago: Montgomery Ward, January 1874), front page. For first quote, see *Catalogue No. 12, Fall and Winter 1874–1875* (Chicago: Montgomery Ward, 1875), front inside cover. For second quote, see *Catalogue No. 15, Winter and Spring, 1876,* back inside cover.

19. See flyer dated 1893, no title, in Montgomery Ward, 8008–87–01–30, box 1, folder "Advertisements," AHC.

20. For trial-order information, see *Catalogue No. 28, Fall and Winter 1880* (1880), 3. For quote, see *Catalogue No. 10,* last page.

21. For cash with order, see *Catalogue No. 19, Fall and Winter, 1877–78* (1877), inside front cover. For grange validation, see ibid., 2. For blacklist, see *Catalogue No. 12, Fall and Winter, 1874–1875* (1874), 3.

22. *Our Silver Anniversary. Being a Brief and Concise History of the Mail Order or Catalogue Business, Which Was Invented by Us a Quarter of a Century Ago* (1897), in Montgomery Ward, 8008–87–01–30, box 27, folder "Newspaper and Magazine Clippings, 1849–1959," AHC.

23. *Montgomery Ward & Co.'s Price List of Groceries, No. 252, September 17th, 1888,* last page.

24. First quote in *Descriptive Illustrated Price List No. 31, Spring and Summer, 1882* (1882), back cover. Second quote in *Seasonable Suggestion Series,* vol. 2, in Montgomery Ward, 8008–87–01–30, box 1, folder "Advertisements," AHC.

25. Quote from interview at Omaha Exhibition of 1898, in pamphlet written by W. B. Leffingwell, advertising manager of Ward in 1898, in Montgomery Ward, 8008–87–01–30, box 3, books, AHC. Leffingwell pledged that they would never sell via urban retail outlets.

26. For Thayer visit and comments, see Ward internal journal *Among Ourselves* 3, no. 1 (1906): 18. For rising prejudice, see Danbom, *Born in the Country,* chap. 7.

27. For figures, see *Catalogue Nos. 41–45,* inside front covers.

28. Story cited in *The First 100 Years,* a history commissioned by the firm. See Montgomery Ward, 8008–87–01–30, box 13, folder "Manuscript, Alfred Lief" 30–31, AHC.

29. Montgomery Ward, 8008–87–01–30, box 13, folder "Manuscript, Alfred Lief" 61, AHC.

30. For Nicholson, see *Among Ourselves* 1, no. 7 (1905): 313. For other examples, ibid. 1, no. 11 (1905): 572; and 1, no. 12 (1905): 639. For Kaufman letter, ibid. 3, no. 1 (1906): 18.

31. For transactions, see Griswold Family, papers, 1814–1943, box 1: "Diaries," and box 4: "Account books, bank books, etc.," ISHL. These figures probably underestimate the volume of sales. Griswold noted on 7 March 1892 that he mailed off $38.61 for barbed wire, but the bank statement did not specify Montgomery Ward but only a debit logged to "Self & B. W. Collins for barbed wire." His diary confirms that the order was sent to Ward's. He wrote on 6 March: "Sent to Montgomery Ward & Co. for 1100 lbs barb wire $2.97 per hundred." If Griswold failed to "double-enter" other transactions in both his bank book and diary, then the number of Ward sales could be underrepresented. Also note that Griswold's aggregate purchases, from 1889 to 1904, of $657 was more than he earned for the entire year of either 1873 or 1875.

32. *Catalogue No. 14, Wholesale, Fall and Winter 1875–1876* (1875), 1.

33. See Leif manuscript, 63–67, in Montgomery Ward, 8008–87–01–30, box 13, folder "Manuscript, Alfred Lief" AHC; and "Remembrances of T. E. Donnelley," in Montgomery Ward, 8008–87–01–30, box 13, folder "Manuscript, Donnelley-Ward Association," AHC.

34. For agents, see *Catalogue and Price-List No. 22, Fall and Winter, 1878* (1878), 3. For Milwaukee store, see *Catalogue No. 28, Fall and Winter, 1880* (Chicago: Montgomery Ward), 160. For retraction, see *Descriptive Illustrated Price List No. 31, Spring and Summer, 1882* (1882), inside back cover, stating: "Having withdrawn our Milwaukee Retail Store, we would inform our Trade that we have no Branch Stores, and employ no Agents."

35. For questionnaire, see R. S. Thain, *New Light on an Old Subject, No. 2* (Chicago: Howard & Wilson, 1899), page titled "Question No. 9—Mail Orders." For Thorne quote, see Leif MS 63 in Montgomery Ward, 8008–87–01–30, box 13, folder "Manuscript, Alfred Lief," AHC.

36. See Louis E. Asher and Edith Heal, *Send No Money* (Chicago: Argus, 1942); Rae Elizabeth Rips, "An Introductory Study of the Role of the Mail-Order Business," Ph.D. diss., University of Chicago, 1938, 26–27; and Boris Emmet and John Jeuck, *Catalogs and Counters: A History of Sears, Roebuck and Company* (Chicago, 1950), 56–59.

37. Asher and Heal, *Send No Money*, 21.

38. Ibid., 3, 52.

39. Ibid., 21, 42–45, 56; Sears, Roebuck, *Consumer Guide, No. 111* (1902), 476.

40. *Among Ourselves* 1, no. 10 (1905): 502, 540; and *Descriptive Illustrated Price List No. 41, Spring and Summer, 1887* (1887), inside front cover. While Sears claimed as early as 1895 that his company surpassed Ward's in sales, it was not until the offer was printed on the back cover of the 1907 catalog that he posted the $10,000 challenge. See Rips, "An Introductory Study of the Role of the Mail Order Business," 34.

41. Montgomery Ward, *Catalogue No. 72* (1904), index. A methodological note should be made regarding the specific products highlighted in this chapter. Expensive goods such as stoves, pianos, and carriages, or products unrepresentative of a broad market, such as parlor furniture, china, or silverware, were not considered. Historians

such as Daniel Boorstin, Alfred Chandler Jr., and Jackson Lears refer to the popularity of bicycles, sewing machines, and patent medicines. For a specific reference on the desirability of sewing machines, see Boorstin, *The Americans,* 113–29; on patent drugs, see Lears, *No Place of Grace,* 52–56; on bicycles, see Alfred Chandler Jr., *The Visible Hand, The Managerial Revolution in American Business* (Cambridge, Mass.: Belknap/Harvard University Press, 1977), 230. As these products were both affordable and desirable, they are compared here. Finally, the catalogs that featured these products were available for purposes of comparison. For these reasons, bicycles, sewing machines, and patent drugs are the three instances used to demonstrate the advertising styles of the two corporations.

42. See Montgomery Ward, *Bicycles and Cycling Sundries, Catalogue M (1895),* 1–4.

43. All references are Sears, Roebuck and Co., *Bicycle Announcement* (1898), n.p.

44. Apparently it was quite common for both catalogs to be in one home. See *Mr. Sears Catalog,* The American Experience, videocassette (60 min.).

45. Sears, Roebuck, *Consumer Guide* (1902), 721.

46. For the terms and conditions of the various lines, ibid., 721; and Montgomery Ward, *Catalogue No. 73* (1904), 11–26.

47. Sears, Roebuck, *Consumer Guide* (1902), 721.

48. For both listings, see Sears, Roebuck, *Consumer Guide* (1902), 722; and Montgomery Ward, *Catalogue No. 73* (1904), 13.

49. The repeated use by Sears of the terms *neighbor* and *neighborhood* suggests an attempt to use the pressure of conformity or pride to promote sales. As the prices of the various models increased, the focus on the beauty of the cabinet as parlor furniture also climbed.

50. Sears listed the Minnesota at $23.20 and offered the set of attachments for $.75. For the Sears copy, see Sears, Roebuck, *Consumer Guide* (1902), 740; for Ward's, see Montgomery Ward, *Catalogue No. 73* (1904), 26.

51. "The Drug Division," *Among Ourselves* 2, no. 1 (1905): 27. See Montgomery Ward, *Drugs, Patent Medicines, and Toilet Preparations Catalogue D* (1894–95); Montgomery Ward, *Drug Catalogue* (1902); Sears, Roebuck, *Consumer Guide* (1897); and Sears, Roebuck, *What We Furnish for the Asking* (1903).

52. For Montgomery Ward, see *Drugs, Patent Medicines, and Toilet Preparations Catalogue D* (1894–95), 91; for Sears, Roebuck, *Consumer Guide* (1897), 33. All of the products mentioned can be found on a single page, suggesting the vast expanse of their advertising imagination. See Sears, *Consumer Guide* (1897), 27. Many other examples exist in the catalogs of these types of claims, including the Women's "Bust Developer and Bust Cream and Food," which combine fanciful claims, grand assurances, and pictures of "cured" individuals as evidence.

53. Montgomery Ward, *Drug Catalogue* (1902), back page.

54. Montgomery Ward, *Catalogue No. 482, Price List of Groceries* (July–August, 1903), back cover.

55. Asher and Heal, *Send No Money,* 36. Neil Harris, introduction to *The Land of Contrasts: 1880–1901,* ed. Neil Harris (New York: Braziller, 1970), 7–9.

56. David Potter, *People of Plenty: Economic Abundance and the American Character* (Chicago: University of Chicago Press, 1954), 170–71; for a brief understanding of "reason why" advertising, see Lears, "From Salvation to Self-Realization," in Fox

and Lears, *Culture of Consumption,* 18. Ward quote in *Among Ourselves* 1, no. 10 (1905), 540.

57. See Lears, "From Salvation to Self-Realization," 6–11; and Roland Marchand, *Advertising the American Dream: Making Way for Modernity, 1920–1940* (Berkeley: University of California Press, 1985), xvii–xviii.

58. For quote, see "Modern Development," n.d. (c. 1947), in Montgomery Ward, 8008-87-01-30, box 45, folder "Catalog History," AHC.

59. For the development of brand names, see Susan Strasser, *Satisfaction Guaranteed: The Making of the American Mass Market* (New York: Pantheon, 1989); Thomas Schlereth, *Victorian America: Transformations of Everyday Life, 1876–1915* (New York: Harper-Collins, 1991); and Richard S. Tedlow, *New and Improved: The Story of Mass Marketing in America* (New York: Basic, 1990).

60. Fifty-six percent of the respondents were from the states of Illinois, Michigan, Iowa, Indiana, Ohio, and Wisconsin. For the study, see Thain, *New Light on an Old Subject.*

61. "Question No. 7—Stove Polish," ibid.

62. For Ward quote, see Montgomery Ward, 8008–87–01–30, box 13, folder "Manuscript, Alfred Lief" 43, AHC; see also *Among Ourselves* 1, no. 6 (1905), 240–41.

63. See "Modern Development," n.d. (c. 1947), in Montgomery Ward, 8008–87–01–30, box 45, folder "Catalog History," AHC.

64. For the seventh annual conference, see Montgomery Ward, 8008–87–01–30, box 37, folder "Anniversary Dinners," AHC.

Conclusion

1. James Fallows, "Caught in the Web," *New York Review of Books* 42, no. 3 (1996): 14–18.

2. The Internet suffers from this very same paradox. While some still hope that this innovation will create a "global village," electronic isolation is just as likely. One merely need witness the computer center of a major university, where operators "interact" with their video screens while remaining insulated and physically cloistered within individual cubicles. This powerful image of connectivity—even if one makes allowance for the fact that people need private work-space—highlights the challenges of total access to information. We are more comfortable with ideas that conform to our own preconceptions, and the thousands of home pages available make it easy to find the few that accommodate us. The inevitable result is an erosion of shared experiences. See Fallows, "Caught in the Web."

3. See Lynd, *Middletown,* and Robert S. and Helen M. Lynd, *Middletown in Transition: A Study in Cultural Conflicts* (New York: Harcourt, Brace and World, 1937).

INDEX

Abbot, Asa, 36–37
Adams, Charles Francis, 125
Adams, Henry, 53
Adams, Dudley, 129–30
Adler, Jeffrey, 79
advertising, 136–37, 140, 148; location of advertisers, 142–42, 149–50; methodology, 137–39, 227–32; regional composite, 147–50; and targeted consumer, 141, 148–49; types of products in, 140–41, 150
agents, 47–50, 63–65, 67–69, 217; and credit and market information, 86–90; and inventory control, 80–82; and manufacturers, 83–85; pricing by, 82–83; and risk management, 79–80; and rural consumerism, 90–93; and transportation, 85–86
agrarian consumerism. *See* rural consumerism
agrarian myth. *See* rural republicanism
agricultural press, 3–4, 30, 35–37, 39, 64, 105. See also *Prairie Farmer*
agriculture, 35, 44–45; and agents, 68–73; and the Civil War, 57–59; commercial considerations, 25, 44–45; and cooperation, 104–5; mechanized, 25, 27–28, 37–42; postwar problems in, 57–63; subsistence farming, 22–23; tenancy, 24
Alexander, Howell & Co., 89–90
American Agriculturalist, 64
Anderson, Sherwood, 3–4
Applegate, Bartholomew, 63
Asher, Louis, 202, 210

Barron, Hal, xi, 6, 8, 97
Beeson, Isaac, 107–8
Bellamy, Edward, 3
Bennett, John, 82
Blair, William, 88

Blake, Charles R., 86
Blakely, Herbert, 46
Bogue, Allan, xi, 24, 27, 45
book farming. *See* scientific farming
Boughton, Myron and Jane F., 38
Boughton, Willis, 46
Boyton, Albert, 69–70
Bradford, Mary, 31–32
Breen, T. H., 9
Brewer-Bonebright, Sarah, 13, 42, 72
Burroughs, H. P., 103–4
Bush, Andrew, 55

Calder, Lendol, 4
Cayton, Andrew R. L., xi, 8, 14, 23
Chandler, Alfred C., 145
Chase, Thurston, 70
Chase Western Rural Handbook, 39
Chicago Evening Journal, 111
Chicago Tribune, 59, 64, 91, 114, 139–40, 184–86, 227–32; advertising in, 140–50
Civil War, 53–59; and commecial farming, 57–59; and the midwest, 53–54; servicemen and consumer goods, 54–59; women and, 56
Clagett, Thomas W., 52
Clark, Adeline, 61–62
Clark, Christopher, 8, 9
Clark, William, 12
Cohen, Ruth Schwartz, 40
Cohen, Lizabeth, 5
commercial agriculture. *See* agriculture
consumer culture, 4, 45; consumer demand and, 31–32; historiography, 4–5; cooperation, 18–19, 98, 100–101; and commercial agriculture, 104–5; 35, 44–45; and agents, 68–73; and cooperation, 104–5 cooperative stores, 132–33; and farmers' clubs, 109–13; and purchasing agencies, 100–103